365: aiga year in design 21

about aiga

2000 aiga medal

communication graphics 21

50 books. 50 covers. of 1999

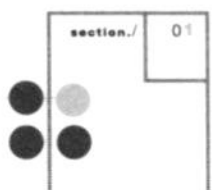

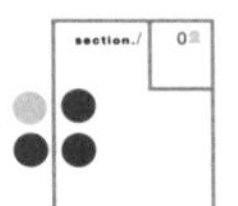

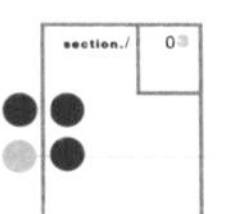

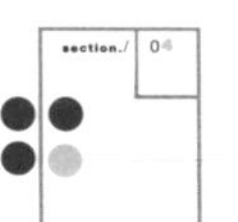

¶01 "The venue for Laurie Haycock and P. Scott Makela's first encounter was auspicious, a coming together of design with things unconventional, imaginative and wobbly. The occasion was the 'first and last' annual Jell-O mold competition, organized by the Los Angeles chapter of AIGA in 1985. 'Everybody brought Jell-O molds—about 25 of them—some absolutely gross and some fantastical,' recalls April Greiman, who was vice president of events for the L.A. chapter at the time. 'When you meet somebody at an important event like that, it has to be fate.' The event did not go over well with the senior members of the chapter, and never took place again. Its only lasting legacy was the 14-year relationship between Haycock and Makela, a partnership that produced—much as when you mix water with gelatin and fruit flavors—more than the sum of its parts. When friends, colleagues and peers describe the Haycock-Makela phenomenon, a picture emerges of two very different and independent sensibilities that came together in a remarkable fusion. By the time they became the resident cochairs of 2-D design at Cranbrook Academy of Art in 1997, each had a firmly established reputation. If Makela was known for his loud, vibrant, high-tech approach to design, Haycock was known for her thoughtful experimentalism and refined typography. Greiman describes the combination as upper body (Haycock)/lower body (Makela), though this, of course, depends on where you stand." (From "Truly, Madly, Deeply: Laurie Haycock and P. Scott Makela" by Peter Hall, page 20) ¶02 "Fred Seibert's career proves that it is not necessary to be a Yale/Cranbrook/RISD/SVA-educated, AIGA/Type Directors/Art Directors Club-award-winning, bona fide/pedigreed/certified graphic designer, or any other kind of designer, to create the most indelible visual identities for some of the most visible pop culture media in the world. You just have to be a fan. A fervent, ardent, passionate devotee of 'people who do fantastic work in music and visual stuff,' as Seibert puts it. Oh, yeah, you also have to have the vision thing." (From "The Instigator: Fred Seibert" by Steven Heller, page 34) ¶03 "'When it comes to design, I like to do it all,' says Michael Vanderbyl, whose lifelong goal has been to merge traditionally segregated design forms like graphic design, product design and interior architecture. As evidenced by the work that has emerged from his San Francisco-based studio over the course of his 27-year career, Vanderbyl has attained this goal—and more. A century ago, Otto Wagner, Vienna's pioneering modernist architect/designer, coined the famous term "Gesamtkunstwerk"—the total work of art—to describe what he believed was the ultimate creative attainment in the modern age. One hundred years later, Vanderbyl's talent and achievements seem to fulfill the Viennese master's criteria with startling accuracy." (From "A Man For All Seasons: Michael Vanderbyl" by Zahid Sardar, page 48) ¶04 "It is a recurring truth that when the economy does well, design awareness tends to increase in mainstream culture. Think back to the 1950s, when postwar plenitude brought forth the giddy production—and consumption—of shiny new cars and brightly decorated homes; or to the go-go '80s, when Armani suits and Memphis furniture meant prosperity writ large in the popular imagination. Well, wealth is back—at least for the moment—and material culture is flourishing. While bright colors (think orange) and flamboyant form (think Apple's iMac and Chrysler's PT Cruiser) are the hallmarks of three-dimensional hip, the graphic cultural moment is clearly dominated by minimalism. Gone are the messy, expressionistic soul-searchings so common to the early-to-mid '90s—the poststructuralist assaults on legibility, those slaps in the face to Swiss-school stricture. Instead, large, restrained type and stark photography vie for attention in a number of this year's 'Communication Graphics' entries. Indeed, there is an uncanny uniformity in much of the creative community's production—which might just make sense. If necessity is indeed the mother of invention, then innovation tends to get short shrift in flush times." (From "Up Close and Personal: Design in Detail" by Andrea Codrington, page 63) ¶05 "Faced with the threat of redundancy—or at least charges of anachronism—in a culture increasingly skewed to the digital, book designers seem to be reinventing and repositioning themselves as editors, curators and shapers of content in an effort to validate their practice. When the designers of one of the winning entries in this year's '50 Books/50 Covers' contest were asked how the advent of electronic books would affect their work, their reply hinted at some kind of genetic evolution of the designer: 'We will have to design smarter and better to make the books worth printing.' It seems that many designers are already designing 'smarter and better,' and the result is a breed of books that is intelligent, beautiful and somehow more relevant and vital than ever." (From "The Book: Rumors of its Death Are Greatly Exaggerated" by Alice Twemlow, page 193) ¶06 "Recently, I got an e-mail from Jeff Bezos, CEO of amazon.com. Bezos was contacting Amazon users to request our advice on the company's website design. It seems that Amazon is growing, transforming itself from a seller of books to a seller of, well, everything, and this requires a redesign of the site navigation. After courteously explaining to us what 'navigation' is (those little tabs at the top of every page), the letter asked us to go to a specially created area of Amazon's site and review some of the design options. So it's come to this: the original powerhouse of e-commerce, the company that practically invented it, is asking us, its customers, how best to design for e-commerce. It's curious enough to see Bezos throw up his hands and effectively ask, 'So where do you want the buttons to be?' But Amazon's query was especially striking when considered alongside the results of the most recent 'Communication Graphics' competition. This year, a multidisciplinary jury of seasoned designers looked at a field of 271 websites, and—for the first time since the competition began accepting websites—selected not a single one to honor as exemplary." (From "WWW: Where Were the Websites?" by Andrea Moed, page 355)

365: AIGA Year in Design 21

Written by Andrea Codrington, Peter Hall, Steven Heller, Andrea Moed,
Zahid Sardar and Alice Twemlow
Designed by Jennifer Sterling Design, San Francisco
Production by Pamela Aviles and Nicolas Simon
Photography by Svend Lindbaek; photography pp. 162-163 by Christian Tuempling
Edited by Andrea Codrington

copyright information

365: aiga year in design | 21

AIGA National Staff

Deborah Aldrich, director, corporate partnerships
Pamela Aviles, director of production
Kelley Beaudoin, director of events
Molly Beverstein, project manager
Cynthia Chan, operations manager
Andrea Codrington, editorial director
Maureen DeLorenzo, information management associate
George Fernandez, membership coordinator
Sue Gordon, chapter liaison
Richard Grefé, executive director
Gabriela Mirensky, director, competitions and exhibitions
Andrea Moed, web editor
Lauren Neefe, program coordinator
Sara Padilla, customer service associate
Alice Twemlow, program director
Marc Vassall, finance and administration associate
Johnny Ventura, facility assistant
Denise Wood, chief experience officer

copyright information

365: aiga year in design | 21

copyright information

365: aiga year in design | 21

Available through DAP/Distributed Art Publishers, Inc., 155 Sixth Avenue, 2nd
floor, New York, NY 10013; 212 627 1999 phone, 212 627 9484 fax

ISBN: 1-884081-01-0

First printing, 2001

Distributed outside of the United States and Canada by HarperCollins
International, 10 E. 53rd Street, New York, NY 10022; 212 207 7691 phone,
212 207 7654 fax

Printing and binding: Syl, Barcelona, Spain
Color separation: Syl, Barcelona, Spain
Paper: Fox River Starwhite Sirius 100 pound text
Typefaces: Colonna, Console, Dead History, Emigre, Futura, Frutiger, Helvetica,
Madrone, Trebuchet and Trixie

¶01 Andrea Codrington is editorial director of AIGA, and a critic specializing in contemporary design and visual culture. Before coming to AIGA, she was a columnist for the New York Times and contributed to such publications as I.D. magazine, the Washington Post and Harper's Bazaar. She is coauthor of Pause: 59 Minutes of Motion Graphics (Rizzoli/Universe, 2000), and is currently working on a monograph about Kyle Cooper.

¶02 Peter Hall is a journalist and design critic based in New York. He wrote and co-edited the book Tibor Kalman: Perverse Optimist (Princeton Architectural Press, 1998) and coauthored Pause: 59 Minutes of Motion Graphics (Rizzoli/Universe, 2000). He writes regularly for Metropolis, The Guardian, I.D. magazine, Men's Journal, Print, Architecture and Interiors, and has contributed essays to the books Sex Appeal (Allworth, 2000) and Architecture and Film (Princeton Architectural Press, 2000). He is a lecturer at Yale School of Art and has appeared as a design critic on BBC Radio 4, Greater London Radio and Sky TV. Currently, Hall is writing a book with the graphic designer Stefan Sagmeister, and consulting on a national design TV series in development.

¶03 Steven Heller, art director of the New York Times Book Review, is the founder and cochair of the School of Visual Arts MFA/Design program. He is the author of more than 70 books on graphic design and popular art, including Paul Rand (Phaidon, 1999), Typology: Type Design from the Victorian Era to the Digital Age (Chronicle Books, 1999), Letterforms: Bawdy Bad and Beautiful (Watson Guptill, 2000) and the Allworth Press books Design Literacy (1997), Design Dialogues (1998), Sex Appeal: The Art of Allure in Graphic Design and Advertising Art (2000) and The Swastika: Symbol Beyond Redemption (2000).

¶04 Svend Lindbaek is a New York-based photographer specializing in portraits and still life for advertising and editorial. His work has been featured in such publications as Cosmopolitan, Glamour, Spin, Time Out, Stuff, Details and Seventeen magazine. Lindbaek, who is originally from Denmark, is also engaged in an ongoing personal project of documenting the United States in portraits. His most recent trip was to Memphis.

¶05 Andrea Moed is the web editor of AIGA. She has been a writer and content developer of websites since 1995, specializing in cultural and educational sites for children and adults. She has also written extensively on design and digital culture for such publications as Print, Interiors, Metropolis and If/Then. Moed is currently completing a master's degree at New York University's Interactive Telecommunications Program.

contributor bios
365: aiga year in design | 21

¶06 Zahid Sardar is the architecture and design editor of the San Francisco Examiner Magazine, and writes for Metropolis, Architecture and other design magazines. He has won several design awards for his pieces on Bay Area architecture and interiors and has also been on several design juries. Sardar is the author of San Francisco Modern Interiors, Architecture & Design (Chronicle Books, 1998).

¶07 Jennifer Sterling is a member of AGE, the SFMOMA's Architecture and Design Accessions Board, and is the founding partner of Sterling Design in San Francisco. Her work regularly appears in such publications as Communication Arts, I.D. magazine and Graphis, and is included in the permanent collections of the Smithsonian Institute, Nationale de France, Museum Für Kunst und Gewerbe Hamburg, The Library of Congress and the SFMOMA, which is hosting an exhibit of her work in Spring 2001. This exhibit will coincide with the release of a monograph on her work and studio. Recent projects include branding for a coalition under the direction of Hillary Clinton and Madelaine Albright, along with the launch of her own product line.

contributor bios
365: aiga year in design | 21

¶08 Alice Twemlow is the director of programming at AIGA. She is program director for "Voice: AIGA 2001 National Design Conference." Twemlow earned a master's degree in design history from a joint program of the Royal College of Art and the Victoria & Albert Museum in London. She has worked previously as a freelance curator and lecturer and has written about design for AIGA Journal, Eye, Graphics International, I.D. magazine, Metropolis, Print and Typographic.

ABOUT AIGA / **left page** AIGA's National Design Center at 164 Fifth Avenue in New York City showing façade designed by Tod Williams Billie Tsien Architects. Photograph © Peter Mauss/Esto.

AIGA

| a = american

| g = graphic

| a = arts

yr founded 03

| i = institute

AIGA: Stimulating Thinking About Design

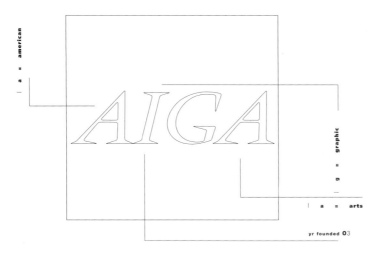

¶01 The purpose of AIGA is to further excellence in design as a broadly defined discipline, strategic tool for business and cultural force. The association is committed to stimulating thinking about design through the exchange of ideas and information, the encouragement of critical analysis and research and the advancement of education and ethical practice.

¶02 AIGA stimulates thinking about design within the creative community by focusing on innovative practices, celebrating excellence and raising critical issues for discussion among professionals. It stimulates thinking about design among the media, the business community and the public by illuminating the challenges of the design process, the role of the designer and the value of effective design.

¶03 AIGA is the oldest and largest membership association for professionals engaged in the discipline, practice and culture of visual communication and graphic design. AIGA was founded in 1914 and now represents over 15,000 designers through national activities and local programs developed by more than 40 chapters and 80 student groups. The next generation of designers is eager to be involved in this window on the profession; more design students are members of AIGA than any other design organization in America.

¶04 In the past year, AIGA has been transformed from a club to a hub, eschewing exclusivity for a role in advancing the interests of design. Members of AIGA include professional designers, educators and students engaged in type and book design, editorial design, communications and corporate design, posters, interaction and web design, as well as new-media and motion-graphics design. The vision and range of AIGA is the result of the perspective of a broadly representative, nationally elected board of directors.

¶05 AIGA serves as a hub of information and activity within the design community using a coordinated set of channels to its audiences: conferences, competitions, exhibitions, publications, educational activities and the web. While many activities are open to both members and the public, AIGA also enables many focused conversations among designers about the issues facing the profession and society. AIGA organizes communities of interest around specific design disciplines for those designers whose preferred community consists of designers dealing with the same challenges. These communities are national in scope and conduct national conferences, arrange activities in many cities through local chapters and maintain active e-groups. These communities can be easily developed at the initiative of interested members. Currently, there are communities of interest focusing on experience design (a more expansive view of interaction design), brand design, design education, typography, illustration and design for film and television.

¶06 As the design process has required the involvement of new disciplines on problem-solving teams, AIGA has welcomed these new professions. The organization's activities now address the challenges of design that is driven by problems that are more strategic and conceptual than before and often require three-dimensional solutions, whether that involves time, space or motion.

¶07 The role of AIGA's local chapters is both integral and complementary to the organization's national role. Chapters provide AIGA members with local forums for meeting, exchanging ideas and information and creating traveling programs of national import to designers and the public. In addition, chapters play a primary role in the growth, expanding service base and creative vitality of AIGA. The energy and relevance of AIGA will always come from its structure in reflecting, through the chapters, the perspective and interests of its members.

¶08 AIGA is a national not-for-profit educational organization incorporated under Section 501 (c) (3) of the Internal Revenue Code in the State of New York.

ABOUT AIGA / **left page** AIGA's exhibition of "Communication Graphics 20" selections at the National Design Center, designed by watersdesign.com. Photograph © Jennifer Krogh **01 - 07** from Thinking Inside the Box, AIGA's brochure on guidelines for its new brand identity, designed by Crosby Associates.

about aiga

365: aiga year in design | 21

Type

There are two families of type that should be used for all "permanent" AIGA materials, including stationery, business cards, forms, membership cards and signage: Filosofia and Interstate. These typefaces may also be used wherever else they may be appropriate, but chapter promotional materials and publications are not limited to these fonts and should be produced in the typefaces that are most appropriate to the subject matter being presented.

Both of these type families are available for PC and Macintosh. Filosofia is available from Emigre Fonts (www.emigre.com). Interstate is available from Font Bureau (www.fontbureau.com).

abcdefghijklmnop
ABCDEFGHIJKLM
01234567890

abcdefghijklmnopq
ABCDEFGHIJKLMN
01234567890

abcdefghijklmno
ABCDEFGHIJKL
01234567890

abcdefghijklmn
ABCDEFGHIJ
01234567890

abcdefghijklmn

n 01

AIGA

cational.
ed·u·ca·ble (ej′ŏŏ kə bəl), *adj.* of being educated or trained. —
bil′i·ty, *n.*
ed′u·cate′ (-kāt′), *v.t.*, -cat·ed, -
1. to develop the faculties and p
(a person) by schooling; teach

n 02

Sequential all-cap abbrevi
MD, DC are set in 8 pt Filos

Logo
Color:
Chapter's choice from the
"AIGA" reversing out to wh

Size on letterhead and env
45 points x 45 points.

Size on business cards and
37 points x 37 points.

n 03

about aiga

365: aiga year in design | 21

educating. 2. the result produced
struction, training, or study. 3. the
or art of teaching. —ed′u·ca′tion
—ed′u·ca′tion·al·ly, *adv.*
e·duce (i dōōs′, i dyōōs′), *v.t.*,
e·duc·ing. 1. to bring out; elicit.

AIGA

n 04

AIGA

nstitute of Graphic
rancisco Chapter

n 05

about aiga

365: aiga year in design | 21

AIGA

4515 C

AIGA

716 U

n 06

American Institute

AIGA

n 07

ABOUT AIGA / **left page** "Communication Graphics 20" exhibition as seen through AIGA's Fifth Avenue façade. Photograph © Jennifer Krogh.

aiga chapters and chapter presidents 2000-2001

Laura Von Gluck	Arizona
Peter Borowski	Atlanta
Sean Carnegie	Austin
Carl Cox	Baltimore
Jennifer Tatham	Birmingham
Amy Strauch	Boston
Patrick Short	Charlotte
Lance Rutter	Chicago
Rondi Tschopp	Cincinnati
Linda Brown	Cleveland
Clare Kelly	Colorado
John J. Conley	Dallas
Michael Hilker	DC
Bruno Hohmann	Detroit
Stacey Leong	Honolulu
Dylan Moore	Houston
Lori Long	Indianapolis
Karen Beach	Iowa
Bonnie Barnes and Steve Shepherd	Jacksonville
Michael Lamonica	Kansas City
Kenneth White	Knoxville
Alfred Herczeg	Las Vegas
Noreen Morioka	Los Angeles
Jonathan Gouthier	Miami
Joelle Anderlik	Minnesota
Brenda Lyman	Nebraska
Christy Bracken	New Orleans
Janet Froelich	New York
Marj Crum	Upstate New York
Casey Twenter	Oklahoma
Yamini Prabhakar	Orange County
Valerie Sloan	Orlando
Rosemary Murphy	Philadelphia
Bernard Uy and Paul Schifino	Pittsburgh
Catherine Healy	Portland
Christy White	Raleigh
Jason Burton	Richmond
Linda Sullivan	Salt Lake City
MaeLin Levine	San Diego
Diane Carr	San Francisco
Tan Le and Laura Zeck	Seattle
Steve Hartman	St. Louis
Jeff Pulaski	Wichita
Ken Hanson	Wisconsin

aiga board of directors 2000-2001

aiga chapters and chapter presidents 2000-2001

Michael Bierut	president
Beth Singer	secretary/treasurer
Richard Grefé	executive director
Bart Crosby	director
Marc English	director
Peter Girardi	director
Bill Grant	director
Eric Madsen	director
John Maeda	director
Clement Mok	director
Jennifer Morla	director
Emily Oberman	director
Mary Scott	director
Sam Shelton	director
Thomas Suiter	director
Petrula Vrontikis	director
Douglas Powell	chapter presidents' council representative

aiga board of directors 2000-2001

AIGA 2000 Activities

JANUARY

National Design Center Opened

¶09 Located in the historic Flatiron district of New York City, the AIGA National Design Center provides a central place from which the organization can support the profession and articulate the value of design to the public through its programs around the country. Renovation of the lower Fifth Avenue building—a 1918 structure—was completed in January and involved architectural commissions from Tod Williams and Billie Tsien (storefront façade), EFM Design (mezzanine and fourth floors) and Pentagram Architecture (third floor) in order to demonstrate different approaches to solving related design issues.

¶10 The building's renovation has garnered a considerable amount of press, including articles in the New York Times, Interiors, Abitare, Metropolis and I.D. magazine. It has become a favorite location for the meetings of international and national working groups interested in the issues of design and has hosted the Smithsonian's National Design Awards jury and the National Academy of Science's "IT and Technology" working group.

AIGA Identity Relaunched

¶11 In January, AIGA board member Bart Crosby presented the organization with a redesign of its logo. In honor of AIGA's past, the new logo retains the spirit of the previous identifier designed by Paul Rand. Because the old logo had a tendency to become lost among accompanying type and graphics, the redesign carries with it a bold background: a box that gives it more presence in cluttered environments.

FEBRUARY

AIGA Communication Graphics 20

February 3-March 10

¶12 This year's exhibition of AIGA's "Communication Graphics 20" competition selections provided 2,151 visitors with a vibrant, eye-catching array of contemporary creative visions. The exhibition's cleverly conceived design was created by watersdesign.com and featured a softly glowing, canvas-covered S-curve that was on 24 hours a day and provided a backdrop for the competition's 107 winners, which were suspended like parachutists on white cables. The exhibition design created an atmosphere of tactile engagement, where people were encouraged to pick up the magazines, brochures and assorted print pieces and leaf through them, or play with several interactive projects that were embedded in the ends of the S-curve display. The gallery's street-front etched-glass window promoted the show's contents to many passersby, who entered the exhibition out of sheer curiosity.

Graphic Design USA: 20

¶13 The 20th edition of Graphic Design USA was published in February. This year's jacket was designed by Fred Woodward of Rolling Stone magazine and the body of the book was designed by Beth Crowell of Cheung/Crowell Design in Rowayton, Connecticut. Annual 20 showcased the winning design work of AIGA's 1998-1999 competition season, including "Communication Graphics 20" and "50 Books/50 Covers" of 1998. The book also chronicled all visiting exhibitions at the National Design Center—including "A Century of Innovative Book Design," "Heavyweight Titles" and "Brand Design 50"—as well as AIGA conferences "Design for Film and Television" and "America: Cult and Culture."

¶14 AIGA's 1999 Medalists—Steven Heller, Tibor Kalman and Katherine McCoy—were profiled, as was Alfred A. Knopf, winner of AIGA's Design Leadership Award. Insightful essays written by Paula Scher, Veronique Vienne and Lorraine Wild accompanied these honors, as did a representative sampling of their life's work.

AIGA Website Redesigned

¶15 Phase I of AIGA's ambitious new website was launched to much acclaim in early February with a robust design and information architecture created by a team headed by Lance Rutter, Joseph W. Juhnke and Orin Fink. As with all web projects, the AIGA site is a work in progress and will change over time. Future implementations include an overhaul of the membership directory and a National Job Bank in Phase II; the inclusion of a dynamic events calendar in Phase III; member discussion forums in Phase IV; and the launch of an open-source content management system in Phase V. In this final incarnation, AIGA will serve as an "infomediary," connecting people to people and people to ideas. The activity generated in this digital agora will be a value engine based on the people and ideas important to the design profession. An idea directory that organizes online discussion forums and links to resources on topics of user interest will offer an opportunity to develop a unique resource of substantial scale that will provide AIGA with the reputation of being the Internet's most comprehensive resource about design theory and practice.

MARCH

Reputedly Illiterate: The Art Books of James Castle

March 30-May 12, 2000

¶16 This spring, the AIGA National Design Center presented "Reputedly Illiterate: The Art Books of James Castle," an exhibition curated by Tom Trusky that featured the work of the visionary deaf-and-mute artist James Castle. Castle (Idaho, 1900-1977) produced an astonishing variety of hermetic, graphically coded drawings, books and objects in a career spanning more than 50 years. As a child in central Idaho's remote Garden Valley, James Castle refused to learn to read, write or sign, although his family developed a system of hand gestures for communication. His parents provided him with what amounted to

 left page AIGA's "Minnesota" conference room and a view to the third-floor offices designed by James Biber of Pentagram Architecture. Photograph © Peter Mauss/Esto.

aiga chapters and chapter presidents 1999-2000

David Rengifo	Arizona
Peter Borowski	Atlanta
Sean Carnegie	Austin
Carl Cox	Baltimore
Jennifer Tatham	Birmingham
Amy Strauch	Boston
Lance Rutter	Chicago
Tim Smith	Cincinnati
Sheila Hart	Cleveland
Clare Kelly	Colorado
John J. Conley	Dallas
Bruno Hohmann	Detroit
Jon Sueda	Honolulu
Shawn Collier	Houston
Lori Long	Indianapolis
Karen Beach	Iowa
Florence Haridan	Jacksonville
Michael Lamonica	Kansas City
Kenneth White	Knoxville
Andrew Hershberger	Las Vegas
Moira Cullen	Los Angeles
Maggy Cuesta	Miami
Douglas Powell	Minnesota
Brenda Lyman	Nebraska
Christy Bracken	New Orleans
Paula Scher	New York
Marj Crum	Upstate New York
Casey Twenter	Oklahoma
Anthony Colombini	Orange County
Caren Lipkin and Rosemary Murphy	Philadelphia
Bernard Uy	Pittsburgh
Susan Agre-Kippenhan	Portland
Christy White	Raleigh
Donald McCants	Richmond
Linda Sullivan	Salt Lake City
Maelin Levine	San Diego
Diane Carr	San Francisco
David Betz and Richard Smith	Seattle
Steve Hartman	St. Louis
Tamera Lawrence	Washington
Jeff Pulaski	Wichita

aiga board of directors 1999-2000

Michael Bierut	president
Beth Singer	secretary/treasurer
Richard Grefé	executive director
Sean Adams	director
Maxey Andress	director
Bart Crosby	director
Michael Donovan	director
Marc English	director
Peter Girardi	director
Eric Madsen	director
Clement Mok	director
Jennifer Morla	director
Emily Oberman	director
Lana Rigsby	director
Mary Scott	director
Thomas Suiter	director
Mark Oldach	chapter presidents' council representative

aiga chapters and chapter presidents 1999-2000

aiga board of directors 1999-2000

a studio and a variety of art supplies, which Castle used to create his earliest drawings and book constructions.

¶17 "Reputedly Illiterate," which was seen by 1,665 visitors, included 87 Castle books—twice as many as have ever been displayed before. Of these works, 77 had never been on exhibit. The exhibition also featured an important selection of key artworks figured with enigmatic codes, symbolic figures and haunting letterforms. Castle found source materials in the rural post office and general store his family operated. Through the mail and from the family's bookshelves, the artist culled liturgical calendars, almanacs, farm journals and mail-order catalogues and transformed them into art.

AIGA Journal of Graphic Design: vol. 17, no. 3

Winter 2000

¶18 "Design As a Main Course" was the topic of interest in this issue, which dealt with food, glorious food—and the design of its packaging and consumer presentation. Guest coedited by Katharine Weese, this issue provided an intense exploration of how food brands vie for attention on crowded supermarket shelves, and of the multitude of ethical dilemmas facing today's packaging designers.

Grow: AIGA Design Business Seminar

¶19 In late February and early March, AIGA prepared a series of seminars in its New York offices run by Recourses, Inc., to help designers grow and manage their businesses. Each sold-out seminar was limited to 30 attendees, which provided an intimate atmosphere for learning. Seminars featured such topics as "How to Implement a Profitable Production/Traffic System," "Leadership Development: Managing the Creative Process (and People)," "How to Position/Market/Sell Your Services," "Making Your Work Strategic" and "Taking Your Firm to the Next Level." The "Grow" instructors included David C. Baker, Cameron S. Foote and David C. Morgan.

¶20 A second series of "Grow" seminars were held during AIGA's "Risk/Reward" conference in San Francisco (see "October"), where David C. Banker and Shel Perkins explored topics like "Marketing Your Services," "Monitoring and Benchmarking Your Practice," "Managing Your Design Practice to the Next Level" and "Implementing a Production/Traffic System."

APRIL

Collision: AIGA Conference on Design for Converged Media

April 12–14, 2000

¶21 In April, AIGA hosted another successful conference event, this time on the hot-button topic of converged media. This sold-out conference was organized by AIGA program director Alice Twemlow and an advisory committee headed by Peter Girardi (Funny Garbage) that included Fred Graver (MTV Networks Online), Andy Proehl (Sony Electronics, Inc. Design Center), Nathan Shedroff (Vivid Studios), Karen Sideman (Children's Television Workshop Online) and Gong Szeto (Rare Medium).

¶22 With the trenchant and witty guidance of moderator Steven Johnson, editor of the webzine FEED and author of the critically acclaimed book INTERFACE CULTURE: HOW NEW TECHNOLOGY TRANSFORMS THE WAY WE CREATE AND COMMUNICATE, the 500-strong audience of designers, journalists and technophiles noodled their way through such compelling questions as "Do designers need to be more savvy technically or do technicians need to be more savvy about design?" and "At what point does the integration of content and advertising become propaganda?"

¶23 Although most presentations were concerned with the convergence of traditional media such as television and radio with the Internet, and speakers included such high-tech luminaries as Brenda Laurel, Andy Proehl and David Small, the audience seemed to appreciate the conference's low-tech moments the most. MIT Media Lab guru John Maeda's humorous rant against the tyranny of computers and the limitations of buggy software—accompanied by hand-scribbled notes on an overhead projector—hit a nerve, as did game designer and theorist Eric Zimmerman's pass-the-balloon competition. The "Collision" party, which was hosted by MTV Interactive at the cavernous white space of SoHo's Ace Gallery, provided conference-goers with great music, delicious food and plenty of opportunity to meet new people and continue conversations initiated at the conference.

MAY

Minnesota Annual Design Review

May 25–June 21

¶24 The 21st annual celebration of design excellence from the AIGA/Minnesota chapter took place in the National Design Center in May. Competition selections made by a panel of distinguished jurors that included Marc English, Kathy Schanno, Sarah Spurr and Jack Summerford were enjoyed by 882 visitors, who were lured into the gallery by the irreverent wit and visual pyrotechnics of the Mosquito state's finest designers.

JUNE

AIGA Journal of Graphic Design: vol. 18, no. 1

Spring 2000

¶25 The state of illustration today was the focus of "Pictures To the Rescue." Despite a seeming renaissance in certain segments of visual culture, guest coeditor Marshall Arisman maintained that illustration is actually under siege. Often misunderstood by art directors and overshadowed by photographers, illustrators seem to be a dying breed. Renowned designers and illustrators like Milton Glaser, Dugald Stermer and James McMullan weighed in on the struggles

ABOUT AIGA / **left page** Exhibition view of "Stripes and Stars: A Visual History of an American Icon," designed by Kit Hinrichs. Photograph © Luca Pioltelli. **01** Poster for "Collision" conference, designed by Scott Stowell with illustration by Chip Wass. **02** Invitation to AIGA's "Minnesota Annual Design Review" exhibition, designed by Laurie DeMartino/Studio d Design. **03** Program brochure for "Collision" conference, designed by AdamsMorioka with illustration by Chip Wass. **04** Exhibition view of "Communication Graphics 20" showing "Disney Go Home" poster designed by James Victore Inc.

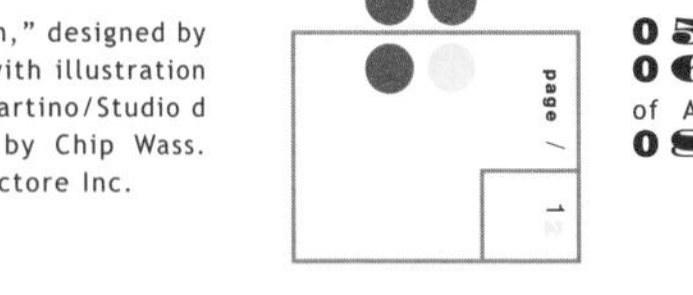

05 Invitation to "Reputedly Illiterate: The Art Books of James Castle," designed by watersdesign.com. **06** Exhibition view of "50 Books/50 Covers of 1999," designed by studio blue. Photograph © Jennifer Krogh. **07** Cover of AIGA Journal of Graphic Design, vol. 18, no. 1, designed by John Fulbrook III with illustration by Joel Holland. **08** Invitation to "50 Books/50 Covers of 1999," designed by studio blue.

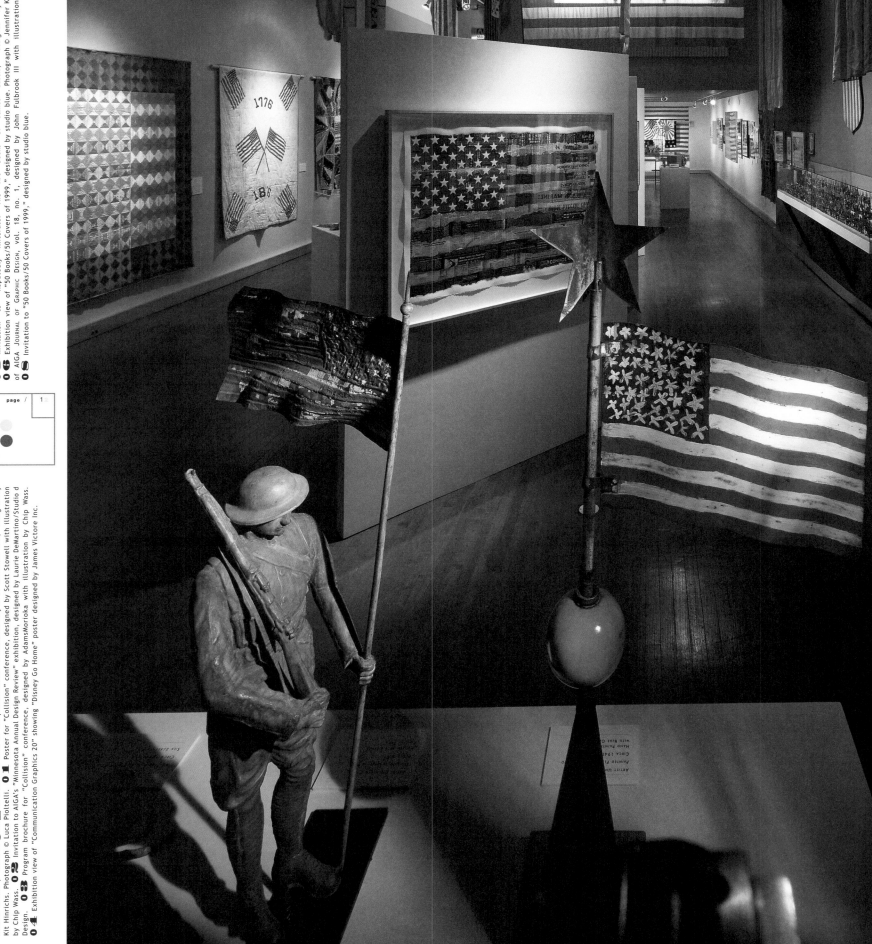

inherent in the field of illustration, and gave their opinion on whether there was hope for this age-old art.

JULY

Stripes and Stars: A Visual History of an American Icon

June 29–August 25, 2000

¶26 This summer, the AIGA National Design Center presented "Stripes and Stars: A Visual History of an American Icon." Originally shown at the San Jose Museum of Art, this exhibition vividly documented America's enduring affair with a true national icon. With little in the way of legal guidelines to limit graphic applications of the nation's flag, Americans have freely and proudly displayed the "stripes and stars," as it was originally known, on many common objects—from embroidery on blankets to lapel pins. Despite various legal restrictions enacted by Congress to regulate popular interpretations of the flag, its motif has continued to appear in many forms.

¶27 Drawn exclusively from the extensive collection of internationally recognized graphic designer Kit Hinrichs, the exhibition attracted 1,741 visitors with a wide variety of objects that celebrated our national symbol and ranged from small historical campaign buttons to kitsch to modern-day sculptural interpretations that incorporate unconventional materials.

Get Out the Vote Posters

¶28 Last summer, AIGA printed 23 different posters that were created by the nation's leading designers in an effort to encourage voter participation. These posters demonstrated the power of effective communication design in stirring public action and reinforced the commitment of the design profession to civic responsibility.

¶29 Posters have a distinguished history in mobilizing public opinion, yet they are often associated with revolutionary or propaganda efforts. In this country, they have not been a highly visible element of the political process—except for on convention floors—for 40 years.

In partnership with Yupo paper, AIGA printed 25,000 posters that were posted in public places in communities across the country by member designers as part of the design profession's national "Get Out the Vote" campaign. The posters began appearing in August and September in an effort to be up by the traditional beginning of the national election campaign on Labor Day.

AUGUST

Advance for Design 3: AIGA Summit on Experience Design

August 11-13, 2000
Telluride, Colorado

¶30 Through provocation and resolution, this "Advance for Design" forum aimed to advance the objectives the group first articulated in its two previous summits, including: Defining the character of experience design and a vocabulary for this emerging discipline, communicating to the business community the nature of experience design in system-integration projects and planning programming activities that will stimulate thinking about experience design. The discussion focused largely on defining a center for this community of practice: Describing what experience designers have in common and what makes this group different from others. Several members have created conceptual models of experience design, some of which were presented and questioned.

¶31 As a preliminary step toward articulating, participants made an effort to discover the "DNA" of the community by profiling those 80 members who were present. Several people offered a preliminary synthesis of the answers given, and it was agreed to refine the results for publication. Other strategies were considered for expanding the discussion to other designers and to those in related disciplines. The group agreed to form a steering committee and subcommittees to coordinate efforts in education, developing regional meetings and activities, case study development and public communications.

SEPTEMBER

AIGA 50 Books/50 Covers of 1999

September 7-October 13, 2000

¶32 This perennial exhibition celebrated selections from AIGA's annual "50 Books/50 Covers" competition, which has recognized excellence in book design and production since 1923. The Chicago-based design firm studio blue created a stunning visual setting for the show, which included books and book covers designed between January 1 and December 31 of the previous year in categories as wide-ranging as trade, reference and juvenile books, as well as university and museum publications and special editions. Separating the show into several different "chapters" by the innovative use of Tyvek banners, studio blue immersed the viewer in an environment that physically expressed the experience of interacting with a book's narrative and design.

AIGA/Aquent Survey of Design Salaries 2000

September 2000

¶33 This survey was conducted on behalf of the AIGA as part of a comprehensive program of activities to serve the professional designer by providing sources of inspiration and strategies for success. The AIGA/Aquent Survey of Design Salaries 2000 updated the last in the series, published in 1998. Based on results drawn from an expanded pool of designers and others allied to the profession, it featured an expanded array of job titles, new data about compensation beyond salary/wages, plus more detailed results at the regional and metropolitan area levels. A particular effort was made to include web-related design and production positions. The survey was conducted on AIGA's

n 01

n 02

n 03

n 04

n 05

n 06

n 07

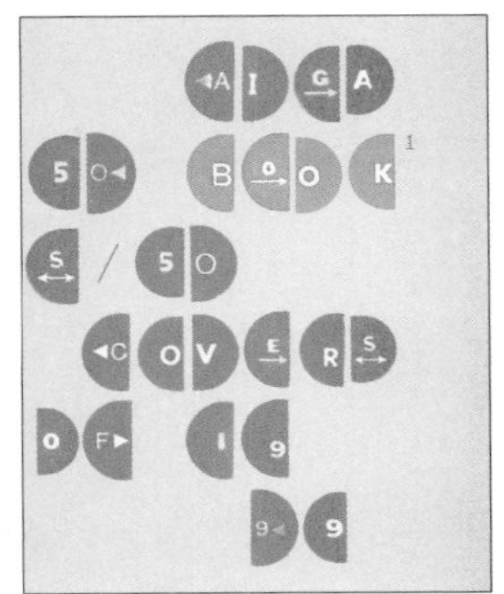

n 08

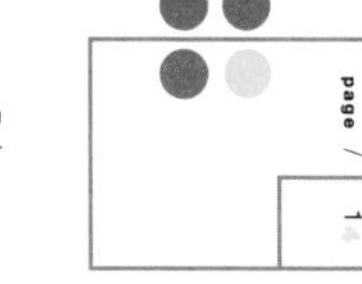

left page AIGA's mezzanine, designed by EFM Design with donor wall by Jennifer Sterling. Photograph © Peter Mauss/Esto. **01** Detail of Untitled Book (Highway Matches: Two Year Catalogue Book) by James Castle. Courtesy A.C. Wade Collection, L.P., and J. Crist Gallery. **02** Political and propaganda flag buttons from 1895-1945, from "Stripes and Stars." **03** "Get Out the Vote" poster, designed by Chris Froeter. **04** Cover of call for entries brochure for AIGA's "Communication Graphics" and "50 Books/50 Covers" competitions, designed by Landor Associates—Frank Mueller.

05 Detail of "Risk/Reward" program guide, designed by Pentagram Design. **06** Detail of "Advance for Design Forum 3" brochure, designed by Sapient. **07** Cover of premier issue of Gain: AIGA Journal of Design for the Network Economy, designed by Sapient.

behalf by Readex, Inc., an independent research company in Stillwater, Minnesota.

OCTOBER

Risk/Reward: AIGA Biennial National Business and Design Conference

October 6-8, 2000
Yerba Buena Gardens, San Francisco

¶34 In early October, AIGA put on "Risk/Reward," a conference that explored the often overstated risks corporations take in investing in sound design and the rewards that successful design solutions bring in terms of market success. The conference took place at the Yerba Buena Center for the Arts, located in the heart of downtown San Francisco's cultural neighborhood and within walking distance of Union Square, the financial district and the South of Market area.

¶35 Presenters included world-renowned architect Frank Gehry and Art Center College of Design president Richard Koshalek, who talked about their current experimental collaboration with students at Art Center; industrial designer Ayse Birsel and Herman Miller research director Jim Long, who explored how they mediated risk and innovation during the development of Herman Miller's new systems-furniture product; and annual-report guru Bill Cahan, who revealed his special approach to making deadly financial statistics come to life.

¶36 Spectacular parties at SFMOMA and the Yerba Buena Center for the Arts—replete with the culinary sophistication of the Bay Area—provided a special sensual contrast to the conference's hard-edged business focus.

NOVEMBER

Gain: AIGA Journal of Design for the Network Economy

November 2000

¶37 Gain is a new journal that was launched in November and will be published twice a year. Dedicated to the topic of interactive and experience design, Gain intends to reach an audience of corporate decision-makers who need to understand how design can simplify the complex in the new network economy. The first two issues of Gain are edited by David Brown (formerly president of Art Center College of Design) and sponsored and designed by Sapient. Gain is published simultaneously on the web and in print. The web edition demonstrates both the power and economy of the medium and the capacity for web-based editorial design. The print version seeks to get the attention of many business leaders and potential clients, with cross-references to the web edition.

Loop: AIGA Journal of Interaction Design Education

¶38 Loop is an interactive, web-only journal providing a forum for presenting research that illuminates and advances understanding of the relationship between practice and pedagogy in the emerging discipline of interaction and visual interface design. Having gone live in October, this academic journal was created by Steve Hoskins and Roy McKelvey of Virginia Commonwealth University in conjunction with AIGA, and resides on the AIGA website.

¶39 Loop serves those people who are investigating new methods of constructing meaningful communication in the new digital environment. Special emphasis has been made on the role of interactivity and nonlinear, multithreaded structures of information design and narrative sequencing.

¶40 As an online publication, Loop regularly publishes articles as well as timely reviews of books, websites and interactive artifacts. It also includes a moderated discussion list allowing for debate of issues raised by contributors and readers.

AIGA Journal of Graphic Design: vol. 18, no. 2

Autumn 2000

¶41 Long-time editor Steven Heller took a bow in this final issue of the journal, which examined the troublesome topic of "Truth in Media Culture." Heller and guest coeditor Milton Glaser posed the perennial question of whether design is an ethically neutral activity. Cultural critics like Kurt Andersen, Denise Caruso, Naomi Klein and Kalle Lasn examine the ways in which truth has been displaced in contemporary society by artificial reality, big business and commercialism—and how designers are partly to blame for our overly hyped culture of consumption.

Art is Work: Milton Glaser Retrospective

November 1-December 28, 2000

¶42 The largest retrospective show ever held of the work of the American graphic designer Milton Glaser, "Art is Work" coincided with the publication of Glaser's new book, a comprehensive survey of his work over the past 25 years. From the famous Bob Dylan poster of 1967 and the universally imitated "I Love NY" logo to the cutting-edge design of his new websites and his masterful illustrations for Dante's Purgatory, Glaser has created some of the most powerful and enduring visual art of our time.

¶43 The extraordinary variety of subject matter and style exhibited in this show, which drew 4,334 visitors, demonstrates why Glaser has been called "the Picasso of graphic arts." The exhibition included his posters, magazine and newspaper designs, interior designs, corporate logos, record albums, magazine illustrations and typography, as well as watercolors, drawings, prints and illustrated books.

n 01

n 02

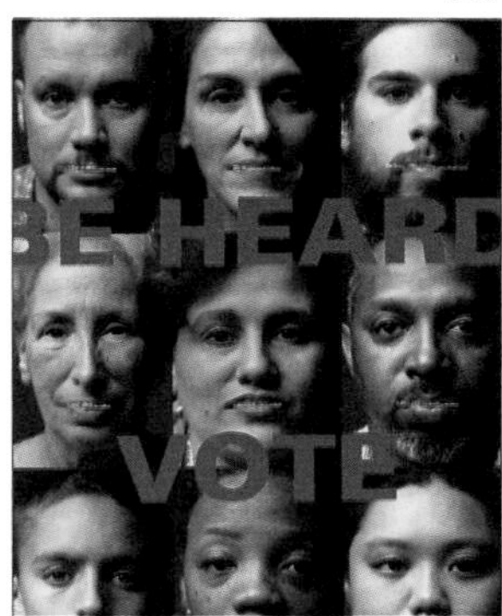

n 03

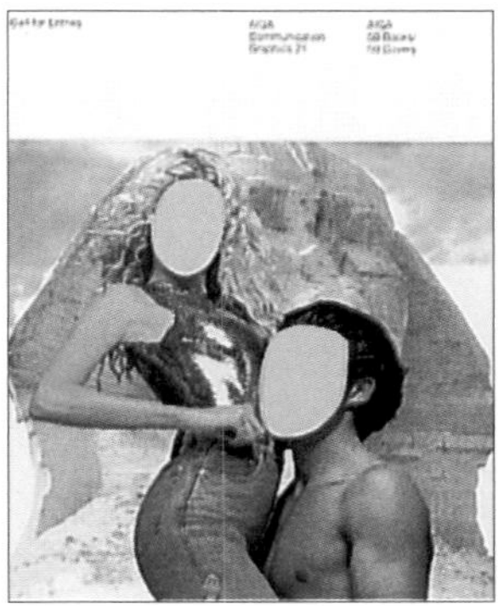

n 04

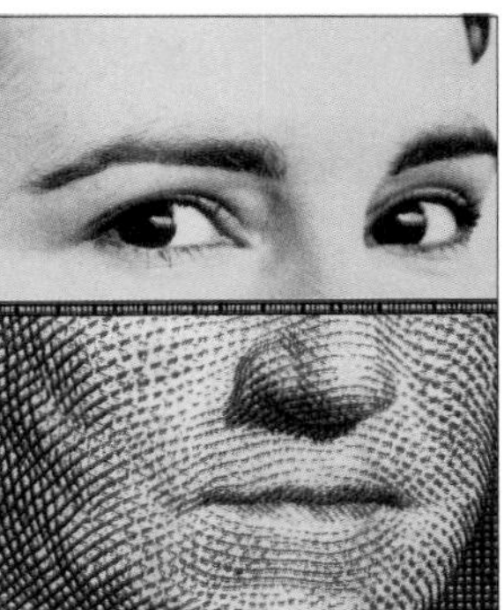

n 05

n 06

n 07

ABOUT AIGA / **left page** Exterior view of AIGA showing "50 Books/50 Covers of 1999" exhibition, designed by studio blue. Photograph © Jennifer Krogh. **01** Milton Glaser illustration for Dante's PURGATORIO, displayed in "Art is Work" exhibition. **02** Detail of invitation to "AIGA Communication Graphics 20" exhibition, designed by watersdesign.com **03** Detail of cover of GRAPHIC DESIGN USA: 20, designed by Fred Woodward (interior designed by Cheung/Crowell Design). **04** Exhibition view of "50 Books/50 Covers" exhibition, designed by studio blue.

05 "Get Out the Vote" poster, designed by Robynne Raye. **06** Detail of invitation to "AIGA Communication Graphics 20" exhibition, designed by watersdesign.com. **07** Exhibition view of "Stripes and Stars," designed by Kit Hinrichs. Photograph © Luca Pioltelli.

Draw: AIGA Seminar on Illustration

November 21, 2000
Galapagos, Brooklyn

¶44 AIGA believes that illustration is an integral and important element of graphic design—although one that has not received as much discrete attention in recent years as it deserves. This event, which took place in a building that used to house a mayonnaise factory, examined issues vital to the culture and practice of illustrators and designers who use illustration.

¶47 Cochaired and organized by Nicholas Blechman (illustrator and art director, formerly of the New York Times op-ed page) and Christoph Niemann (illustrator), "Draw" consisted of three theme-based panel discussions that provided lots of opportunity for audience participation.

n 01

n 02

n 03

n 04

n 05

n 06

n 07

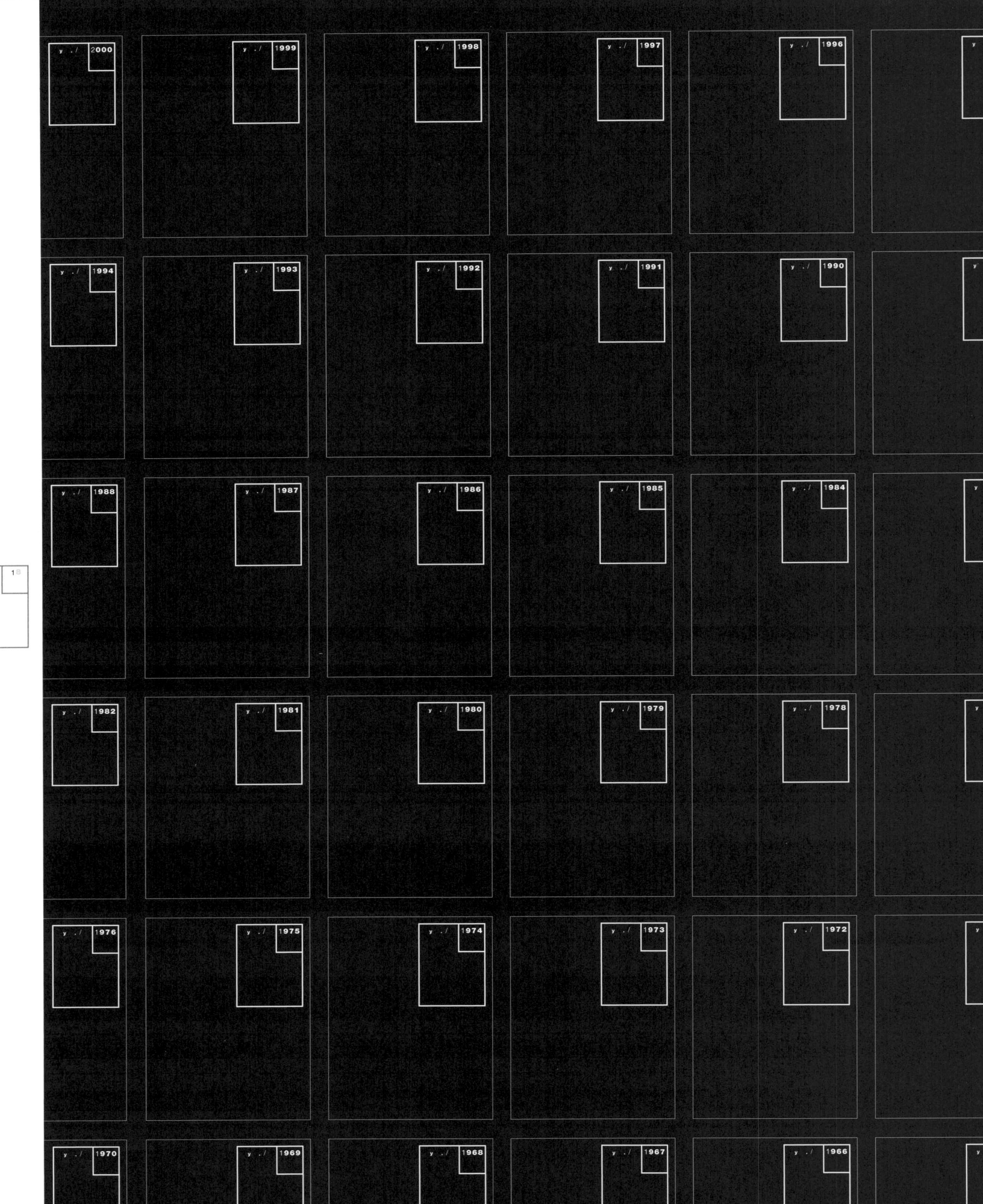
y ./ 2000
y ./ 1999
y ./ 1998
y ./ 1997
y ./ 1996
y ./ 1994
y ./ 1993
y ./ 1992
y ./ 1991
y ./ 1990
y ./ 1988
y ./ 1987
y ./ 1986
y ./ 1985
y ./ 1984
y ./ 1982
y ./ 1981
y ./ 1980
y ./ 1979
y ./ 1978
y ./ 1976
y ./ 1975
y ./ 1974
y ./ 1973
y ./ 1972
y ./ 1970
y ./ 1969
y ./ 1968
y ./ 1967
y ./ 1966

Introduction to AIGA Medal

¶01 The medal of AIGA, the most distinguished in the field, is awarded to individuals in recognition of their exceptional achievements, services or other contributions to the field of graphic design and visual communication. The contribution may be in the practice of graphic design, teaching, writing or leadership of the profession. The awards may honor designers posthumously.

¶02 Medals have been awarded since 1920 to individuals who have set standards of excellence over a lifetime of work or have made individual contributions to innovation within the practice of design.

¶03 Individuals who are honored may work in any country, but the contribution for which they are honored should have had a significant impact on the practice of graphic design in the United States.

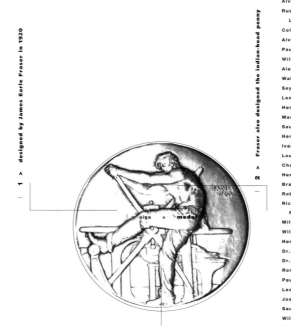

aiga medal recipients

years. | 1920 - 2000

previous medal recipients

P. Scott Makela and Laurie Haycock Makela. Fred Seibert. Michael Vanderbyl.	y 200 -0
Tibor Kalman. Steven Heller. Katherine McCoy.	y 199 -9
Louis Danziger. April Greiman.	y 199 -8
Lucian Bernhard. Zuzana Licko and Rudy VanderLans.	y 199 -7
Cipe Pineles. George Lois.	y 199 -6
Matthew Carter. Stan Richards. Ladislav Sutnar.	y 199 -5
Muriel Cooper. John Massey.	y 199 -4
Alvin Lustig. Tomoko Miho.	y 199 -3
Rudolph de Harak. George Nelson. Lester Beall.	y 199 -2
Colin Forbes. E. McKnight Kauffer.	y 199 -1
Alvin Eisenman. Frank Zachary.	y 199 -0
Paul Davis. Bea Feitler.	y 198 -9
William Golden. George Tscherny.	y 198 -8
Alexey Brodovitch. Gene Federico.	y 198 -7
Walter Herdeg.	y 198 -6
Seymour Chwast.	y 198 -5
Leo Lionni.	y 198 -4
Herbert Matter.	y 198 -3
Massimo and Leila Vignelli.	y 198 -2
Saul Bass.	y 198 -1
Herb Lubalin.	y 198 -0
Ivan Chermayeff and Thomas Geismar.	y 197 -9
Lou Dorfsman.	y 197 -8
Charles and Ray Eames.	y 197 -7
Henry Wolf. Jerome Snyder.	y 197 -6
Bradbury Thompson.	y 197 -5
Robert Rauschenberg.	y 197 -4
Richard Avedon. Allen Hurlburt. Philip Johnson.	y 197 -3
Milton Glaser.	y 197 -2
Will Burtin.	y 197 -1
Herbert Bayer.	y 197 -0
Dr. Robert R. Leslie.	y 196 -9
Dr. Giovanni Mardersteig.	y 196 -8
Romana Javitz.	y 196 -7
Paul Rand.	y 196 -6
Leonard Baskin.	y 196 -5
Josef Albers.	y 196 -4
Saul Steinberg.	y 196 -3
Wilhelm Sandberg.	y 196 -2
Paul A. Bennett.	y 196 -1
Walter Paepcke.	y 196 -0
May Massee.	y 195 -9
Ben Shahn.	y 195 -8
Dr. M. F. Agha.	y 195 -7
Ray Nash.	y 195 -6
P. J. Conkwright.	y 195 -5
Will Bradley. Jan Tschichold.	y 195 -4
George Macy.	y 195 -3
Joseph Blumenthal.	y 195 -2
Harry L. Gage.	y 195 -1
Earnest Elmo Calkins. Alfred A. Knopf.	y 195 -0
Lawrence C. Wroth.	y 194 -8
Elmer Adler.	y 194 -7
Stanley Morison.	y 194 -6
Frederic G. Melcher.	y 194 -5
Edward Epstean.	y 194 -4
Edwin and Robert Grabhorn.	y 194 -2
Carl Purington Rollins.	y 194 -1
Thomas M. Cleland.	y 194 -0
William A. Kittredge.	y 193 -9
Rudolph Ruzicka. J. Thompson Willing.	y 193 -5
Henry Lewis Bullen.	y 193 -4
Porter Garnett.	y 193 -2
Dard Hunter.	y 193 -1
Henry Watson Kent.	y 193 -0
William A. Dwiggins.	y 192 -9
Timothy Cole. Frederic W. Goudy.	y 192 -7
Burton Emmett.	y 192 -6
Bruce Rogers.	y 192 -5
John C. Agar. Stephen H. Horgan.	y 192 -4
Daniel Berkeley Updike.	y 192 -2
Norman T. A. Munder.	y 192 -0

1 > designed by James Earle Fraser in 1920

2 > Fraser also designed the indian-head penny

aiga = medal

3 > medal depicts a printing pressman at work

aiga medal recipients

years. | 1920 - 2000

aiga medal recipients

years. | 1920 - 2000

previous medal recipients

previous medal recipients

previous medal recipients

previous medal recipients

p. scott and laurie haycock makela.

aiga medal. | 01

p. scott and laurie haycock makela.

aiga medal. | 01

p. scott and laurie haycock makela.

aiga medal. | 01

Truly, Madly, Deeply: P. Scott and Laurie Haycock Makela | By Peter Hall

¶01 The venue for Laurie Haycock and P. Scott Makela's first encounter was auspicious, a coming together of design with things unconventional, imaginative and wobbly. The occasion was the "first and last" annual Jell-O mold competition, organized by the Los Angeles chapter of AIGA in 1985. "Everybody brought Jell-O molds—about 25 of them—some absolutely gross and some fantastical," recalls April Greiman, who was vice president of events for the L.A. chapter at the time. "When you meet somebody at an important event like that, it has to be fate."

¶02 The event did not go over well with the senior members of the chapter and never took place again. Its only lasting legacy was the 14-year relationship between Haycock and Makela, a partnership that produced—much as when you mix water with gelatin and fruit flavors—more than the sum of its parts. When friends, colleagues and peers describe the Haycock-Makela phenomenon, a picture emerges of two very different and independent sensibilities that came together in a remarkable fusion. By the time they became the resident cochairs of 2-D design at Cranbrook Academy of Art in 1997, each had a firmly established reputation. If Makela was known for his loud, vibrant, high-tech approach to design, Haycock was known for her thoughtful experimentalism and refined typography. Greiman describes the combination as upper body (Haycock)/lower body (Makela), though this, of course, depends on where you stand.

¶03 It was Haycock's passion that struck Lorraine Wild when she first encountered the designer during an interview at California Institute for the Arts for a faculty position. "When I came to see what was going on at CalArts, I watched Laurie teach and thought, This is a brilliant teacher," says Wild, an L.A.-based designer-educator who was chair of graphic design at the school from 1985 to 1991. "She was one of those people who was very engaged with what is in front of her in the classroom. She could draw the best out of the students and be their best advocate, and through advocacy, and haranguing them, essentially dare them to do better work." Haycock and Wild subsequently collaborated on design projects, including a series of books for the Getty Center for the History of the Arts and Humanities, the Getty's academic press. The content of the series was dry and arcane—what Wild calls "extreme scholarship"— but Haycock managed to breathe some life into the essays by treating them as malleable forms. "Laurie's instinct was to deal with the sensual, physical quality of the text," says Wild. "Even with three levels of subnotes she could be incredibly inventive."

¶04 Wild subsequently hired Makela, who moved to Los Angeles after graduating from Minneapolis College of Art and Design (MCAD), to teach a sophomore class at CalArts. "He was just a barrel of energy," she recalls, offering one of many variations on the zesty descriptives that have been attached to Makela. His distinctive design sensibility did not emerge, however, until he left L.A. with Haycock to attend the post-graduate program at Cranbrook. The definitive Makela project came after graduation: the Minneapolis College of Art and Design's catalogue for the 1992-93 academic year. Produced with a "100 percent digital process," according to Makela's extensive technical analysis of the project in I.D. magazine, it featured all the future hallmarks of the designer, an early adopter if ever there were. It was produced in a high-energy frenzy (on a two-week design and production schedule) on the latest computer equipment and software available (Hi-8 video, continuously crashing 60 MB Quark files, Fontographer, Freehand and PhotoShop). With rich, dimensional montages and bold, custom-made typefaces, the catalogue beat its metaphorical head against the limitations of the available time and technology with unmitigated enthusiasm. "The speed required to produce this project on deadline, together with the creation of digital imagery, became a valuable aesthetic underpinning for the catalogue's design," wrote Makela in I.D. He made no attempt to hide the technology, but let it define the aesthetic, which in turn was guided by his perception of the audience, "17-to-24 year-olds interested in choosing an undergraduate art school but who were more familiar with MTV and computers than with Rapidograph pens and firing kilns."

¶05 Across town at the Walker Art Center, Haycock—now Laurie Haycock Makela—had taken the position of design director and was working to redefine the contemporary arts institution. With the departure of the center's venerated design director Mildred (Mickey) Friedman and her husband, Martin, came the opportunity to address the institution's visual identity, until now characterized by an unwavering adherence to the clinical International Style. With the support of the museum's new director, Kathy Halbreich, Haycock Makela hauled the institution's mailers, catalogues and publications into the 1990s, introducing new typefaces like DIN, Imago and her husband's Carmela, and "shutting down the white space," as she told I.D. in 1993. At root was a desire to reflect the museum's culturally diverse program in its visual language. As design director, she also had an opportunity (albeit short-lived) to revise the center's publication Design Quarterly, most memorably in the Winter 1993 issue, where three designers were asked to submit unreleased typefaces—experimental, in-progress or discarded. Ed Fella delivered the hand-rendered Out West on a 15 Degree Ellipse—now an Emigre font—while Zuzana Licko provided the spiky serif face Quartet, and Matthew Carter sent Sophia, inspired by letterforms from sixth-century Constantinople. "It was interesting in that Laurie did not commission typefaces but asked what we had in the bottom drawer," reflects Carter. "I wish more people would do that." The experiment

AIGA MEDAL. P. SCOTT AND LAURIE HAYCOCK MAKELA / **left page** "Cranbrook Design: The New Discourse" poster, 1990. **01** Detail from Minneapolis College of Art and Design's DEFINE catalogue, 1996. **02** Detail from Walker Art Center "Juneteenth" lecture series poster, 1994. **03** Detail from "The Wild Next" poster and magazine cover, 1994. **04** Detail from "Digital Campfires: Stories of Life and Liberty" project, 1996. **05** Detail from "Cranbrook Design: The New Discourse" poster, 1990.

06 Detail from Minneapolis College of Art and Design catalogue, 1993. **07** Detail from Walker Art Center "Musicians of Jajouka" poster, 1994.

ART science

Nothing pulls you into the territory between art and

the new discourse

the new CRANBROOK DESIGN discourse

n 01

n 02

n 03

n 04

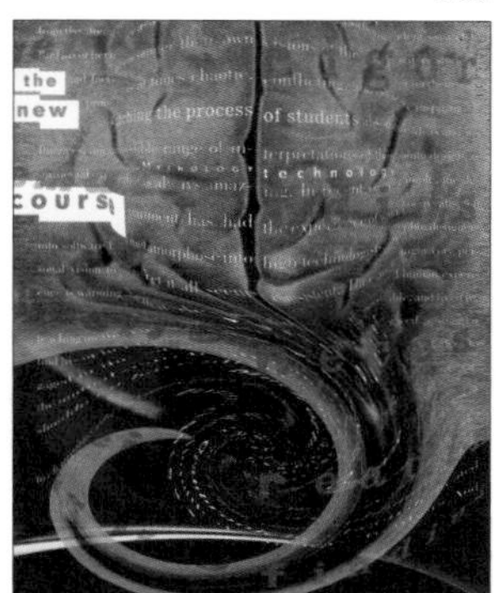

n 05

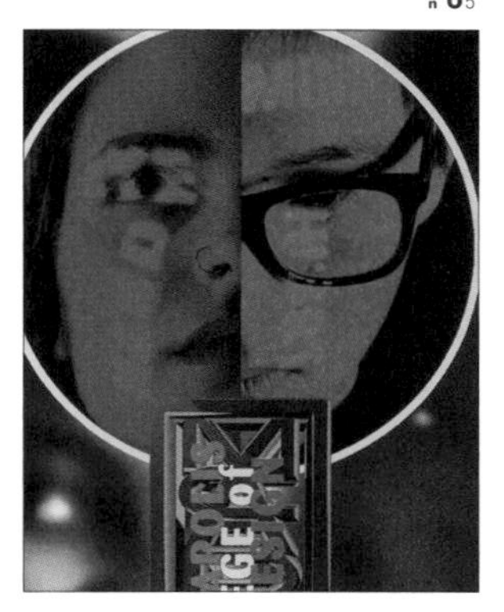

n 06

n 07

MAKELA P. SCOTT

BURN

PAPER + CATHODE

(new graphic design for print, film and global digital media)

an exhibit at Kendall College of Art and Design

opening reception Feb 15, 4-6pm

and on the internet at http://www.grfn.org/~makela/

FEBRUARY 15 - MARCH 15 1995

gallery talk wed, feb 15, 2:30pm

...upport of the Michigan Council for Arts and Cultural Affairs, The Etheridge Company, Modern Imaging, Central Michigan Paper Company, Veenstra Reproductions, Herman Miller Inc., Grand Rapids Public Library, Grand Rapids Freenet ... The Imaging Network. Film preparation done on Scitex equipment. Film output on a Scitex Dolev 800.

AIGA MEDAL. P. SCOTT AND LAURIE HAYCOCK MAKELA / **left page** "Burn/Born" poster announcing exhibition of Makela's work at Kendall College of Art and Design, 1995.

proved particularly fruitful when Haycock Makela recognized that Carter might also provide the solution to the problem of finding an identity system for the Walker that could reflect its polymorphous outlook. By requesting a flexible, modular house typeface instead of a conventional, monolithic logo, she paved the way for Carter's historic Walker, with its snap-on serifs. "I came up with a few ideas, none of which I had much confidence in at the time," recalls Carter. "I listened to Laurie and Kathy Halbreich shoot down these trial balloons, and knew what I had to do: a typeface that could be modified by its user."

¶06 In the years before joining their careers at Cranbrook in 1997, Haycock and Makela separately developed interests and methodologies that increasingly came to resemble each other's. Makela, by now on the international lecture circuit as a multimedia design star ("while everybody is standing around contemplating multimedia, Makela is doing it," noted EMIGRE founder Rudy VanderLans in 1993), embarked on a collaboration with video and commercial director Jeffery Plansker. His bulging, hybrid typefaces appeared in two memorable Plansker spots: for the TV channel UTV and for Vans shoes, the latter a series of compelling live-action optical tricks that included a double-sided card printed with apparently random letters (in Makela's Dead History typeface) spinning to spell the phrase "think twice." Haycock, meanwhile, was not only putting Makela's fonts to good use in Walker catalogues like IN THE SPIRIT OF FLUXUS (1993), she was turning up the volume in her print work. Her design with Kristen McDougall of a 1994 Bruce Nauman exhibition catalogue featured fragments of a Nauman video blown up to almost (but not quite) unintelligible proportions, with large display type rotated and pushed to the page's edge until the letter tops were sliced off. While the designers' stated aim was to create a book that reflected the "purity and vigor of a mathematics textbook and a spiritual text," the proximity of Makela's approach clearly had some effect in firing up their methodology. Type gains the power of image, and image becomes texture—at least on the covers. In Makela's work the layering was more extreme. As he put it in 1992 in EMIGRE, "I am trying to grab a chunk of experience and have that bleed off all edges."

¶07 The Makelas' ideas about running Cranbrook's design department were often as unconventional—and controversial—as their work. While it was expected that department chairs would continue their professional careers, some students and outside observers questioned the Makelas' blurring of boundaries between the classroom and the commercial world. Cranbrook was even called a "sweatshop" after a Nike commission for Words + Pictures, the commercial arm of the Makelas, became a studio assignment (students were paid for their contributions). The Makelas also incorporated student work in their public presentations, which pleased the more extroverted people in the class, but displeased those who wished to maintain a strong sense of ownership, and downright pissed off those whose work was never chosen for the shows.

¶08 On the other hand, many students and visiting lecturers came away from the campus in Bloomfield Hills, Michigan, as if they had received an adrenaline shot. Among them is Stefan Sagmeister, who recently chose to embark on a year's "nonclient work" inspired to no small extent by what he saw and experienced during a visit to Cranbrook. "The program was unbelievable when I saw it, because the students were truly mature—they had five years of work behind them and could do honest experimentation. Two or three days there definitely had something to do with my year without clients. I felt that what they were doing was very healthy."

¶09 The Makelas' methodology, immortalized in their 1998 book and website project WHEREISHERE, was symbolized by a circle surrounded by three words—Obsession, Means, Audience—and penetrated by a fourth, (De)material. Candidates interviewing for a place at Cranbrook would be asked by a panel of current-year students and the Makelas, "What is your obsession?" The essence of the program was for students to use their obsession—"your ignition, swag, food and payload"—to drive a creative project toward its audience, guided by the chosen tools ("means") and media ("dematerial").

¶10 If WHEREISHERE mystified much of the design world outside Cranbrook, it was because it was a strange hybrid—the Makelas' radically experimental fusion of Eastern and Western ideas and a selection of contemporary design work—without any serious attempt at explication. In the Western tradition were the obsessions—technology and sex, how they define us and shock us—represented in the cover, an out-of-focus detail of a photograph of interracial anal sex. "Scott's question was always, 'What will shock people?' And then, 'How can you get it into stores in Singapore?'" says Warren Corbitt, a Cranbrook student who also worked at Words + Pictures (including on the design of the book). In the Eastern tradition was a devotion to Buddhist philosophy (Haycock's brother is a Buddhist monk), a belief that eternity can be experienced in a moment and that wordless teaching can be sublime.

¶11 The best illustration of the Makelas' fusion of Western ideas of technology and sexuality and Eastern philosophy is Haycock's shocking story, told in WHEREISHERE, of her brain hemorrhage, a "congenital time bomb" set off by "three sequential orgasms in the ladies room of a trendy restaurant in SoHo, New York." The text, set in Carmela type opposite a scan of her injured brain, starts off in vivid imagistic fashion, littered with medical terminology and blunt detail, and ends with a mystical explanation of the phrase-word that became the book's title. "The Zen

LM: A PUBLICATION CALLED . . .

FLUXUS,

GM: AND THAT'S IT, THAT WAS GOING TO BE LIKE A BOOK, WITH A TITLE, THAT'S ALL.

AIGA MEDAL. P. SCOTT AND LAURIE HAYCOCK MAKELA / **left page** Cover of In the Spirit of Fluxus book for Walker Art Center, 1993. **01** Cover of Empathy, Form and Space book created by Haycock Makela and Lorraine Wild for the Getty Center for the History of the Arts and Humanities, 1992. **02** Detail from "Flesh & Fluid" poster, 1990. **03** Detail from In the Spirit of Fluxus, 1993. **04** Cover of Modern Architecture: Otto Wagner book created by Haycock Makela and Lorraine Wild for the Getty Center for the History of Arts and Humanities, 1989.

05 and 06 Details from "Brilliant: New Art from London" printed ephemera for Walker Art Center, 1995.

n 01

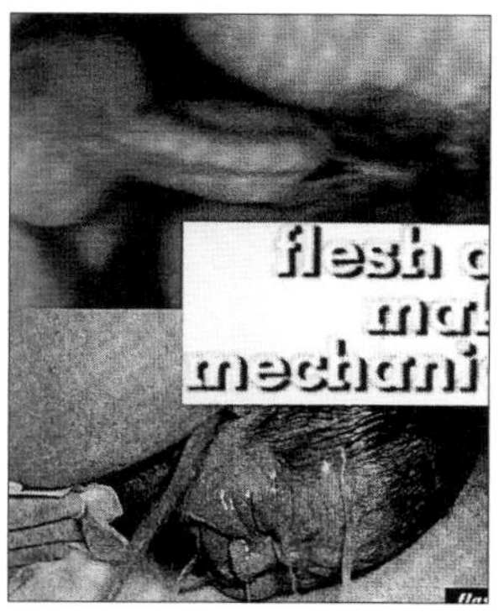

n 02

n 03

n 04

n 05

n 06

1 Pay Attention (1973), lithograph on Arjomari paper, 38 ¼ x 28 ¼ in. (97.2 x 71.8 cm). Published by
G.E.L., Los Angeles.
PAUL SCHIMMEL
Bruce Nauman's relationship to the view
only makes art for us but also tells us how to see it. He creates
extended concentration from the viewer. In Pay Attention (1973
printed in reverse in stacked block letters: "PAY ATTENTION MOTHE
before we know it. "By describing both our experience and its spec
You has written, "Pay Attention . . . successfully integrates our a
what we see."1 Throughout Nauman's career he has baited, controll
angered, imperiled, experimented with, and manipulated us—his
within his parameters. He establishes a uniquely instructional
meaning of the piece is what it does to us.
In a 1971 interview Nauman described
metaphor to explain its effect on the viewer:
It had to do with going up the stairs in the
step and you take the step, but you are al
stairs and expecting there to be another st
seems that you always have that jolt and i
these pieces work they do that too. Someth
it happens every time. You know why, and
the same thing. It is very curious.2
More recently, Nauman described his "jolt" to the audience as a feeling "
bat. Or better, like getting hit in the back of the neck. You never see it com

AIGA MEDAL. P. SCOTT AND LAURIE HAYCOCK MAKELA / **left page** Detail of spread from BRUCE NAUMAN book for Walker Art Center, 1994.

master uses a technique called the koan to sharpen the mind," writes Haycock. "'What is this?' he might ask the student, holding up one finger. With the speed and precision of dueling swords, the student answers 'this.' 'Where is here?' he asks, looking the student in the eye. The student answers 'here.'" The intent of the koan is to encourage mindfulness—an awareness of the present moment. The significance of the phrase "whereishere" is intensified by Haycock's own story; her survival was celebrated by a neurologist to a class of Cornell medical students. "What is the most important fact of this case?" the doctor asked. The answer: "She is here!"

¶12 Makela's own interpretation of "whereishere" was perhaps more a craving for a moment of intense awareness brought on by something resembling an orgasm, epiphany and system overload. His last and most important project win was for Rossignol, a Vermont-based snowboard and ski maker. A passionate snowboarder, Makela fended off competition from much larger advertising agencies with the sheer energy of his presentation, which dwelt on the sublime nature of the sport. "Scott loved snowboarding and mountain biking," says Paul Schneider, a Cranbrook student who took on the Rossignol project. "He had always meditated, but he once told me that finding these activities allowed him to meditate at a speed which felt comfortable to his mind."

¶13 Schneider recently left Words + Pictures to form his own L.A.-based firm, which he named Wide Open Spaces in homage to P. Scott Makela's love of the great outdoors. Corbitt, who collaborated with Schneider, has a lasting impression of Makela: "Scott was a power-chord designer. He'd get the biggest amp and pick you could find and go blam. I remember seeing him in his studio with Swiss trance stuff playing over Real Audio, working on MTV stuff while a snowboarding video was on the television and [the Makelas' daughter] Carmela running around. He always had to have so many data streams going on. He never had the time to get bored by one thing."

¶14 Makela never, in fact, slowed down. During his last year at Cranbrook, he and Haycock landed an MTV project to design and direct on-air spots. "Scott locked himself in a room with an Avid editor and came out with 16 different cuts in just about an hour. Each five- or six-second version was so wild I worried MTV wouldn't be able to run them," remembers Schneider. "These things were fast even by the quickest video-game-teen-attention-deficit-standard. The MTV editor was shell-shocked, and Scott was beaming with delight. I always felt those spots were just about normal in their pacing with relation to his mind."

¶15 The frenetic pace of Makela's life ended tragically in May 1999, with his death at age 39 of complications from a viral infection. It was an untimely end, to say the least. At Cranbrook, the Makelas had just begun to send out the first waves of influence, with their first class of first-year students nearing graduation. As partners of a commercial practice, they were winning increasingly prestigious and coveted jobs, from the film titles for David Fincher's FIGHT CLUB to the advertising and marketing campaign for Rossignol. As a couple, they had two children, aged eight and six months, and a flourishing musical project. "They were just starting to hit a good stride, starting to make a giant wave," adds Greiman. "They were a powerful combination, a couple where one plus one does not equal two, but three."

¶16 In awarding a medal to Haycock and a posthumous medal to Makela, it would be easy to convey the wrong impression—that AIGA thinks the show is over. This would underestimate the strength and autonomy of Haycock, who will continue to chair the design department at Cranbrook through the end of this year while raising a family and pursuing her music and performance career. In effect, a new chapter has begun, and the design world waits to see where her next steps lead.

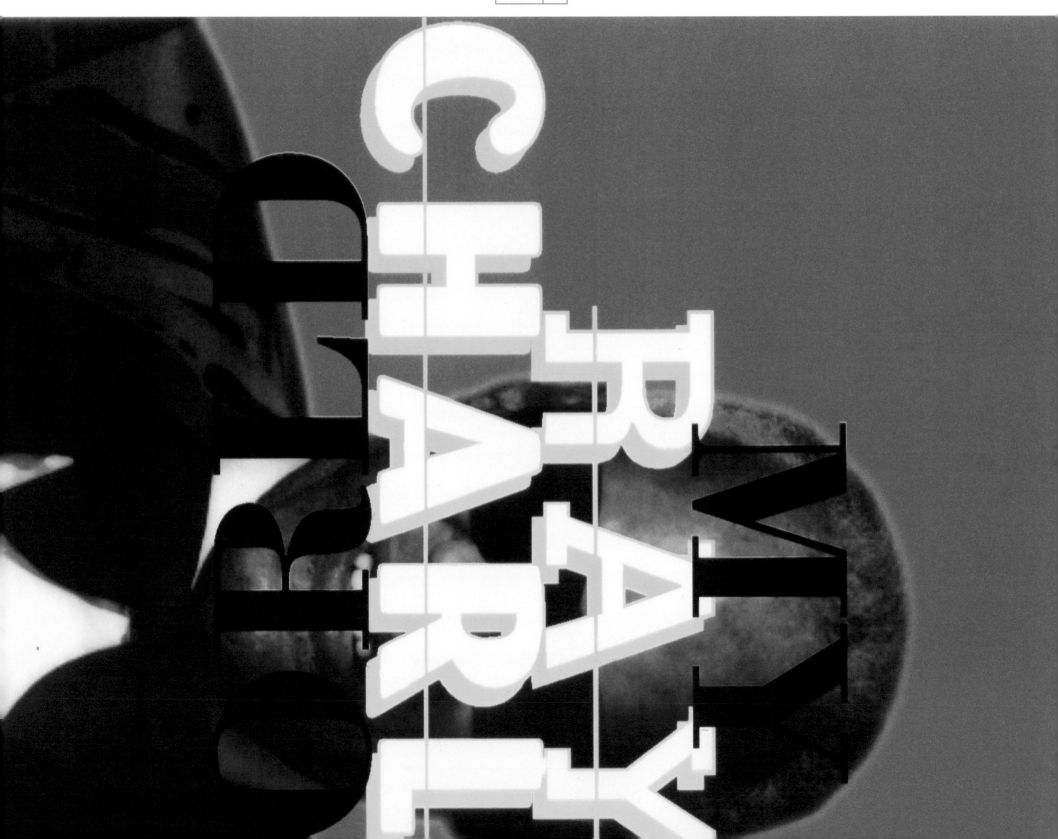

AIGA MEDAL. P. SCOTT AND LAURIE HAYCOCK MAKELA / **left page** Detail from CD cover created for Ray Charles' My World, 1992. **01** Detail from Willem de Kooning: The Late Paintings, The 1980s book for Walker Art Center, 1995. **02** Still from "Lotus: This is Notes" TV advertisement, 1995. **03** Detail from "10ls" poster for the 10th issue of Eye magazine, 1993. **04** Detail from corporate identity for Propoganda Films, 1995. **05** Detail from CD cover created for David Sylvian's Everything+Nothing, 1995.

06 Detail from CD cover created for Todd Levin's DeLuxe, 1995. **07** Detail from "Living Surfaces" conference poster for the American Center for Design, 1993.

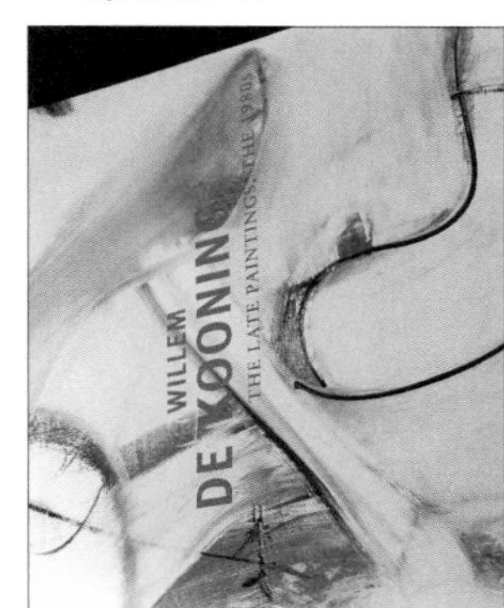

n 01

n 02

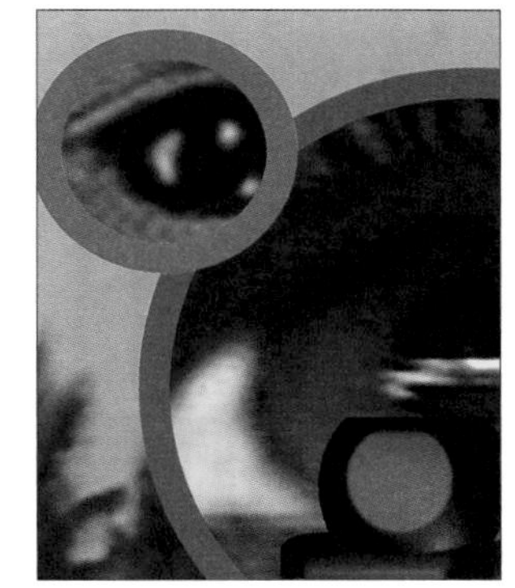

n 03

n 04

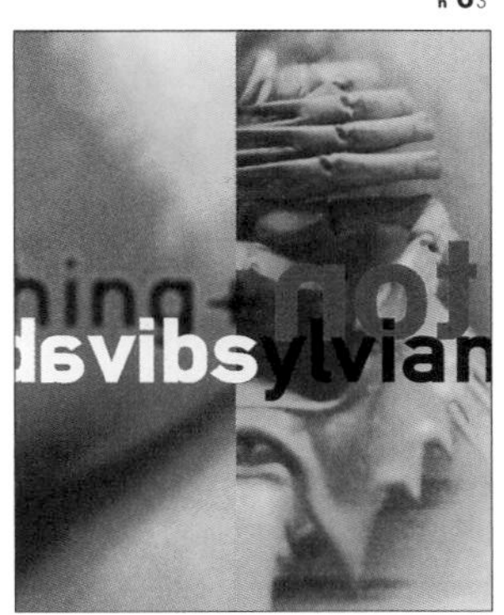

n 05

n 06

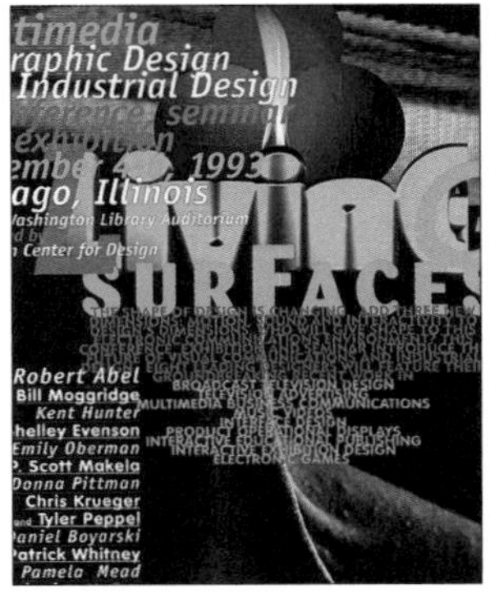

n 07

left page Still from Michael and Janet Jackson's "Scream" music video, 1995. **01** Cover of In What Style Should We Build? book created by Haycock Makela and Lorraine Wild for the Getty Center for the History of the Arts and Humanities, 1992. **02** Type detail from Michael and Janet Jackson's "Scream" music video, 1995. **03** Page detail from In the Spirit of Fluxus, 1993. **04** Page detail from Willem de Kooning: The Late Paintings, The 1980s, 1995.

05 Concept for "Nomadic Work Station" created with Don Carr for Nynex Media Lab, 1991. **06** Cover from Bruce Nauman, 1994. **07** Page detail from In What Style Should We Build?, 1992.

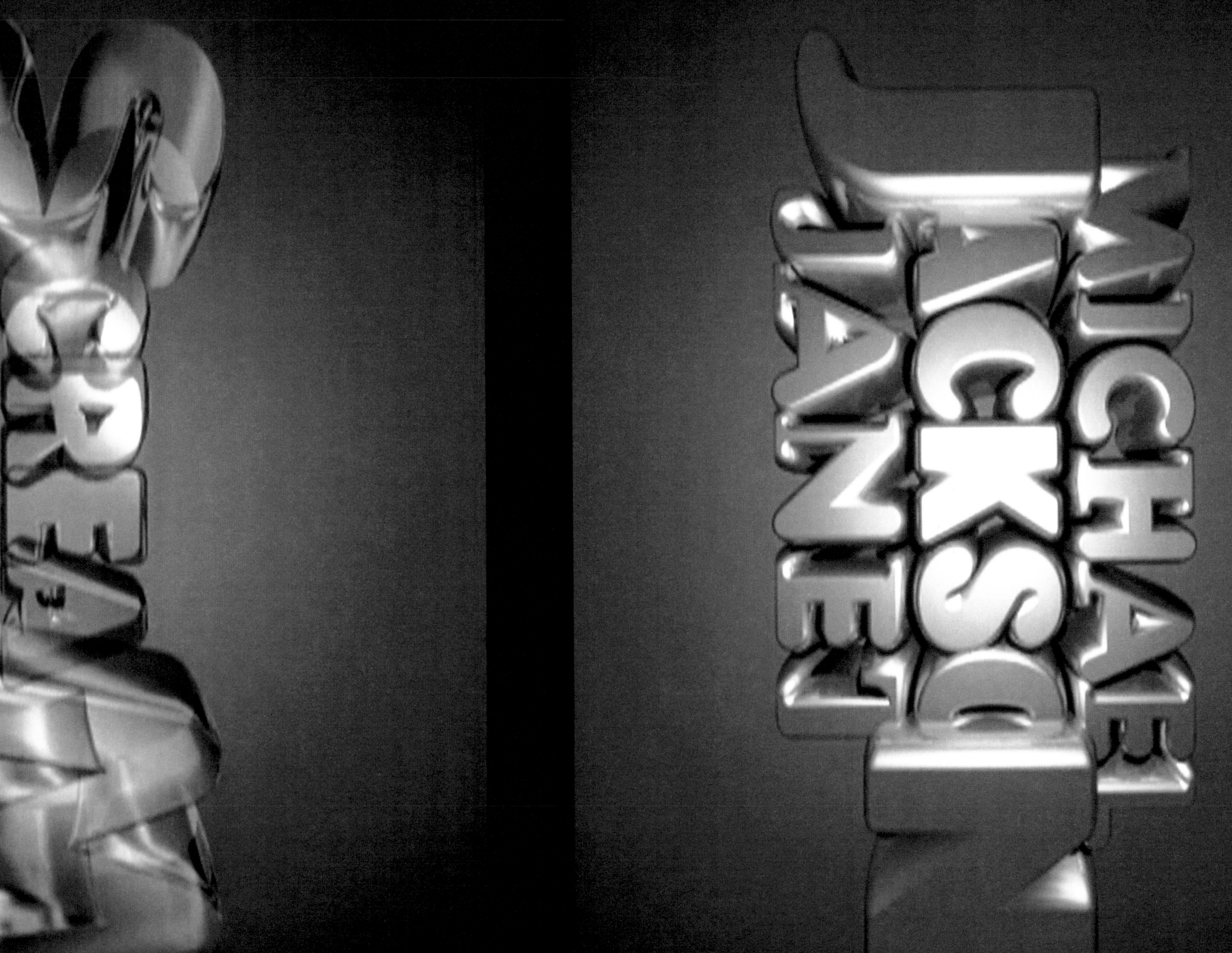

n 01

n 02

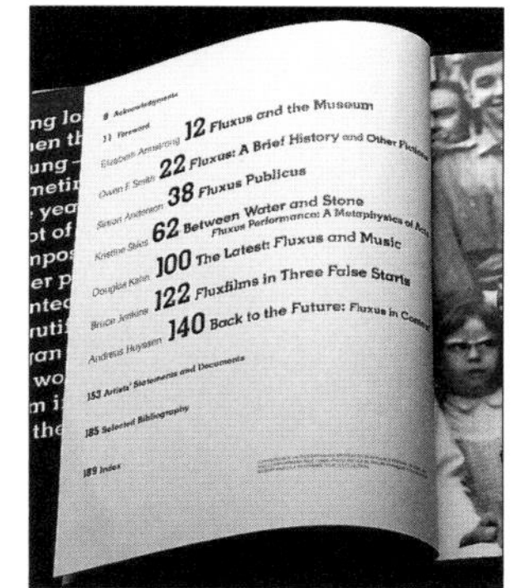

n 03

n 04

n 05

n 06

n 07

fred seibert.

aiga medal. | 02

fred seibert.

aiga medal. | 02

fred seibert.

aiga medal. | 02

The Instigator: Fred Seibert | **By Steven Heller**

¶01 Fred Seibert's career proves that it is not necessary to be a Yale/Cranbrook/RISD/SVA-educated, AIGA/Type Directors/Art Directors Club-award-winning, bona fide/pedigreed/certified graphic designer, or any other kind of designer, to create the most indelible visual identities for some of the most visible pop culture media in the world. You just have to be a fan. A fervent, ardent, passionate devotee of "people who do fantastic work in music and visual stuff," as Seibert puts it.

¶02 Oh, yeah, you also have to have the vision thing.

¶03 Without vision, and the talent, know-how and ambition to realize it, Seibert might have become a tie-dyed-in-the-wool Dead Head selling pot brownies from the back of a psychedelicized microbus. Instead, he instigated, orchestrated, facilitated and otherwise dreamed up the nascent visual personas of MTV and Nickelodeon, back when they were truly vanguards of the pop-cultural revolution. In the ensuing years he has exerted a significant influence on the look and content of animated cartoons, first as president of Hanna-Barbera and later as the founder of Frederator, a cartoon production company that provides programming to the Cartoon Network. If these accomplishments were not enough for one lifetime, he was also president of both MTV Networks Online and Nickelodeon Online, where he had a hand in transforming the Internet by provoking, stimulating and triggering numerous creative collisions. Seibert recently left to commit himself full-time to further developing Frederator.

¶04 "Seibert may not fit the accepted definition of a graphic designer, but he practices design in the emerging sense of the term, as a producer of ideas," says Forrest Richardson, a graphic designer and a member of the 1999 AIGA Medal selection committee. "Seibert designs in the broadest sense by enlisting other people who create unprecedented ideas. Just look at what he has spawned."

¶05 What he spawned was a series of environments—at MTV, Nickelodeon, Hanna-Barbera and the Cartoon Network—where creative misfits were able to create unconventional film and animation that otherwise would have had few, if any, outlets. And possessed with a keen ability to see beyond the current thing to the next big thing, and even a few things beyond that, Seibert has a knack for predicting what the public will like, because as a fan he likes it too. In a formal sense, he constructs complex matrices of interconnected concepts designed to support overarching visual communications that project mnemonic identifying images. More simply put, he matches the right person with the best project to get extraordinary results. Moreover, he understands the distinction between integration and interference and rarely asks creative people to slavishly execute his own ideas. "They will do it grudgingly, and expensively," he explains. Rather, he defines contexts, provides opportunities and encourages individual points of view that are used as components of larger programs. He employs those people—young and old, neophyte and veteran—who can interpret a basic blueprint and transcend its confines. So in addition to being an ersatz designer, Seibert is a full-blown impresario. He is also the proverbial whiz kid, the one who always dreamed of making great things.

¶06 "The Beatles proved that you could zig and zag through various polarities and still be the thing that you were," recalls Seibert, who was born in 1951 and heard the Beatles for the first time when he was 12 years old. He still speaks of that defining moment with breathless enthusiasm. "It was a really inspiring thing for me to know that you could go from Sergeant Pepper's to the White Album, from 'I Want To Hold Your Hand' to 'A Day In The Life,' from Rubber Soul to Let It Be. I also found inspiration in the fact that they were the ultimate 20th-century media thing. They wanted to be a beast of the media and appeal to millions and millions and millions of people, and make trillions and trillions and trillions of dollars, but they did not think that that was in any way counter to making art."

¶07 Seibert always wanted to be in the music business. In his early 20s he had a brief stint as a DJ on a college radio station and later produced avant-garde jazz records for a small independent label. Yet he failed to attain his goal of pop record producer because, he laments, "I didn't smoke enough dope." At 27 he stumbled into the promotion side of the radio business and was hired by adman Dale Pon, who introduced him to Bob Pittman. Pittman was a 25-year-old radio programmer who had just switched over to the cable TV business to shepherd a new venture: a channel that would show music videos 24 hours a day. Pittman invited Seibert to join him in the venture that would become MTV, and with trepidation he complied. "I watched television, I didn't make it," Seibert says about his initial misgivings. And yet all those hours spent in front of the tube had left him with a natural affinity for the medium.

¶08 The cable business was so new that virtually anything Seibert tried earned praise. One of his first promos was a kinetic montage of images cut to the beat of claps in the song, "Car Wash." "They [the bigwigs] thought it was an amazing thing," he reports. "I guess television didn't usually do things to the beat." Virtually unfettered, Seibert continued to intuitively brand the emerging channel through quirky spots and bumpers. "In those days, we didn't know the word 'brand,' and so we broke many of the rules that had governed television's identity for decades," he remembers. Seibert, with his friend and MTV colleague Allen Goodman, used cable TV as a laboratory for a slew of unprece-

AIGA MEDAL. FRED SEIBERT / **left page** Bubbles, Blossom and Buttercup from the Cartoon Network series "The Powerpuff Girls," 1995. **01** Detail of MTV logo stenciled on a cow, 1983. **02** Detail of Nickelodeon logo in action as an arrow, 1985. **03** Detail from sequence showing TNN's "We've got pop" tagline, 2000. **04** Detail of Blossom from "The Powerpuff Girls," 1995. **05** Detail of the Nickelodeon logo as a pack of howling dogs, 1985.

06 Detail of the Comedy Central logo dropped into a parking lot, 1991. **07** Detail from sequence showing TNN's "We've got pop" tagline, 2000. **08** Detail of an early logo for the Lifetime channel, 1987.

n 01

n 02

n 03

n 04

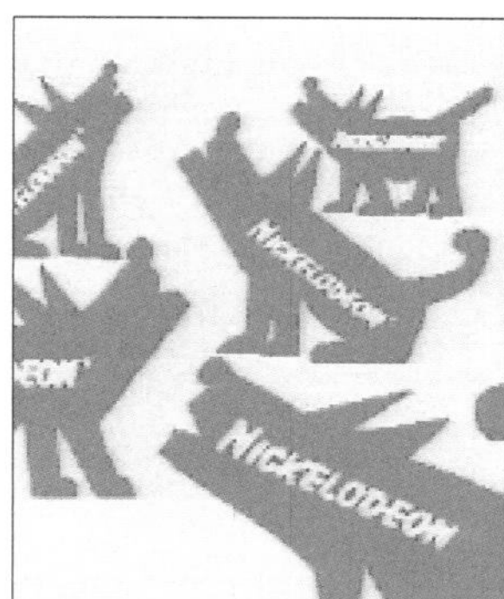

n 05

n 06

n 07

n 08

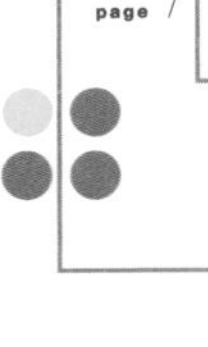

AIGA MEDAL. FRED SEIBERT / **left page** Whistler's famous mother forms the basis for a Ha! TV Comedy Network sequence, 1989. (Ha! became Comedy Central in 1991.)

dented animations. The idea was to entertain rather than push sales pitches down the audience's throats. And in the process, Seibert wanted to unleash the talents of creative people he had always admired.

¶09 As a teen, Seibert was inspired by the wellspring of innovative graphic design and packaging that came out of Columbia Records during the '60s and early '70s. He particularly admired the work of art director John Berg who, he explains, "created a language that reflected the wildly diverse sensibilities of type design, photographic imagery and portraiture of the time. And yet there was this amazing consistency, a quality of ideas that went through the whole thing." (Inspired by this work, Seibert taught himself to "design" covers for his own company, Oblivion Records, which he founded while working at MTV.) When he launched the promotions for MTV, his model was not Lou Dorfsman's legendary advertising for CBS Television, which was considered the industry standard, but Berg's art direction for Columbia. "I wanted the MTV visuals to be like album covers for television," he says.

¶10 Seibert began his work at MTV with the idea that since music was multifaceted, the network should avoid projecting a rigid corporate persona or, for that matter, anything corporate-looking. The television industry revered the sanctity of logos: the CBS Eye (1951), NBC Peacock (1956) and ABC circle (1961) embodied the networks' respective ethos and were thus immutable and inviolable. So Seibert's first instinct was to avoid the I.D. firms that churned out the most expensive corporate identity systems. Instead, he commissioned a childhood friend, Frank Olinsky, who was a principal, along with Pat Gorman and Patti Rogoff, in Manhattan Design, a very small graphics and illustration office tucked behind a tai chi studio in Manhattan's Greenwich Village. Although they had no previous corporate-identity experience, Seibert chose them "because I'd been friends with Frank since I was four years old, and he was talented even then." He also loved rock and roll. Luckily, Bob Pittman agreed that the logo could take any form as long as the "call letters" were readable.

¶11 The first version of the "M" was inspired when Patti Rogoff walked past a graffiti-scrawled schoolyard wall. At that moment she realized MTV's logo had to be made of three-dimensional letters that exuded street culture. After many false starts, Pat Gorman finessed a large M and hand-scrawled a little "TV" onto it, which Olinsky thought was ugly. He argued that if the concept was going to work, a better rendering of "TV" was imperative. But their real breakthrough came when Gorman and Olinsky decided that the M could be something like a screen on which various images could be "projected." And the M could become an object—a birthday cake, a bologna sandwich, or whatever else they wanted to make it. The shape of the M could be transformed into anything, as long as it continued to look like an M.

¶12 Back at headquarters, MTV executives were troubled by the solution. They felt that the M was not legible. And their lawyers argued that a mutable logo would require repeated registration each time a different iteration was used. Seibert, however, was not concerned. Five variations of the logo were pinned up on his wall for weeks because he couldn't make up his mind which one he liked best. Finally, he decided it would be "very rock and roll" to use them all in animated sequences. It seemed like the problem was solved.

¶13 Still, the head of sales lobbied to kill the logo because he didn't want to send such a flagrantly unconventional design to potential advertising buyers. Seibert recalls that he was asked by the muckety-mucks if he really thought that this logo would last as long as the CBS Eye. His answer was a resounding "No." "Why would I think that a rock thing would stand up to the icon of TV logos?" The executives insisted that Seibert approach some "real" designers, including Push Pin Studios and Lou Dorfsman, which he did. But Seibert kept total faith in the original idea and slyly admits, "I sandbagged the assignment. They all did terrible work and then we were out of time." So with a small type variation on the "Music Television" subtitle, the original was approved a few weeks before the new channel went on the air, on August 1, 1981.

¶14 The televised MTV logo was the perfect embodiment both of raucous rock and roll and of MTV's promise to change forever ordinary viewing (and listening) habits. Its animated mutability made it as anticipated a feature of daily programming as the music videos themselves. Over time, various illustrators were hired, including John van Hammersveld, Mark Marek, Lynda Barry and Steven Guarnaccia, to transform the basic prop into mini-metaphors. But the most important vehicle for establishing the logo's supremacy were 25 10-second animated spots in which the logo changed design and meaning. This included the most recurring and iconic spot, an appropriation of the famous photograph of the first man landing on the moon with a vibrating, ever-changing MTV logo used in place of the American flag. "Ultimately," recalls Seibert, "we did three or four hundred promos that were the real heartbeat of the 'newness' of MTV."

¶15 Four years after MTV launched, Seibert and Allen Goodman helped restructure a foundering Nickelodeon, transforming it from a repository of stale cartoons to a content-driven destination of original entertainment for young and old. Unlike network TV, where programming aims for high ratings at all costs (by filling the air with trendy action heroes or "When Pets Attack"), Nickelodeon was determined to do things right, with stories and characters that were good from a kid's point of view. "If we did that well, then we'd make money," says

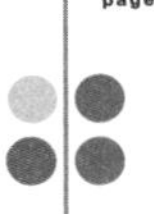

AIGA MEDAL. FRED SEIBERT / **left page** MTV's iconic moon-landing sequence, which used the music network's logo in the place of the American flag, 1981. **01 - 07** Details showing the ever-changing contexts for the MTV logo, 1981-83. (Note that 07 depicts a claymation Fred Seibert interacting with the logo)

n 01

n 02

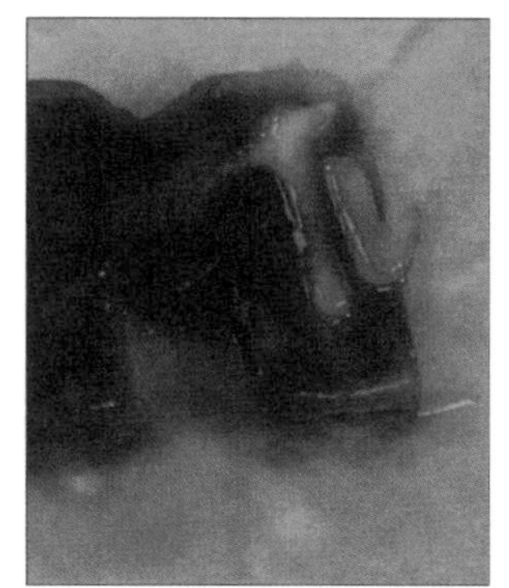

n 03

n 04

n 05

n 06

n 07

AIGA MEDAL. FRED SEIBERT / **left page** Rudy Tabootie from the Nickelodeon series "Chalkzone," 1998.

Seibert. Within a year, the channel's ratings had made a huge jump. The duo also devised Nick at Nite, a brilliant scheme to broadcast reruns of baby-boom TV classics during the time slots when younger kids were in bed. For Seibert, this was more than a retro gimmick—it was a move to philosophically position the channel as a repository of great pop culture. "Back then, old television was considered even more disposable than old music," he explains, "and I was determined to prove—even to Gerry Laybourne, who ran Nickelodeon—that it wasn't junk, that it has cultural value."

¶16 Which is the reason why, in 1992, he accepted the top job at Hanna-Barbera, the cartoon studio known for its pioneering "limited-animation" style, yet which for decades had been churning out mediocre reprises of its cartoon classics, which included "The Flintstones," "The Jetsons," "Yogi Bear" and others. Seibert understood that with the success of Matt Groening's "The Simpsons" and John Kricfalusi's "Ren and Stimpy," a new generation of cartoon creators was waiting to be tapped. He immediately altered the archaic internal organization of Hanna-Barbera, which emphasized production over concept and technicians over artists. His model was based on creative teams that enabled new ideas to take precedence over old chestnuts. He soon oversaw the creation of HB's first new series in decades, "Two Stupid Dogs." The cartoon did not do well, yet out of this failure he devised a unique concept called "What A Cartoon." Instead of investing a lot of money in one 13-show series, he used the same capital to produce 48 speculative cartoons, each made by one artist and a team of production people. "What A Cartoon" was an anthology of speculations, and the most successful ones were spun off into series, later produced by Frederator. The successes included such current hits as "Dexter's Laboratory," "The Powerpuff Girls," "Cow and Chicken" and "Johnny Bravo."

¶17 Seibert is a product of 1960s mass media, and he admits to a somewhat schizophrenic relationship with the branding that he has done so well. "I am deeply cynical about the goals of branding, which to me, in its purest form, means higher CPMs [cost-per-thousand] for advertising. But I realize that what I am looking to change through the work that I do ultimately gives value to advertising. That's the cynical side." The other side of the relationship is more deeply rooted: "I feel like a '60s child, always attracted to things that were disenfranchising to me," he says. And this is what comes through in the music, cartoons and comics he has fervently tried to integrate into today's mainstream. "I was very resentful of the fact that, in the '60s, people said that the music I liked was 'disposable.' It definitely wasn't disposable to me. So one of the things in the back of my mind in the work I was doing at MTV was, 'I'll make them listen!' and give this stuff new value."

¶18 MTV and Nickelodeon are wildly successfull today. And given the current reach of cable and satellite TV, their identities may be more recognized internationally than all the networks combined. Irreverent, oddball and sometimes gross cartoons also fill television now more than ever. Seibert must be given credit for a fair share of this.

¶19 Yet Seibert's chronic restlessness prevents him from basking too long in the glow of previous accomplishments. For the past three years he has been working in the newest mass medium, as a player in the Internet. After his stint at Hanna-Barbera, he became president of MTV Networks Online, a position he held until recently at Nickelodeon Online. He confides: "I don't have a bottom-of-my-toes feeling yet" about the new media. Yet complete mastery of a medium has never been a handicap for him before. Rather, his unflagging enthusiasm for the creative potential of the medium is what makes him invaluable. "What I do with the Internet is find unbelievably talented people, the way I always have, put them in a room where the best ideas can come out, then defend their right to have ideas and fail or succeed." As a fan, he adds, "I follow these great people and I've found myself attracted to places where great people are attracted. I figured that by the rub-off of their greatness, I could feel better."

¶20 Seibert's modesty is not false. His exposure to a legion of creative people who have worked for him has definitely enriched his life. But in the final analysis, because Seibert has spent his career instigating creative people, the media, popular culture and the mass audience have been greatly enriched, too.

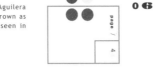

 Detail of an early VH1 logo, 1986. **01** Singer Christina Aguilera as seen in SonicNet.com's "Me Music" campaign, 2000. **02** Detail of the VH1 logo, 1986. **03** Singer James Brown as seen in SonicNet.com's "Me Music" campaign, 2000. **04** Detail of the VH1 logo, 1986. **05** Singer Jewel as seen in SonicNet.com's "Me Music" campaign, 2000.

06 Detail of the VH1 logo, 1988. **07** Singer Sting as seen in SonicNet.com's "Me Music" campaign, 2000.

n 01

n 02

n 03

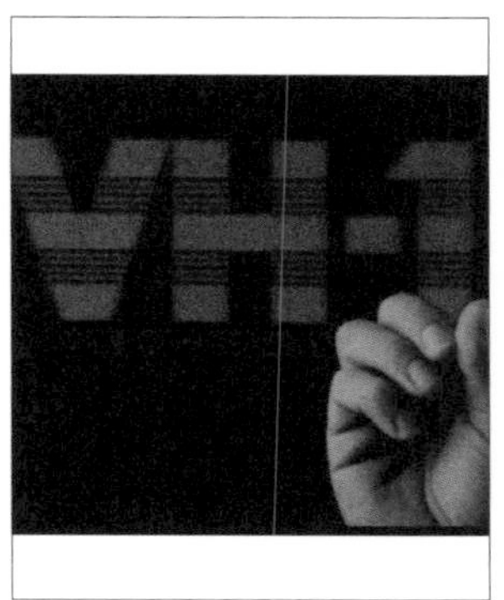

n 04

n 05

n 06

n 07

AIGA MEDAL. FRED SEIBERT / **left page** The MTV logo receives emergency medical attention, 1982.
01-07 Details from various TNN spots showing the "We've got pop" tagline, 2000.

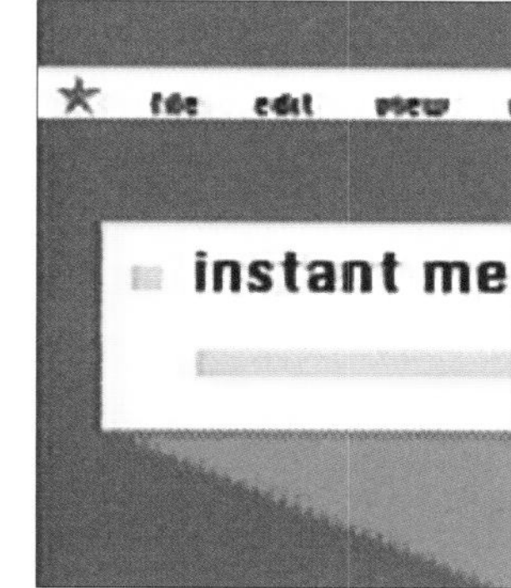

n 01

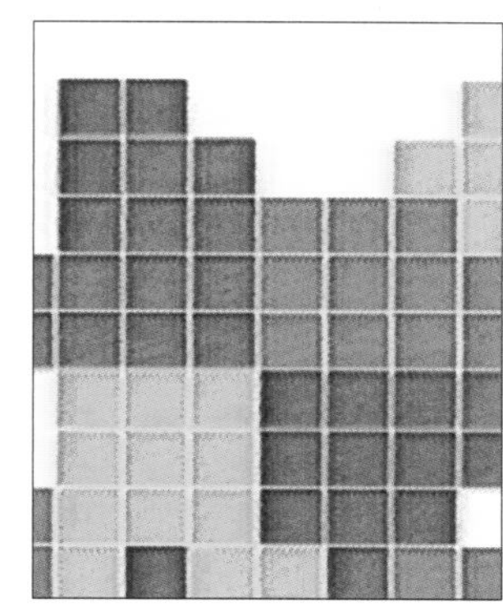

n 02

n 03

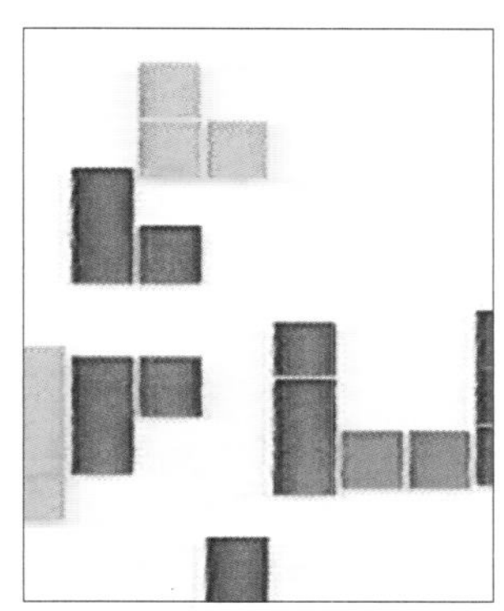

n 04

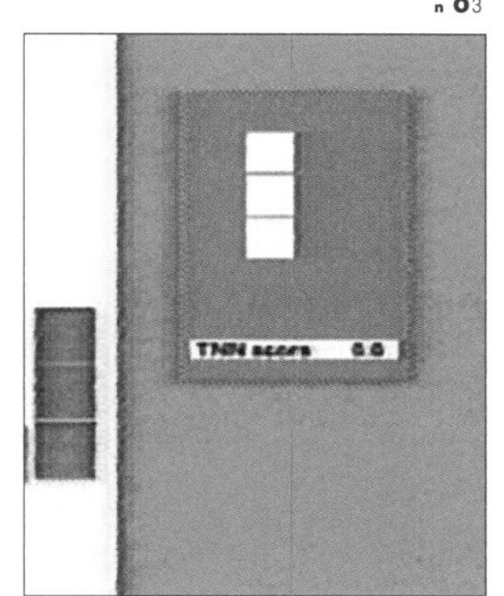

n 05

n 06

n 07

Michael Vanderbyl with pieces from the Vanderbyl Collection for HBF, 2000

michael vanderbyl.

aiga medal. | 03

michael vanderbyl.

aiga medal. | 03

michael vanderbyl.

aiga medal. | 03

A Man For All Seasons: Michael Vanderbyl | **By Zahid Sardar**

¶01 "When it comes to design, I like to do it all," says Michael Vanderbyl, whose lifelong goal has been to merge traditionally segregated design forms like graphic design, product design and interior architecture. As evidenced by the work that has emerged from his San Francisco-based studio over the course of his 27-year career, Vanderbyl has attained this goal—and more. A century ago, Otto Wagner, Vienna's pioneering modernist architect/designer, coined the famous term "Gesamtkunstwerk"—the total work of art—to describe what he believed was the ultimate creative attainment in the modern age. One hundred years later, Vanderbyl's talent and achievements seem to fulfill the Viennese master's criteria with startling accuracy.

¶02 Fin-de-siècle Vienna and 1960s San Francisco may seem worlds apart at first glance, but they were both 20th-century ground zeros in terms of sociocultural foment and shifting sexual mores. San Francisco was the seedbed for an American youth culture that found expression in the underground graphics of the times—psychedelic posters, comic books and hot rods. The hippie mind-set of communal living that promoted Arts and Crafts production and a union of art, music and literature influenced Vanderbyl, who became a proponent of cultural synthesis. As a graphic designer, he grew into a part of the very marketing and merchandising machinery that made counterculture America one with the mainstream. In that vein, it is illuminating to observe that the voluble, opinionated Vanderbyl—a graduate of the California College of Arts and Crafts (CCAC)—is now also dean of the design faculty he has assembled at his alma mater.

¶03 "When I started to teach in 1980, I could see what art schools needed to do for designers," he says. Standing in front of a class helped Vanderbyl shape, as well as assert, his views. "What I had learned intuitively had to be dissected in great detail," he observes, "and this allowed me to look at my own work." Vanderbyl soon began to articulate a mission from atop this soapbox: to bring graphic design into any serious discussion about art.

¶04 Vanderbyl began to encourage his students to think of the "real possibilities" present for designers: They could create not just graphics, but products and store environments as well. All of these commercial endeavors were as important as any other "art" discipline, he suggested. "I find a great irony that the world of fine art has claimed all of art history as its own," Vanderbyl says. Art for art's sake as a leisurely, aristocratic concept is only about 120 years old. "When you think of great painters before the Impressionists, they were essentially painting for clients who also commissioned buildings and other designs. I tell my students, 'Michelangelo's day was a lot like yours is going to be. The Pope was very much a client. He presented problems that had to be solved.'"

¶05 Vanderbyl's consistently crisp, witty graphics and designs amplify this idea. They have won him trophies and speaking engagements; his work was even listed in Time magazine among 1987's best design triumphs. Alongside Vanderbyl's work, the magazine listed other "winners"—a skyscraper, an airline terminal, a theater and a subway station—putting graphic design squarely on par with architecture, one of Vanderbyl's personal passions. In 1992, he chaired the National Endowment for the Arts' Presidential Design Awards at the White House and in 1997 was featured on the PBS series, "The Creative Mind."

¶06 There was a time when the marketing and media capitals New York and Los Angeles dominated the communication arts. But artists like Vanderbyl helped to diversify the playing field. Drawing inspiration equally from such masters as turn-of-the-century architect Josef Hoffman and designers Joseph Muller-Brockman, Milton Glaser and other members of New York's Push Pin Studio, Vanderbyl evolved a distinctive visual shorthand to communicate ideas and information. A typical Vanderbyl poster, designed for California Public Radio, demonstrates the speed with which a good design delivers its message. The image, composed of geometric and symbolic forms, is a metaphor for radio: a man in silhouette (a favorite Vanderbyl device), speaking and listening, but not seeing. A blue bar covers the man's eye, while two red arrows funnel sound into his ear and out of his mouth. For Vanderbyl, it isn't enough to consider graphics in the convention of the time—as spartan abstractions—but as a form that employs color and pictorial expression.

¶07 The hippie/rock graphics that had brought many native West Coast graphic artists to prominence in the late 1960s didn't translate well on the other side of the country. Even in California, it wasn't until the mid-1970s that mainstream designers began to incorporate those ideas to form a separate identity, distinct from New York-centered trends.

¶08 According to past AIGA president Lucille Tenazas, a CCAC alum who also currently teaches there, Vanderbyl's work—and his influence—was key to this development. "Everybody in New York was still just using black, white and red in the modernist Swiss tradition," recalls Tenazas. But by the time she arrived at Cranbrook in 1980, she was able to use a lot of color. "Because of Vanderbyl and his peers, I understood that there could be other colors in design," she says. "It was an exciting time. People began to refer to the influence of the new California Wave, Pacific Wave or Nuevo Wave."

AIGA MEDAL. MICHAEL VANDERBYL / **left page** Archetype Collection for McGuire Furniture, 2000. **01** Archetype Collection for McGuire Furniture, 2000. **02** Vanderbyl Collection for HBF, 2000. **03** Hosiery designs for Esprit, 1988-89. **04** Archetype Collection for Baker Furniture, 1996. **05** Vanderbyl Collection for HBF, 2000. **06** Esprit bed linen designs, 1986-90. **07** Flute series of ceramic tabletop ware for Pentimento, 1997. **08** Archetype Collection for Baker Furniture, 1996.

ILLUSTRATIONS **top to bottom** Logo for Windquest Yacht Racing Syndicate, 1992; Logo for D'icilà cosmetics, Shiseido, 1991; Logo for California Conservation Corps, 1978.

n 01

n 02

n 03

n 04

n 05

n 06

n 07

n 08

 / **left page** Teknion Chicago Showroom, 1999.

ILLUSTRATIONS **top to bottom** PID (Personal Information Dirigible) for experimental exhibit at the San Francisco Museum of Modern Art, 1999.

¶09 Vanderbyl's early posters began to include whimsical postmodernist axonometric renderings and architectural imagery, hinting at the range of his later work, which would leap into three dimensions as he began to practice architecture. "I always had this underlying need for 3-D," recalls Vanderbyl. "In high school I wanted to be an architect, but my counselor told me I wasn't smart enough."

¶10 Lifting graphic design off the page and applying it to a line of sheets and towels for Esprit during the early 1980s was a baby step toward exploring ideas three-dimensionally. These days, Vanderbyl bridges several worlds, providing multiple solutions for the same client—from identity systems to lighting and furniture, showrooms and office interiors. "If I were just facing an 8 1/2-by-11-inch sheet of paper, I wouldn't be doing this anymore," Vanderbyl says. He alludes to historic precedents for this broad reach—architects like Frank Lloyd Wright, who didn't hesitate to fashion chairs, textiles and home accessories, and the designers Charles and Ray Eames, who jumped at the chance to practice architecture.

¶11 "When you do a product, the brochure and the exhibit space, you can make the idea clearer rather than spend time fighting different factions and identities," Vanderbyl says, indicating that a need for design clarity and consistency are what propel him to seek control over every design detail for a client. "Nowadays they like to call [such design control] branding. A branding awareness simply demands consistency between one medium and another," he explains. Vanderbyl's work as a teacher serves him well when the time comes to educate those clients who need to understand clearly what he can offer them. "They are learning, and as their designer you can help."

¶12 For instance, in 1983, when Vanderbyl's graphics client Hickory Business Furniture (HBF) couldn't afford an architect to design its showroom at the Chicago Merchandise Mart, Vanderbyl got the chance to apply his 3-D ideas. "I look at spaces as emotional identities," he explains. In keeping with the traditional look of HBF's contract furniture, he freshened up the original logo, a cameo of President Andrew Jackson (who was nicknamed "Old Hickory"), simply by enlarging its scale. To reiterate this "traditional" concept in HBF's brochures, all of its products were rendered as large-scale cameos. The showroom, Vanderbyl decided, needed to suggest updated tradition as well; black-and-white checkered floors straight out of Vermeer and stylized architectural elements, such as columns and pediments set against bright white walls, helped create a classical atmosphere and pulled the company's products and visual identity into a cohesive whole. "When it won an award, it shocked them and me," says Vanderbyl. "I realized I could apply graphics concepts to interiors as well."

¶13 Nine years later, when he produced HBF's Los Angeles showroom on an even slimmer budget, Vanderbyl continued the use of traditional motifs with a modern twist. Canvas backdrops for the latest furniture suspended from the ceiling were printed with computer reproductions of Michelangelo's Eritrean Sybil from the Sistine Chapel. Other clients besides HBF—such as Bernhardt, Baker and McGuire (furniture companies with showrooms in North Carolina), as well as Teknion in Chicago—give Vanderbyl ample opportunity to shape interior architecture using translations of graphics he has created for those companies.

¶14 "It is exciting to tilt things off the flat surface, and that's why I got into furniture design as well," Vanderbyl says. The Cambridge chair, one of a group of six seating designs for HBF, has not only won awards; it landed in the San Francisco Museum of Modern Art's (SFMOMA) permanent collection. "For me, HBF was an art patron," Vanderbyl exclaims.

¶15 When Vanderbyl and several other San Francisco designers including Michael Manwaring and Michael Cronan—loosely dubbed "The Michaels"—were acknowledged as proponents of a West Coast style in a 1992 SFMOMA show of their work called "In The Public Eye," they made news. They were the first graphic designers working within the same city (but not together) to be featured at the museum. Unlike previous shows of graphic design, which essentially were showcases for poster art, their exhibit demonstrated the wide-reaching influence of commercial art. Their prolific output, in the tradition of the Eameses, blurred the boundaries between print and three-dimensional design and helped to disseminate the lighthearted but elegant, colorful and decorative views of West Coast designers.

¶16 Vanderbyl's diverse client list remains an unexpected mix: vases for Pentimento, showrooms for contract- and residential-furniture maker Keilhauer and fabrics for Luna Textiles. In 1996, he created an AIGA award trophy given to companies for ecological awareness, made of scrap aluminum parts that can be disassembled and recycled. For the San Francisco Design Center's 1998 Idea House, he created a new SFDC corporate identity and a startlingly simple shopping bag graphic: a child's rebus incorporating the image of an eye, the letter "D" and a house.

¶17 While the conceptual range of Vanderbyl's graphics work has not changed much since the early days, it has become surprisingly austere, relying more on his signature black-and-white stripes, checks and a New Age minimalism not seen in his earlier work. Vanderbyl's all-white office in downtown San Francisco typifies his current visual direction (which is undoubtedly tempered by the constraints of furniture and product manufacturing). Stripped to bare elements, it is itself an infor-

AIGA MEDAL. MICHAEL VANDERBYL / **left page** Bernhardt Los Angeles showroom, 1998. **01** Esprit New York shoe showroom, 1988. **02** Keilhauer Chicago showroom, 1998. **03** Teknion Chicago showroom, 1999. **04** Esprit New York shoe showroom, 1986. **05** Robert Talbott store in Carmel, California, 1996. **06** Shaw Contract showroom in Chicago, 1998. **07** Robert Talbott Store in Carmel, California, 1996.

ILLUSTRATIONS **top to bottom** Winery design for White Loon Vineyards in Niagara-on-the-Lake, Canada, 2001.

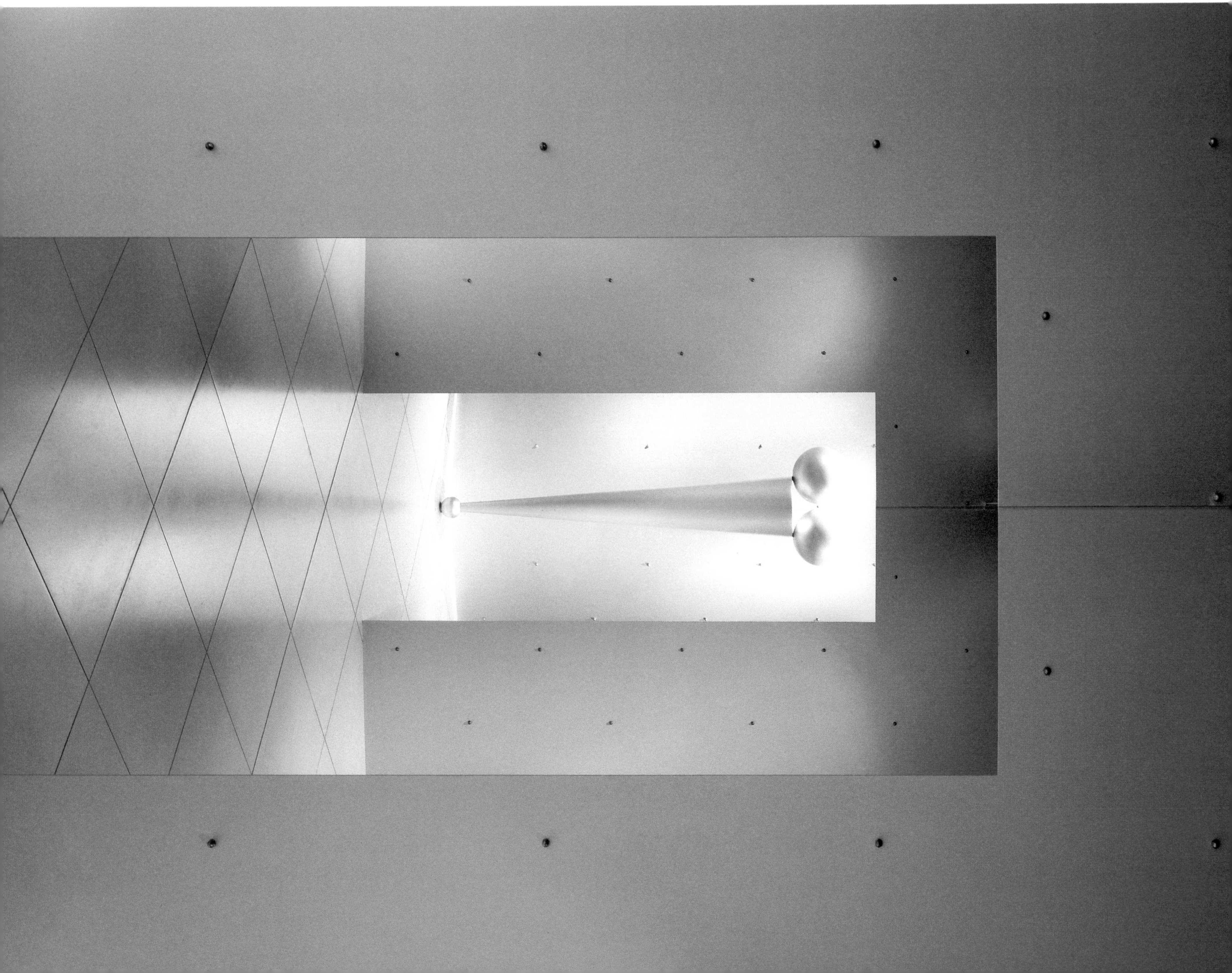

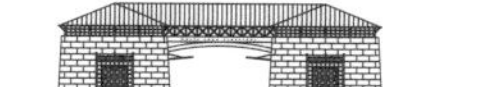

n 01

n 02

n 03

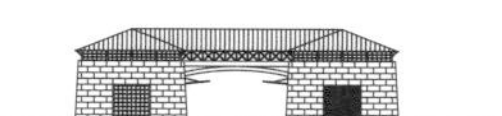

n 04

n 05

n 06

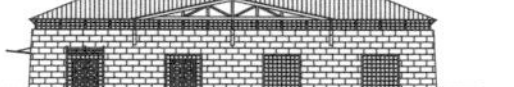

n 07

ILLUSTRATIONS **top to bottom** Hull and logo designs for AmericaOne/America's Cup Challenge, 2000.

AMERICAONE

mation graphic, saying "office" with the childlike clarity that has become the hallmark of the deliberately small studio. Instead of dots, stripes and checks, Vanderbyl uses planes of black, white or gray: a dark receptionist's counter; white canvas chairs for visitors; a row of black drawing tables for six designers; a round white table for spreading out design ideas.

¶18 Vanderbyl's versatility and success in so many design fields over the past three decades has given him stature and provided a powerful pulpit to direct the way present-day graphic designers are perceived. With pieces in the collection of the Cooper-Hewitt National Design Museum as well as at SFMOMA, Vanderbyl continues to influence new generations of designers while shifting perceptions of where the best American design is. His designs have also been extremely profitable for his clients. When he gave image makeovers to HBF and Bernhardt Furniture, the companies' revenues and profits jumped. As IBM president Tom Watson once famously declared, "Good design is good business."

¶19 Vanderbyl offers further insight in a large, stylish portfolio of career highlights. "At the outset, I thought of design as one thing: a way of communicating," he writes. "However, my work has evolved to include environments and products, each informed by the principles of graphic design." Mainly, Vanderbyl has discovered that good design communication needs few rules. An avid sailor, he often employs nautical fittings in his furniture-showroom designs. And his motif of green crosshatched spikes for fiberglass sporting-boat hulls and uniforms for America One, America's cup 2000 in New Zealand, is proof that graphic designers can go well beyond the confines of the printed page.

¶20 "There is design with a sharper deconstructivist edge than mine—a more subversive message," he admits. "Yet I believe that my work is no less meaningful because it honors history, no less serious because it has humor. Design can be intuitive, and not everything needs to be understood." Vanderbyl chuckles. "Design is fun."

AIGA MEDAL. MICHAEL VANDERBYL / **left page** L.J. Skaggs and Mary C. Skaggs Foundation annual report, 1988. **01** L.J. Skaggs and Mary C Skaggs Foundation annual report, 1987. **02** California College of Arts and Crafts 1999-2001 catalogue. **03** Identity and stationery system for Archetype (a Canadian printing company), 1997. **04** Esprit bed and bath packaging, 1987-89. **05** Pischoff Sign Company identity and stationery program, 1990. **06** Teknion Advanced Concepts brochure, with cover made of heat-sensitive film, 2000. **07** Spread from Teknion Advanced Concepts brochure, 2000.

08 Style brochure for the Robert Talbott Company (one in a series), 1998.

ILLUSTRATIONS **top to bottom** Logo for Robb Murray and Company (screen printers), 1998; Logo for Rocket Science (marketing and consulting firm for technology and biotech industries), 1998; Logo for Copia: The American Center for Wine, Food and the Arts in Napa, California, 1998.

n 01

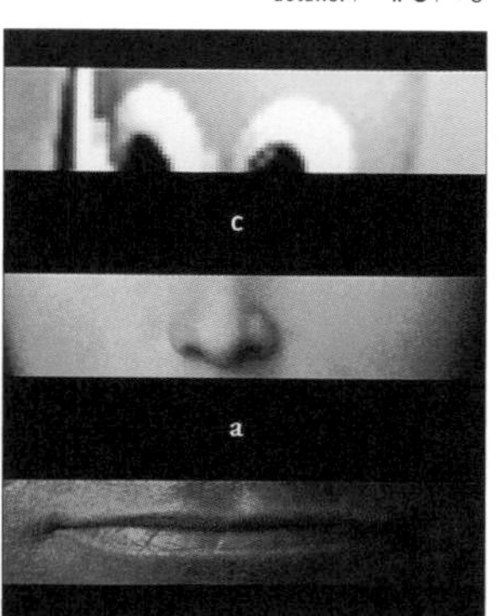

n 02

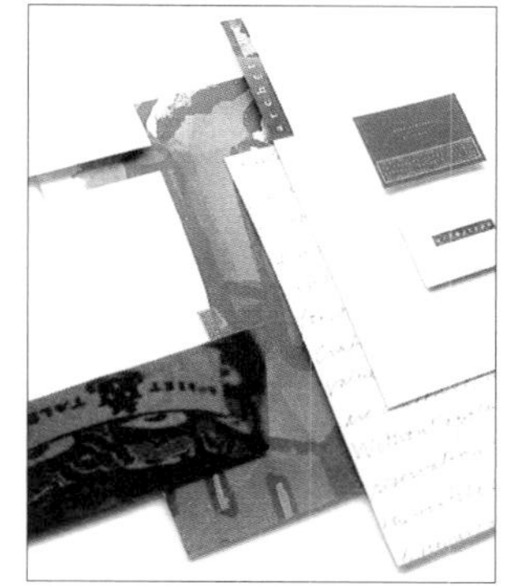

n 03

n 04

n 05

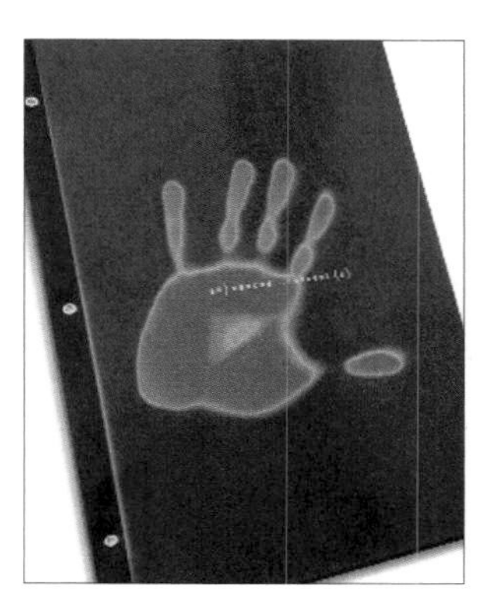

n 06

n 07

n 08

AIGA MEDAL. MICHAEL VANDERBYL / **left page** Bus shelter poster for design lecture series featuring French designers, sponsored by SFMOMA and SF AIGA, 1993. **01** Poster for California Public Radio, 1997. **02** Poster for the annual "Exhibitor Show," sponsored by EXHIBITOR magazine, 1992. **03** Esprit bed and bath packaging, 1987-89. **04** California College of Arts and Crafts art exhibition poster, 1990. **05** "Passion" brochure for the California College of Arts and Crafts Capital Campaign, 1997. **06** Spread from "Passion" brochure, 1997. **07** California College of Arts and Crafts 2001-2003 catalogue.

08 Poster for Polaroid Europe, 1988. **09** Poster for the annual "Exhibitor Show" sponsored by EXHIBITOR magazine, 1999.

ILLUSTRATIONS **top to bottom** Logo for Makani Kai residential development in Hawaii, 1991; Logo for Lascaux Restaurant in San Francisco, 1986; Logo for Na Pali Haweo residential development in Hawaii, 1989.

LES ENFANTS TERRIBLES
THE 1993 SAN FRANCISCO
MUSEUM OF MODERN ART
DESIGN LECTURE SERIES
PRESENTED BY THE
AMERICAN INSTITUTE
OF GRAPHIC ARTS
SAN FRANCISCO CHAPTER

n 01

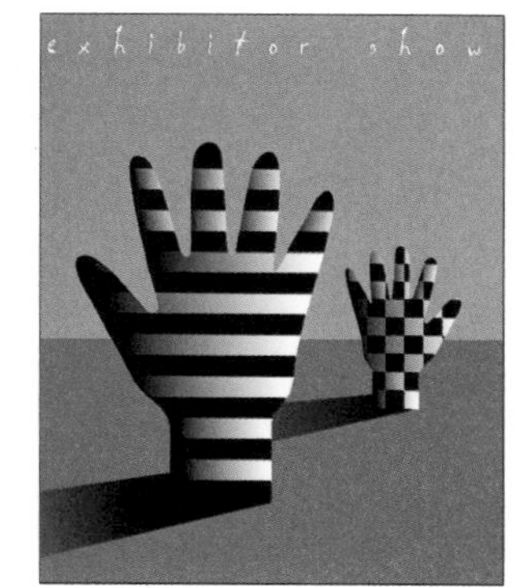

n 02

n 03

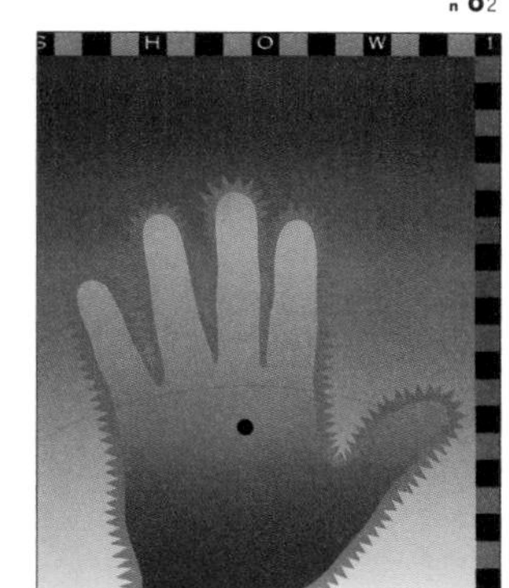

n 04

n 05

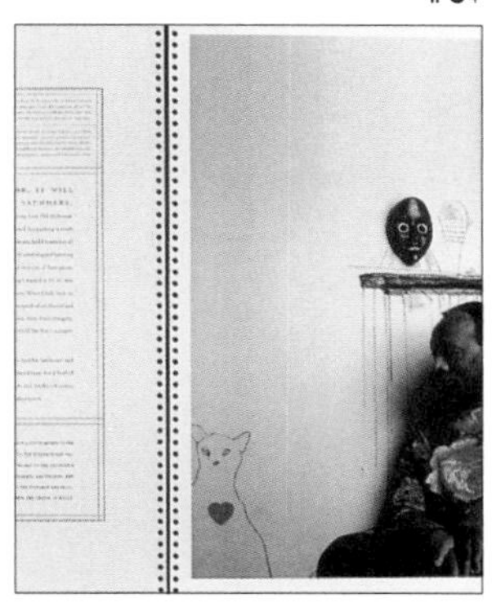

n 06

n 07

n 08

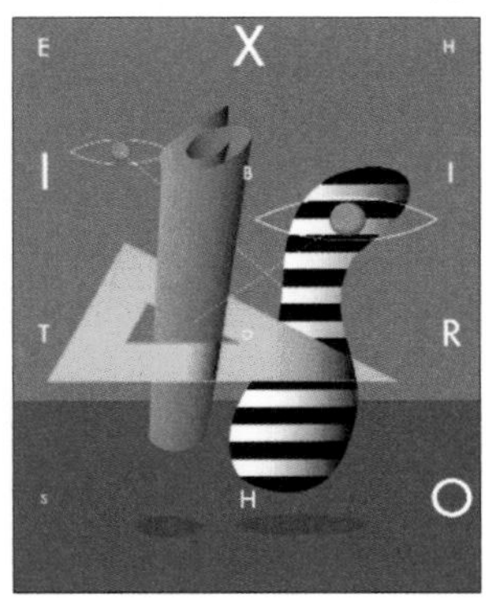

n 09

03. CONTEXT ESSAY 01 / **left page** AIGA's exhibition of "Communication Graphics 20" selections at the National Design Center, designed by watersdesign.com. Photograph © Jennifer Krogh.

communication graphics

context essay. | 01

communication graphics

context essay. | 01

communication graphics

context essay. | 01

Up Close and Personal: Notes on Design in Detail | By Andrea Codrington

¶01 It is a recurring truth that when the economy does well, design awareness tends to increase in mainstream culture. Think back to the 1950s, when postwar plenitude brought forth the giddy production—and consumption—of shiny new cars and brightly decorated homes; or to the go-go '80s, when Armani suits and Memphis furniture meant prosperity writ large in the popular imagination.

¶02 Well, wealth is back—at least for the moment—and material culture is flourishing. While bright colors (think orange) and flamboyant form (think Apple's iMac and Chrysler's PT Cruiser) are the hallmarks of three-dimensional hip, the graphic cultural moment is clearly dominated by minimalism. Gone are the messy, expressionistic soul-searchings so common to the early-to-mid '90s—the poststructuralist assaults on legibility, those slaps in the face to Swiss-school stricture.

¶03 Instead, large, restrained type and stark photography vie for attention in a number of this year's "Communication Graphics" entries. Indeed, there is an uncanny uniformity in much of the creative community's production—which might just make sense. If necessity is indeed the mother of invention, then innovation tends to get short shrift in flush times.

¶04 What does come into play is a great attention to detail—a working of the surface that leaves the viewer sensually satisfied despite the stripped-down aesthetic. The majority of pieces selected this year displayed such a high level of tactility that their evaluation entailed as much sensual interaction as intellectual engagement. At a time when digital media has grabbed the spotlight from "traditional" design disciplines, it seems telling—if not sweetly ironic—that the lure of butter-smooth paper and letterpressed type proved to be greater than the bells and whistles of Flash-enabled websites.

¶05 This is the face of luxury today—consumption wrapped in an austere, near-spiritual package. The opening copy in a catalogue created by the New York studio Design: M/W for the Japanese store Takashimaya sums it up well: "Life is a gift. In return we must take advantage of all it has to offer, heightening experience and seducing the senses into grateful complicity."

¶06 With their exquisite detailing and precision typography, the designers at Design: M/W could well be considered the patron saints of low-key luxury. Juxtapositions, a brochure they designed to showcase Mohawk Satin and Vellum, has more in common with fashion-culture magazines like Purple and Visionaire than with the paper samplers of yesteryear. Delicately perforated pages, peek-a-boo die cuts and deadpan Dutch photography lend a high-concept aura to this workhorse genre. In a saturated marketplace, visual cues of luxury are all-important in any brand's initial seduction or fight for sustained allegiance—whether those cues are selling Prada or paper.

¶07 Interestingly, another Mohawk promo—this one created by Oh Boy of San Francisco—hones in even more on the contemporary zeitgeist. "For the discerning, indulgence is necessity," reads the first line of Covetables: A Catalogue of Indulgence and Necessity, which goes on to lay out stunning dolce vita details in elegant, minimalist layouts. Granted, pleasures come in all shapes and sizes—from a vintage Indian motorcycle to a day spent reading in bed—but their preternaturally cool presentation flattens them out, blurring the line between purchasable pleasure and transcendent personal experience.

¶08 But this is in keeping with the drift of contemporary culture. Increasingly, everything we wear, drive and live with is becoming an extension of ourselves. The old German maxim "Mann ist was mann isst" ("You are what you eat") takes on new relevance when consumption is done with mind, body and soul. There is a transference of identity between object and subject, between consumed and consumer. If you consume luxury—if you buy items that are branded with the idea of luxury—then you are luxury.

¶09 One cover for the New York Times Magazine that was praised by the jurors expressed just this. For an issue exploring the relationship between clothing and identity, art director Janet Froelich features an image of supermodel Shalom Harlowe wrapped in a dress that bears her own face. The tagline reads "It's So You."

¶10 Although all of this has the subtle effect of objectifying the individual, subjectivity is oftentimes the visual trope. In fact, the face—up close and personal—seemed to be a reoccurring visual leitmotif this year. It could be that the work of art photographers like Thomas Ruff and Rineke Dijkstra, who have focused on the unsmiling human visage for years, has trickled down into the designer's visual subconscious. Or it could be that the preponderance of shoulder-up portraiture indicates a corporate attempt to move away from "faceless" global interest toward a more humanized identity. This would certainly account for the fact that annual reports seem to be the premier vehicle for such imagery.

¶11 The face seemed to hold particular iconic interest for corporations that were involved in technology, like General Magic, a company that leads the market in voice-enabled telecommunications services. Cahan and Associates' 1998 annual report for the company features a cover line that reads "The human voice is our most natural means of expression," followed by a series of close-cropped, full-bleed images from the news of people in the process of speaking, yelling, crying or singing. (In this case, pictures truly must speak a thousand words.) SamataMason's report for NCR similarly uses the repeating theme of the human face in an effort to relay that the company "helps its customers discover millions of markets of one."

03. CONTEXT ESSAY 01 / **left page** AIGA's exhibition of "Communication Graphics 20" selections at the National Design Center, designed by watersdesign.com. Photograph © Jennifer Krogh.

communication graphics

context essay. | 01

communication graphics

context essay. | 01

communication graphics

context essay. | 01

¶12 It makes sense that in an age of proliferating media and consumer options the central case for purchasing or relating is the subjective. After all, MTV Interactive runs TV commercials of Sting and Jewel scatting "Me, me, me, me, me, me, me" to tout its customizable "Me Music" option. Levi's offers "original spin" jeans, form-fit to the individual's body specifications. And New York University advertises its continuing education courses with a tag line that reads: "I Am the President of Me, Inc." One question remains, though. If radical subjectivity is the rule in contemporary culture, why does everything look so much the same?

n 01

n 02

n 03

n 04

n 05

n 06

n 07

communication graphics

margaret youngblood, chair. | juror 01

n 01-03 Details from company brochure for Agilent Technologies, 1999. 04 Margaret Youngblood. 05 and 07 Details from identity campaign for the French entertainment media group, Pathé, 1999.

n 06 Details from identity campaign for the San Francisco Exploratorium, 1998.

01 CG. MARGARET YOUNGBLOOD / Margaret Youngblood is creative director of corporate identity and a principal of the firm Landor Associates, where she has directed identity programs for such companies as Lucent Technologies, Hewlett Packard, Netscape, Old Navy and Pathé, the French entertainment media group. Prior to joining Landor, Youngblood was a designer with Allied International Designers Ltd. in Paris. A native of Ann Arbor, Michigan, she received her BFA from the University of Arizona and in 1981 earned a degree in French and French civilization from the Sorbonne in Paris. Her design work has received awards of excellence and recognition, including those from the Grand Palais (Paris, France), Graphis, AIGA, Society of Typographic Arts, Communication Arts, Print, Society of Environmental Graphic Designers and Los Angeles Art Director's Club. Youngblood serves on the advisory board of AIGA's San Francisco chapter and of New Langton Arts, an internationally acclaimed alternative arts institution.

communication graphics

thomas geismar. | juror 02

n 01

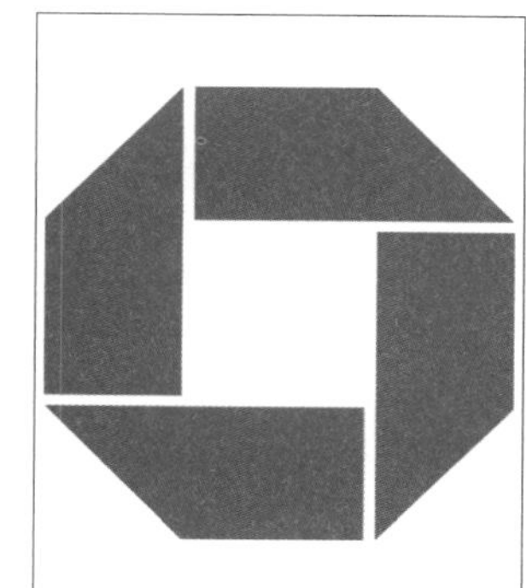

n 02

n 03

n 01 Poster for "Graphic Arts USA" exhibition organized for tour in former Soviet Union, 1963. 02 Logo for Chase Manhattan Bank, 1960. 03 Exhibition display created for Ellis Island, 1990. 04 Logo for Mobil, 1964. 05 Thomas Geismar.

n 04

n 05

n 06 "Peace" poster for "Images for Survival" exhibition at Shoshin Society, 1985. 07 Detail from "Graphic Arts USA" poster, 1963.

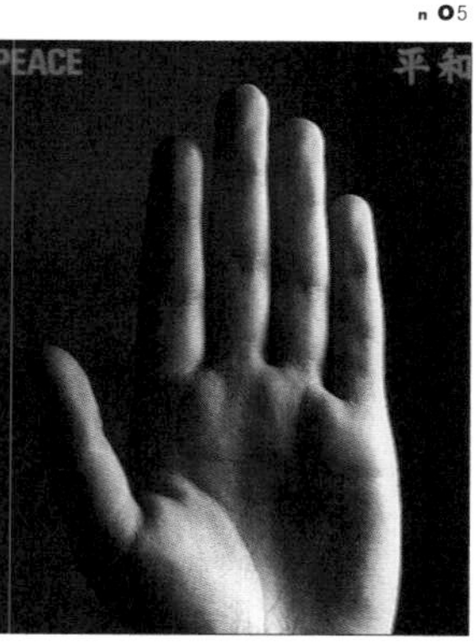

n 06

n 07

02 CG. THOMAS GEISMAR / As a principal of Chermayeff & Geismar Inc., the New York firm he founded with Ivan Chermayeff in 1960, Thomas Geismar has been responsible for the design of over 100 corporate identification programs for major U.S. businesses and institutions, including Mobil Oil and the Museum of Modern Art in New York. Geismar has also been extensively involved in designing and curating museum exhibitions, including at such national landmarks as the new Statue of Liberty Museum, the Ellis Island Immigration Museum and the Harry S. Truman Library and Museum, currently under development in Independence, Missouri. In 1979, with Chermayeff, Geismar received AIGA's highest honor, the Gold Medal. In 1983 they shared the First International Design Award from the Japan Design Foundation and in 1985 received the Yale Arts Award Medal. Geismar has served as director and vice president of AIGA and is a member of the Alliance Graphique Internationale. He attended Brown University and the Rhode Island School of Design concurrently, then attended Yale's School of Art and Architecture, where he received an MA in graphic design.

03 03. Russ Haan / It's been over a decade since Russ Haan founded After Hours Creative in Phoenix. Since then, the agency has moved from a run-down house to a run-down warehouse to a swanky office to a run-down industrial complex. Fortunately, the firm's work has not followed the trend. Purposely small (five employees at this time), After Hours has served clients that include GE Capital, AT&T, Intel, Cox Interactive Media, Lucent Technologies, the Children's Television Workshop and many more. The firm works in all media. Of late, it has primarily served the needs of web-based start-ups, Fortune 100 and various consumer-product companies. The firm and its creative teams have won Clios, New York Art Director's Awards, National Addys, One Show Pencils, Athenas and more, as well as recognition from Communication Arts, Graphis, Print, Affiche, Archive and from local and national chapters of AIGA. In addition to working for its present clients, the firm also manufactures, sells and licenses its designs across a range of products. But that's another story.

n 01

n 02

THE COTTON CENTER

n 03

n 04

n 05

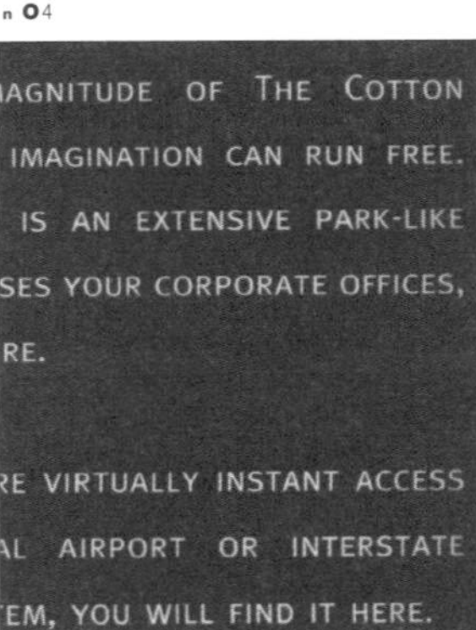
AGNITUDE OF THE COTTON
IMAGINATION CAN RUN FREE.
IS AN EXTENSIVE PARK-LIKE
SES YOUR CORPORATE OFFICES,
RE.
RE VIRTUALLY INSTANT ACCESS
AL AIRPORT OR INTERSTATE
TEM, YOU WILL FIND IT HERE.

n 06

n 07

communication graphics

russ haan. | juror 03

n 01-03 and 05-07 Details from brochure for the Cotton Center, a business park being built in former cotton fields, 1997.

04 Russ Haan.

communication graphics

gayle christensen. | juror 04

n 01

n 02

n 01, 02 and 04-07 The ubiquitous purple-and-orange FedEx logo applied in various contexts.

n 03

03 Gayle Christensen.

n 04

n 05

n 06

n 07

04 CG. GAYLE CHRISTENSEN / Born in Alabama but raised in Southern California, Gayle Christensen began her career with FedEx in 1978 as a sales representative in San Francisco. For the past 18 years, Christensen has been responsible for the global-identity system design and implementation for FedEx Corporation, including management of the 1994 award-winning identity change from Federal Express to FedEx and the recently announced FedEx brand-extension design and implementation. In addition, she manages sports sponsorships and the development and distribution of customer communications. Christensen lives on the Mississippi River in Memphis, Tennessee, with two dogs and two cats. She travels extensively and is the sole proprietor of Niya Arabians, a farm dedicated to the breeding of pure Egyptian Arabian horses.

communication graphics

karin fong. | juror 05

05 CG. KARIN FONG / Karin Fong is a creative director and partner at the Hollywood-based conceptual design and production company Imaginary Forces, where she directs and designs for film, broadcast projects and commercials. Her recent work at Imaginary Forces includes the main title sequence for Dead Man on Campus, which has won numerous awards including Best of Category in I.D. magazine's Annual Design Review. Other work includes main title sequences for The Avengers, Stuart Little and 28 Days, teaser trailers for 8MM and 102 Dalmatians, on-air graphics for MTV and commercial campaigns she directed for Qualcomm, Janus Mutual Funds and Coors Light. Fong has been featured in I.D.'s I.D. Forty, Metropolis, Idea and Fox's "fxm Dailies." Her other professional honors include awards from AIGA, Art Directors Club, Broadcast Design Association, Monitor Awards, New York Advertising Festival and the Type Directors Club.

n 01

n 02

n 03

n 04

n 05

n 06

n 07

n 01-03 and 05-07 Scenes from the Imaginary Forces trailer of 102 Dalmatians for Buena Vista Distribution Company, 2000.

04 Karin Fong with friend.

communication graphics

maira kalman. | juror 06

n 01 Maira Kalman. Photograph © Karen Kuehn.
02, 03 and 06 Details from illustrated article about the Paris couture shows for the NEW YORK TIMES MAGAZINE, 2000.

n 01

n 02

n 03

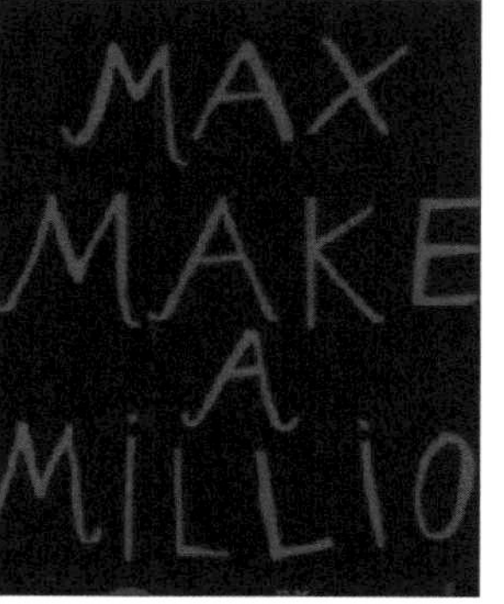

n 04

n 04 Cover detail of MAX MAKES A MILLION for Viking, 1990. 05 Cover of (UN)FASHION book for Harry N. Abrams, 2000.

n 05

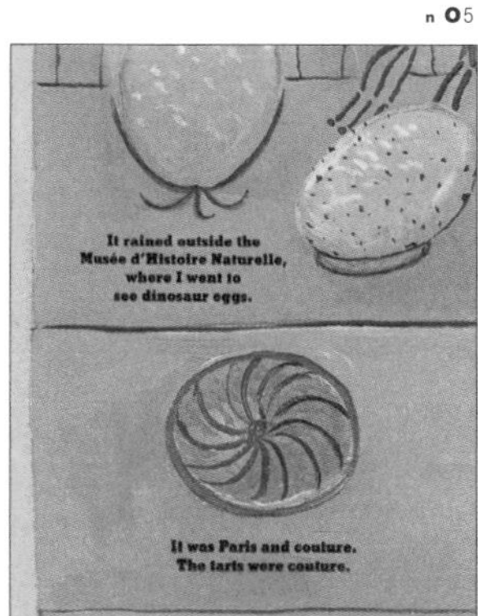

n 06

06 06. MAIRA KALMAN / Maira Kalman was born in Tel Aviv, Israel, and moved to New York during the 1950s. Kalman is the author/illustrator of 10 children's books (published by Penguin Putnam), including the celebrated series about Max Stravinsky, the poet dog who travels around the world. She was commissioned to do a series of murals housed in Grand Central Terminal during its historic renovation. These murals are now featured in Kalman's latest book, NEXT STOP GRAND CENTRAL. She is a frequent contributor to many publications, including the NEW YORKER, the NEW YORK TIMES, ATLANTIC MONTHLY and TRAVEL & LEISURE.

She has designed fabrics for Isaac Mizrahi and mannequins for Ralph Pucci. A permanent exhibit of Kalman's work is housed in the Children's Museum of Manhattan. The Museum of Modern Art sells a line of M&Co products and has made the 10-one-4 watch part of its permanent collection. Kalman is now the CEO, vice president and secretary of M&Co, a multidisciplinary design studio whose clients include the Museum of Modern Art, Barnes & Noble, Vitra and Creative Time. She currently lives in New York with her two children and her faithful dog, Pete.

01 CG. A TENEMENT STORY / The museum needed a signature publication to be sold in the shop. Originally I'd envisioned a comprehensive historical overview of tenement life. The client pared down the scope and shifted the focus to include museum background material. I then decided to alter column widths and margins in each of the sections to reflect what I saw as differing voices within the text. In keeping with the low budget—and art of widely varying quality—I was drawn to some site photos documenting the dilapidation and the textures of the building in its original state.

01

DESIGN FIRM	Angela Voulangas, Brooklyn, NY
DESIGNER	Angela Voulangas
WRITERS	Stuart Miller, Sharon Seitz, Angela Voulangas
TYPEFACES	Scala, Giza families
TRIM SIZE	7 x 9 1/2 inches
CLIENT	Lower East Side Tenement Museum
PRINTER	Cosmos Communications, LIC

detail. / n 02

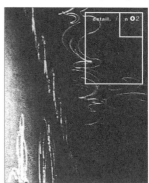

design firm. angela voulangas

communication graphics. | NO. 01

detail 01

detail. / n 02

detail 02

design firm. angela voulangas

communication graphics. | NO. 01

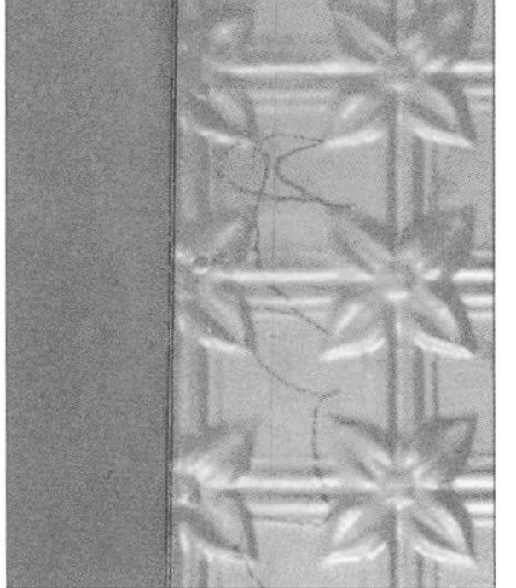

detail 03

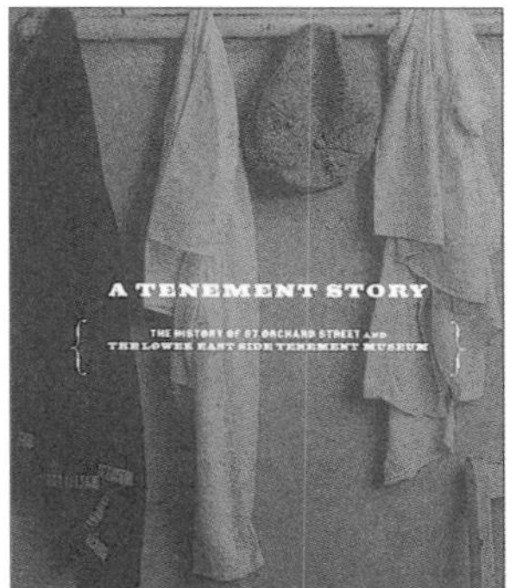

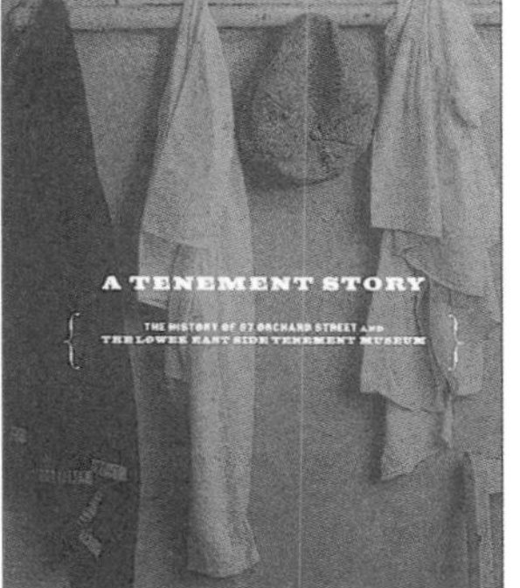

detail 04

PART I FOUND

ONE

Years fle
time Josephi
Side to shop

detail 05

design firm. angela voulangas

communication graphics. | NO. 01

detail 06

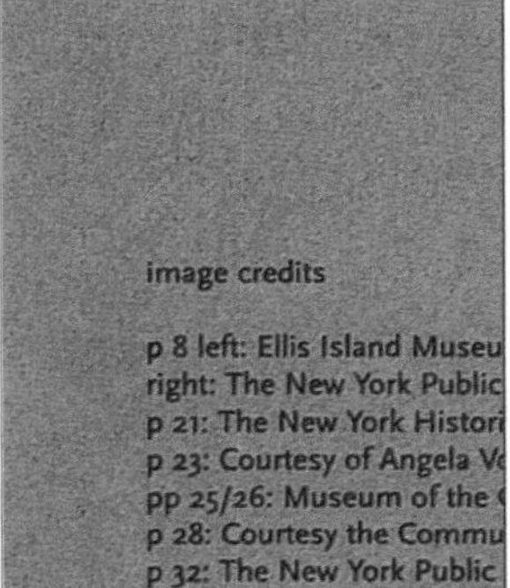

detail 07

02 03. MOHAWK SUPERFINE PROMO / Our concept for the promotion was inspired by Charles Eames' slideshow "The New Covetables," in which he denounced the consumption of manufactured objects in favor of the raw products from which end-use items are made. We immediately saw Superfine as a covetable itself, and decided to create a catalogue that defined other things and experiences one might covet. The book became a sort of manifesto for Oh Boy's philosophy: that as designers, the things we create should be, or become, artifacts.

02

DESIGN FIRM	Oh Boy, A Design Company, San Francisco, CA
ART DIRECTOR	David Salanitro
DESIGNER	Ted Bluey
PRINT PRODUCTION	Elizabeth Cutter
PHOTOGRAPHER	Scott Peterson, except where noted in book
WRITER	Ross Viator
PRINTER	Anderson Lithograph
PAPER	Mohawk Superfine
CLIENT	Mohawk Paper Company

detail. / n 06

VASE

Vases by Jonathan Adler
$110 and $210

Buying a piece of original art can be a life-enriching experience. This is especially true of art that is functional as well as beautiful. Such is the case with Jonathan Adler's ceramic vases. Each piece is handmade by the New York potter, and all are as beautiful holding flowers as they are when empty. Adler's vases can be found in San Francisco at Zinc Details

design firm. oh boy, a design company

communication graphics. | NO. 02

Cozy up in a den painted a rich, earthy brown; have tea in a sunny yellow
car in a garage that's fire-engine red. Ralph Lauren paints come in a range
an 400 hues and five distinctly beautiful color families—from the rich tones
h interiors to the soothing shades of country life. Indulge yourself.

detail O1

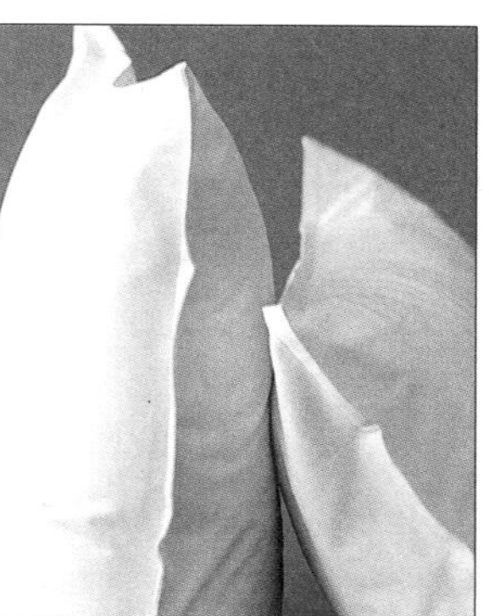

detail O2

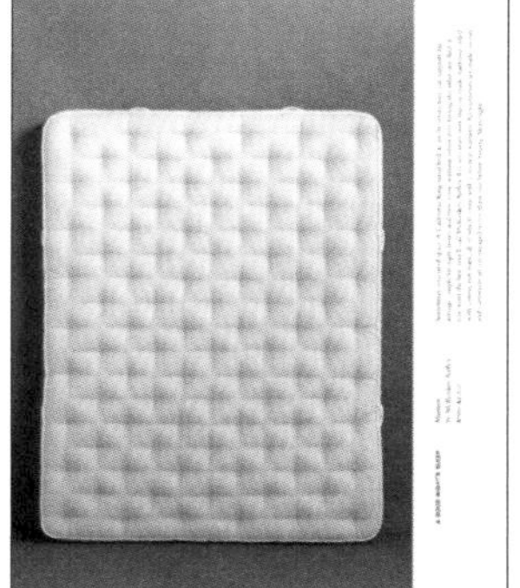

detail O3

design firm. oh boy, a design company

communication graphics. | NO. 02

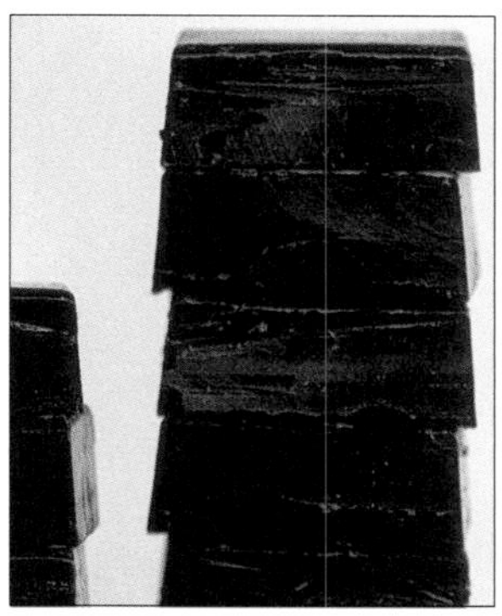

detail O4

COVETABLES

A Mohawk Superfine Promotion

detail O5

design firm. oh boy, a design company

communication graphics. | NO. 02

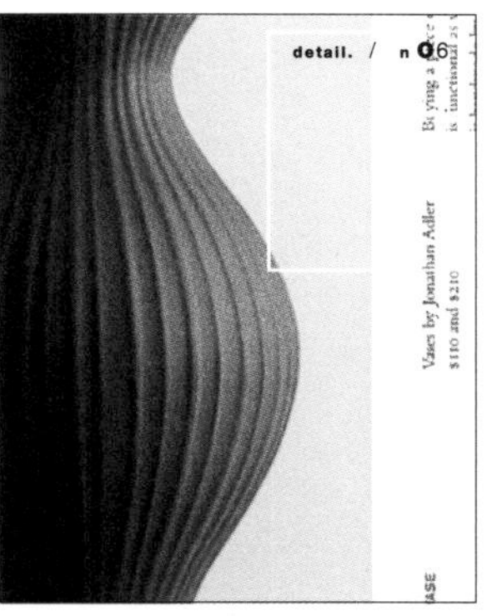

detail O6

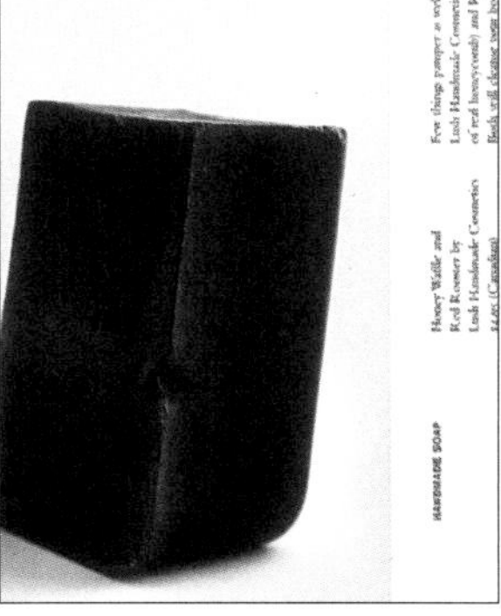

detail O7

03

DESIGN FIRM	Design: M/W, New York, NY
CREATIVE DIRECTORS	Allison Williams, J. Phillips Williams, Mats Hakansson
PHOTOGRAPHER	Blommers and Schumm
TYPEFACE	Din
TRIM SIZE	7 1/4 x 13 1/4 inches
PRINTER	Hennegan
PAPER	Mohawk Satin and Vellum
CLIENT	Mohawk Paper Company

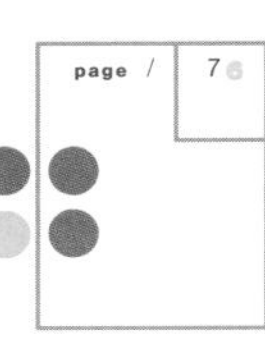

[**26**] MOHAWK SATIN, WARM WHITE, 80 TEXT
FOUR-COLOR PROCESS

design firm. design: m/w

communication graphics. | NO. 03

detail 01

detail 02

design firm. design: m/w

communication graphics. | NO. 03

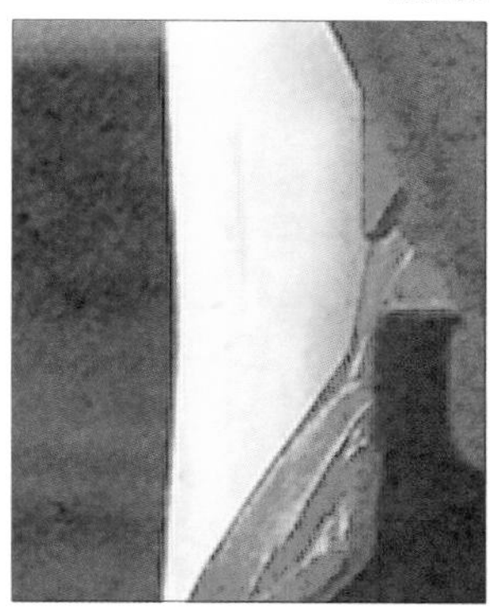

detail 03

detail 04

design firm. design: m/w

communication graphics. | NO. 03

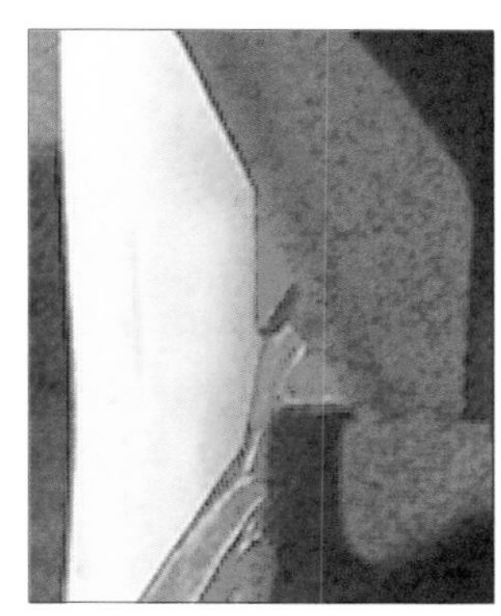

detail 05

detail. / n 06

[26] MOHAWK

FOUR-COLOR

detail 06

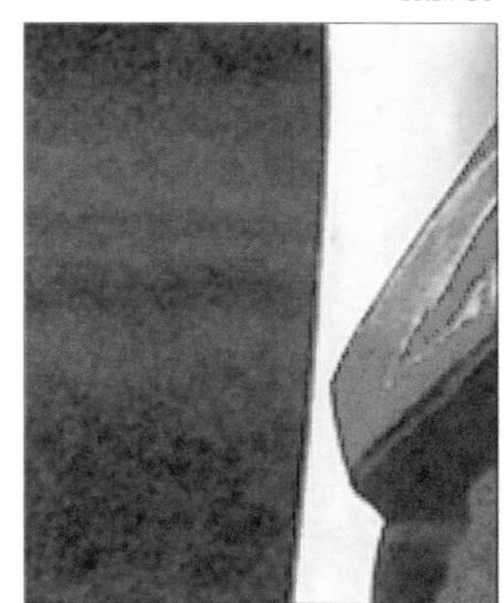

detail 07

04 09. EAI 2000 CALENDAR / We wanted to create a holiday gift that people wouldn't throw away for our studio's clients and friends. Inspired by an old Chinese calendar, we finally hit on the idea of making a year 2000 calendar with word/picture combinations that explore the effect context has on meaning.

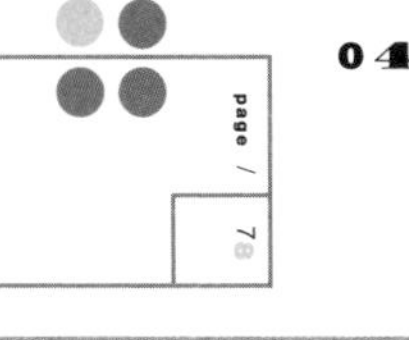

04

DESIGN FIRM	EAI, Atlanta, GA
CREATIVE DIRECTOR	Matt Rollins
DESIGNER	Courtney Garvin
PRINT PRODUCTION	Julie Midkiff
ILLUSTRATORS	Courtney Garvin, Ian Watts
TYPEFACE	Trade Gothic
TRIM SIZE	5 x 7 inches
PRINTER	Seiz Printing
PAPER	French Durotone 60 pound text, Gilbert Voice 100 pound

detail. / n 04

2000

design firm. eai

communication graphics. | NO. 04

detail O1

detail O2

design firm. eai

communication graphics. | NO. 04

detail O3

detail O4

detail O5

design firm. eai

communication graphics. | NO. 04

detail O6

detail O7

05 CG.FRENCH STACK O'PACKS PROMOTION / We were charged to develop a promotion for French's heavyweight paperboard for graphic designers to use in packaging applications. We chose to create a series of pop-art packaging posters that poke fun at different categories of packaged goods, along with consumerism itself.

05

DESIGN FIRM	Charles S. Anderson Design Company, Minneapolis, MN
ART DIRECTOR	Charles S. Anderson
DESIGNER	Jason Schulte
ILLUSTRATORS	Jason Schulte, Charles S. Anderson
WRITER	Lisa Pemrick
TYPEFACES	Various
PRINTER	Anderberg-Lund
FABRICATOR	Terry, Kim and Brian French
PAPER	French Muscletone
CLIENT	French Paper Company

Weighing in at a hefty 140 lbs., Muscletone is so sturdy you could use it to build a house. But unlike laminated sheets, it won't crack, buckle, or warp when scored. Which means that you can now fold, spindle, and staple without fear of mutilation.

HANG TAG

detail. / n 04

FRENCH PAPER
140 lb. MUSCLETONE papers

detail. / n 06

place glue on this tab

muscletone

BOX 2

THIS IS ONE STAND-UP PAPER. Unlike laminated sheets, French Muscletone won't crack under pressure.

design firm. charles s. anderson design company

communication graphics. | NO. 05

detail O1

detail O2

detail O3

design firm. charles s. anderson design company

communication graphics. | NO. 05

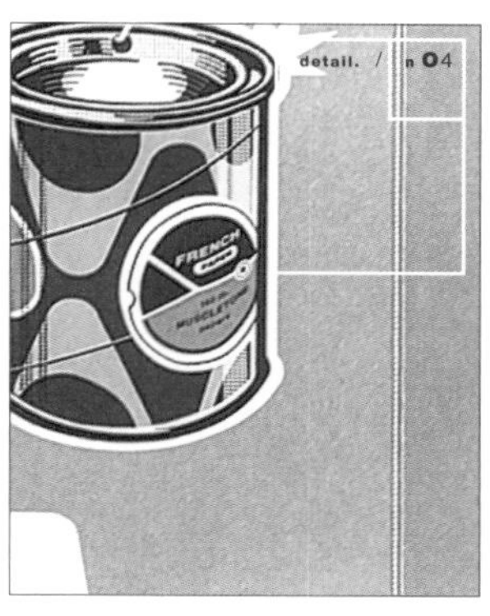

detail O4

detail O5

design firm. charles s. anderson design company

communication graphics. | NO. 05

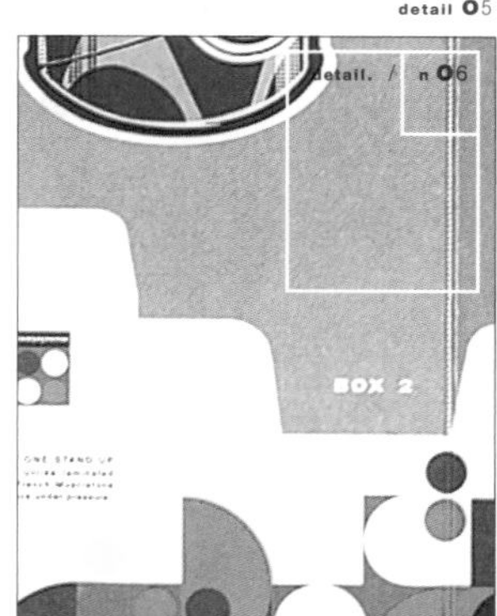

detail O6

detail O7

06 CG. CALIFORNIA COLLEGE OF ARTS & CRAFTS CATALOGUE / The design challenge for the California College of Arts & Crafts catalogue was to show the college in its best light to prospective students, highlight the individual departments and to provide an experience of the school, curriculum and people. The approach was to talk about the school in a bold way by utilizing the insight of graduates and professors and presenting the students' voices and points of view through portraits and handwritten statements.

06

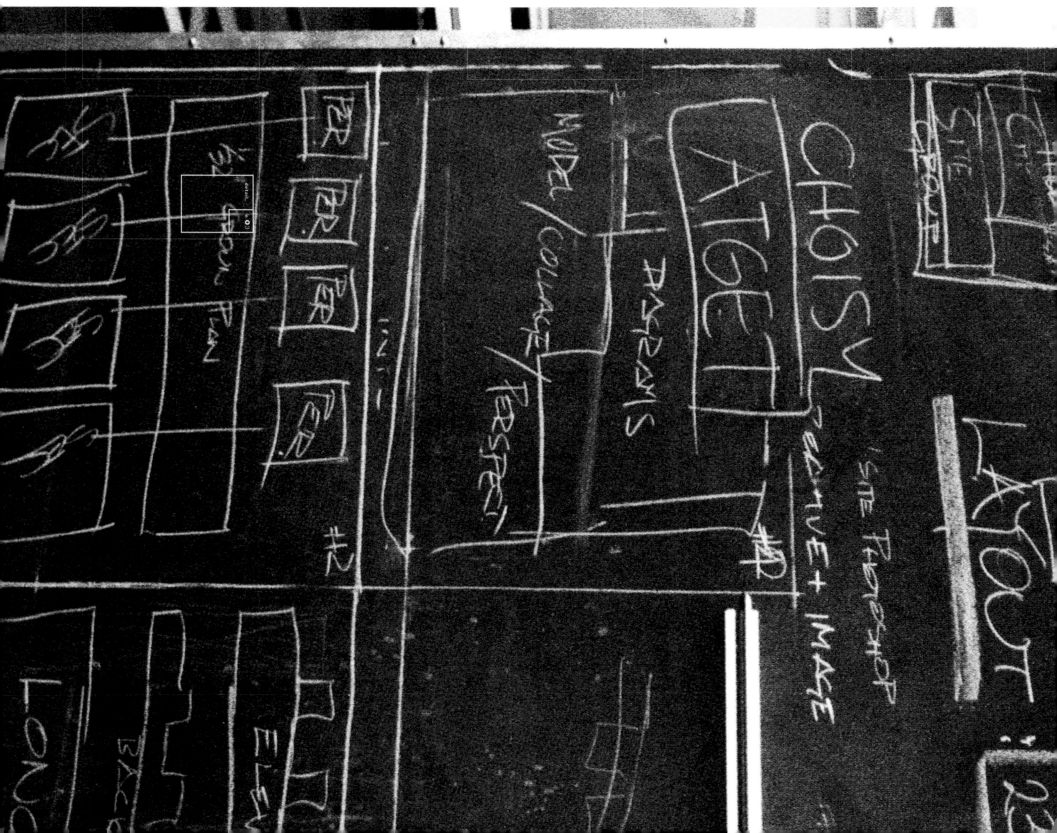

DESIGN FIRM	Michael Vanderbyl Design, San Francisco, CA
CREATIVE DIRECTOR	Michael Vanderbyl
DESIGNER	Karin Myint
PHOTOGRAPHERS	Todd Hido, David Peterson
WRITER	Mind Power
PRINTER	The Campbell Group
TYPEFACES	Handlettering, Officina, Garamond expert
CLIENT	California College of Arts & Crafts

detail. / n 03

design firm. michael vanderbyl design

communication graphics. | NO. 06

detail 01

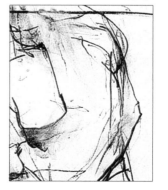

detail 02

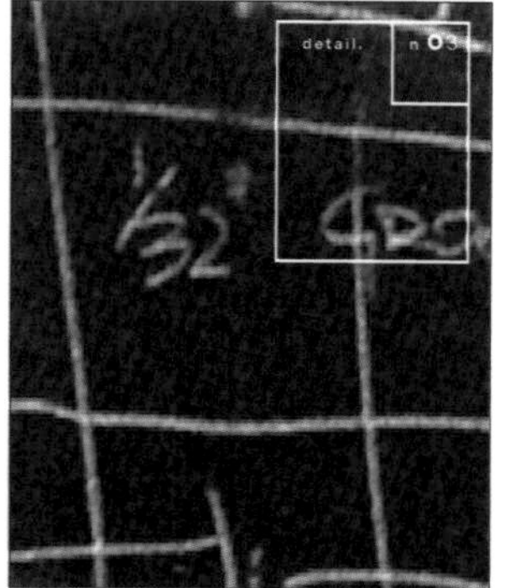

detail 03

design firm. michael vanderbyl design

communication graphics. | NO. 06

detail 04

detail 05

design firm. michael vanderbyl design

communication graphics. | NO. 06

detail 06

detail 07

detail 08

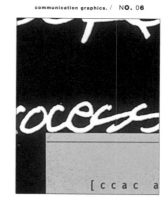

detail. / n08

It's been five days since you left our living room.

19

page / 8

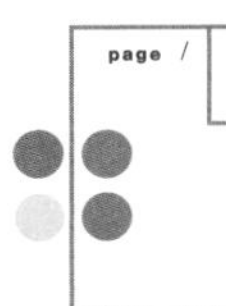

07 CG. PBS 1999 ANNUAL REPORT / PBS wanted to use the annual report to speak to the general managers of all broadcasting stations across the country and show that it has stood behind its word to promote quality, inspirational, informative and entertaining programming. The solution was to communicate the quality of PBS programming by featuring letters from viewers stating how programs affected their lives and stayed with them long after the television was turned off.

07 DESIGN FIRM Cahan and Associates, San Francisco, CA
ART DIRECTOR Bill Cahan
DESIGNER Bob Dinetz
PHOTOGRAPHER Ken Probst
WRITERS David Stone, Bob Dinetz

TYPEFACE Helvetica
TRIM SIZE 10 1/2 x 12 3/4 inches
PRINTER Graphic Arts Center
PAPER Potlatch McCoy
CLIENT PBS

design firm. cahan and associates

communication graphics. | NO. 07

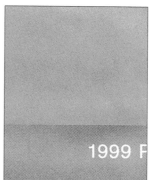

design firm. cahan and associates

communication graphics. | NO. 07

detail 01

1999 F

detail 02

rwriters of the PE
rporation / Alfred
st Company Fou
undation / Fidelit
Corporation / Iom
Lilly Endowmen

detail 03

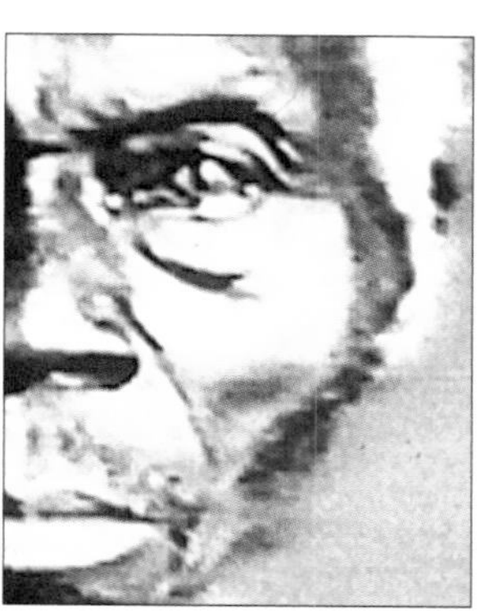

detail 04

978

984

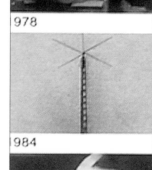

detail 05

design firm. cahan and associates

communication graphics. | NO. 07

detail 06

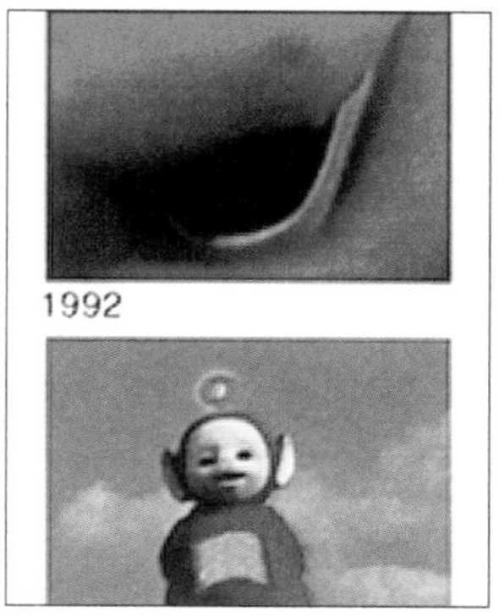

detail 07

08 03. THE COMPLETE LESTER YOUNG STUDIO SESSIONS ON VERVE / We needed to figure out how to create innovative and economical packaging on a very low budget. We chose to create a new package that had never been done before. We printed and embossed to simulate wood effect, and printed direct to plate in order to save on film costs.

08

DESIGN FIRM	The Verve Group, New York, NY
CREATIVE DIRECTOR	Hollis A. King
DESIGNER	Isabelle Wong/Isthetic
PRINT PRODUCTION	Sherniece Johnson-Smith
ILLUSTRATOR	David Stone Martin
PHOTOGRAPHER	Herman Leonard (cover)
LETTERING	Paul Shaw
PRINTER	Tower Communications
PAPER	Strathmore

detail. / n07

design firm. the verve group

communication graphics. | NO. 08

detail 01

detail 02

detail 03

design firm. the verve group

communication graphics. | NO. 08

detail 04

detail 05

design firm. the verve group

communication graphics. | NO. 08

detail 06

detail 07

09 09. MERCURY INTERACTIVE 1999 WORLDWIDE USER CONFERENCE MATERIALS / Mercury Interactive, the worldwide leader in enterprise application testing solutions, asked Oh Boy to design the collateral for its 1999 worldwide user conference. The goal of the materials was to convey the complex subject matter of the conference in a manner that was neither overly simplistic nor difficult to comprehend. To that end, Oh Boy avoided the overly technical look and feel of most mail received by IT managers and computer analysts and utilized everyday objects, photographed with an urban sensibility and complemented by two-word phrases like "Increase function."

09

DESIGN FIRM	Oh Boy, A Design Company, San Francisco, CA
ART DIRECTOR	David Salanitro
DESIGNER	Ryan Mahar
PRINT PRODUCTION	Elizabeth Cutter
PHOTOGRAPHERS	Various
WRITER	Carol Baxter
PRINTER	Hemlock Printers
PAPER	Various
CLIENT	Mercury Interactive

design firm. oh boy, a design company

communication graphics. | NO. 09

design firm. oh boy, a design company

communication graphics. | NO. 09

design firm. oh boy, a design company

communication graphics. | NO. 09

detail O1

detail O2

detail O3

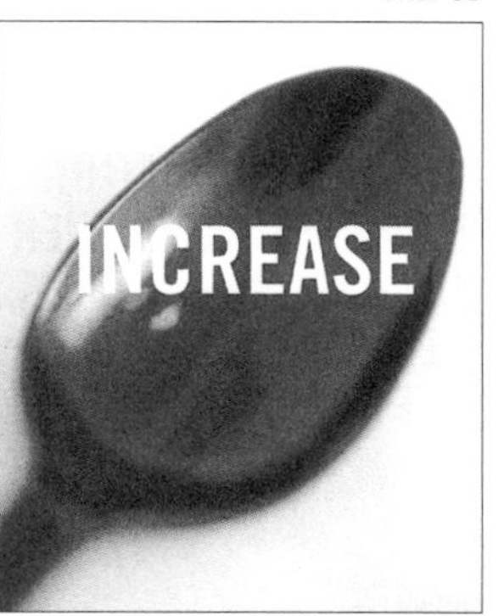

detail O4

detail O5

IN 1997
THE WORLDWIDE
ACKAGED SOFTWAR
MARKET GREW TO
35 BILLION. BY 200
T IS ESTIMATED TO
CEED $228 BILLIO

detail O6

10 03. METROPOLIS MAGAZINE / The challenge was to design the last "oversize" issue of METROPOLIS, which for 18 years has been the largest format design magazine in America. METROPOLIS has always been one of my favorite magazines, so I was honored and pleased to get asked to design an entire issue, especially on that huge format. I chose to use only the area that the new page size (beginning with the next issue) would be. Each page, starting with the cover, has crop marks and a white band across the page indicating the area to be lost with the new size.

10

DESIGN FIRM	Metropolis Magazine, New York, NY
ART DIRECTOR/ DESIGNER/ PHOTOGRAPHER	David Carson
PRINT PRODUCTION	Jim Goss
TYPEFACE	
DESIGNER	Jens Gehlhaar
TRIM SIZE	11 x 17 inches
PRINTER	Brown Printing
PUBLISHER	Bellerophon Publications

OLIS

detail. / n 01

OCTOBER 199

A MONSTER PROJECT FOR MANHATTAN'S FINAL FRONTIER?

MICKEY MOUSE CONSTRUCTION IN CELEBRATION, FLA

EZRA STOLLER'S TWENTIETH CENTURY

PLUS:

WRIST PHONES, PORN PALACES, AND BEN KATCHOR ON THE SLUG-BEARERS OF KAYROL ISLAND

design firm. metropolis magazine

communication graphics. | NO. 10

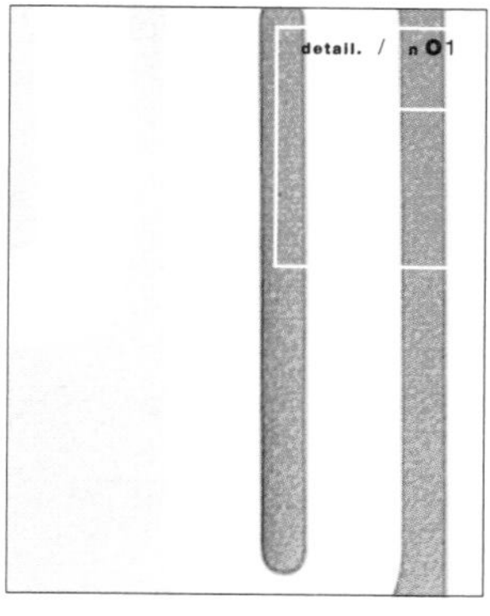

detail 01

detail 02

detail 03

design firm. metropolis magazine

communication graphics. | NO. 10

detail 04

detail 05

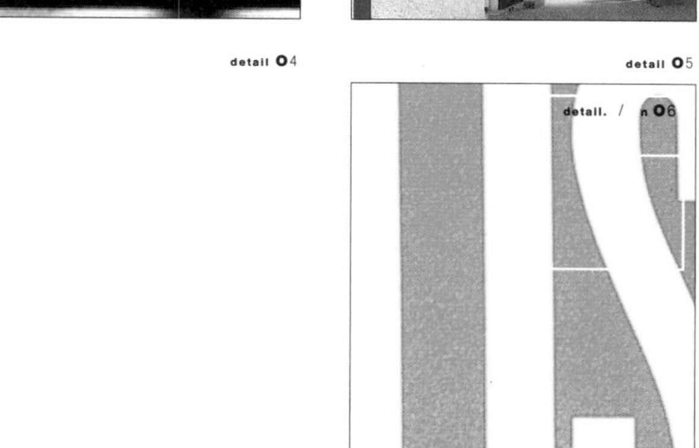

design firm. metropolis magazine

communication graphics. | NO. 10

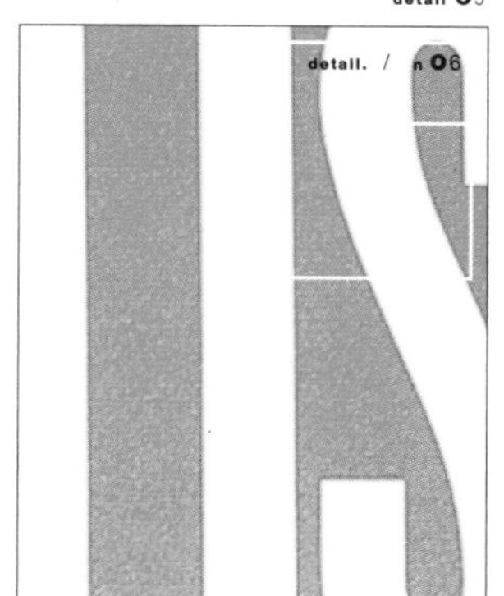

detail 06

detail 07

THROUGH YOUR EYES: WALKER ART CENTER ANNUAL REPORT 1998–1999 / The Walker is a ary contemporary arts museum in Minneapolis, and this year's annual report is meant to summarize a four-year dollar grant initiative to diversify our audiences to include more low-income visitors, people of color and teens. a varied cross-section of visitors and collaborators and gathered thoughts about their experience with the Walker. ts were taken and coupled with excerpts of each person's commentary.

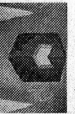

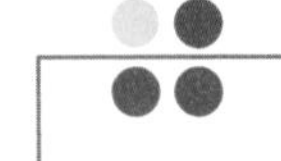

11

DESIGN FIRM	Walker Art Center Design Department, Minneapolis, MN
DESIGN DIRECTOR	Andrew Blauvelt
DESIGNER	Aaron King
PRINT PRODUCTION	Michelle Piranio
TYPEFACE	News Gothic Condensed
TRIM SIZE	10 1/2 x 7 3/4 inches
PRINTER	Ambassador Press
PAPER	Champion
CLIENT	Walker Art Center

itions 19 59–1999

CATALOGUE RAISONNÉ

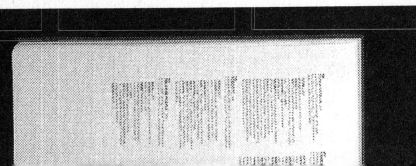

2

3

design firm. walker art center

communication graphics. | NO. 11

detail O1

detail O2

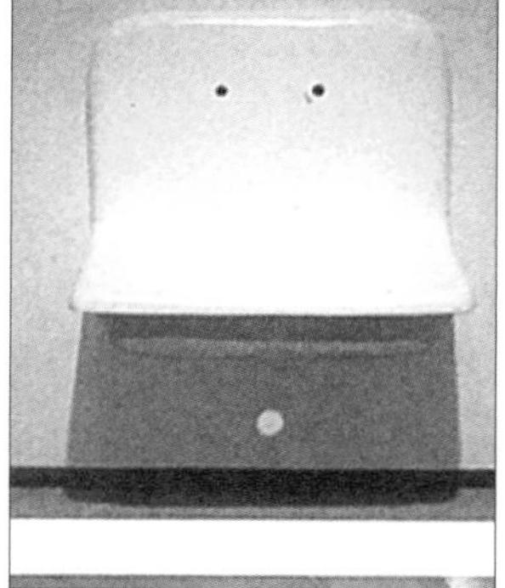

detail O3

design firm. walker art center

communication graphics. | NO. 11

detail O4

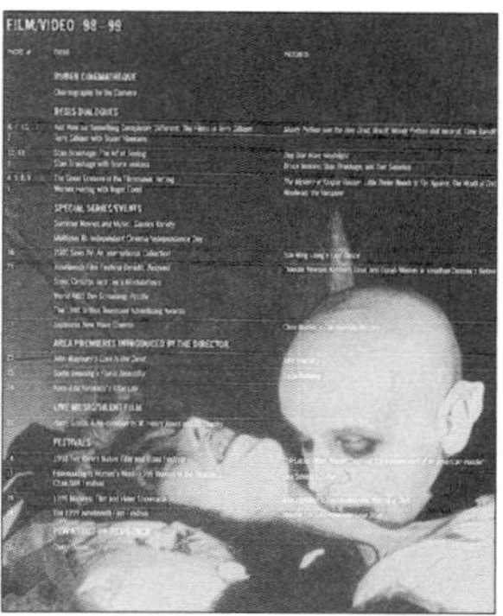

detail O5

design firm. walker art center

communication graphics. | NO. 11

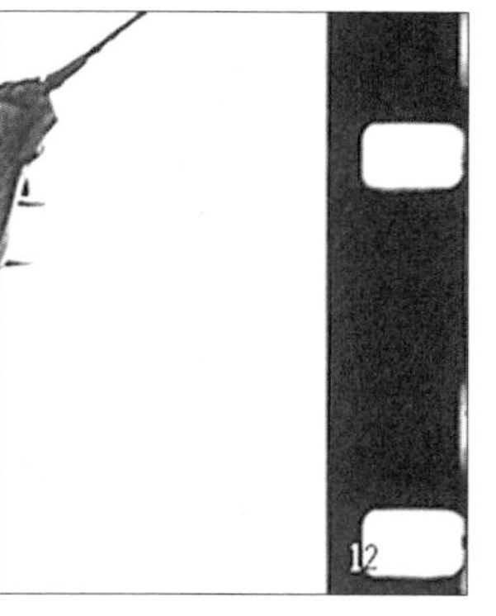

detail O6

detail O7

12 CG. AIGA/SF 1999 SHOWOFF CALL FOR ENTRIES / The goal with the 1999 fundraiser was to increase attendance. The event was slated to be an open show for each designer to submit one piece of work. Turner & Associates developed the concept of providing attendees with "praise and scorn" stickers. Guests then individually judged work by adhering stickers to the matte around each submission. There were few projects that were untouched by both praise and scorn from the community. In order to promote the event, a large brochure and small mailer were crafted around a theme of biblical proportions.

page / 9

12

DESIGN FIRM	Turner & Associates, San Francisco, CA	WRITERS	Paul Roberts, Phil Hamlett, Stephen Turner
CREATIVE DIRECTOR	Stephen Turner	TYPEFACES	HTF historicals
DESIGNERS	Laurie Carrigan, Angela Hughes	PRINTER	Hennegan
ILLUSTRATOR	Chad Cameron	PAPER	Various
PHOTOGRAPHER	Kevin Irby	CLIENT	AIGA San Francisco

detail. / n 01

design firm. turner & associates

communication graphics. | NO. 12

detail. / n O1

detail O1

DAY OF THE
e last year of
f every kind,[2]
cended upon
hey had been
to join in a

detail O2

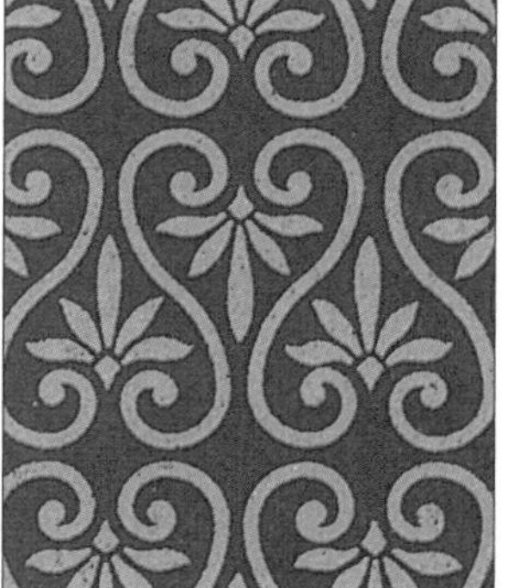

detail O3

design firm. turner & associates

communication graphics. | NO. 12

1
MOST RIG
first amo
so that th
eyes in its

2
DIVINE T
and woos

detail O4

detail O5

design firm. turner & associates

communication graphics. | NO. 12

reat Festival.[5] And they were give
ons.[6] And they feasted upon victuals
om seed-bearing plants and fatted
And when they had their fill, they
orth about the Great Hall[8] and s
e toil[9] of their brethren, and they
udgement.[10] And that Work whic
bserved as good,[11] thus they pro
. And that which was deemed un
hus they smote it down.[13] This w
ith great care, as the creators of ea
ere present, and did watcheth over.
And yea, though there was much
f hair and gnashing of teeth,[14] soon
ade merry, and even more veri
efore. For the wine flowed freely,
pirits kindred, and all did know

detail O6

4
PROPHETIC
clearly fore
doing in te

5
BRAZEN Th
respect for

6
HEATHEN T

detail O7

13 CG. NEWENERGY CONNECTIONS BROCHURE / In order to capture the attention of corporations that use lots of power, this brochure was designed to be large in format, clean and full of information. Each page of the brochure carries a single significant image, with an understated tagline that gives the name of a high-profile client such as Saks Fifth Avenue, CBS or the U.S. Department of Defense. We focused on making the connection between NewEnergy and its clients in addition to making connections in the design of facing pages.

13

DESIGN FIRM	Cahan and Associates, San Francisco, CA
ART DIRECTOR	Bill Cahan
DESIGNER	Michael Braley
PROJECT MANAGER	Katie Kniestedt
PHOTOGRAPHERS	Robert Schlatter, William Mercer McLeod
WRITER	Nanette Biers
TYPEFACES	Goudy, Garamond
PRINTER	ColorGraphics
PAPER	McCoy Cougar
CLIENT	NewEnergy

design firm. cahan and associates

communication graphics. | NO. 13

the connection

detail 01

detail 02

design firm. cahan and associates

communication graphics. | NO. 13

detail 03

detail 04

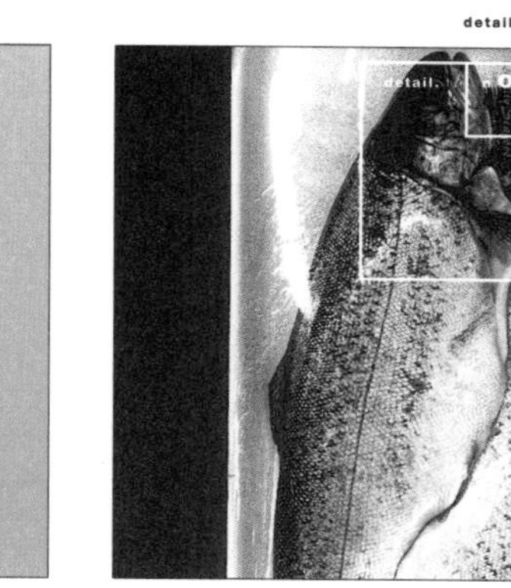

detail 05

design firm. cahan and associates

communication graphics. | NO. 13

detail 06

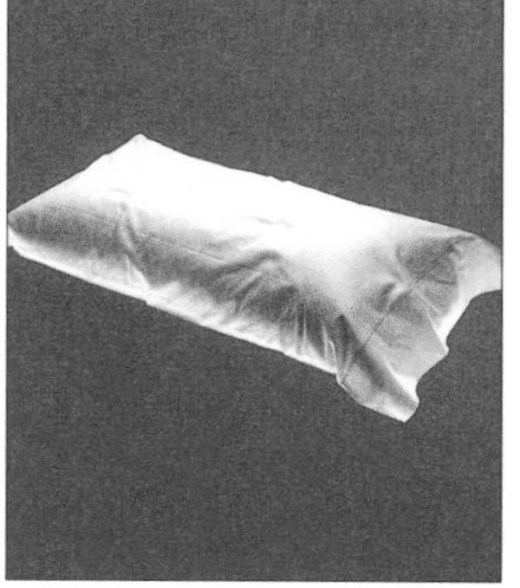

detail 07

WHOSOEVER DESIRES CONSTANT SUCCESS MUST CHANGE HIS CONDUCT WITH THE TIMES.

detail. / n 03

I DON'T KNOW THE KEY TO *SUCCESS*, BUT THE KEY TO FAILURE IS TRYING TO PLEASE EVERYBODY.

Bill Cosby

Niccolo Machiavelli

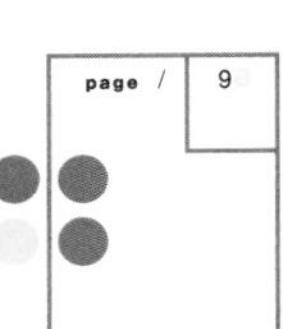

page / 9

14 CG. THE PROGRESSIVE CORPORATION 1999 ANNUAL REPORT / Much about Progressive is not what you'd expect from an insurance company. To illustrate this concept, we commissioned artist Gregory Crewdson to investigate the idea of the end of status quo with his evocative photographs. To further explore the notion of the end of status quo, attributed quotes that ranged in attitude were juxtaposed front to back on translucent papers. Colors were inspired by the saturated palette of the artwork, and text was pulled from the body of the report to emphasize Progressive's philosophy of questioning the status quo.

14

DESIGN FIRM	Nesnadny + Schwartz, Cleveland, OH
ART DIRECTORS	Mark Schwartz, Joyce Nesnadny
DESIGNERS	Joyce Nesnadny, Michelle Moehler
ARTIST	Gregory Crewdson
WRITER	Peter B. Lewis, the Progressive Corporation
PRINTER	Fortran Printing Inc.
PAPER	Various
CLIENT	The Progressive Corporation

design firm. nesnadny + schwartz

communication graphics. | NO. 14

detail 01

design firm. nesnadny + schwartz

communication graphics. | NO. 14

detail 02

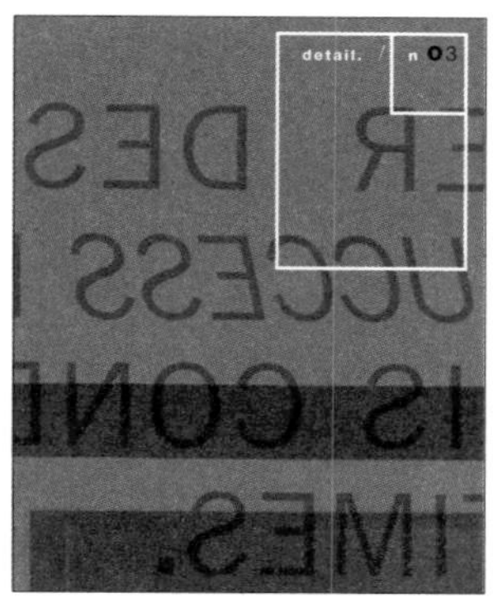

detail 03

detail 04

design firm. nesnadny + schwartz

communication graphics. | NO. 14

detail 05

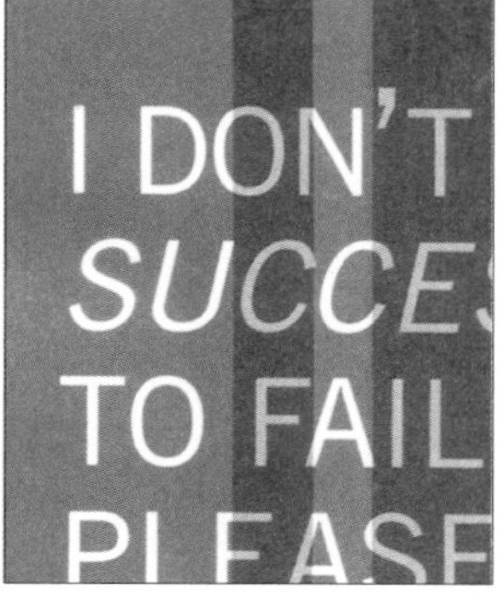

detail 06

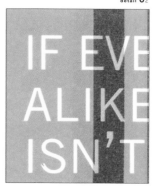

15 03. VALENTIS 1999 ANNUAL REPORT / Valentis is a biotechnology company developing a broad technology platform consisting of several in-vivo, non-viral gene delivery systems. The small format of the book was continued from the previous year and worked well given budgetary limitations. The strong geometric shapes and colors serve as a backdrop for the company's message to a target audience of stockholders, partners and employees.

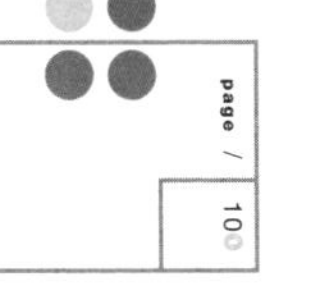

15

DESIGN FIRM	Cahan and Associates, San Francisco, CA
ART DIRECTOR	Bill Cahan
DESIGNER	Sharrie Brooks
PROJECT MANAGER	Kerrie Claeys
WRITER	Bennett Weintraub
TYPEFACE	Trade Gothic
TRIM SIZE	5 1/2 x 7 inches
PRINTER	ColorGraphics
PAPER	McCoy Cougar
CLIENT	Valentis

VALENTIS

detail. / 07

detail. /

design firm. cahan and associates

communication graphics. | NO. 15

detail 01

detail 02

design firm. cahan and associates

communication graphics. | NO. 15

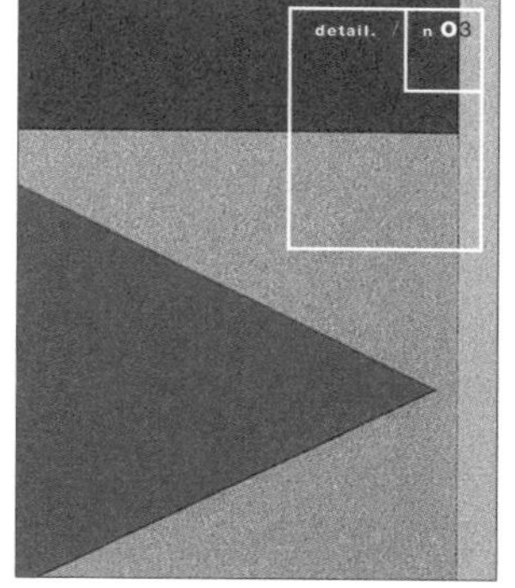

detail 03

detail 04

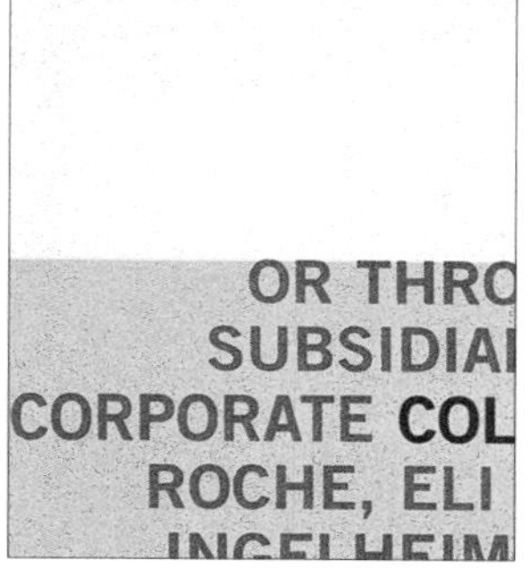

detail 05

design firm. cahan and associates

communication graphics. | NO. 15

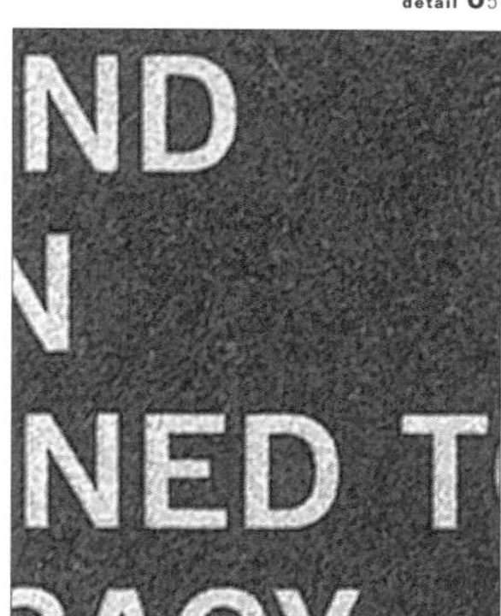

detail 06

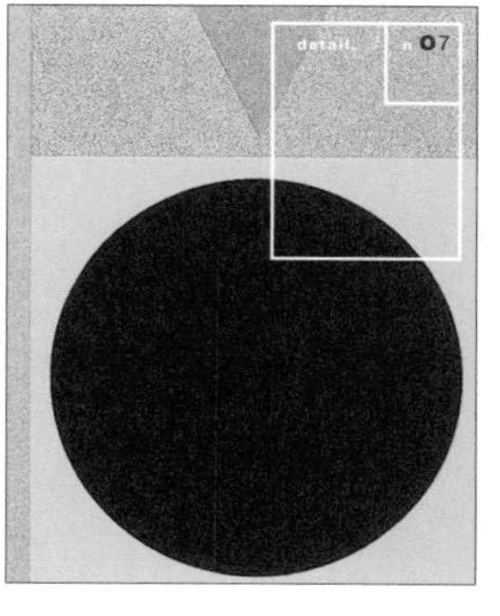

detail 07

A PERSON SPENDS AN AVERAGE OF 3 MINUTES READING AN ANNUAL REPORT.

16 GEORGIA-PACIFIC 1999 ANNUAL REPORT PARTY INVITATION / We wanted to come up with a clever invitation to a party for those involved in creating annual reports. Everyone in the design business has heard the statistic that the average person spends about three minutes with an annual report. We tried to put that time frame into perspective.

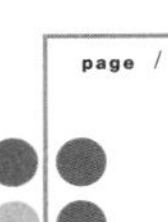

16

DESIGN FIRM EAI, Atlanta, GA
ART DIRECTOR David Cannon
DESIGNER Samantha Davenport
PROJECT MANAGER Katie Wright
PHOTOGRAPHER Scott Lowden

TYPEFACE Franklin Gothic
TRIM SIZE 6 x 8 inches
PRINTER ColorGraphics
PAPER Nekoosa Solutions 80 pound text
CLIENT Georgia-Pacific Papers

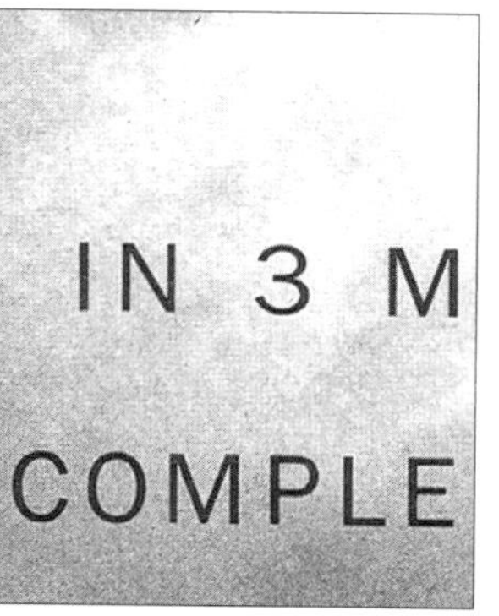

design firm. eai

communication graphics. | NO. 16

detail O1

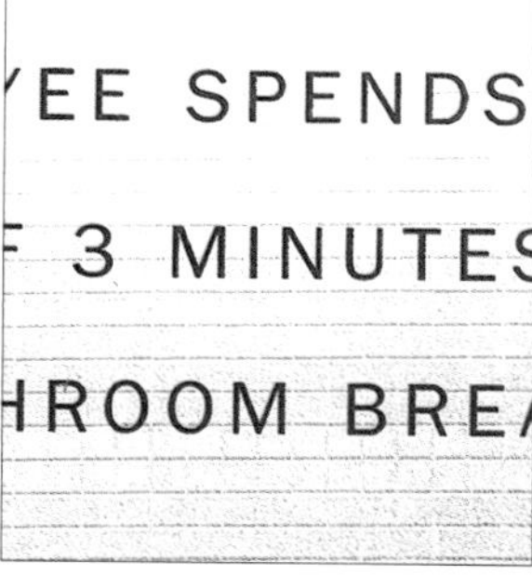

design firm. eai

communication graphics. | NO. 16

detail O2

detail O3

detail O4

design firm. eai

communication graphics. | NO. 16

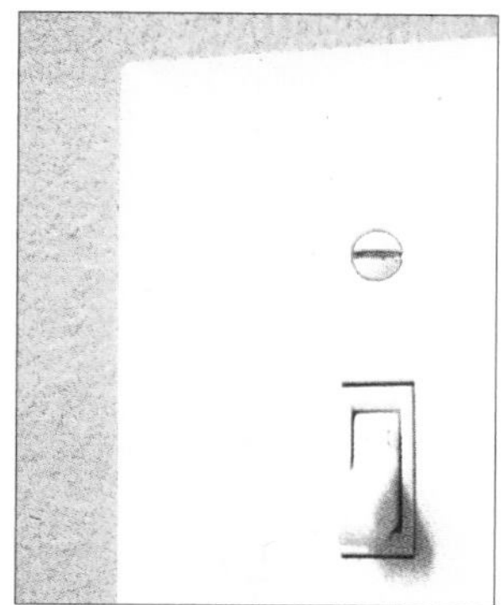

detail O5

detail O6

17 06. DOCKERS K-1 CLOTHING TAGS / The graphic language we developed for this collection is rooted in the simplicity we found in materials created by the army in the 1930s and '40s. We tried to remain true to how "undesigned" those materials look by only using one or two typefaces, little color and real simple lock-ups. We used industrial materials like sheet metal for the jacket tags, heavy duty chip board for the pant tags, industrial rubber bands for the belts and even K-Ration-like bags to package the T-shirts. Even the printing techniques got no fancier than silk screening and crude letterpress printing.

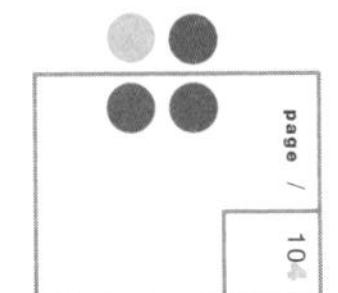

17

DESIGN FIRM	Templin Brink Design, San Francisco, CA
CREATIVE DIRECTOR	Gaby Brink
DESIGNERS	Gaby Brink, Jason Schulte
WRITERS	Dann Wilkens, Jesse Zeifman
TYPEFACE	Futura BT
PRINTER/FABRICATOR	KEA, Inc.
PAPER	Chipboard, various
CLIENT	Dockers Khakis

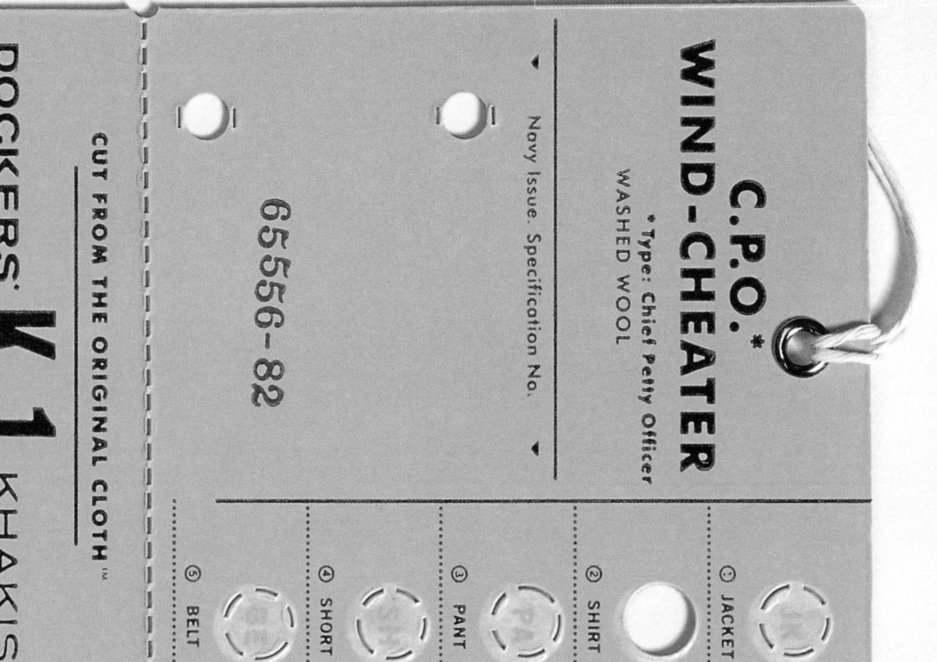

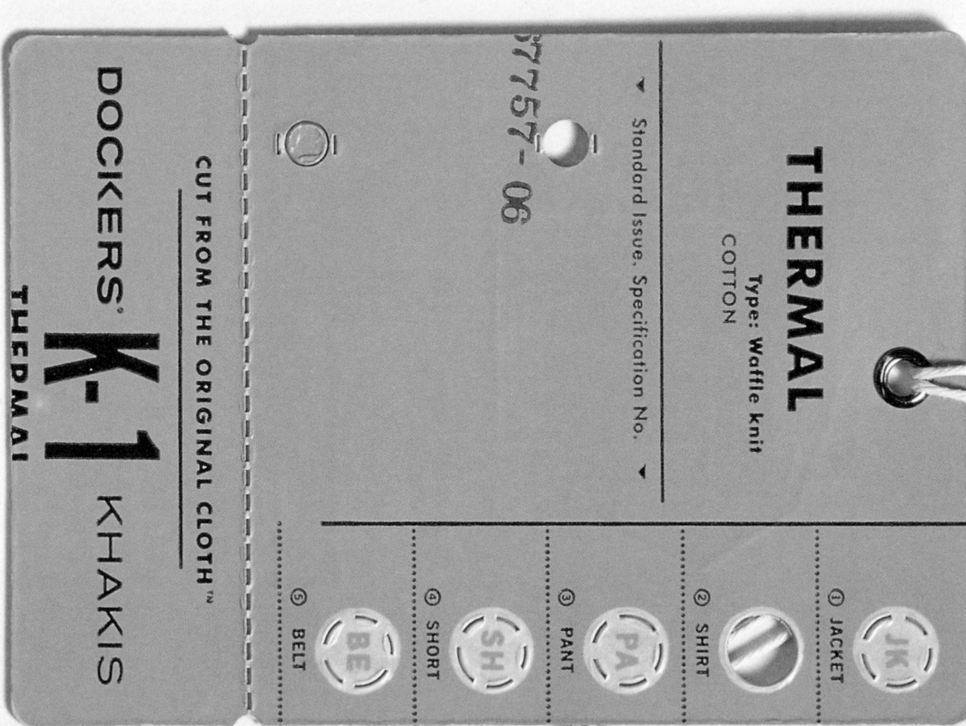

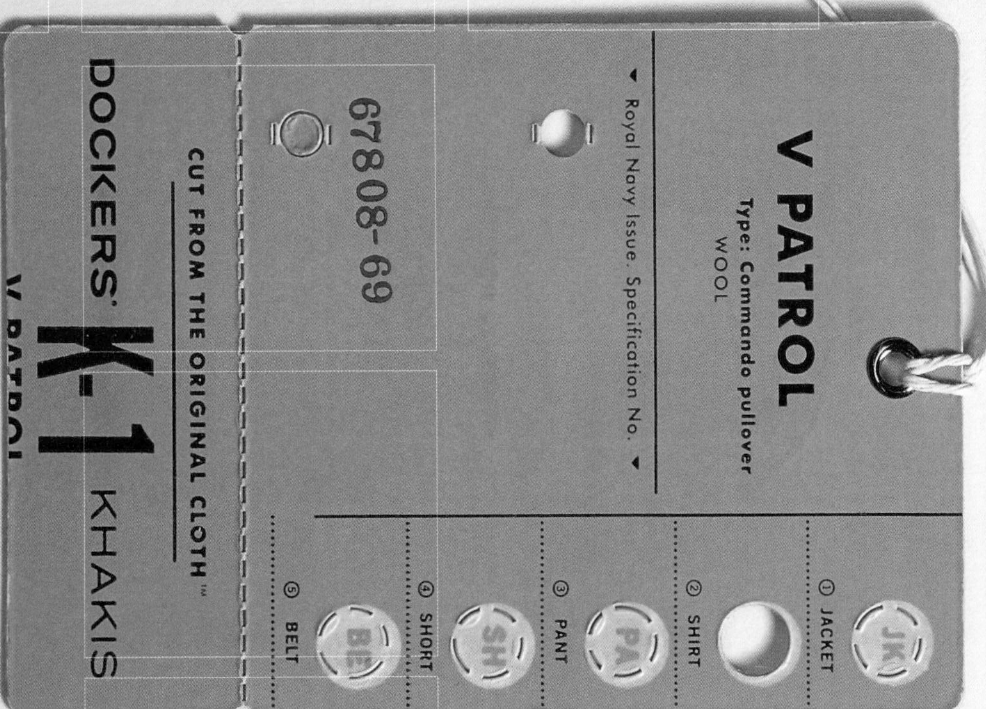

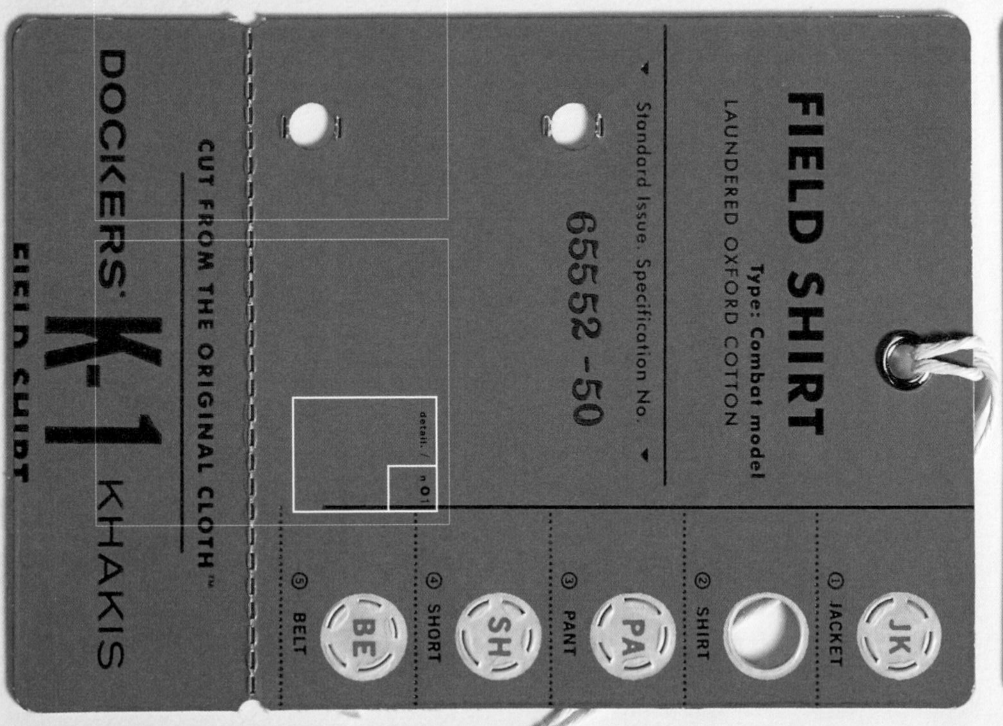

design firm. templin brink design

communication graphics. | NO. 17

detail 01

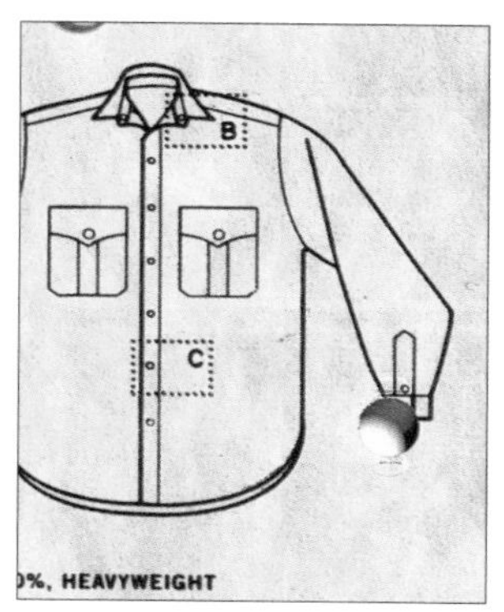

detail 02

design firm. templin brink design

communication graphics. | NO. 17

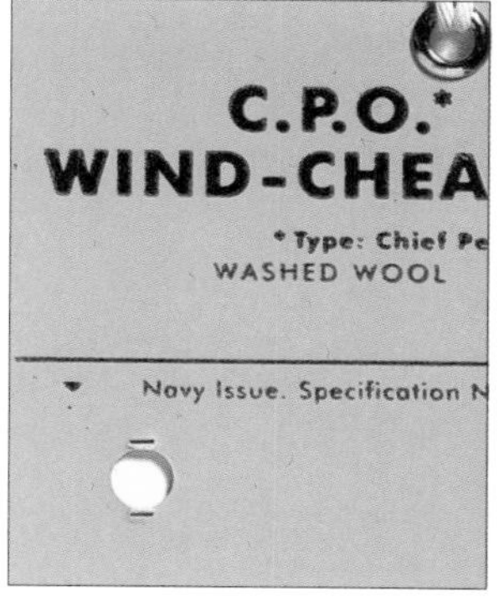

detail 03

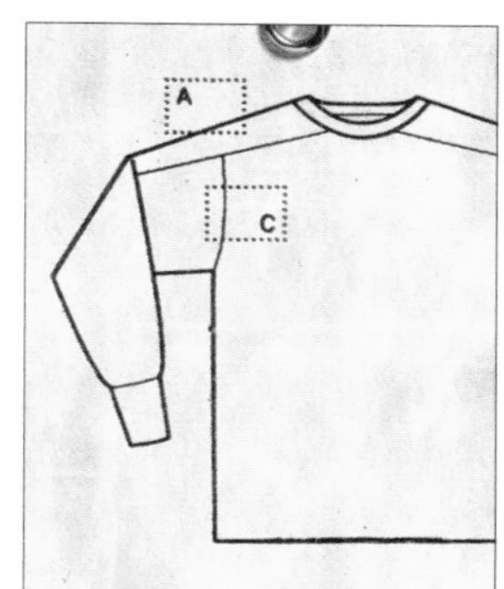

detail 04

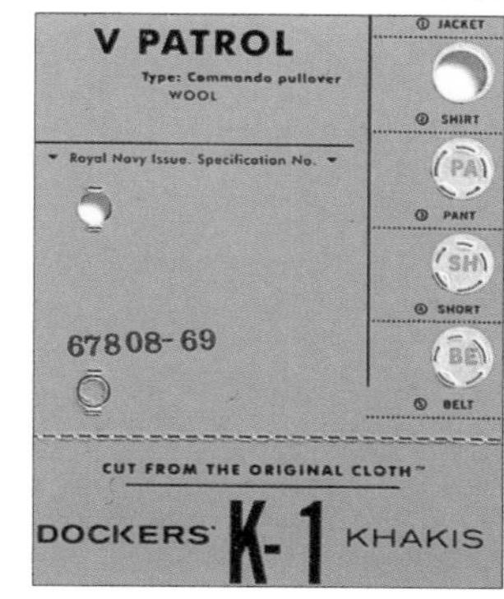

detail 05

design firm. templin brink design

communication graphics. | NO. 17

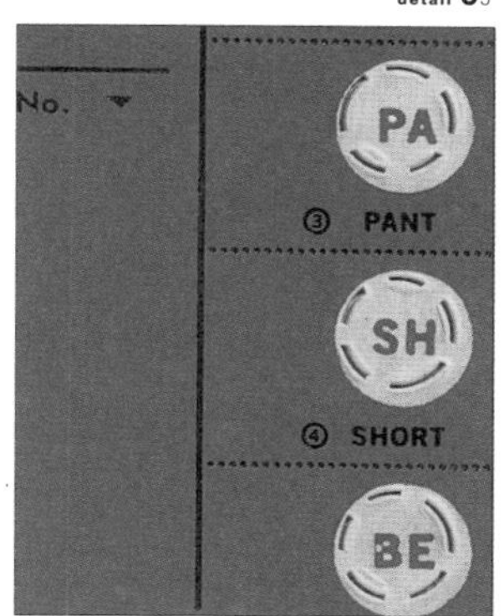

detail 06

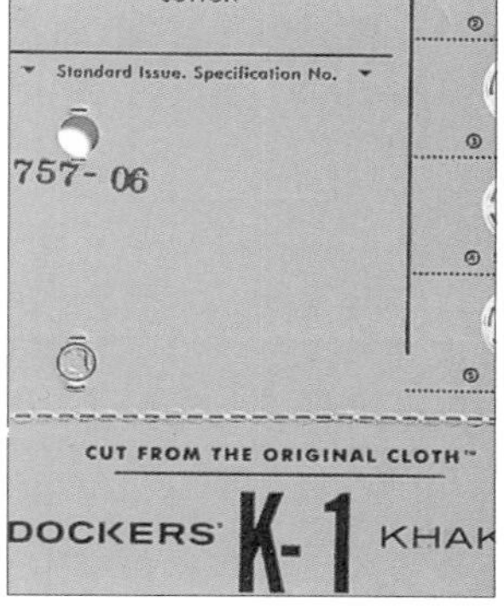

detail 07

18 CG. GLOBAL DESIGN ALLIANCE BROCHURE / Global Design Alliance is the first corporation formed in the network model to serve the built environment. Unlike a conventional organization, Global Design Alliance is a system—a living organism that can expand or contract to exactly the right mix of expertise for the project at hand.

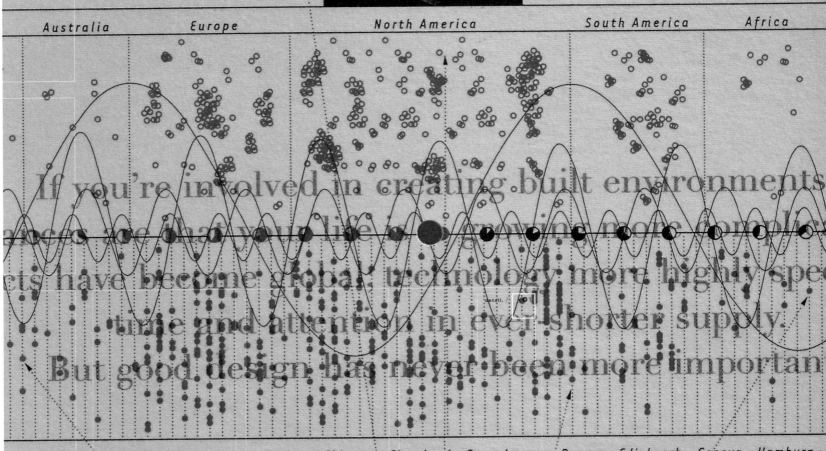

18

DESIGN FIRM	Rigsby Design, Inc., Houston, TX
ART DIRECTOR	Lana Rigsby
DESIGNERS	Lana Rigsby, Pamela Zuckcer
ILLUSTRATOR	Pamela Zuckcer
PHOTOGRAPHER	Various
WRITER	Lana Rigsby
TYPEFACE	Tarzana
TRIM SIZE	7 1/4 x 7 1/4 inches
PRINTER	H. Macdonald Printing
PAPER	Mohawk Superfine
CLIENT	Global Design Alliance

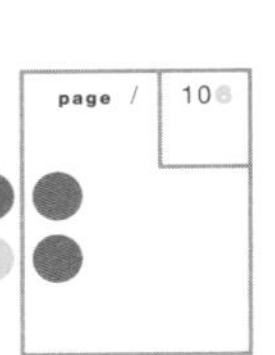

Australia Europe North America South America Africa

If you're involved in creating built environments
...ances are that your life is growing more complex
...cts have become global; technology more highly spec...
time and attention in ever-shorter supply.
But good design has never been more importan...

Atlanta • Berlin • Bonn • Boston • Buenos Aires • Chicago • Cleveland • Copenhagen • Denver • Edinburgh • Geneva • Hamburg •
...salem • Lima • Los Angeles • London • Melbourne • Mexico City • Miami • Montreal • Moscow • New York • Orlando • Oslo • Par...
...an Francisco • Seattle • Seoul • Shanghai • Singapore • Stockholm • Sydney • Tokyo • Topeka • Toronto • Tucson • Washington DC

3 4 5 6 7 8 9 10 11 12 13 14 15 16 17 18 19 20

YOU ARE HERE

design firm. rigsby design, inc.

communication graphics. | NO. 18

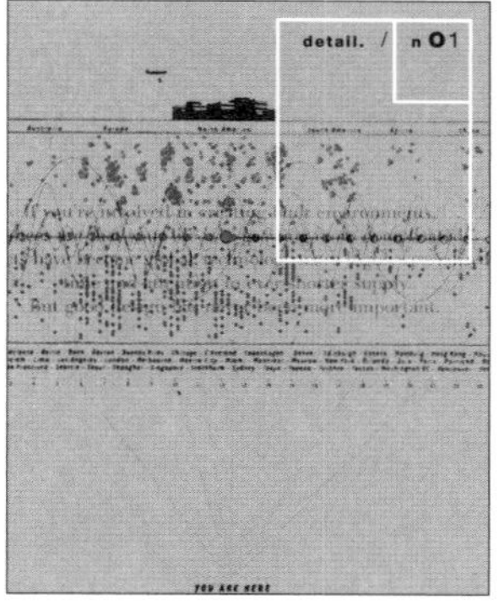

detail O1

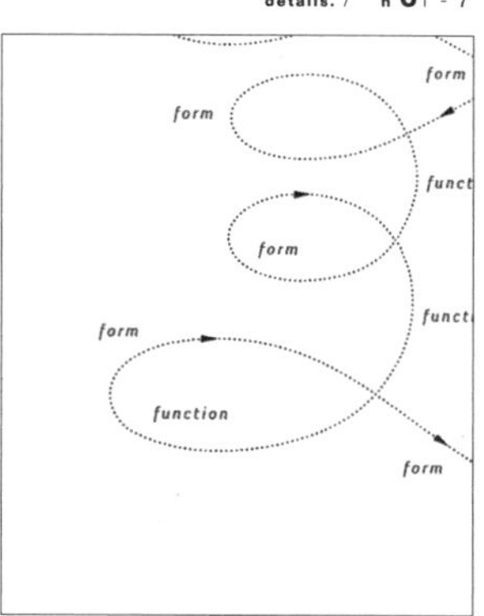

detail O2

design firm. rigsby design, inc.

communication graphics. | NO. 18

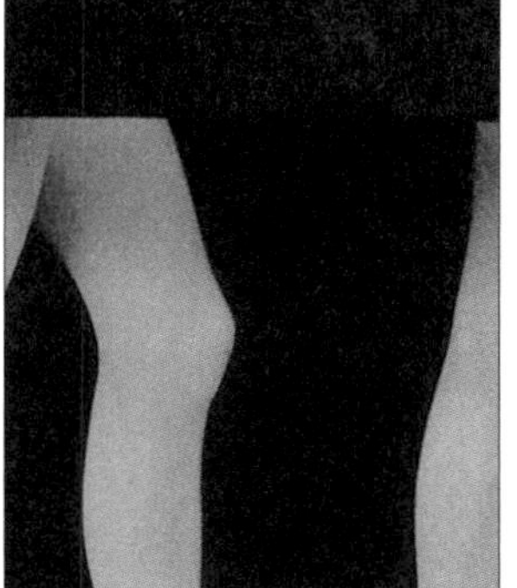

detail O3

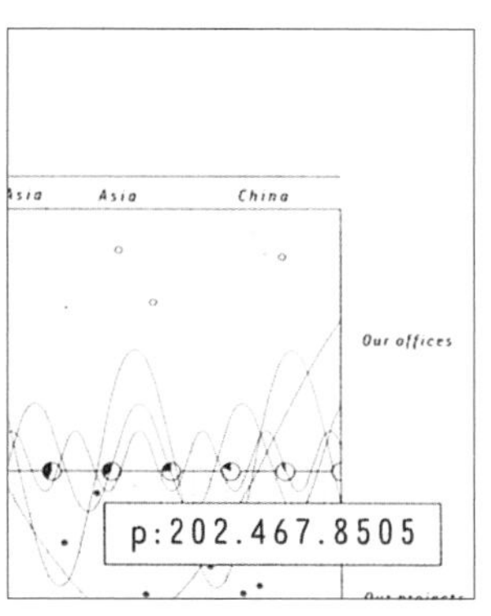

detail O4

detail O5

design firm. rigsby design, inc.

communication graphics. | NO. 18

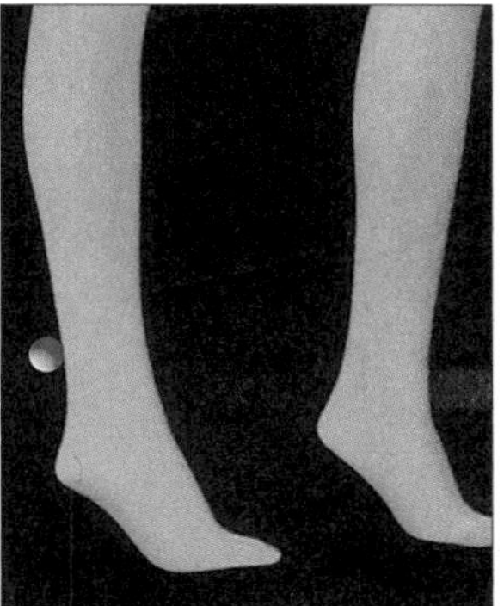

detail O6

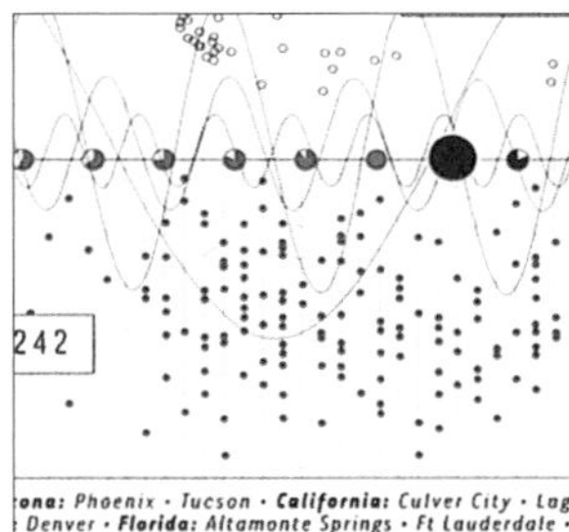

detail O7

19 CG. RETHINKING DESIGN FIVE: THE VISUAL LANGUAGE OF SUBCULTURES / This publication looks at ways that groups of people use the tools of design to create identity—from '50s custom-car enthusiasts to Vatican II-era Catholic nuns to '90s skateboarders. The "Rethinking Design" series was created by Pentagram to demonstrate the beauty of Mohawk's papers to the design community, while raising issues about what designers do and how they do it. To underline the vernacular character of this edition's subject matter, the book takes the form of a standard paperback, complete with a quasi-lurid foil-stamped embossed cover.

19

DESIGN FIRM	Pentagram Design, New York, NY
PARTNER/DESIGNER	Michael Bierut
DESIGNER	Jacqueline Thaw
PHOTOGRAPHERS	Various
ILLUSTRATORS	Andy Cruz and Rich Roat (House Industries), Christoph Niemann

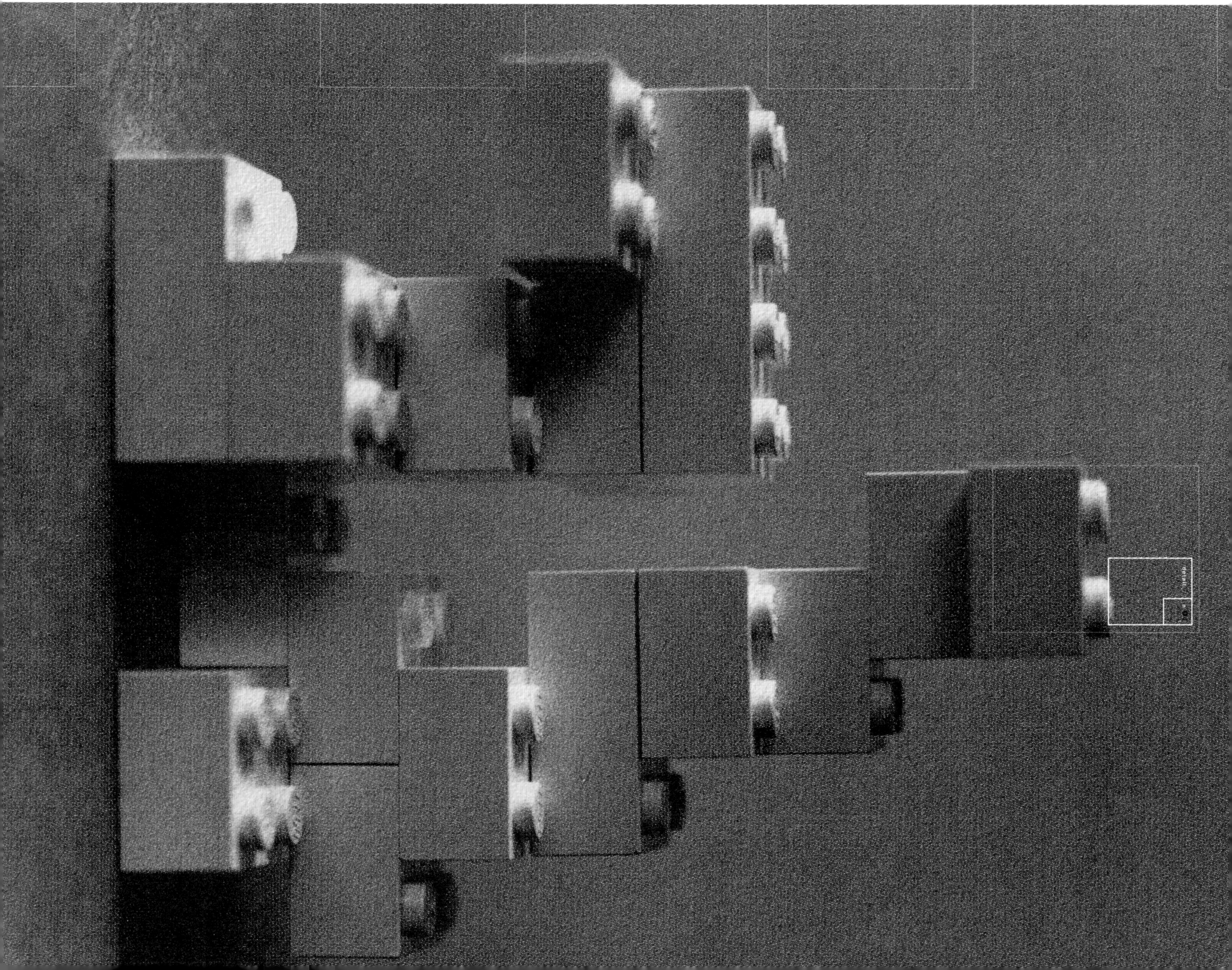

design firm. pentagram design

communication graphics. | NO. 19

detail O1

detail O2

design firm. pentagram design

communication graphics. | NO. 19

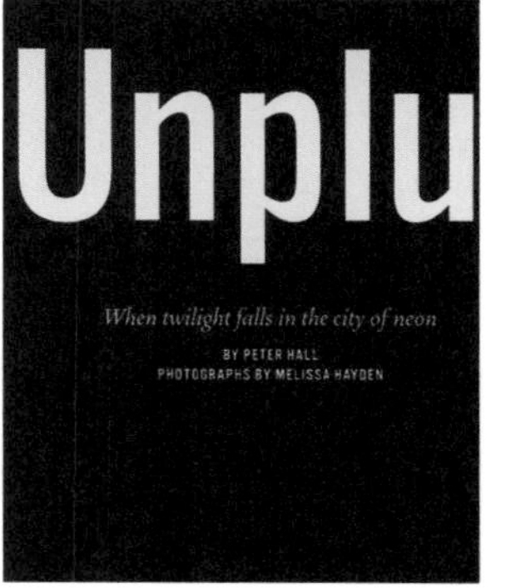

detail O3

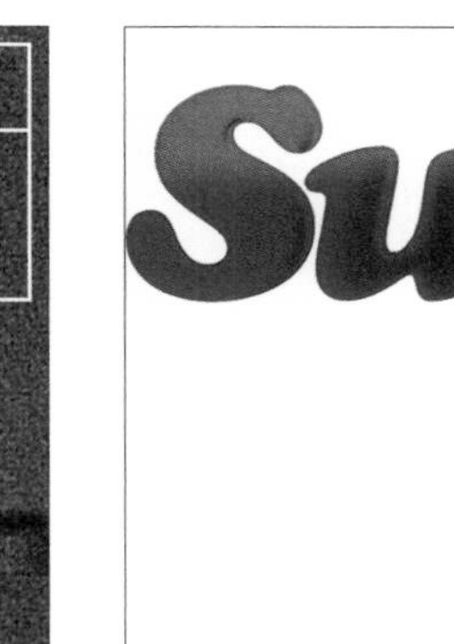

detail O4

detail O5

design firm. pentagram design

communication graphics. | NO. 19

that was bourgeois. And he'd give that student and every other student in the class a stack of Color Aid squares.

Albers had spent the preceding 14 years of his life investigating the problems, if any, of superimposing squares of color on one another. So he was determined that for the first year of your instruction at Yale, you deposited squares of Color Aid paper on top of each other until you got it right.

Now

IN GRAPHICS, THE IDEA OF ANTI-BOURGEOIS purging took place with tremendous speed, first in Europe and then in this country. The Bauhaus, De Stijl, the Constructivists, El Lissitzky, Rodchenko, Jan Tschichold, a whole group of typographers and graphic designers, and above all the Swiss, the people I think of as the Helveticans, put forward this notion that all bourgeois elements should disappear entirely from graphics.

What were these elements? There should be no more

detail O6

Rethinking Design
Number Five:
The Visual Language
of Subcultures

Edited and designed by Pentagram

Published by Mohawk Paper Mills

detail O7

20 03. E*TRADE GROUP, INC. 1999 ANNUAL REPORT / We were hired to create an annual report that would do much more than just tell E*TRADE's story—the report had to position the company in a much bigger context and show how it was truly empowering a revolution in financial services. We created a two-part editorial document. The first segment set up the pivotal moments in history that defined acts of individual expressions of freedom. The second segment showed how E*TRADE breaks through the barriers of time, access and geography by giving individuals the tools they need to take control of their own financial destiny.

20

DESIGN FIRM	Broom & Broom, San Francisco, CA
DESIGN DIRECTOR	Martin McMurray
DESIGNER	Dan Chau
PHOTOGRAPHERS	Various
COPYWRITERS	Various
TYPEFACES	Various
TRIM SIZE	8 1/2 x 10 inches
PRINTER	Anderson Lithograph
PAPER	Cougar 100 pound Opaque Smooth Cover and Book

detail. / n 03

design firm. broom & broom

communication graphics. | NO. 20

detail 01

1967

THEY SAID EQUALITY WAS ONLY FOR SOME OF US

detail 02

design firm. broom & broom

communication graphics. | NO. 20

detail 03

detail 04

COULDN'T BE DONE. TO WHICH
SAY IT
EING DONE

detail 05

design firm. broom & broom

communication graphics. | NO. 20

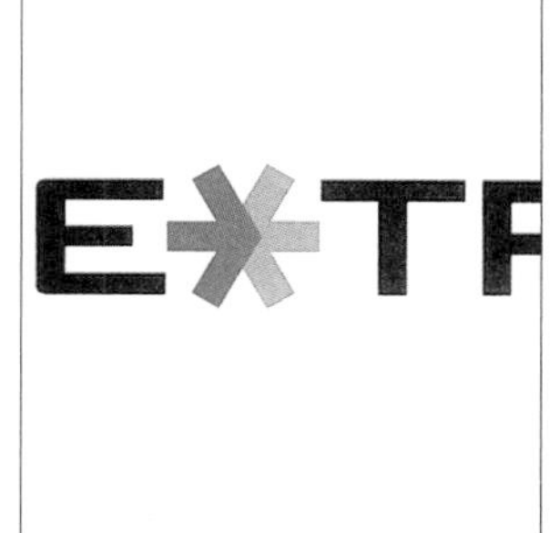

detail 06

detail 07

21 03. EXPOSURE BROCHURE / The client wanted to solicit the involvement of emerging artists and designers in a new hybrid format of exhibition and retail presentation of their work and of Levi's Vintage Clothing. The solution was to create images and text that were simple and straightforward and had a sense of humor. The result was a booklet with posterlike pages that is memorable yet doesn't require a lot of close attention. The title of the show was carried through for the neighborhood map guide, street posters, advertising and PR campaign that followed.

21

DESIGN FIRMS	Pompei A.D. LLC and Me Cozza Studio, New York, NY
CREATIVE DIRECTOR	Michael Gresty (Pompei A.D.)
ART DIRECTOR	Marc Cozza (Me Cozza Studio)
PHOTOGRAPHERS	Marc Cozza, James Smolka
WRITERS	Marc Cozza, Michael Gresty
TYPEFACE	Trade Gothic Bold
TRIM SIZE	6 3/8 x 10 inches
PRINTER	Typogram
CLIENT	Levi's Vintage Clothing

A MAP

& GUIDE

TO YOUR NEIGHBORHOO

WILL BE PRODUC

detail O1

design firm. pompei a.d. llc / me cozza studio

communication graphics. | NO. 21

detail O2

design firm. pompei a.d. llc / me cozza studio

communication graphics. | NO. 21

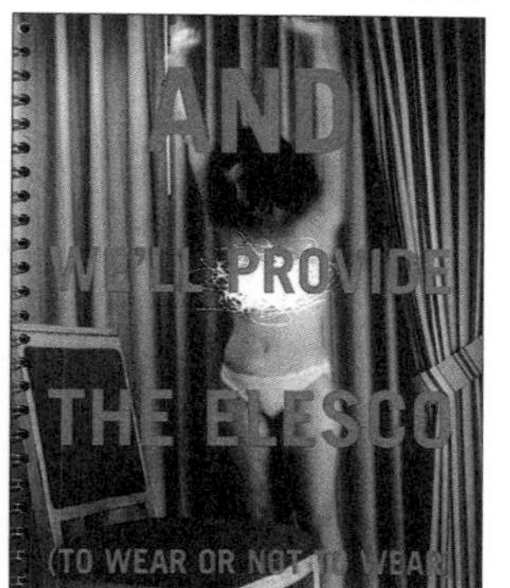

detail O3

detail O4

design firm. pompei a.d. llc / me cozza studio

communication graphics. | NO. 21

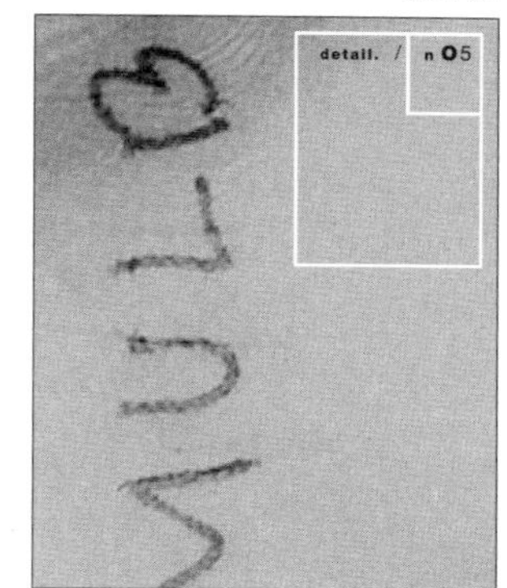

detail O5

detail O6

22 CG. 1999 DEL MONTE ANNUAL REPORT / Del Monte needed to update its "canned" food image, and wanted to implement a look that was contemporary and refreshing. Our design goal was to integrate energy, color and movement on each page and be reflective of life in the new century. We wanted the report to have a simple, yet fast-paced feel—as if the reader were watching a video. Because this was Del Monte's first annual report, the layouts were designed to be flexible. The text was minimal, giving the images a chance to be simple and bold.

22

DESIGN FIRM	Howry Design Associates, San Francisco, CA
ART DIRECTOR	Jill Howry
DESIGNER	Ty Whittingtion
PRINT PRODUCTION	Chris Cincebeaux
PHOTOGRAPHER	Stuart Schwartz
WRITER	Lindsay Beaman
PRINTER	Lithographix
CLIENT	Del Monte Foods

detail. / n01

QUICK

detail. / n 01

detail 01

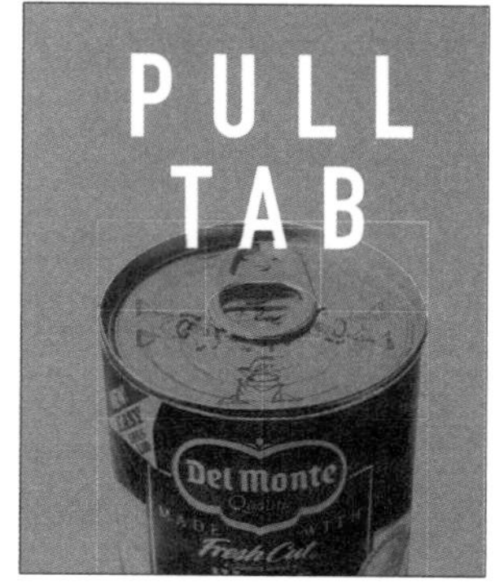

detail 02

DEL MONTE:
SOLUTIONS
LIFESTYLES

detail 03

5. Top with cheese during last 2 minutes.
pasta or rice, if desired

CHEESEBURGER MACARONI

Prep & Cook Time 15 minutes 4 servings

1 lb. ground beef
1 cup chopped onion
1 can (14-1/2 oz.) DEL MONTE® Diced To
Basil, Garlic & Oregano
1 cup elbow macaroni
1-1/2 cups shredded Cheddar cheese

1. Brown meat and onion over medium-h
skillet, drain. Season with salt and peppe

detail 04

detail 05

detail 06

design firm. howry design associates

communication graphics. | NO. 22

design firm. howry design associates

communication graphics. | NO. 22

design firm. howry design associates

communication graphics. | NO. 22

28 06. SUSSMAN/PREJZA & COMPANY SCALE FIGURES TEMPLATE / We decided to create an item that could function as a conceptually innovative promotional piece and as a New Year's greeting. The key idea was to take an ordinary, familiar article and reintroduce it as an object with a clearly defined reference to Sussman/Prejza. Given the fact that scale figure templates are rare or simply do not exist, it became a handy tool to have at one's workstation. Promotionally, the mailing was met with enormous enthusiasm and both humanized and personalized the company to clients, collaborators and others.

28

DESIGN FIRM	Sussman/Prejza & Company, Inc., Los Angeles, CA
PRINCIPAL	Deborah Sussman
CREATIVE DIRECTOR	Niv Kasher
DESIGNERS	Niv Kasher, Tad Hara, Robert Chacko
WRITERS	Niv Kasher, Miles Mazzie
ILLUSTRATOR	Selene Rawls
TYPEFACES	Univers Condensed Regular and Bold
TRIM SIZE	7 1/4 x 12 3/4 inches
PRINTER	Cliff Colors
FABRICATOR	Field Template

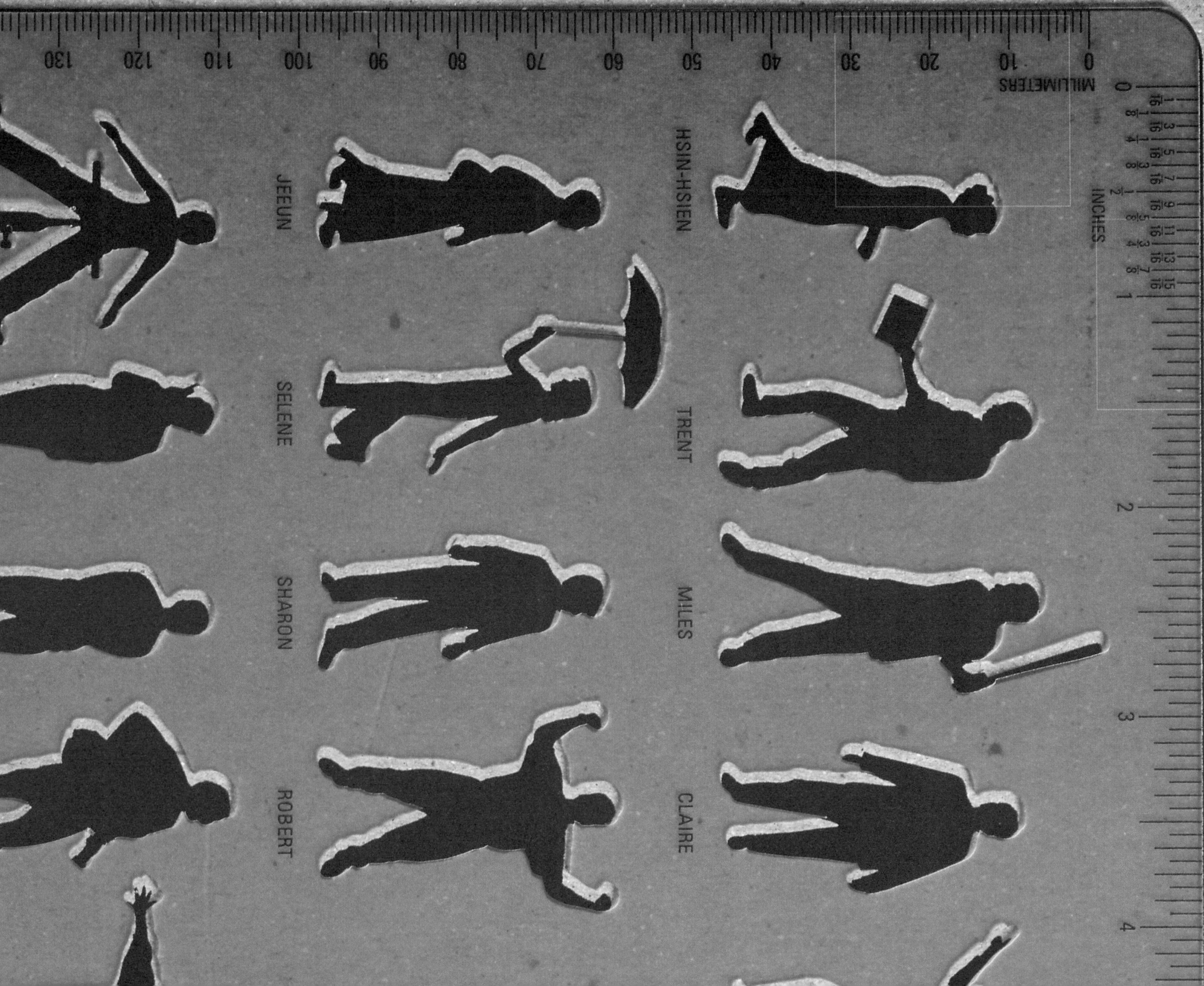

detail / no2

design firm. sussman/prejza & company, inc.

communication graphics. | NO. 23

detail 01

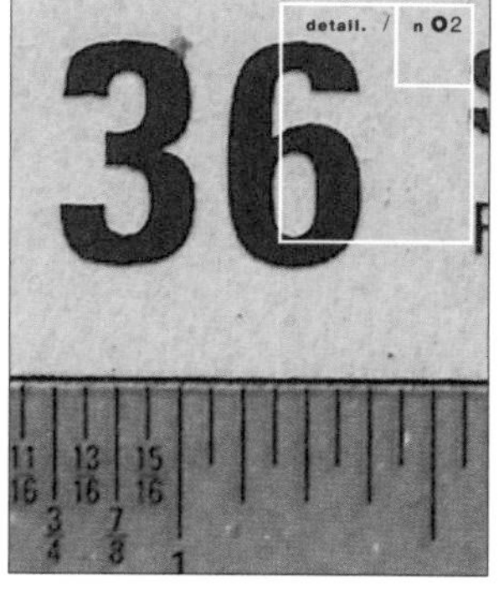

detail 02

design firm. sussman/prejza & company, inc.

communication graphics. | NO. 23

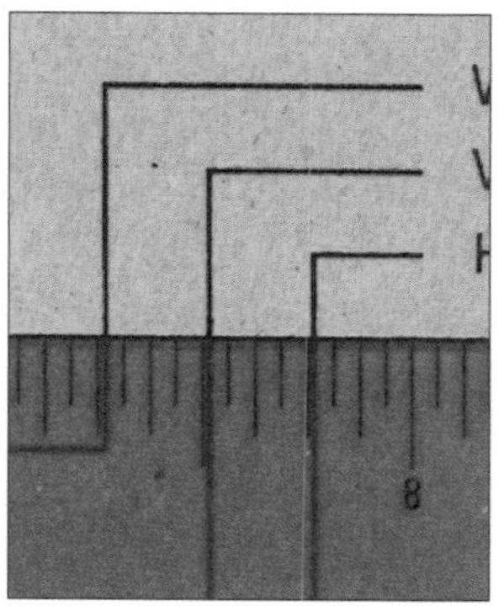

detail 03

detail 04

design firm. sussman/prejza & company, inc.

communication graphics. | NO. 23

detail 05

detail 06

The Anniversary Parade took place on June 2

detail. / n 05

24 06. BOB LEWIS/ANDERSON LITHOGRAPH PROMO PIECE / We needed to promote Bob Lewis, Anderson Lithograph and Appleton Papers using photos of a Fireman's Parade taken by Bob in 1974. We tried to document the event just as the Ramsey Fire Department would. Bob's photographs were paired with descriptions of the event found in the RFD records. (We had hoped to find out more about the event from the fire department, but most of its records were burned by an arsonist in 1981.) Crops were inexact, colors were faded and the words were typed with an old Olympia SM typewriter.

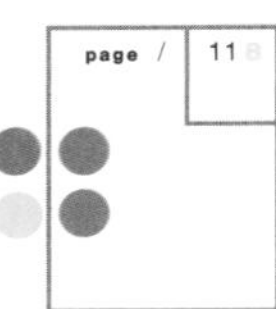

24

DESIGN FIRM	EAI, Atlanta, GA
CREATIVE DIRECTOR	Matt Rollins
DESIGNER	Nicole Riekki
PHOTOGRAPHER	Bob Lewis
WRITER	Bob Lewis, Ramsey Fire Department

TYPEFACE	Olympia SM
TRIM SIZE	8 1/2 x 11 1/2 inches
PRINTER	Anderson Lithograph
PAPER	Various
CLIENT	Bob Lewis, Anderson Lithograph

design firm. eai

communication graphics. | NO. 24

197

detail 01

detail 02

design firm. eai

communication graphics. | NO. 24

taking t
the lens
most inn
were tak
Ramsey,
running
victory
ning tro
Time sus

detail 03

I can remember wh
so suspicious, so
taking their pict
the lens of your
most innocent for
were taken at a F
Ramsey, New Jerse
running and laugh
victory of having
ning trophies, ha
Time suspended. I

detail 04

detail 05

design firm. eai

communication graphics. | NO. 24

detail 06

detail 07

25 CG. NICB ANNUAL REPORT 1998 / With the loss of the National Insurance Crime Bureau's most valuable membership service, the charge was on to restructure its value proposition. We needed to show members why it was so important to continue their association with the NICB. The message is simple: "This year insurance fraud took it on the chin," and the NICB played a major role in the fight. The images of fraud are overwhelming, whereas the images that illustrate the uncovering of the crime are quiet and full of information.

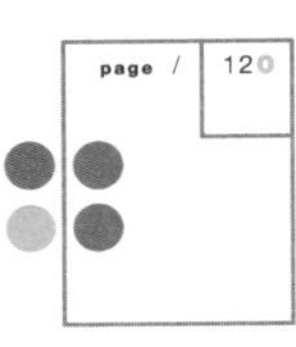

25

DESIGN FIRM	Froeter Design Company, Chicago, IL
CREATIVE DIRECTOR	Chris Froeter
DESIGNERS/ ILLUSTRATORS	Chris Froeter, Heather Crosby
PHOTOGRAPHY	François Robert
WRITER	Jeff Benzing
TYPEFACE	Franklin Gothic
TRIM SIZE	11 x 17 inches
PRINTER	Consolidated Press
PAPER	Appleton Papers Utopia II
CLIENT	National Insurance Crime Bureau

detail. / n

Membership
SIUs led to
his sharing of
case and
owns'
ustomers
adaches.

It's a tale that sounded all too familiar to us
o we quickly let everyone in on the whole sto

Investigative Services State Farm SIU Lee Fink jump-sta
NICB Agent Phil Blessinger after he realized Jane had purposely hit M
insurance policy. They had used different last names to deceive State
The payout led Fink and Blessinger to dig deeper into the Brown's bac

design firm. froeter design company

communication graphics. | NO. 25

detail O1

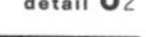

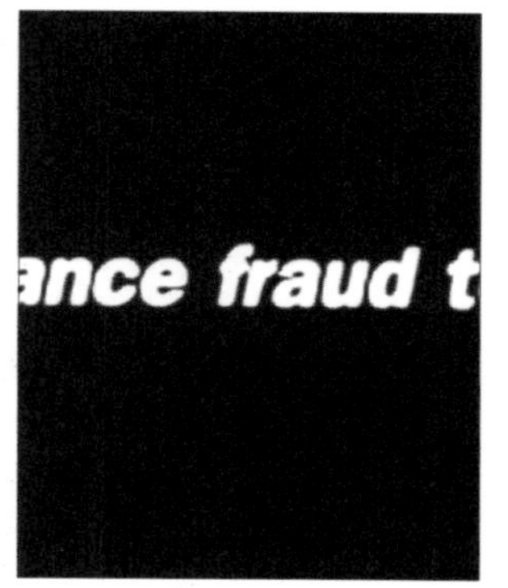

detail O2

detail O3

design firm. froeter design company

communication graphics. | NO. 25

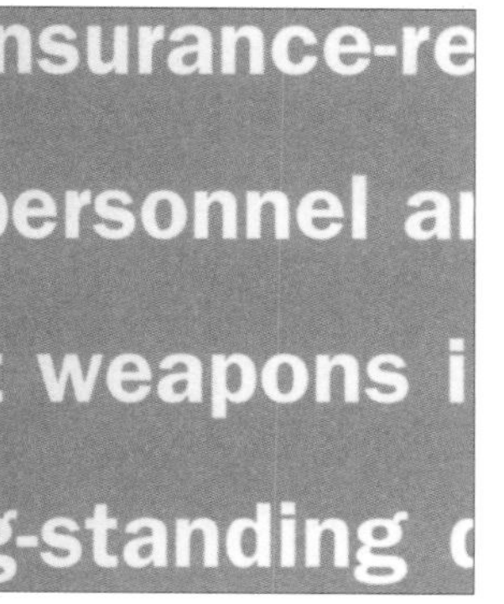

detail O4

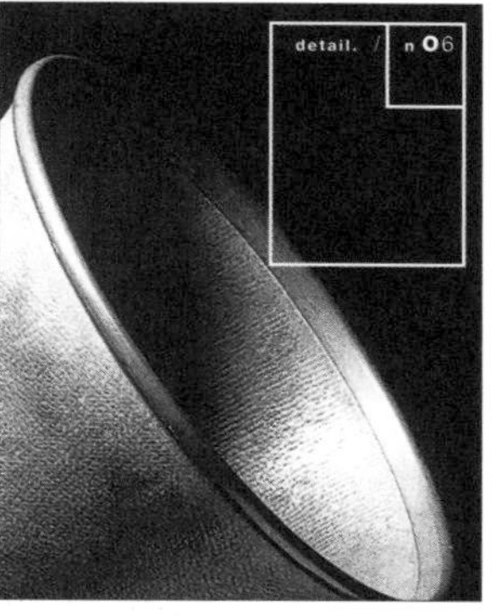

detail O5

design firm. froeter design company

communication graphics. | NO. 25

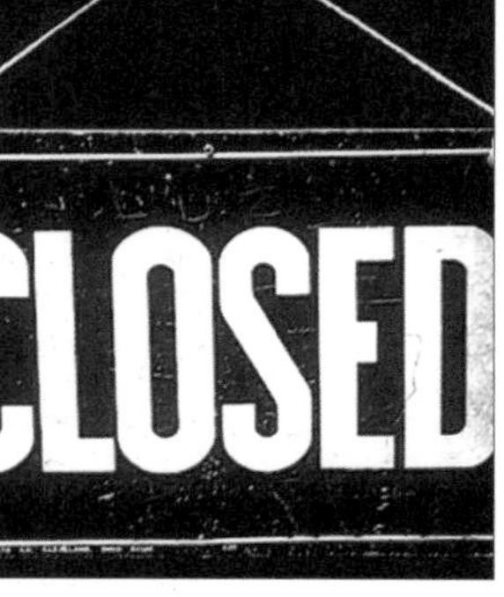

detail O6

detail O7

26 CG.GENERAL MAGIC 1998 ANNUAL REPORT / General Magic wanted to convey the idea that the user voice interface was the next frontier in communication. What seemed most compelling was simply the idea of your own voice being the next interface with the digital environment. Ironically, people have always tried to control their televisions, cars and computers by speaking to them. Now, General Magic wants to make the human voice the logical replacement for the graphical user interface (GUI). We made a case for voice as the most natural way to communicate throughout the world.

26

DESIGN FIRM	Cahan and Associates, San Francisco, CA
ART DIRECTOR	Bill Cahan
DESIGNER	Bob Dinetz
PROJECT MANAGER	Liza Thomson
PHOTOGRAPHER	Various
WRITERS	Thom Elkjer, Bob Dinetz
TYPEFACE	Akzidenz Grotesk
TRIM SIZE	5 1/2 x 7 1/2 inches
PRINTER	Lithographix
PAPER	Potlatch McCoy
CLIENT	General Magic

detail. / n 02

ic is already creating voice-enabled services that use magicTalk. The first one is calle

design firm. cahan and associates

communication graphics. | NO. 26

To Our Valued
In the second y
for voice-enabl
Portico™ virtual
up subscribers

detail 01

design firm. cahan and associates

communication graphics. | NO. 26

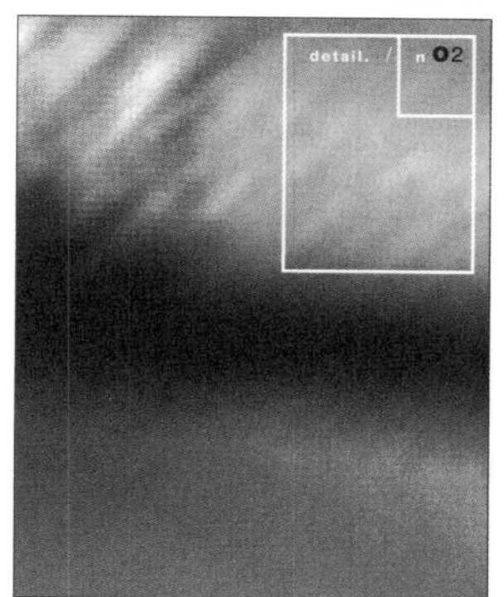

detail 02

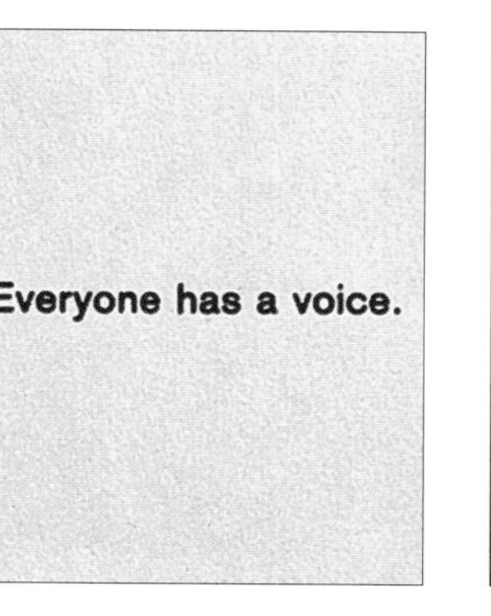

detail 03

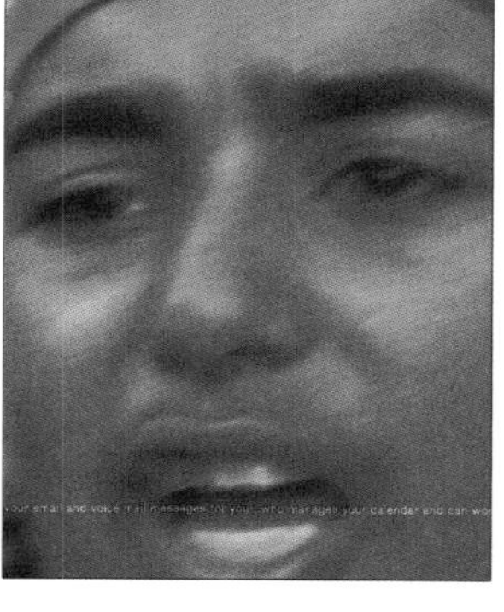

detail 04

design firm. cahan and associates

communication graphics. | NO. 26

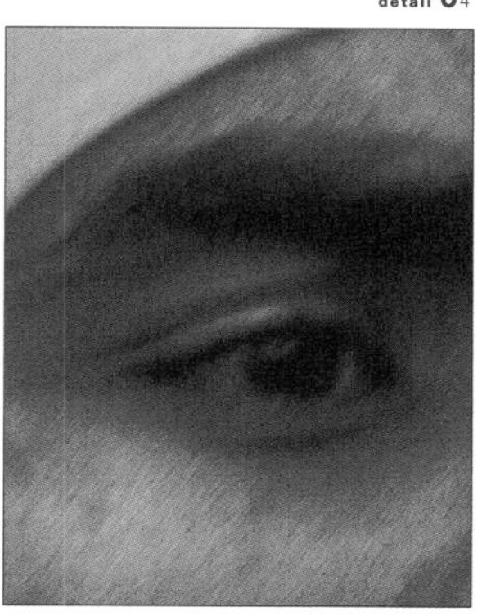

detail 05

detail 06

27 03. TRACY CHANEY WEDDING INVITATION / Oh Boy designed this whimsical and endearing wedding invitation for close personal friends. Drawing inspiration from the location of the wedding reception—the Enoch Pratt Free Library in Baltimore—the invitation takes the form of a 1950s-era grade school primer. Included with the invitation is a report card-style comment card, rating the couple's performance in areas such as "Bouquet toss (distance and height)" and "Apparel and general hygiene," as well as library-style cards as response cards.

27

DESIGN FIRM	Oh Boy, A Design Company, San Francisco, CA
ART DIRECTOR/ DESIGNER	David Salanitro
PRINT PRODUCTION	Elizabeth Cutter
ILLUSTRATOR	Heather Layne
WRITERS	David Salanitro, Ted Bluey
TYPEFACES	Century Schoolbook, Twentieth Century
PRINTER	Expressions Litho, Digital Engraving
PAPER	Mohawk softwhite eggshell

Tracy and Thomas

detail / no 04

design firm. oh boy, a design company

communication graphics. | NO. 27

design firm. oh boy, a design company

communication graphics. | NO. 27

design firm. oh boy, a design company

communication graphics. | NO. 27

detail O1

Thomas loved to sail.

detail O2

detail O3

detail O4

The first time Tracy met Thomas she knew she could talk with him all night long.

Thomas thought that he might like something even more than sailing.

13

detail O5

At five o'clock on July 24th, Tracy will become Thomas' first mate.

15

detail O6

detail O7

DESIGN FIRM Eleven, Inc., San Francisco, CA
CREATIVE DIRECTORS Paul Curtin, Rob Price
ART DIRECTOR Keith Anderson
DESIGNERS Kevin Brown, Druanne Cummins
PHOTOGRAPHER William Abranowicz
WRITER Stephanie Marlis
ACCOUNT PERSON Jessica McCarthy
PRODUCTION MANAGER Jim King
CLIENT Williams-Sonoma

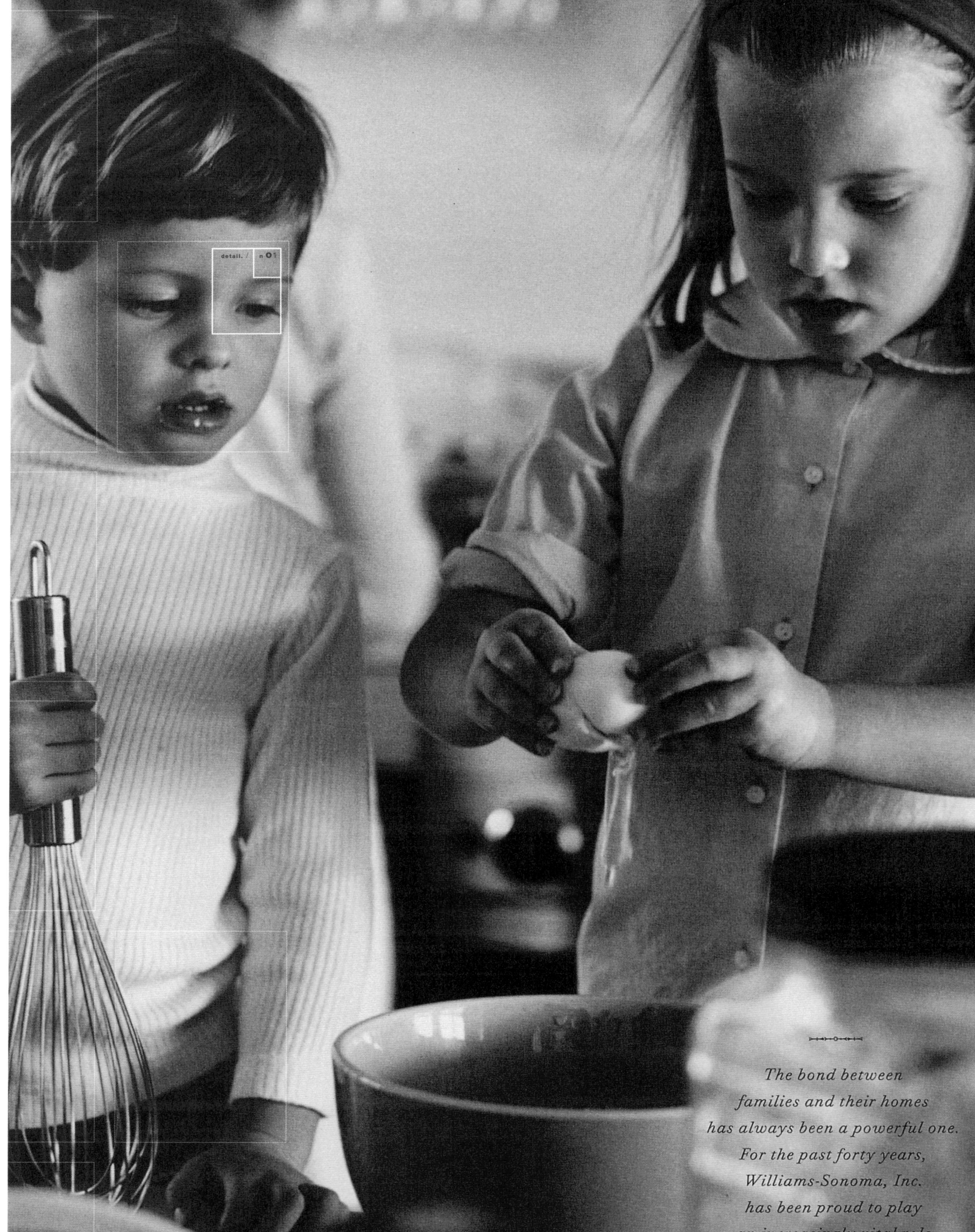

The bond between families and their homes has always been a powerful one. For the past forty years, Williams-Sonoma, Inc. has been proud to play an increasingly vital role

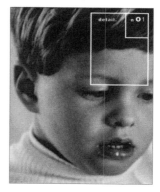

design firm. eleven, inc.

communication graphics. | NO. 28

design firm. eleven, inc.

communication graphics. | NO. 28

design firm. eleven, inc.

communication graphics. | NO. 28

detail. n O1

detail O1

detail O2

By the end of a
Company had
threshold, gro
18 percent inc

detail O3

detail O4

detail O5

WILLIAMS
1998 AN

detail O6

(separately
, 2 1/4 cups cake
milk.
lightly flour
the shorten
til light an

detail O7

29 CG. NCR 1999 ANNUAL REPORT / We wanted to effectively communicate NCR's ongoing business strategy while at the same time reporting on the company's prior year. Building on the corporate idea of transforming transactions into relationships, our idea was to show how NCR helps its customers discover millions of markets of one, rather than one market of millions by focusing on the "one" moment a single transaction is made.

29

DESIGN FIRM	SamataMason, Inc., Dundee, IL
ART DIRECTOR	Dave Mason
DESIGNER	Kevin Krueger
PHOTOGRAPHER	James LaBounty-Sandro (chairman's portrait)
WRITER	Rodger Alexander

TRIM SIZE	6 3/4 x 10 inches
PRINTER	Williamson Printing Corporation
PAPER	Appleton Utopia Two Bluewhite Dull, Weyerhaeuser Cougar Opaque Smooth
CLIENT	NCR Corporation

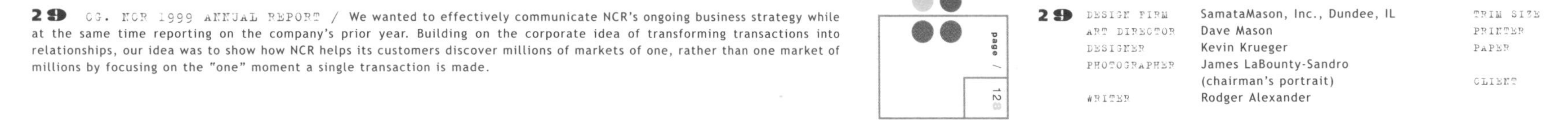
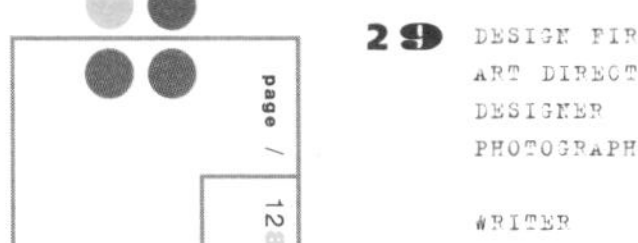
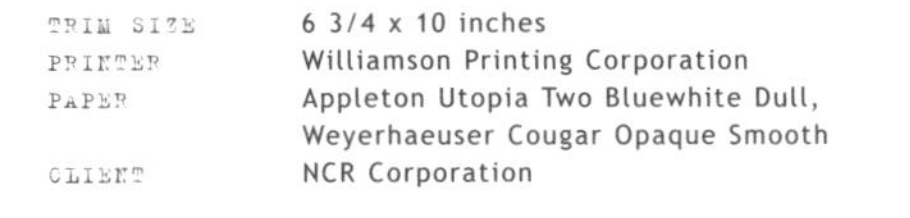
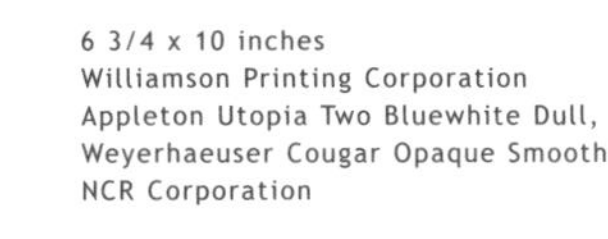
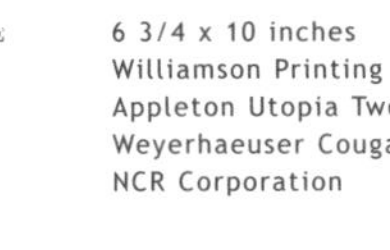
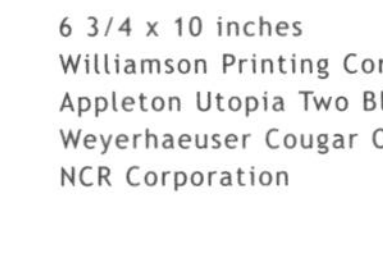

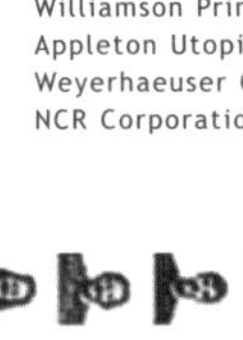

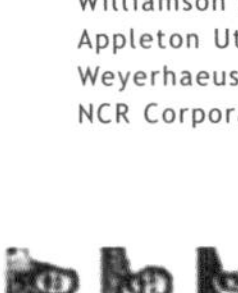

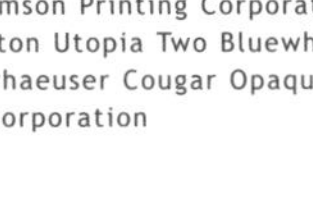
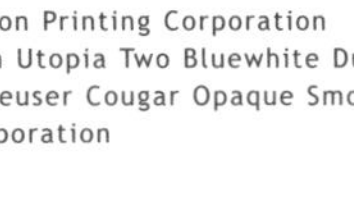

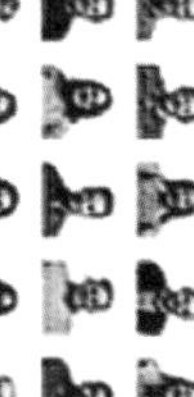

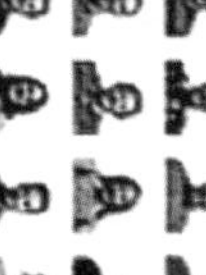

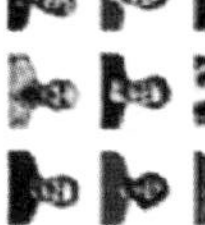

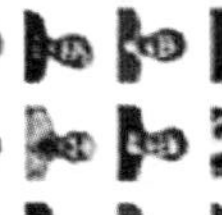

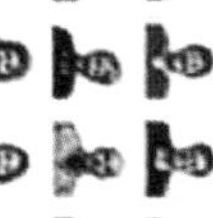
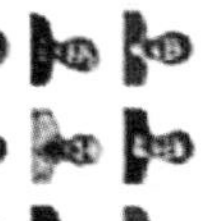

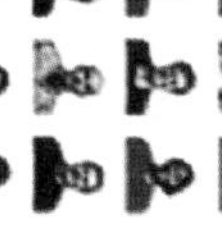
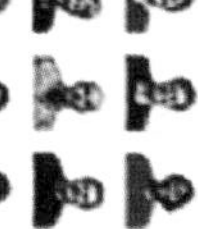

detail. / n 04

design firm. samatamason, inc.

communication graphics. | NO. 29

detail O1

design firm. samatamason, inc.

communication graphics. | NO. 29

detail O2

detail O3

detail O4

design firm. samatamason, inc.

communication graphics. | NO. 29

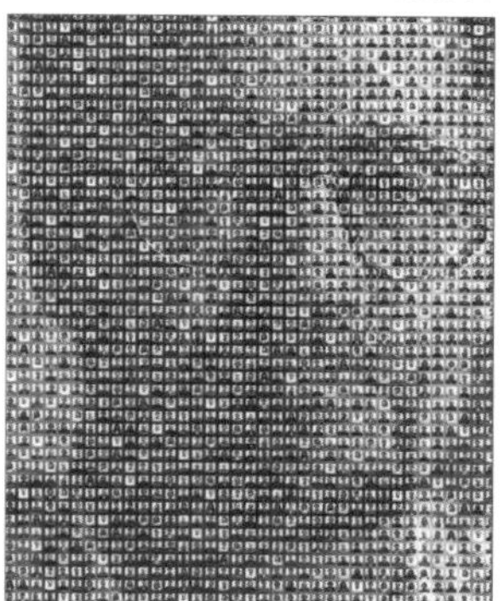

detail O5

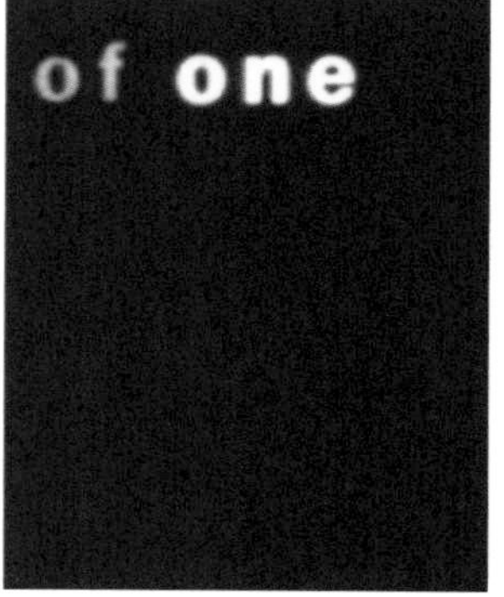

detail O6

30 CC. ALPHABETS PACKAGING / Billing themselves as a "modern general store," Alphabets houses a diverse collection of toys, books and ephemera. Playing off of Alphabets' name, an illustrative style reminiscent of children's "learn-to-read" flash cards represents the store's vast range of products and its whimsical attitude. Keeping in mind the low cost of many items sold in the store, all packaging needed to be relatively inexpensive. Artwork was created that would not only not suffer by inexpensive reproduction, but would be enhanced by it.

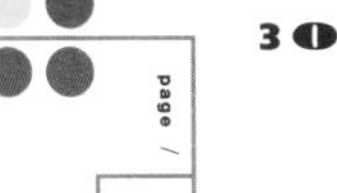

30

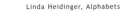

DESIGN FIRM	Lisa Billard Design, New York, NY
DESIGNERS	Lisa Billard, Kate Johnson
ILLUSTRATOR	Various
TYPEFACE	Geometric
PRINTER	Packaging Specialties (shopping bags), Artray (stickers)
CLIENT	Linda Heidinger, Alphabets

design firm. lisa billard design

communication graphics. | NO. 30

detail 01

detail 02

design firm. lisa billard design

communication graphics. | NO. 30

detail 03

detail 04

detail. / n 05
detail 05

design firm. lisa billard design

communication graphics. | NO. 30

detail 06

detail 07

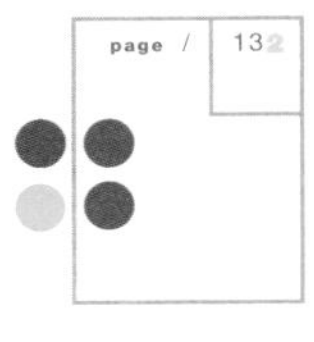

31

DESIGN FIRM: Martha Stewart Living Omnimedia, New York, NY
ART DIRECTOR: Debra Bishop
DESIGNER: Angela Gubler
PRINT:
PRODUCTION: Beth Bartholomew
ILLUSTRATOR: Natasha Tibbott
WRITER: Jennifer Cegielski
TYPEFACES: AT Sackers, MSL Gothic
TRIM SIZE: 3 1/4 x 3 1/2 inches
CLIENT: Martha Stewart Living Omnimedia

ELIZABETH BERRY'S
GALLINA CANYON RANCH
FOR MARTHA BY MAIL®

detail. / n 02

WHITE AZTEC BEANS

NET WEIGHT 16 OZ. (453 G)

design firm. martha stewart living omnimedia

communication graphics. | NO. 31

design firm. martha stewart living omnimedia

communication graphics. | NO. 31

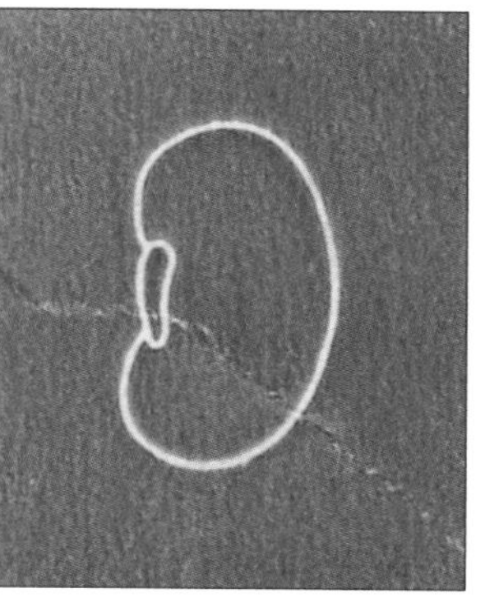

detail O1

detail. / n O2
WHITE AZTEC BEA
NET WEIGHT 16 OZ. (453 G)

detail O2

BEANS

detail O3

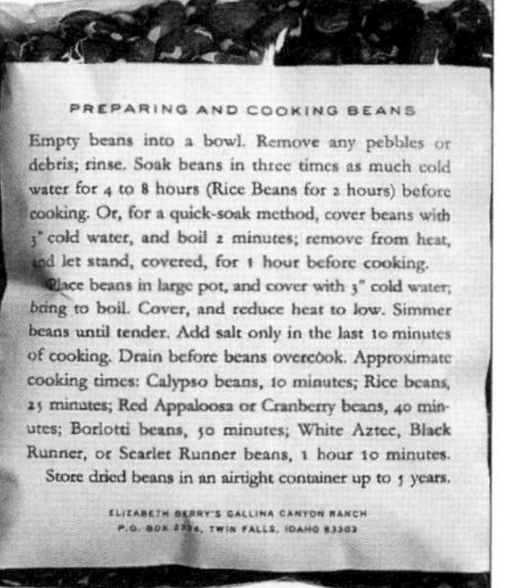
PREPARING AND COOKING BEANS
Empty beans into a bowl. Remove any pebbles or debris; rinse. Soak beans in three times as much cold water for 4 to 8 hours (Rice Beans for 2 hours) before cooking. Or, for a quick-soak method, cover beans with 3" cold water, and boil 2 minutes; remove from heat, and let stand, covered, for 1 hour before cooking.
Place beans in large pot, and cover with 3" cold water; bring to boil. Cover, and reduce heat to low. Simmer beans until tender. Add salt only in the last 10 minutes of cooking. Drain before beans overcook. Approximate cooking times: Calypso beans, 10 minutes; Rice beans, 25 minutes; Red Appaloosa or Cranberry beans, 40 minutes; Borlotti beans, 50 minutes; White Aztec, Black Runner, or Scarlet Runner beans, 1 hour 10 minutes.
Store dried beans in an airtight container up to 5 years.
ELIZABETH BERRY'S GALLINA CANYON RANCH

detail O4

design firm. martha stewart living omnimedia

communication graphics. | NO. 31

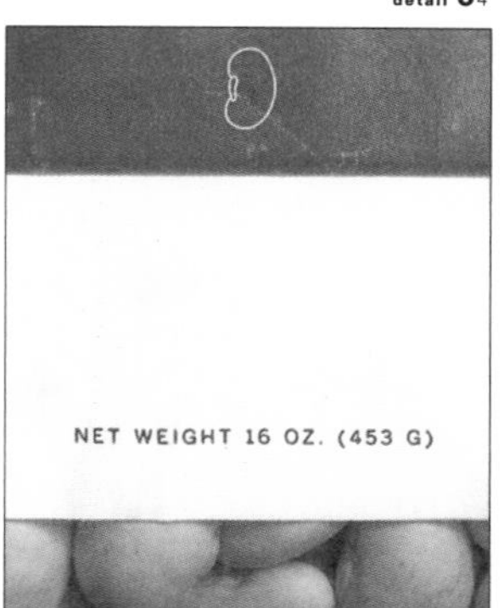
NET WEIGHT 16 OZ. (453 G)

detail O5

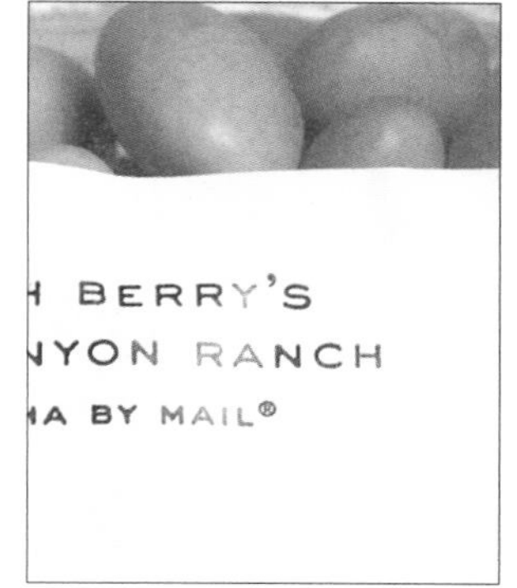
H BERRY'S
NYON RANCH
A BY MAIL®

detail O6

32 03. SCIENT: THE COMPLETE GUIDE TO EBUSINESS INNOVATION. / The design brief called for a way to get 100 CEO's—or "C-level equivalents" of the top Fortune 500 companies—to attend the Scient Summit Conference. We've noticed that people just can't seem to throw away hardbound books, so we decided to masquerade an invitation as a book.

32

DESIGN FIRM	Bielenberg Design, San Francisco, CA
CREATIVE DIRECTOR	John Bielenberg
DESIGNER	Erik Cox
PROJECT MANAGER	Sarah DeMore
WRITER	Rich Binell
TYPEFACE	Garamond
TRIM SIZE	5 5/8 x 6 1/2 inches
PRINTER	Lithocraft
PAPER	Unknown cheap white text paper
CLIENT	Scient

detail / 04

THE COMPLETE GUIDE TO eBUSINESS INNOVATION

design firm. bielenberg design

communication graphics. | NO. 32

THIS IS NOT THE COMPLETE GUIDE TO eBUSINESS INNOVATION.

detail 01

design firm. bielenberg design

communication graphics. | NO. 32

WHY NOT?

detail 02

SO WHERE DO YOU GO TO GET THE BEST, LATEST, MOST EXPERT INFORMATION ON eBUSINESS?

detail 03

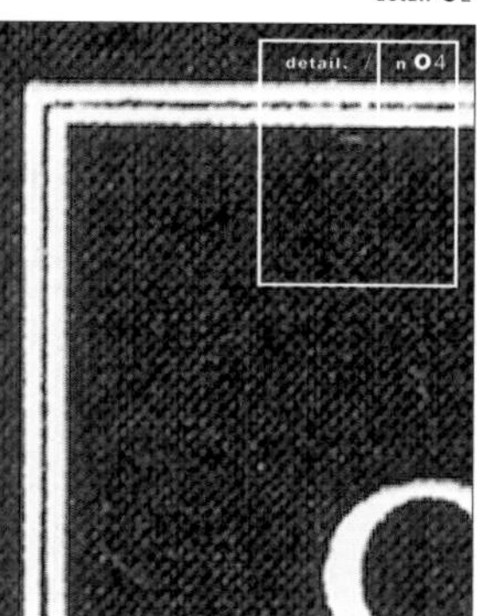

detail 04

design firm. bielenberg design

communication graphics. | NO. 32

E GUIDE

INESS

TION.

detail 05

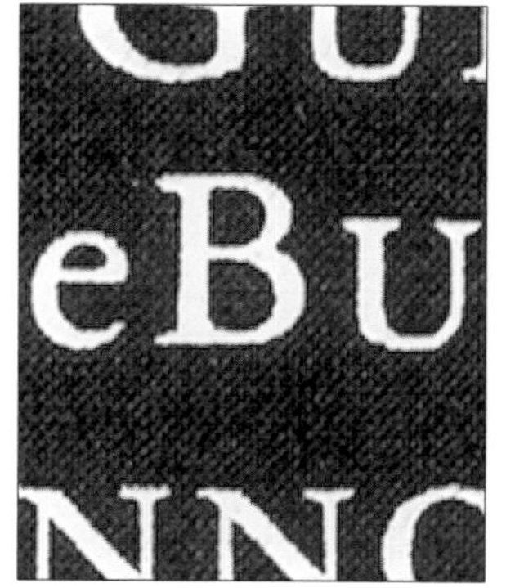

detail 06

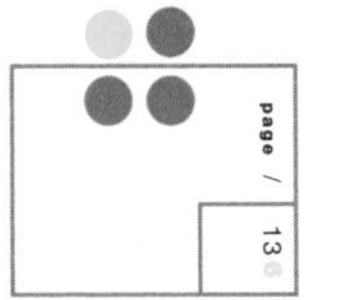

38

DESIGN FIRM	Design: M/W, New York, NY	WRITER	Laura Silverman
CREATIVE DIRECTOR	Allison Williams	TYPEFACE	Akzidenz Grotesk
DESIGNERS	Allison Williams, J. Phillips Williams, Mats Hakansson, Yael Eisele	PRINTER	Lithografix
PHOTOGRAPHER	Anita Calero	PAPER	Gmund (special making) cover, Mohawk Superfine text
		CLIENT	Takashimaya New York

TAKASHIMAYA NEW YORK

FIRST CLASS
PRESORTED
U.S. POSTAGE
PAID
PERMIT NO. 1933
FULLERTON, CA

7

detail.

detail 01

design firm. design: m/w

communication graphics. | NO. 33

detail 02

detail 03

design firm. design: m/w

communication graphics. | NO. 33

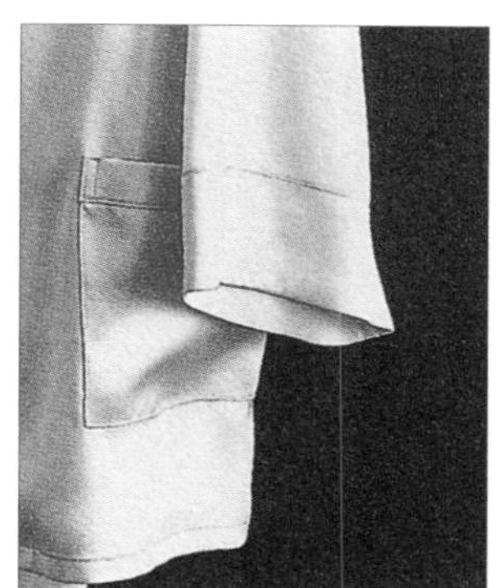

detail 04

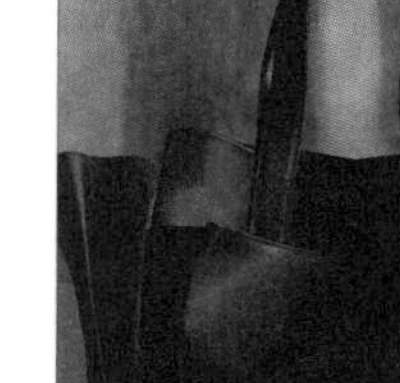

detail 05

design firm. design: m/w

communication graphics. | NO. 33

detail 06

detail 07

34 03. 2000 BOOK / The client wanted us to design a commemorative book for the millennium to be shared with the friends of Williamson Printing Corporation. The design solution was a hardcover book celebrating the theme 2000. We particularly wanted to showcase traditional and specialty printing techniques that are specific to Williamson.

34

DESIGN FIRM	Richards, Brock, Miller, Mitchell & Associates, Dallas, TX
CREATIVE DIRECTOR	Kenny Garrison
ART DIRECTOR	Jim Jacobs
ILLUSTRATOR	Ratchet
PHOTOGRAPHER	Pete Lacker, various
WRITER	Jim Jacobs
TYPEFACE	Adobe Garamond
PRINTER	Williamson Printing Corporation
PAPER	Sappi-Warren Strobe Silk
CLIENT	Williamson Printing Corporation

detail. / n 03

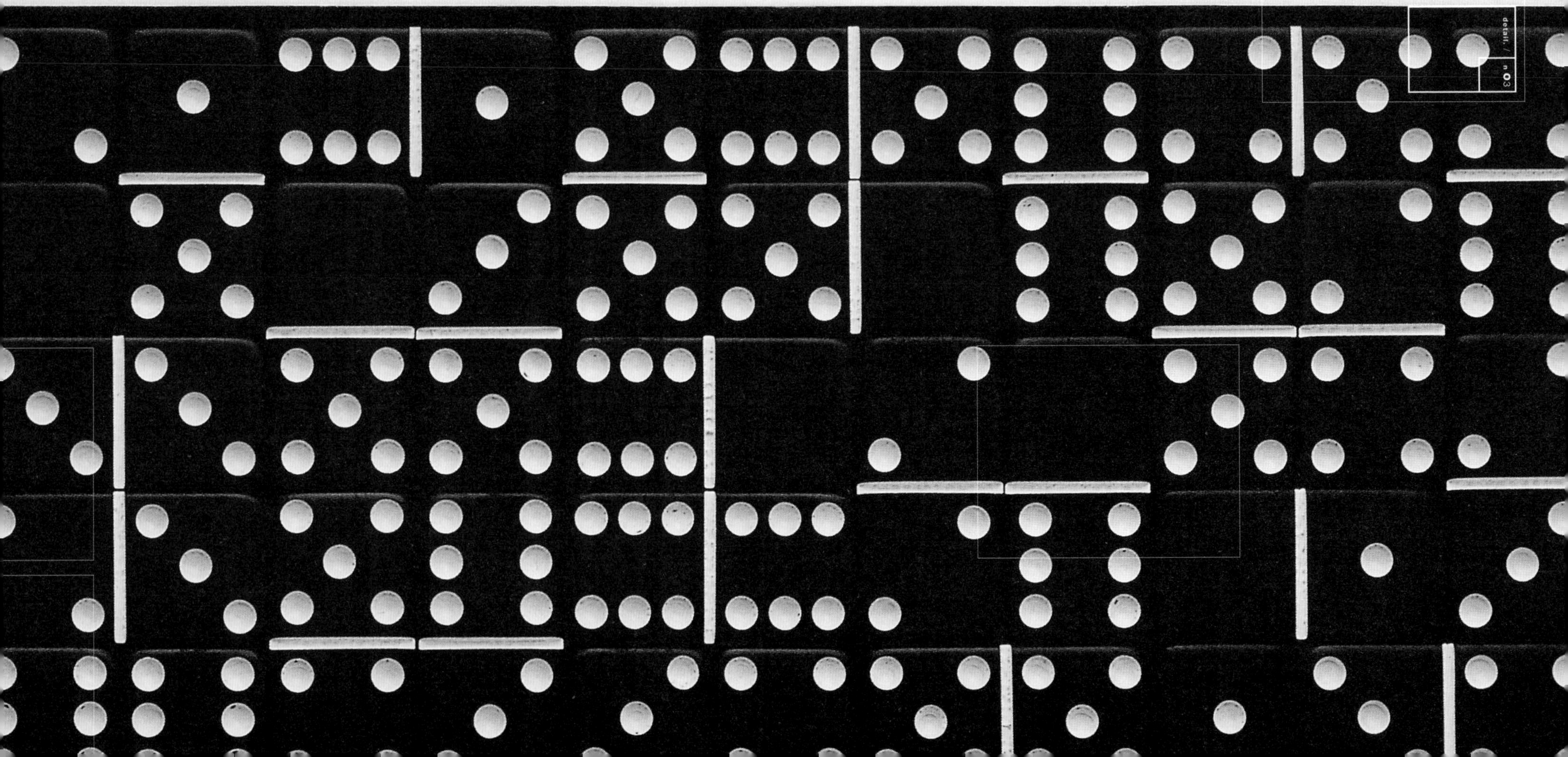

design firm. richards, brock, miller, mitchell & associates

communication graphics. | NO. 34

A Small Celebration of Two Thousand

Williamson Printing Corporation

detail 01

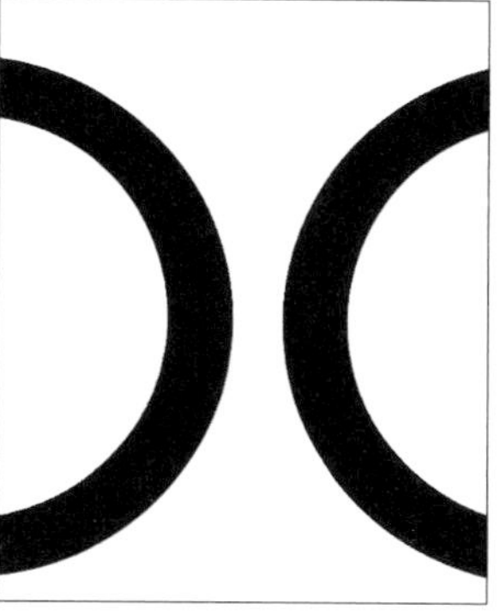

detail 02

design firm. richards, brock, miller, mitchell & associates

communication graphics. | NO. 34

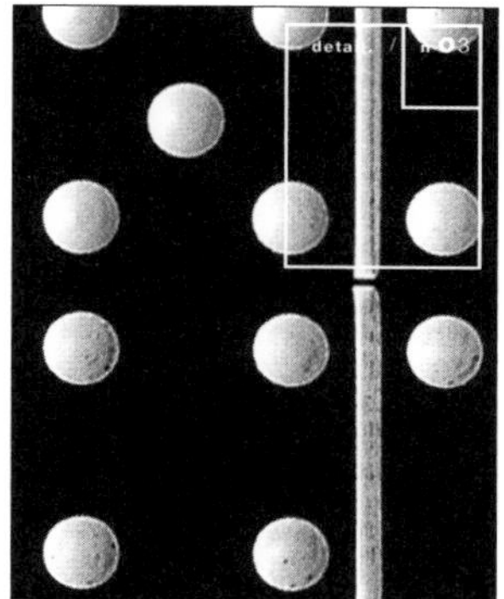

detail 03

Two Tho

detail 04

Two Thousand Little White Dots

detail 05

design firm. richards, brock, miller, mitchell & associates

communication graphics. | NO. 34

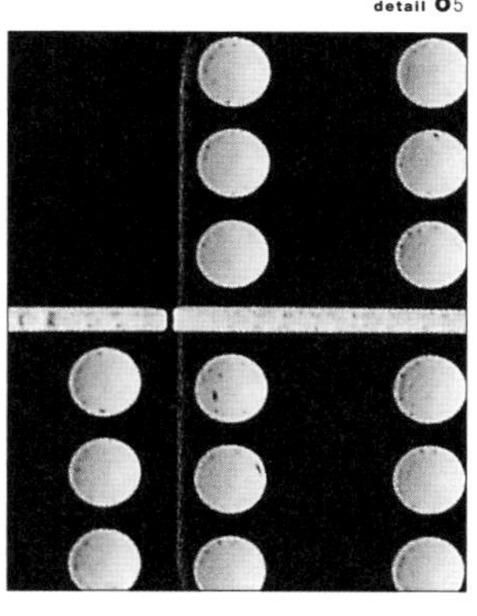

detail 06

Two Thousand Inches

detail 07

03. TUPPERWARE 1999 ANNUAL REPORT / By showing evolution in every aspect of the Tupperware Corporation–from product design and selection to sales force and distribution–I was able to show that the company is up to date. I decided to use the bright colors that are seen in Tupperware products and translucent paper to represent their look and feel.

DESIGN FIRM	SamataMason, Inc., Dundee, IL
ART DIRECTOR	Greg Samata
DESIGNER	Steve Kull
PHOTOGRAPHERS	Sandro (main products), Marc Norberg (executive), Mark Craig
WRITER	Laurence Pearson
TYPEFACES	Bell Gothic, Folio
PRINTER	H. MacDonald Printing
PAPER	Various
CLIENT	Tupperware Corporation

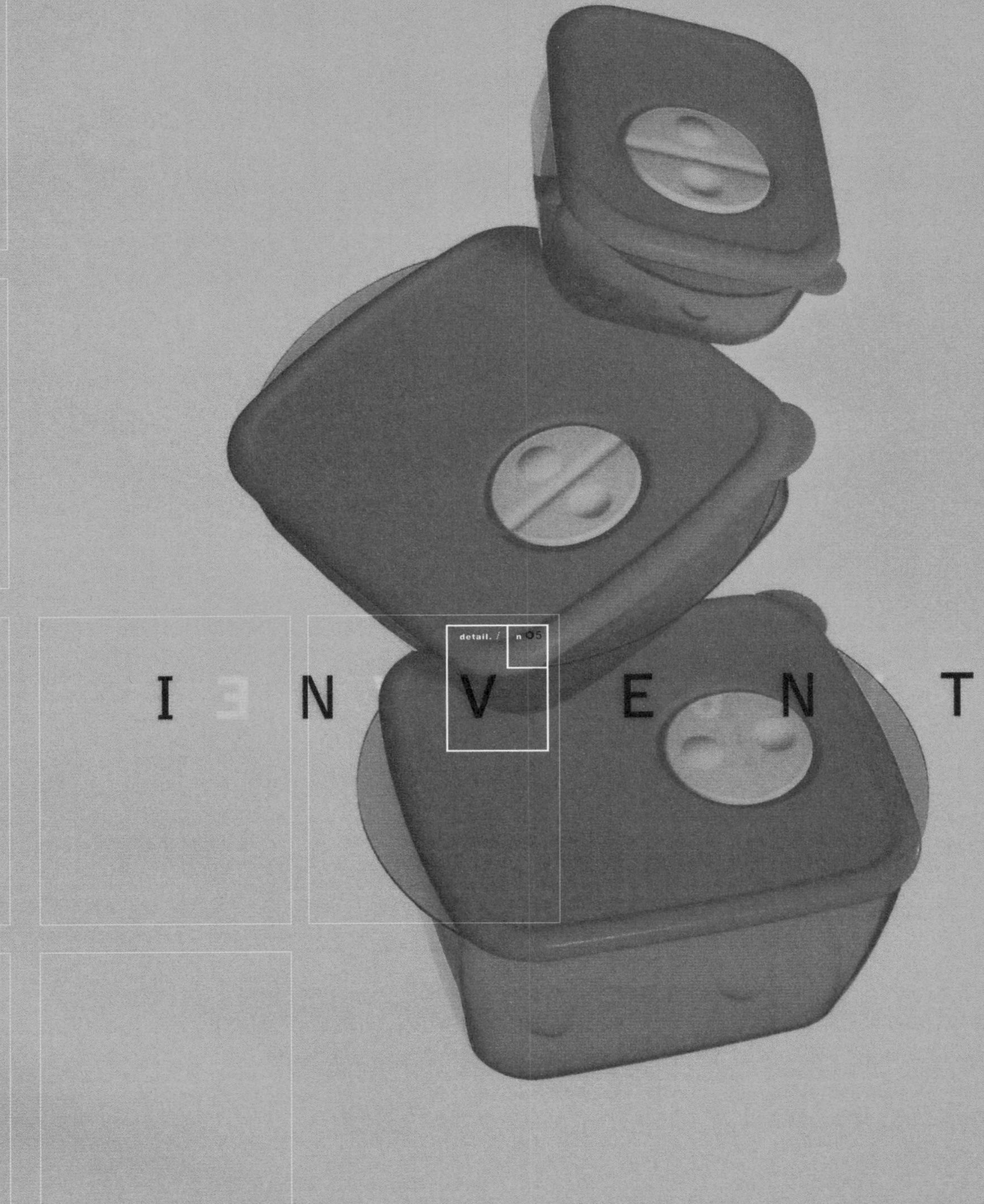

1 **PRODUCT SELECTION**

TUPPERWARE 1999

To meet the needs of consumers in many different cultures, Tupperware combines the local cultural knowledge of our global marketing staff with the inventive skills of our product development groups. Examples range from an innovative electronic home air filter for the Japanese market to an elegant serving dish in Latin America that is ideal for keeping tortillas warm and fresh on the table to our new *Crystal Plus* microwave line in Europe with a stunning transparent look. (shown above)

design firm. samatamason, inc.

communication graphics. | NO. 35

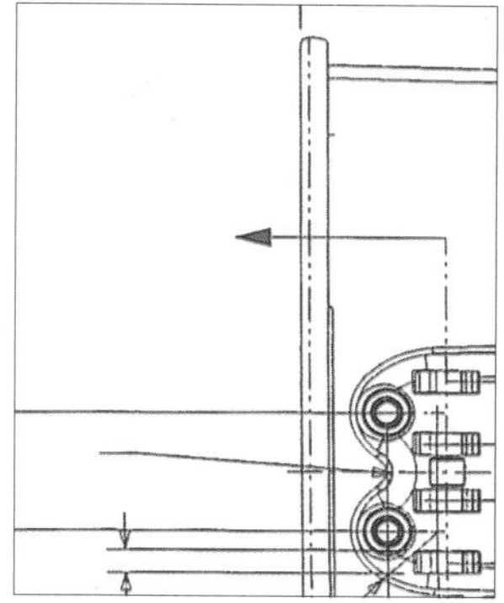

detail O1

detail O2

design firm. samatamason, inc.

communication graphics. | NO. 35

detail O3

detail O4

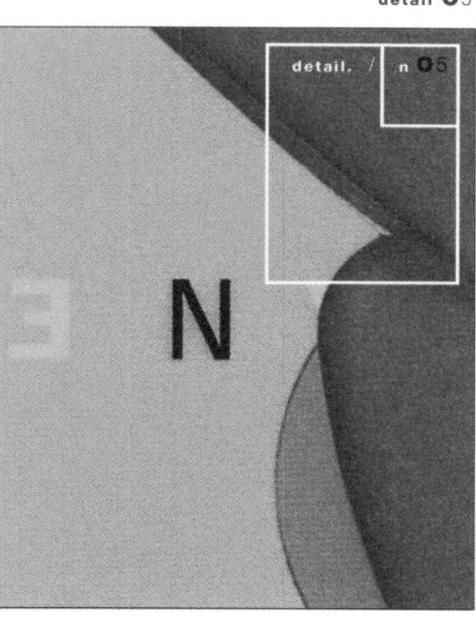

detail O5

design firm. samatamason, inc.

communication graphics. | NO. 35

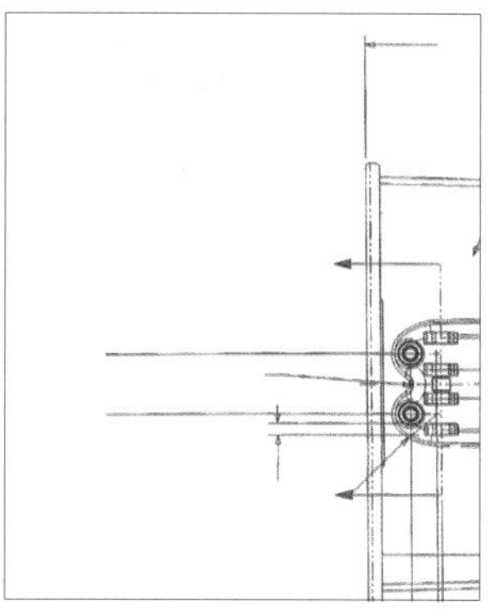

detail O6

detail O7

36 CG. COLLATERAL THERAPEUTICS 1998 ANNUAL REPORT / Collateral Therapeutics approached us to design its first annual report. The company wanted to explore the emotional effects of its product, which is a gene therapy and delivery system for cardiovascular disease. By focusing on the mind-boggling statistics of heart disease, we were able to put a face to the problem and gain the empathy and interest of the reader. Exercises of comparison through multiple series of photographs reveal the potential benefits of gene therapy as a better alternative to existing models of surgery and drug therapy.

36

DESIGN FIRM	Cahan and Associates, San Francisco, CA
ART DIRECTOR	Bill Cahan
DESIGNER	Kevin Roberson
PROJECT MANAGER	Katie Kniestedt
PHOTOGRAPHER	Robert Schlatter
TYPEFACE	Akzidenz Grotesk
TRIM SIZE	6 7/8 x 8 3/4 inches
PRINTER	ColorGraphics
PAPER	Mead Signature
CLIENT	Collateral Therapeutics

detail. / n 05

00:10

THEODORE “TED” STEVENSON

design firm. cahan and associates

communication graphics. | NO. 36

detail 01

~~ACKMAN~~	CANDY R. CLEME
ARKER	JOSIE WOLFE
BATES	~~ERNESTO GONZAL~~
VIDSON	~~HADLEY L. CRES~~
. PETERSEN	GEORGINA M. FA
~~ORRESTER~~	DOUGLAS G. FRE
. BRANTAD	STUART P. RING
. LINCOLN	~~LINDA R. DAVIS~~
~~SMITHSON~~	ELENA R. KISHL
~~COWENS~~	BARNEY H. FLAC
L. LOWE	DENISE G. LAMO
LAWRY	CLYDE F. SINGL
EWMAN	~~NATASHA D. GRE~~
SNEED	~~GAYLE M. PATRO~~

design firm. cahan and associates

communication graphics. | NO. 36

detail 02

STON	~~TONY S. NELSON~~
~~TG~~	F. SCOTT PETERS
~~—~~	J. TODD SIMMONS
E	MATTHEW A. GRAYSON
	~~DOUG P. DARMINSKI~~
~~ES~~	DYLAN S. FREDMONT
NO	LUKE T. PHUE
	~~SHAW C. MERRITT~~
OORE	TOBIAS W. GEBB
S	CHANCE MBUKWA
TANA	~~JOHN YUET LEE~~
DER	LASHONA TORRANCE
~~ZA~~	~~BART HOLMES~~

detail 03

BYPASS GRAFT

detail 04

design firm. cahan and associates

communication graphics. | NO. 36

detail 05

detail 06

37 05. SCHELLA KANN FALL/WINTER COLLECTION ANNOUNCEMENT / Within a very limited budget, the client needed a poster/invitation to announce the presentation of the fall/winter collection of Schella Kann, an Austrian fashion designer. A simple one-color design solution was printed as a poster as well as folded and inserted into glassine envelopes for the direct-mail invitation. The universal icon of the standard coat hanger was printed on pattern drafting tissue in keeping with the modern appeal of Schella Kann's designs.

37

DESIGN FIRM	Susanna Barrett, New York, NY
ART DIRECTOR/ DESIGNER/ ILLUSTRATOR	Susanna Barrett
TYPEFACE	Custom
PRINTER	Tanagraphics
PAPER	Esleck, Fidelity Onion Skin
CLIENT	Schella Kann

SCHELLA KANN FALL/WINTER COLLECTION 2000/01 STYLE INDUSTRIE JAVITS CENTER NEW YORK CITY BOOTH 1116 FEBRUARY 26-29 9AM-6PM

detail. / n 05

design firm. susanna barrett

communication graphics. | NO. 37

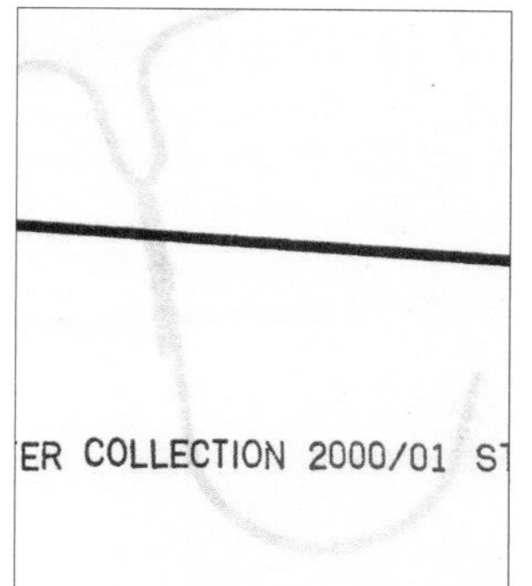

detail 01

design firm. susanna barrett

communication graphics. | NO. 37

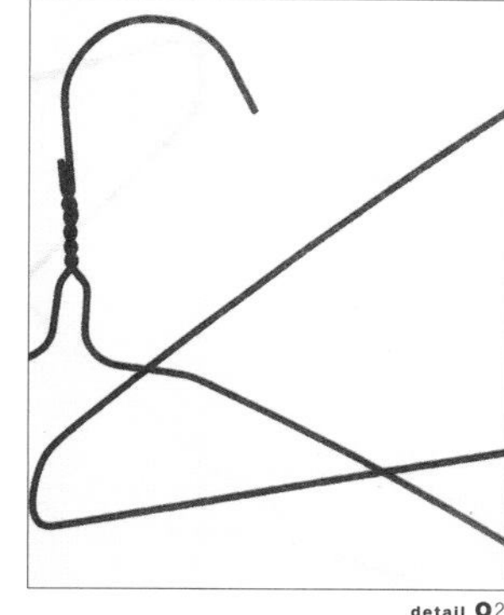

detail 02

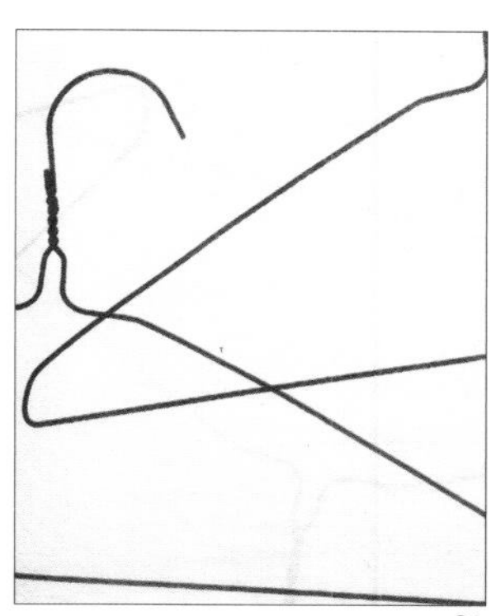

detail 03

detail 04

design firm. susanna barrett

communication graphics. | NO. 37

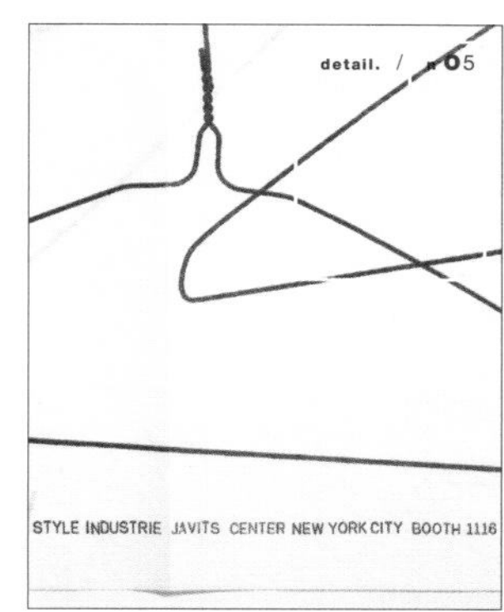

detail 05

detail 06

RAWSON

Kelham

WINEGROWER

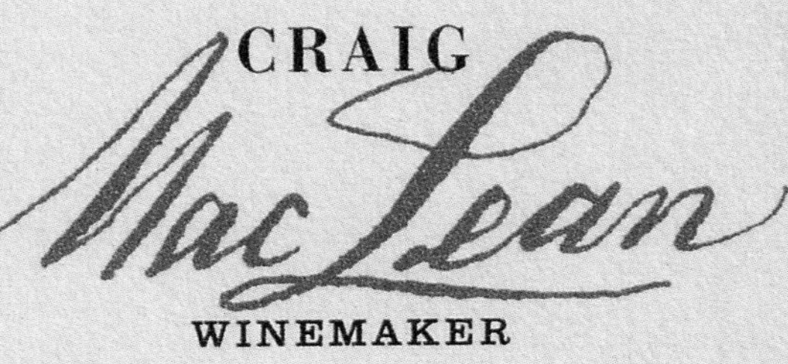

CRAIG

MacLean

WINEMAKER

360 ZINFANDEL LANE

St. Helena, CA 94573

TEL. 707-963-2000

FAX. 707-963-2262

JEFF GERLOMES

PRINCIPAL

detail. / n05

RAWSON

Kelham

WINEGROWER

CRAIG

MacLean

WINEMAKER

360 ZINFANDEL LANE

St. Helena, CA 94573

TEL. 707-963-2000

FAX. 707-963-2262

38 CG. KELHAM MACLEAN STATIONERY / Although Kelham MacLean is a start-up winery, we wanted its stationery system to reflect the quality of the handcrafted wines it produces. We used classic, elegant typography and combined it with a signature-like lettering of the name to speak to the partnership between the two parties. The letterhead has a faded edge, is letterpressed and has a lasercut pin perf to give it rich tactile detail. All the materials are understated and simple.

38

DESIGN FIRM	Templin Brink Design, San Francisco, CA
CREATIVE DIRECTOR	Gaby Brink
CALLIGRAPHER	Elvis Swift
TYPEFACES	Bodoni, Trade Gothic, Clarendon
TRIM SIZE	8 1/2 x 11 inches
PRINTER	Digital Engraving
FABRICATION	Colorbar
CLIENT	Kelham MacLean Winery

design firm. templin brink design

communication graphics. | NO. 38

detail 01

detail 02

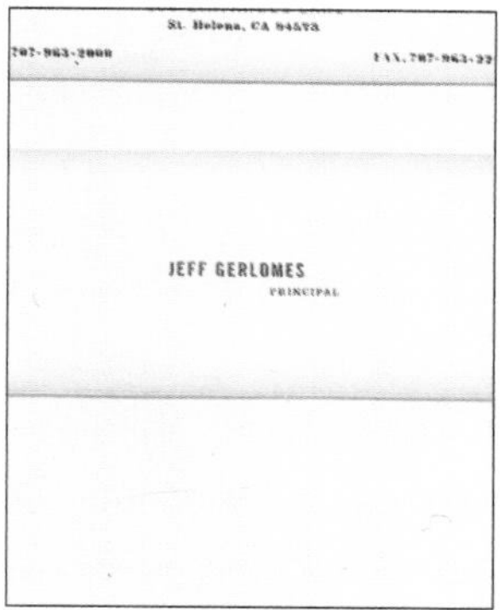

detail 03

design firm. templin brink design

communication graphics. | NO. 38

detail 04

detail. / n 05

detail 05

design firm. templin brink design

communication graphics. | NO. 38

detail 06

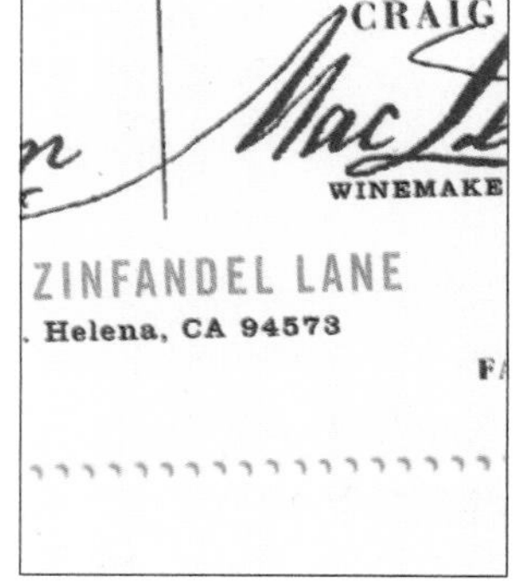

detail 07

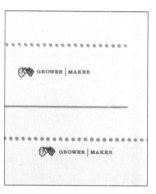

39 06. IDENTIX 1999 ANNUAL REPORT / The dramatic set-up to this annual is the exact situation that Identix is able to protect against—identity fraud. As security threatens the Internet, Identix provides identity authentication and verification through biometrics.

39

DESIGN FIRM	Cahan and Associates, San Francisco, CA
ART DIRECTOR	Bill Cahan
DESIGNER	Michael Braley
PROJECT MANAGER	Kerrie Claeys
WRITERS	Michael Braley, Joanna di Paolo
TYPEFACES	Franklin Gothic, Franklin Gothic Condensed, Emigre Eight
TRIM SIZE	4 1/2 x 6 inches
PRINTER	Lithographix
PAPER	Topkote Dull
CLIENT	Identix

I know your password.

detail. / n 01

design firm. cahan and associates

communication graphics. | NO. 39

I know your password.

detail. / n 01

detail 01

design firm. cahan and associates

communication graphics. | NO. 39

I have your social security number.

detail 02

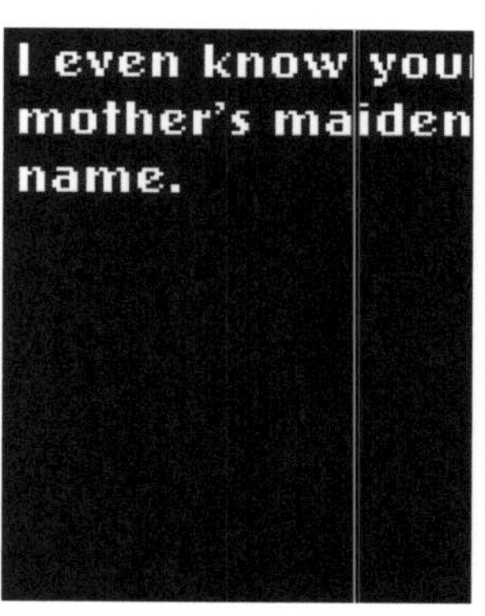

detail 03

detail 04

design firm. cahan and associates

communication graphics. | NO. 39

detail 05

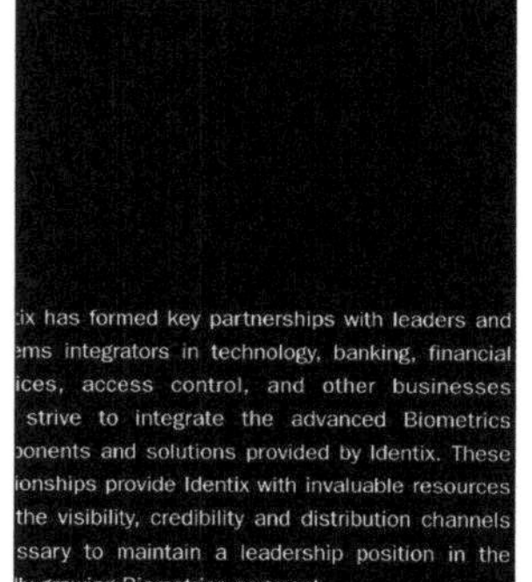

detail 06

40 CG. BLU DOT 2D3D PACKAGING / Rather than do three separate packages for three different products, we designed one package that would fit all three, and printed it in one color on corrugate. The products come in vastly different sizes and proportions, so each one simply slips under the appropriate tabs to lock it in place. The exterior label is applied according to the package contents, and a diecut shows the color of the product inside. A handle makes for easy display and portability.

40

DESIGN FIRM	Werner Design Werks, Inc., Minneapolis, MN
ART DIRECTOR	Sharon Werner
DESIGNERS	Sharon Werner, Sarah Nelson
PRINTER	Menasha Corp.
CLIENT	Blu Dot

design firm. werner design werks inc.

communication graphics. | NO. 40

design firm. werner design werks inc.

communication graphics. | NO. 40

design firm. werner design werks inc.

communication graphics. | NO. 40

communication graphics. / NO. 40

details. / n 01 - 7

detail 01

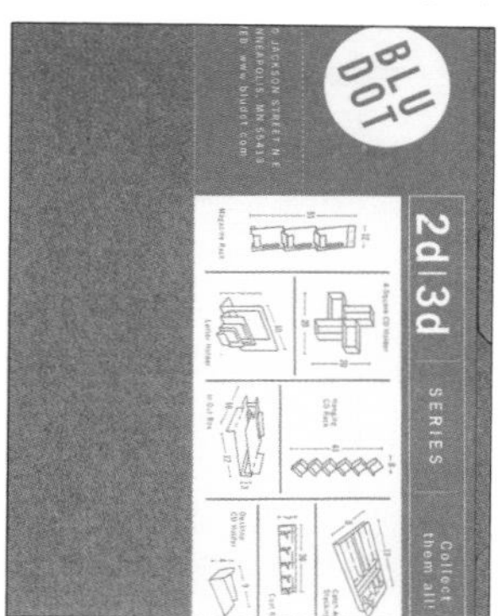

detail 02

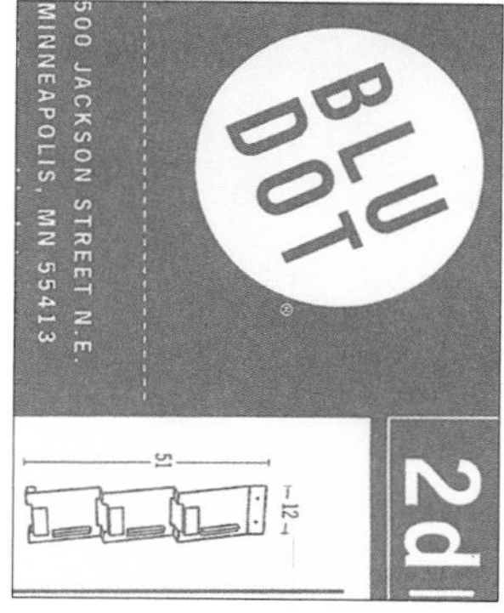

detail 03

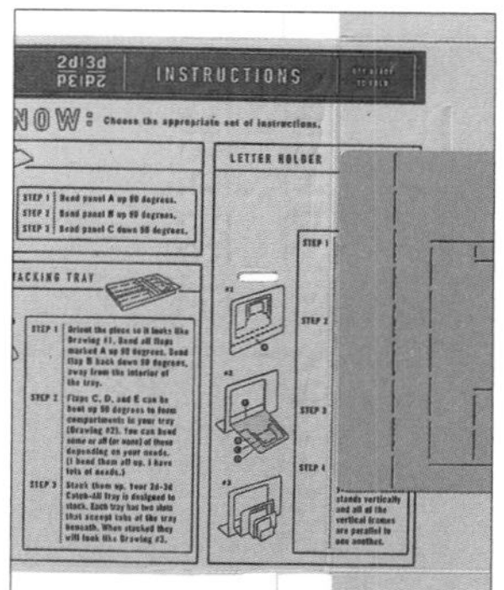

detail 04

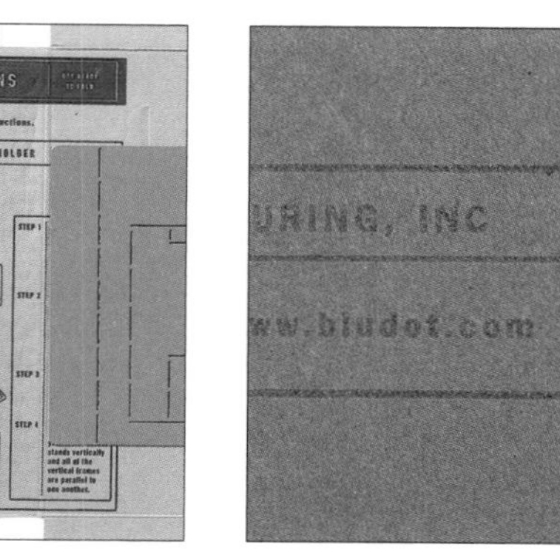

detail 05

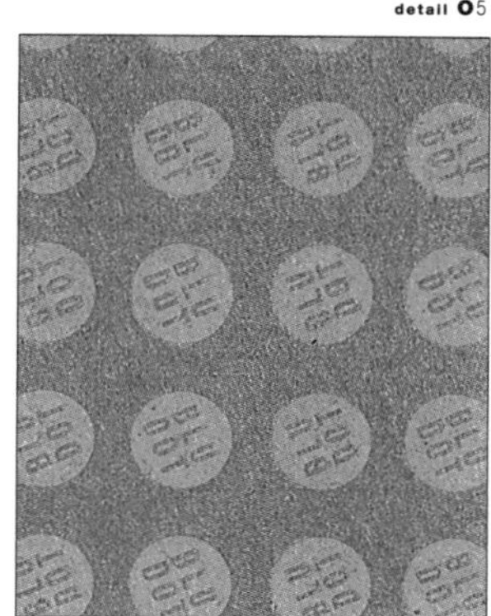

detail 06

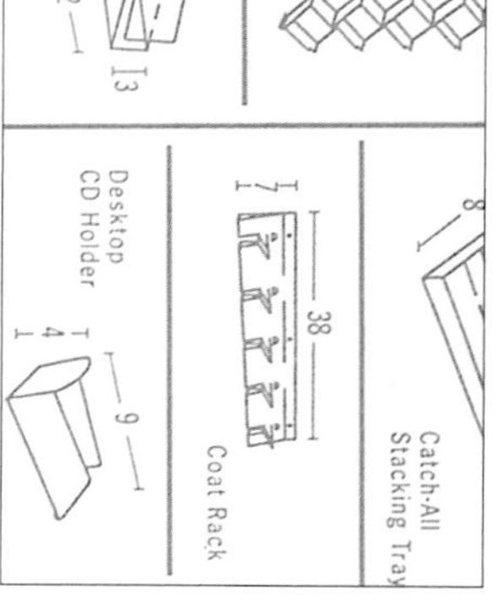

detail 07

41 CG. ERIC STEWART STATIONERY / Eric Stewart asked us to create a new identity for him to reflect a change in his company's name. Our solution was to emphasize what Eric does—write. Rather than focus on the design, we chose to let the subject matter take center stage. We also wanted the business cards to be something that people would remember. Because the business cards were being printed 10-up, we were able to create cards with 10 different messages, with varying degrees of tastelessness to suit the recipient.

41

DESIGN FIRM	Fuller Designs, Inc., Vienna, VA	TRIM SIZE	8 1/2 x 11 inches (letterhead), 2 x 3 1/2 inches (business card), #10 envelope
CREATIVE DIRECTORS	Doug Fuller, Aaron Taylor	PRINTER	Budget Communications
DESIGNER	Doug Fuller	PAPER	French Construction Cement Green
WRITERS	Doug Fuller, Aaron Taylor	CLIENT	Eric Stewart, copywriter
TYPEFACE	ITC Officina Sans		

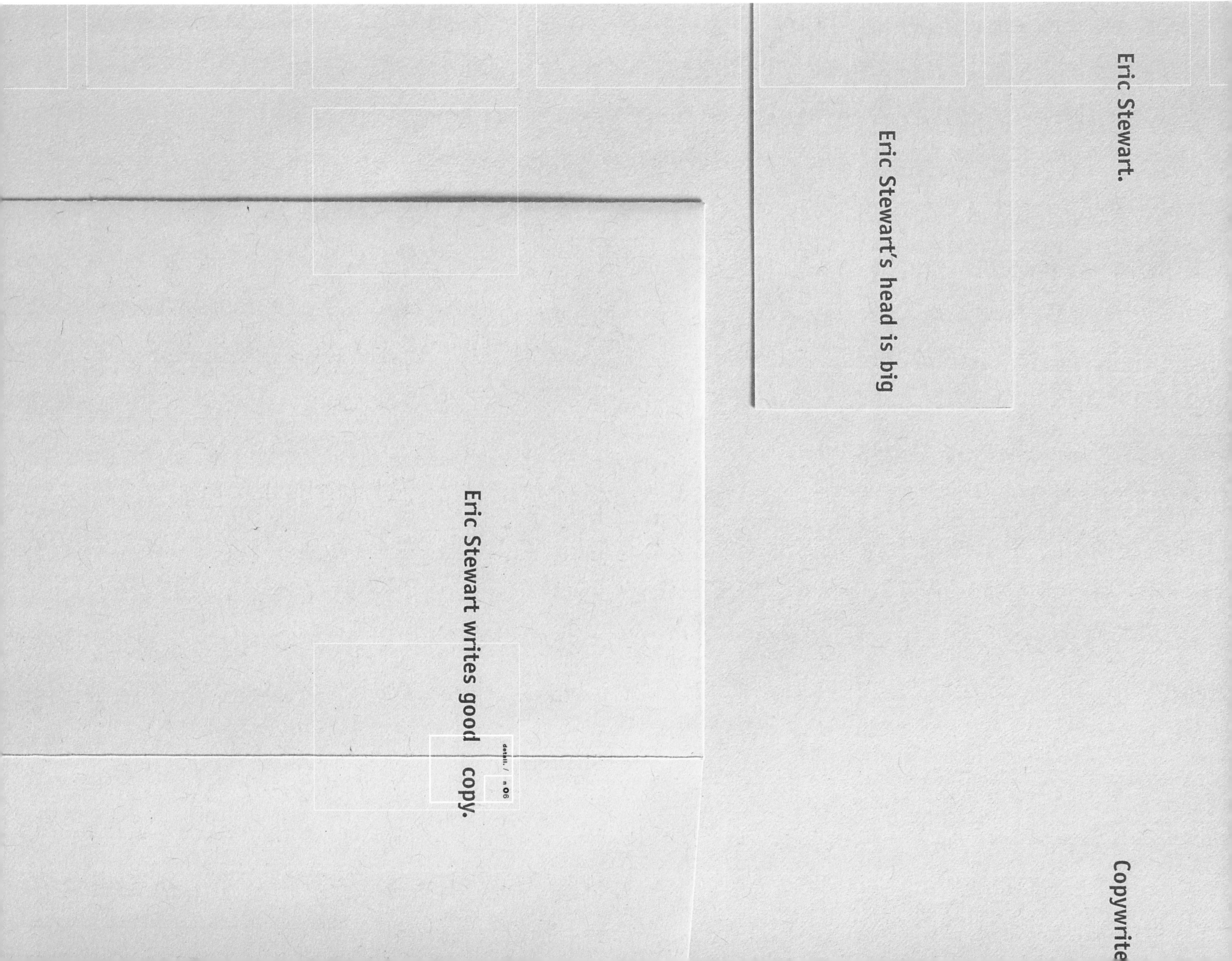

Eric Stewart.

Copywrite

Eric Stewart's head is big

detail. / n 06

Eric Stewart writes good copy.

design firm. fuller designs, inc.

communication graphics. | NO. 41

Eric Stewart is lazy

detail O1

design firm. fuller designs, inc.

communication graphics. | NO. 41

about housework,

Eric Stewart, Copywriter / 1711
Phone 703-528-0018 / Fax 703-5

detail O2

Stewart hates you

detail O3

be unhappy with y

c Stewart, Copywriter / 1711 N. Qu
one 703-528-0018 / Fax 703-528-0

detail O4

design firm. fuller designs, inc.

communication graphics. | NO. 41

py with your copy.

er / 1711 N. Quincy Street / Arlin
/ Fax 703-528-0590 / escopy@min

detail O5

detail O6

42 CG. SILICON VALLEY BANK 1999 ANNUAL REPORT / Silicon Valley Bank provides banking services to entrepreneurs and the companies they build. This year, SVB wanted to celebrate entrepreneurs and demonstrate their understanding of the personal sacrifices a person makes to bring their "big idea" to fruition. The design approach for this piece is intended to be very frank and matter-of-fact, while being fresh and somewhat magazine-like, an aesthetic that the Y-generation entrepreneur might appreciate. The brochure was saddle-stitched to give it a feeling of immediacy and intimacy, something you wouldn't expect from a typical bank.

42

DESIGN FIRM	Cahan and Associates, San Francisco, CA
ART DIRECTOR	Bill Cahan
DESIGNER	Todd Simmons
PRODUCTION ARTIST	Celeste Sartino
PHOTOGRAPHERS	Todd Hido, Jock McDonald
WRITERS	Tim Peters, Jamie McGinley, Todd Simmons
TYPEFACES	Trade Gothic, Champion Gothic
TRIM SIZE	7 x 10 3/4 inches
PRINTER	INSYNC.MEDIA
PAPER	Utopia 2 matte
CLIENT	Silicon Valley Bank

SILICON VALLEY BANCSHARES 1999 YEAR IN REVIEW

I TRADED MY 8-HOUR WORKDAY FOR A 17-HOUR WORKDAY.

ALISON – DIRECTOR OF PRODUCT DEVELOPMENT

design firm. cahan and associates

communication graphics. | NO. 42

detail O1

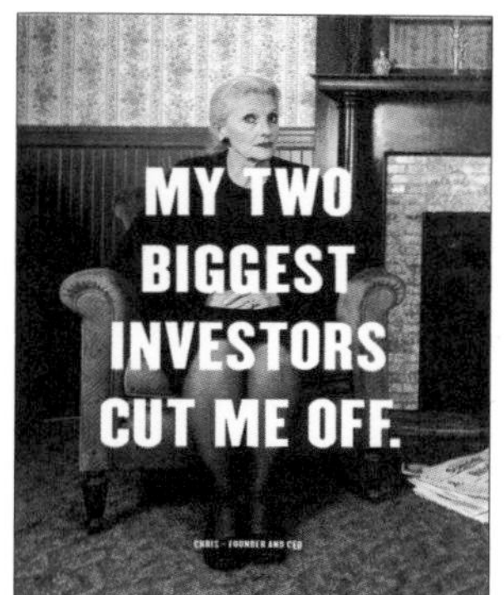

detail O2

design firm. cahan and associates

communication graphics. | NO. 42

detail O3

detail O4

detail O5

design firm. cahan and associates

communication graphics. | NO. 42

K AN ENTREPRENEUR "HOW'S LIFE?" AND YOU PROBABLY WON'T EAR MUCH ABOUT VACATIONS OR THE LATEST HIT MOVIE. STEAD, YOU'LL PROBABLY HEAR ABOUT THEIR NEXT ROUND OF NANCING, NEXT PRODUCT RELEASE OR BUILDING A MANAGEMENT AM – THE ONGOING CHALLENGES IN THEIR ALL-CONSUMING RUGGLE TO TURN A VISION INTO A START-UP AND START-UP INTO SUCCESSFUL ENTERPRISE. THE LIFE OF AN ENTREPRENEUR VOLVES AROUND THEIR WORK – THE CHALLENGES, OPPORTUNI-ES, SETBACKS, AND SUCCESSES.

IAT'S WHY WE DON'T ASK ENTREPRENEURS "HOW'S LIFE?" STEAD, WE ASK, "HOW CAN WE HELP?" FROM IDEA TO IPO (AND YOND) OUR MISSION IS DECIDEDLY SIMPLE: TO HELP OUR IENTS SUCCEED.

detail O6

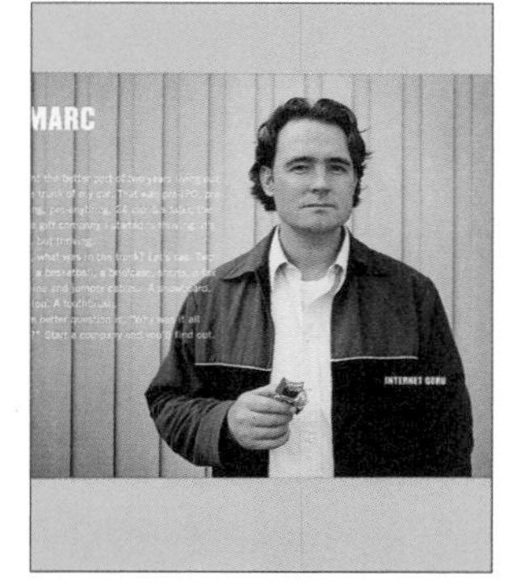

detail O7

43 CG. MELANSON BIRTH ANNOUNCEMENT/INVESTMENT CALCULATOR / With the pressures in today's work world, family life often takes a back seat to seemingly more urgent matters. An investment calculator seemed an appropriate way to illustrate the returns from quality and quantity time spent with the family. I wanted the piece to be insightful, yet humorous. Ike was the perfect client. Unlike other clients, he spit up on my comps only once. In addition, he granted me a lot of creative liberty, which allowed me to maintain the integrity of the original concept.

43

DESIGN FIRM	Meyer & Liechty, Inc., Lindon, VT
CREATIVE DIRECTOR	Thomas Melanson
PRODUCTION MANAGER	Jessica Melanson
WRITER	Brooks Briggs
TYPEFACES	News Gothic, Scala, Lucia
PRINTER	Printing Resource, Inc.
DIE CUTTING	Tru-cut
PAPER	Matrix 12 point C1S
CLIENT	Isaac Thomas Melanson

item #2

detail. / no1

design firm. meyer & liechty, inc.

communication graphics. | NO. 43

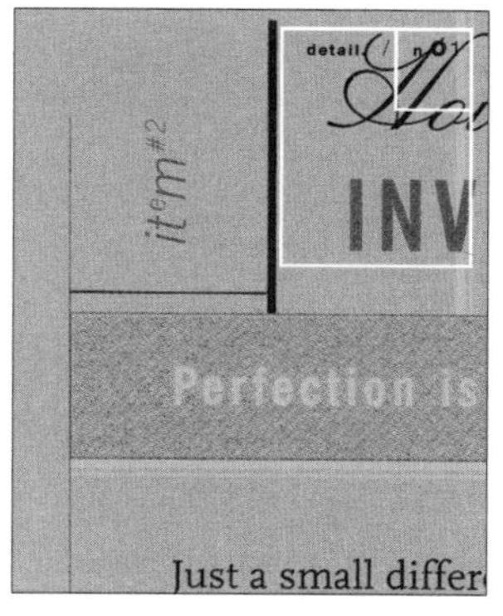

detail O1

design firm. meyer & liechty, inc.

communication graphics. | NO. 43

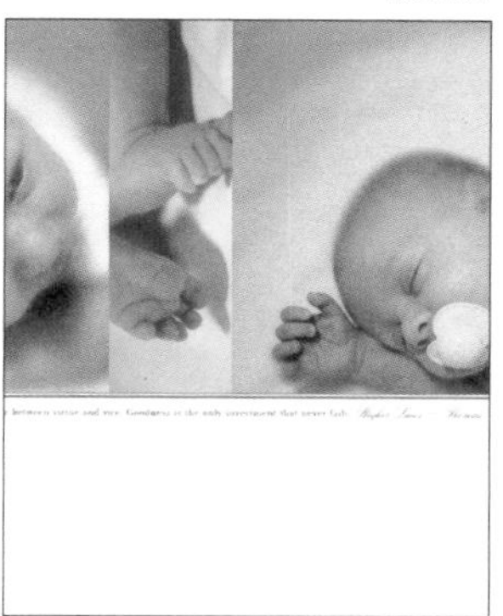

detail O2

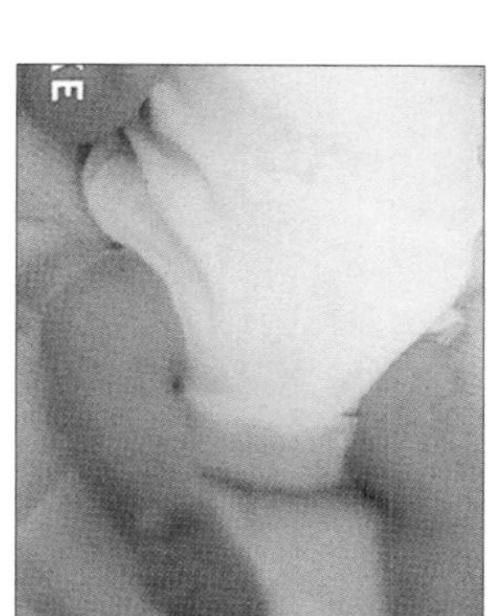

detail O3

detail O4

design firm. meyer & liechty, inc.

communication graphics. | NO. 43

detail O5

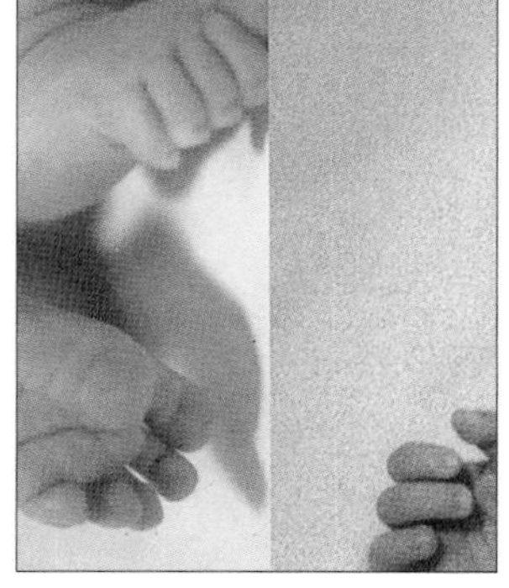
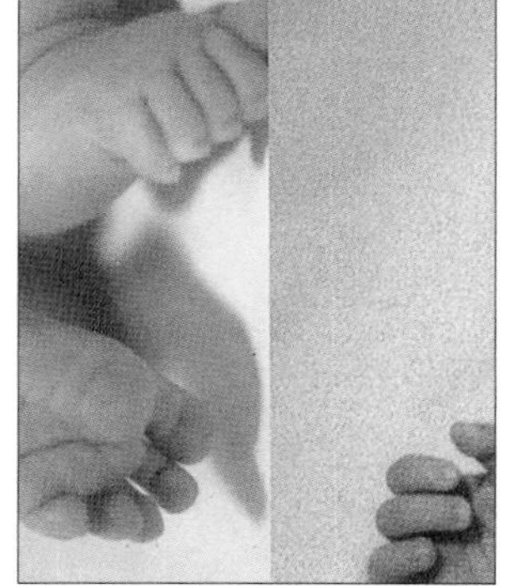

detail O6

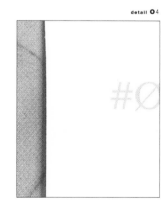

44 OG. INSECTS AND SPIDERS POSTAGE STAMPS / Steve Buchanan was contracted by the Postal Service to create a concept for stamps. Because of the wide selection of insects and spiders to choose from, he did approximately 30 sketches for review. When the committee reviewed the sketches, they were so enthusiastic they approved a full pane of 20 designs. Working closely with Buchanan, Carl Herrman developed the entire pane of stamps, and arranged the insects so that the creatures appeared to be crawling on top of the paper. This was achieved by using shadows and arranging the creatures so they overlapped the adjoining stamps.

44

DESIGN FIRM	U.S. Postal Service
CREATIVE DIRECTOR	Terrence McCaffrey
ART DIRECTOR/ DESIGNER	Carl Herrman
ILLUSTRATOR	Steve Buchanan
TYPEFACES	Trajan (title), Sabon (denomination caption)
TRIM SIZE	7 1/2 x 7 7/8 inches
PRINTER	Ashton Potter

USA
33

1999

design firm. u.s. postal service

communication graphics. | NO. 44

detail 01

design firm. u.s. postal service

communication graphics. | NO. 44

detail 02

detail 03

detail 04

design firm. u.s. postal service

communication graphics. | NO. 44

detail 05

detail 06

THIS IS NOT A METAL BUILDING.

Robertson-Ceco Corporation
1998 Annual Report

45 DESIGN FIRM Oh Boy, A Design Company, San Francisco, CA
ART DIRECTOR David Salanitro
DESIGNER Ted Bluey
PRINT PRODUCTION Elizabeth Cutter
PHOTOGRAPHER Hunter Wimmer
WRITERS Various
TYPEFACES HelveNeuMed, Univers
PRINTER Hemlock Printers
PAPER Mohawk Superfine Ultrawhite Smooth
CLIENT Robertson-Ceco Corporation

45 CG. ROBERTSON-CECO 1998 ANNUAL REPORT / Robertson-Ceco creates highly complex, custom-engineered structures for an ever-expanding range of purposes—from public schools to sports arenas. The report gives its readers varied perspectives of Robertson-Ceco's process and award-winning results while dispelling the outdated notion of corrugated siding and tin roofs. On-site photographs that illustrate the narrative showcase another of Oh Boy's proficiencies—custom photography. Each of the 200 photos were shot by Oh Boy at Robertson-Ceco facilities across the country.

design firm. oh boy, a design company

communication graphics. | NO. 45

NOPE.

detail 01

detail 02

design firm. oh boy, a design company

communication graphics. | NO. 45

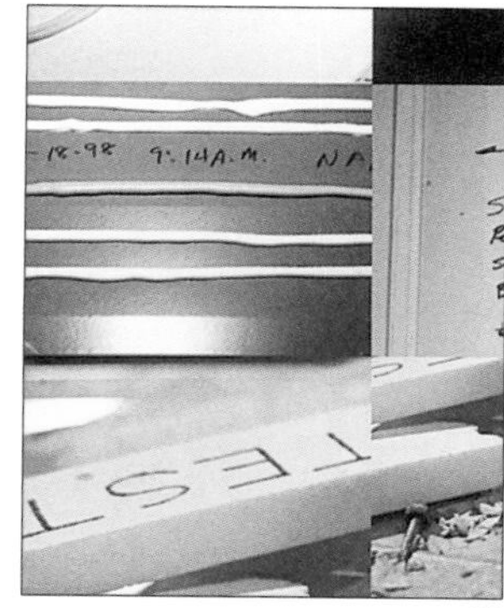

detail 03

NOT A
BUILDIN

detail 04

detail 05

design firm. oh boy, a design company

communication graphics. | NO. 45

detail. / n 06

THIS IS
METAL

Robertson-Ceco Corporation
1998 Annual Report

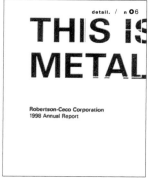

detail 06

detail 07

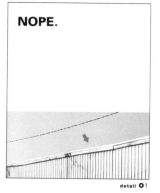

46 OG. HOLIDAY BAG / Instead of giving clients a gift for the holidays, we asked them to give clothing to those who are truly in need. In a global effort, each of our offices—New York, Los Angeles, London, Paris and Sydney—coordinated pickup and delivery of all the donations to chosen charities. Most clients, however, chose to keep their holiday laundry bags and to send their donations in plain bags and boxes. The bag's color is reminiscent of life-savers, traffic cones and safety vests, and holds up to 35 pounds of clothing.

46

DESIGN FIRM	@radical.media, New York, NY
ART DIRECTOR/ DESIGNER	Rafael Esquer
PRINT PRODUCTION	Will Noonan
WRITER	Jon Kamen
TYPEFACES	HouseBroken, HouseBroken Rough
TRIM SIZE	30 x 40 inches
PRINTER	Porcupine Product
CLIENT	@radical.media

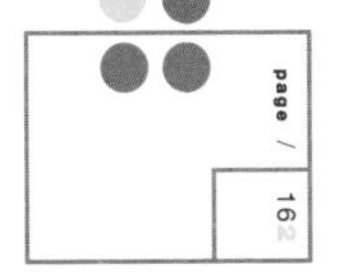

EDIA OFFICES
RDINATING
T TO PROVIDE
OPLE IN NEED
PARTICIPATE
OUR OFFICES
2 462.1590
310 664.4515
6 148.253
4453.2626
9213.6328
PART AND
THE BAGS
THIS HOLIDAY
SEASON
WE INVITE YOU
TO JOIN US AS
@RADICALS
FOR A
GOOD CAUSE
detail. / n04

design firm. @radical.media

communication graphics. | NO. 46

detail O1

detail O2

detail O3

design firm. @radical.media

communication graphics. | NO. 46

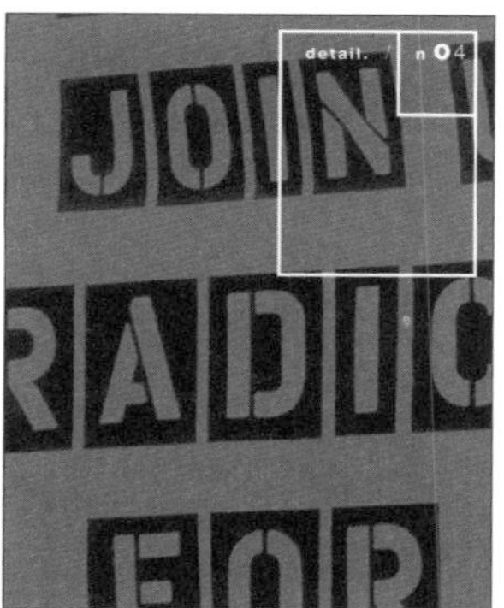

detail O4

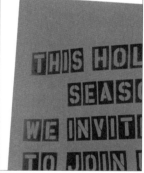

detail O5

design firm. @radical.media

communication graphics. | NO. 46

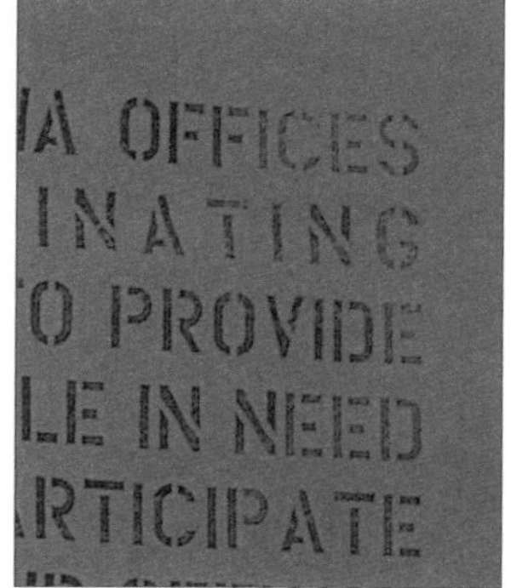

detail O6

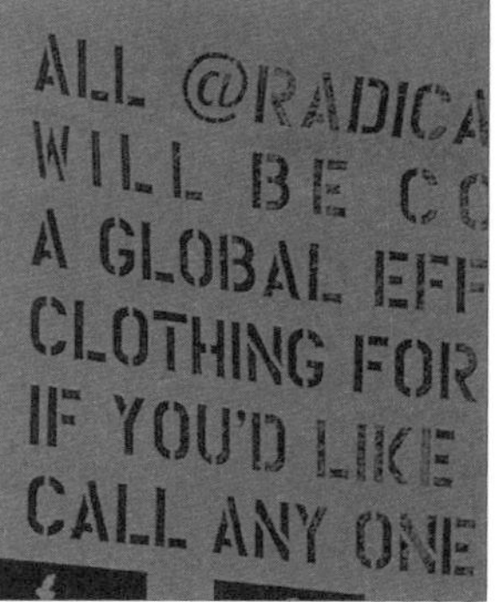

detail O7

47 CG. VH1 HOLIDAY GIFT BOOK / The client requested a holiday gift that would hold CDs and promote the "100 Greatest Songs of Rock and Roll," one of VH1's programming events. In search of divine inspiration, the designer visited several Manhattan cathedrals, broke the Eighth Commandment and through Immaculate Conception created the "Hymns of the Millennium."

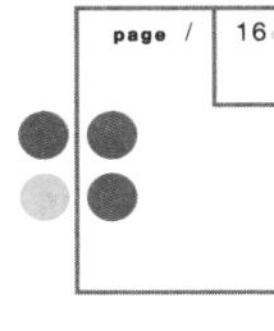

47 DESIGN FIRM MTV Networks, New York, NY
CREATIVE DIRECTOR Monica Halpert
SENIOR ART DIRECTOR Dean Lubensky
DESIGNER Charles Hamilton
PRODUCTION DIRECTOR Russ Pinieri
WRITER Traci Terril
TYPEFACE Garamond
PRINTER Print Promotions, Inc.
PAPER Utopia 3, Skivertex cover

Wild Thing

Words and Music by
CHIP TAYLOR

detail. / n O1

Moderately Slow Rock/Funk
Strum Pattern: No. 3

A D E

CHORUS

A D

(5) 3

Wild Thing, ye

2 2

A D E D A D E

heart sing. Ye make ev'-ry-thing come - ly,

0 2 3 3 0 2 2 2 2

A D E G A G A

To Coda

Tacet

wild thing *Spoketh: Wild Thing,— me - thin*

0 2

A G A G A

Tacet Tacet

Yet I wouldst fain know for sure. *Spoketh: Come—— thou,—— hold m*

design firm. mtv networks

communication graphics. | NO. 47

design firm. mtv networks

communication graphics. | NO. 47

design firm. mtv networks

communication graphics. | NO. 47

ords and Music by
HIP TAYLOR
Moderately Slow
Strum Pattern: N

detail O1

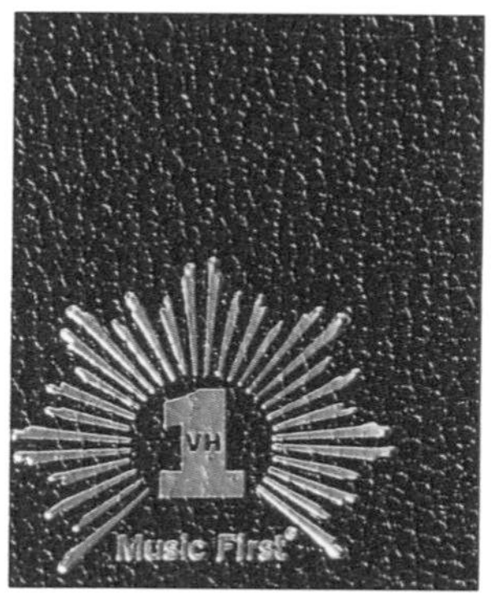

detail O2

Dream On

detail O3

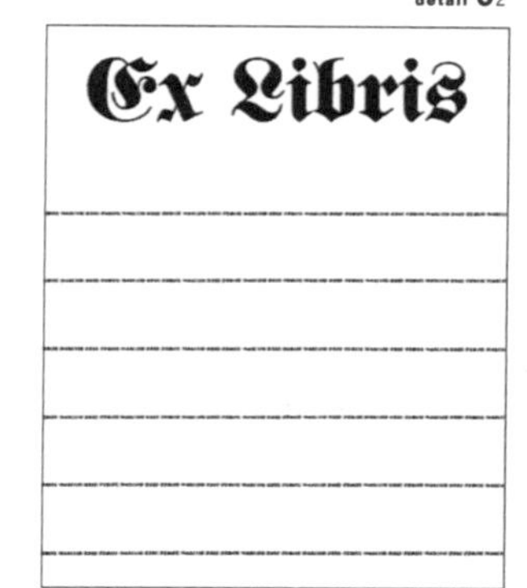

detail O4

detail O5

detail O6

48 03. THINGS THAT MATTER "BIG BOOK" / The idea was to take a holistic look at the soul elements of Herman Miller. We originally wanted to do this via a double truck ad series. Since we didn't have enough money to produce and run the ads, Steve Frykholm (Herman Miller's creative director) suggested a compilation of the ad ideas into one piece. Dan Botruff (Herman Miller's marketing director) got the alternate idea approved and budgeted, and we were off to the races. The only real "but" following the original concept presentation was the "it isn't 8 1/2 x 11" one.

48

DESIGN FIRM	Fairly Painless Advertising, Holland, MI
ART DIRECTORS	Tom Crimp, Steve Frykholm (art), Peter Bell (creative)
DESIGNER	Brian Hauch
PHOTOGRAPHER	Rodney Smith
WRITER	Clark Malcolm
TYPEFACES	Meta Plus Normal, Meta Plus Bold
PRINTER/ FABRICATOR	Hennegan
PAPER	French Newsprint special make
CLIENT	Herman Miller

detail / 05

Things that Matter

design firm. fairly painless advertising

communication graphics. | NO. 48

detail 01

detail 02

design firm. fairly painless advertising

communication graphics. | NO. 48

detail 03

detail 04

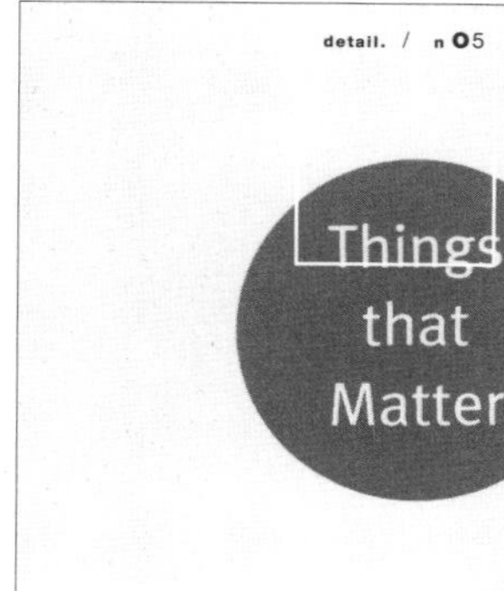

detail 05

design firm. fairly painless advertising

communication graphics. | NO. 48

detail 06

detail 07

49 0G. STEFAN SAGMEISTER LECTURE POSTER / Our brief was to design a poster for a slide lecture given by the designer Stefan Sagmeister. The audience was comprised of graphic design students at Philadelphia's Tyler School of Art. Our solution was to present a playful reference to the headless chicken poster Sagmeister did for an AIGA conference in New Orleans. This particular chicken is a little nervous about Sagmeister's arrival.

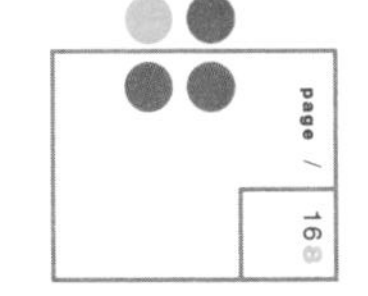
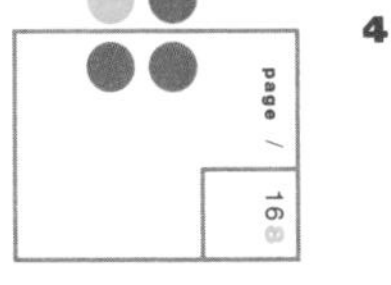

49

DESIGN FIRM	Scorsone/Drueding, Jenkintown, PA
ART DIRECTORS/ DESIGNERS/ COPYWRITERS	Joe Scorsone, Alice Drueding
ILLUSTRATOR	Joe Scorsone
TYPEFACES	Franklin Gothic, handlettering
TRIM SIZE	24 x 24 inches
PRINTER	Colorcomp, Inc.
PAPER	Cross Point Genesis 80 pound text
CLIENT	Tyler School of Art

STeFaN SagmeiSTer is CoMing to TyLEr

RAPHIC DESIGNER STEFAN SAGMEISTER WILL GIVE
N FRIDAY NOVEMBER 12 / 1:30 PM / 110 PENROSE HA

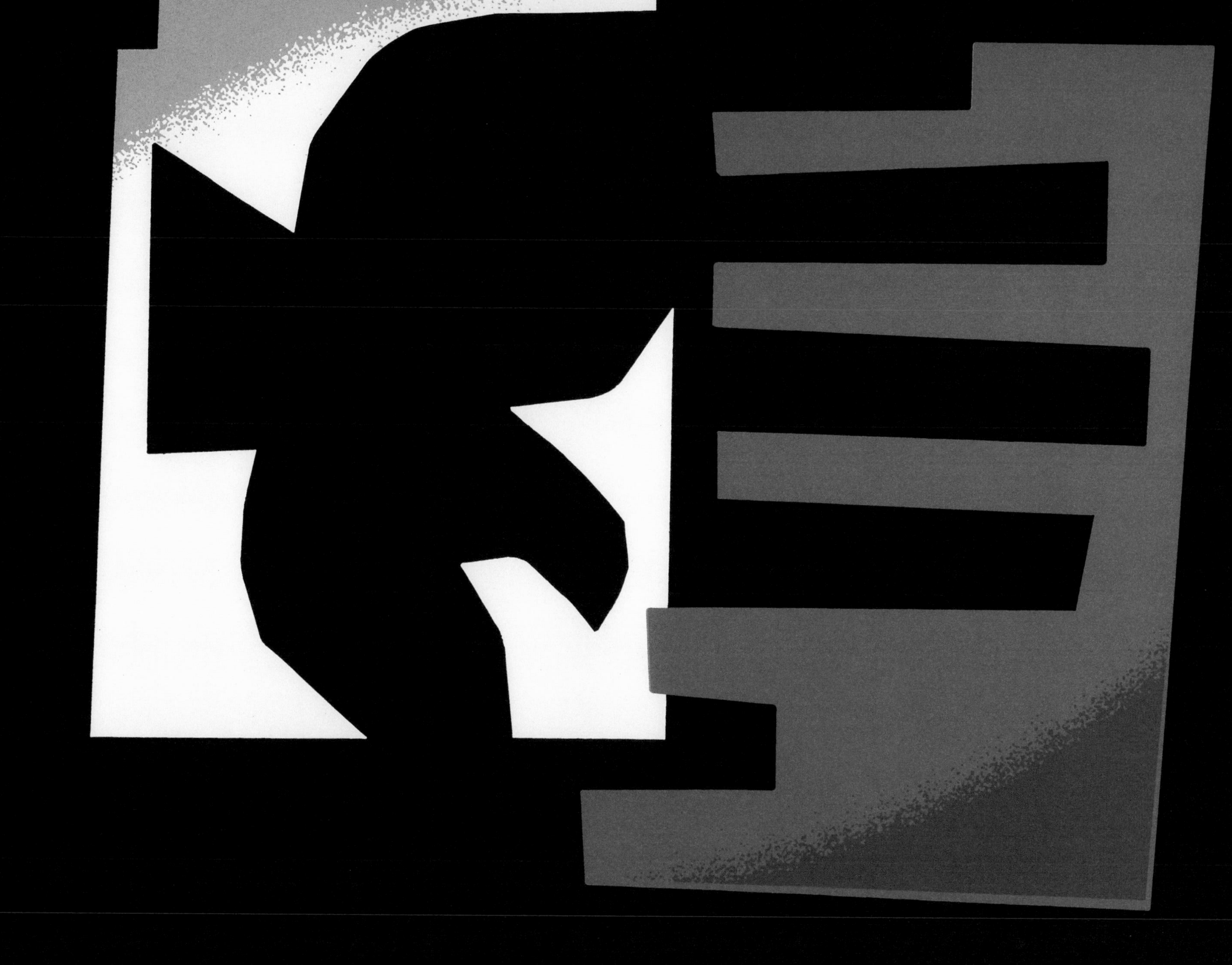

50 06. NATIONAL CAMPAIGN AGAINST YOUTH VIOLENCE POSTER / The National Campaign Against Youth Violence is a new organization that started as a Clinton initiative to build a nationwide infrastructure to help reduce youth violence. Because the poster was designed for people who are making enormous contributions to this important cause, we wanted to give them something unique and relevant to the campaign they are supporting. The poster is a limited edition of 125 prints, and the mechanical was hand-inked in full scale. The design clearly reflects an era that called for revolution and reform while it illuminates the campaign's logo.

50

DESIGN FIRM	Templin Brink Design, San Francisco, CA
CREATIVE DIRECTORS	Gaby Brink, Joel Templin
DESIGNERS	Joel Templin, Gaby Brink, Felix Sockwell
ILLUSTRATORS	Felix Sockwell, Erik Johnson
TYPEFACE	Corpus Gothic
TRIM SIZE	29 3/4 x 41 1/2 inches
PRINTER	Art Real
PAPER	Reeves BFK
CLIENT	National Campaign Against Youth Violence

5 ■ DESIGN FIRM The Washington Post, Washington, D.C.
ART DIRECTOR Jackson Dykman
CARTOGRAPHERS Louis Spirito, William McNulty, Richard Furno
TECHNICAL GURU Patterson Clark

WRITERS/ RESEARCHERS Dita Smith, Robert Thomason
TYPEFACES Postoni, Poynter, Postroman, Map Helvetica
TRIM SIZE 12 1/2 x 22 1/2 inches
PRINTER The Washington Post

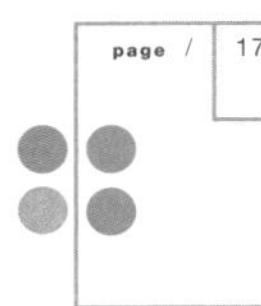

5 ■ C3. KOSOVO MAP / This map of Kosovo documents the expulsion of more than 317,000 ethnic Albanians from their homes and villages. They were sent fleeing across the borders into neighboring Macedonia, Montenegro and Albania. These countries were overwhelmed with the influx, and while NATO, the U.S., the U.N. and private relief organizations launched major aid projects, the situation at the borders became desperate. This map pinpointed locations of harassment, killings or expulsions of ethnic Albanians by Serbian forces and documented the plight of hundreds of thousands of refugees.

Kosovo The Human Crisis

NATO's airstrikes against Yugoslavia have not persuaded Yugoslav President Slobodan Milosevic to agree to a peace deal for Kosovo. Instead, Milosevic's security forces have been systematically emptying Kosovo of its majority ethnic Albanian population, while also battling separatist guerrillas. As the bombing continues, Milosevic is thus changing the ethnic balance in the province, whose population used to be 90 percent ethnic Albanian, by employing his military and security forces to herd hundreds of thousands of people to collection points and then force them toward the borders.

The Scope of the Crisis

The Washington Post collected nearly 150 reports from witnesses, government and aid agencies and the media and analyzed the data electronically.

The results showed that since airstrikes started on March 24:

- Ethnic Albanians have been expelled from at least 100 villages, towns and cities in Kosovo.
- A minimum of 22 villages or neighborhoods have been burned by Serbian forces.
- At least 41,300 ethnic Albanians have been reported missing.
- A minimum of 2,800 ethnic Albanians have been killed by security forces across Kosovo.

Indicates locations that have been the scenes of harassment, killings or expulsions of ethnic Albanians by Serbian forces since March 24.

The Victims

Expulsions: The U.N. High Commissioner for Refugees reports that at least 317,000 ethnic Albanians have been forced across Kosovo's borders—into Albania, Macedonia and the Yugoslav republic of Montenegro—since March 24.

Method: Serbian forces have developed a distinct pattern for clearing neighborhoods and villages of ethnic Albanians:

First, armed and masked Serbs terrorize residents in the streets, forcing them into their homes. Then they enter homes and order residents to leave immediately or risk being killed. Residents are then forced to staging areas, where they are loaded onto trains, sometimes boxcars, bound for the Macedonian border or onto trucks or buses headed for the Albanian border.

Still in Kosovo: At least 260,000 ethnic Albanians are believed stranded in Kosovo without shelter or food, according to aid agencies. Food drops had been considered but then discarded for fear of supplies falling into the hands of Serbian forces.

The Refugees

Since expulsions began on March 24, more than 300,000 ethnic Albanians have moved into neighboring countries.

	Since March 24
In Montenegro	32,000
In Macedonia	115,000
In Albania	170,000

Before March 24 / Since March 24

Morina: Of the 170,000 arrivals since March 24, 22,000 crossed into Albania yesterday. Tens of thousands more are streaming toward the

Blace: More than 60,000 refugees waiting in muddy field

Area where U.S. soldiers were cap

DESEO S.A. presenta:
TODO
SOBRE
MI
MADRE

52 CG. ALL ABOUT MY MOTHER FILM POSTER / The filmmaker Pedro Almodóvar wanted a poster that could be associated with his idiosyncratic style and be easily understood internationally. Firstly, we avoided photography, which is so overused in the world of cinema. The painting is of a proud and "transparent" woman—a mother who could either be interpreted as the protagonist of the film or someone you know. We wanted the image to be easy to reproduce at any size, and we used only flat colors to be economical.

52

DESIGN FIRM	OMB Diseño Gráfico S.L., Madrid, Spain
ART DIRECTOR/ DESIGNER/ ILLUSTRATOR	Oscar Mariné
PRINT PRODUCTION	Curra de la Fuente
TYPEFACE	Compacta
PRINTER	TF Artes Gráficas
PAPER	Fedreigoni Tintoretto Neve 200 grams
CLIENT	El Deseo, S.A

53 CG. THE TAMING OF THE SHREW POSTER /

53 DESIGN FIRM Luba Lukova Studio, New York, NY

ART DIRECTOR/
DESIGNER/
ILLUSTRATOR Luba Lukova

TRIM SIZE 27 x 38 inches

PRINTER Janus Group

CLIENT Center for Theatre Studies at Columbia University

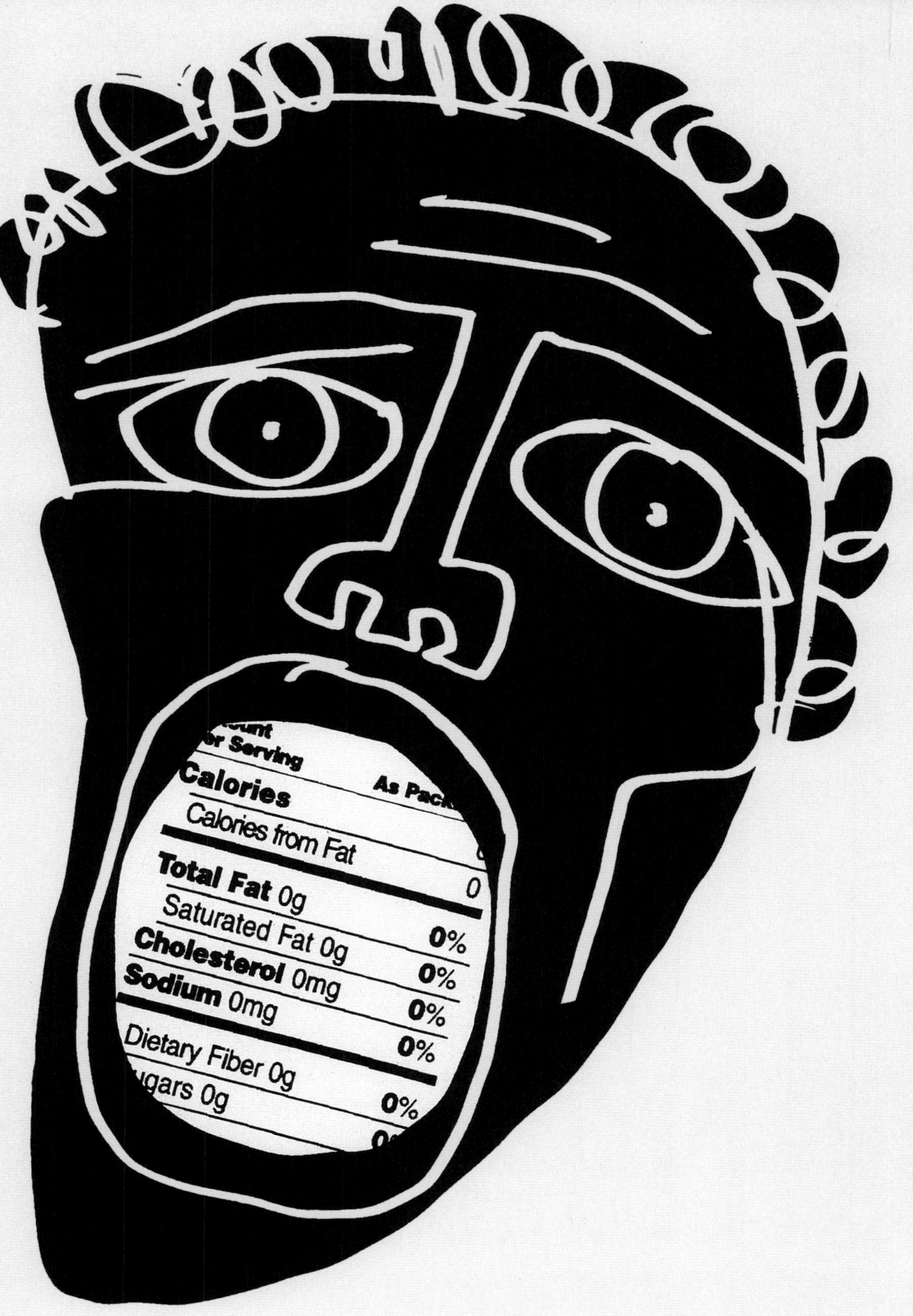

54 CG. SUDAN POSTER /

DESIGN FIRM	Luba Lukova Studio, New York, NY
CLIENT	International Anti-Poverty Law Center
ART DIRECTOR/ DESIGNER/ ILLUSTRATOR	Luba Lukova
TRIM SIZE	27 x 38 inches
PRINTER	Janus Group

55 0G. CAUTION: CHILDREN AT WAR / The poster was created for an initiative by Amnesty International to abolish the use of child soldiers worldwide. The image was inspired by the common "Caution: Children at Play" street signs.

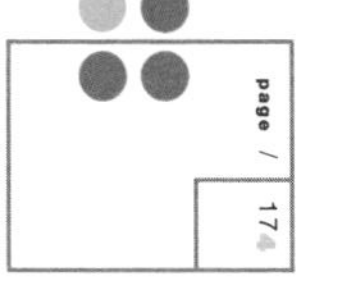

55

DESIGN FIRM	Pentagram Design, New York, NY
PARTNER/ DESIGNER	Woody Pirtle
DESIGNER	Chris Dunn
TYPEFACE	Interstate
CLIENT	Amnesty International

UTION: CHILDREN AT WA

ne use of child soldiers worldwide. Children have the right to be chil

AMNESTY INTERNATIONA

www amnest

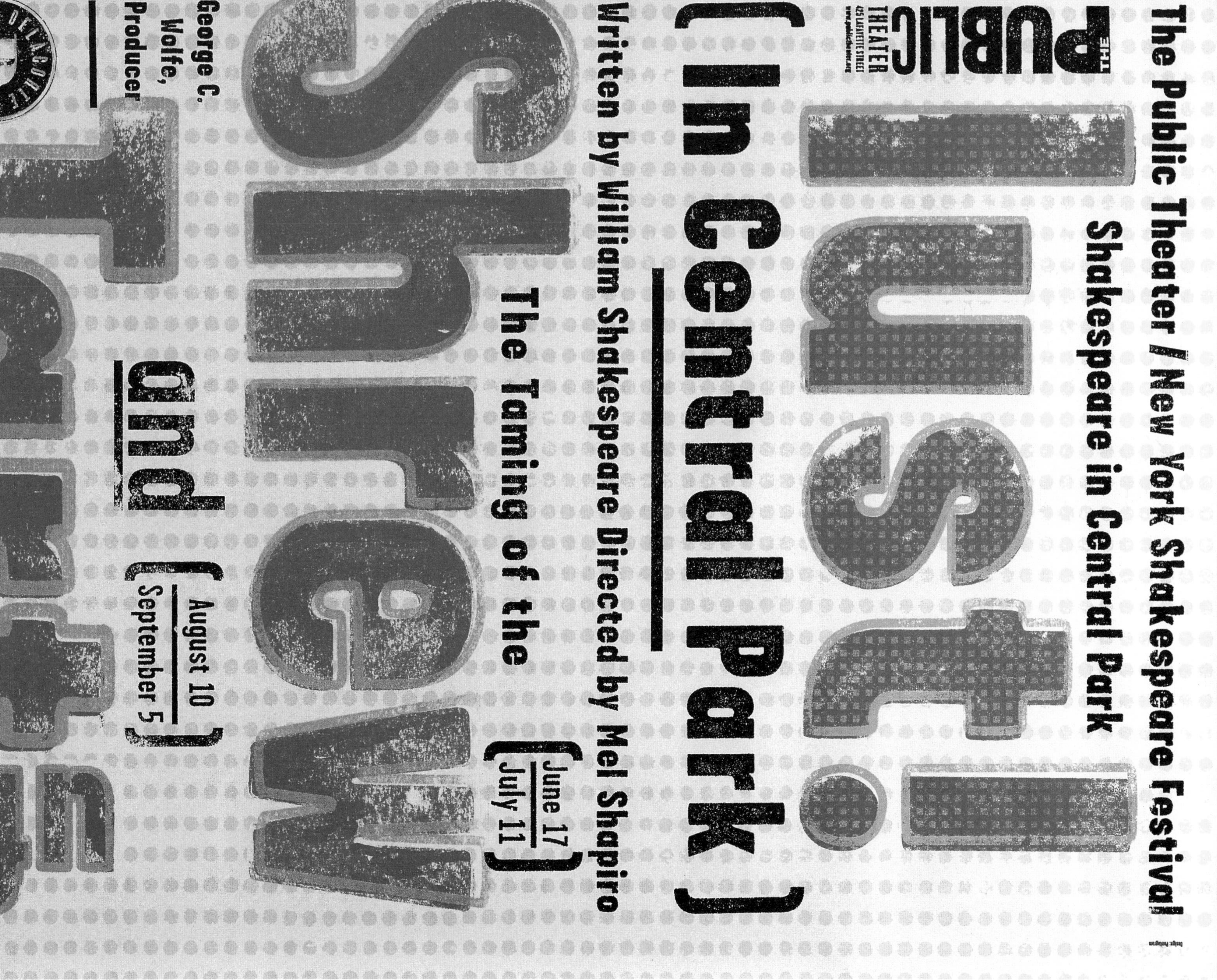

The Public Theater / New York Shakespeare Festival
Shakespeare in Central Park
THE PUBLIC THEATER
425 LAFAYETTE STREET
www.publictheater.org
lust!
(In Central Park)
Written by William Shakespeare Directed by Mel Shapiro
The Taming of the
June 17
July 11
Shrew
George C. Wolfe, Producer
and
August 10
September 5
Tart
DELACORTE THEATER
D

56 06. NEW YORK SHAKESPEARE FESTIVAL POSTER / Since 1994, Paula Scher has been designing colorful typographic posters in the tradition of old-fashioned English theater announcements for this festival. The Taming of the Shrew and Tartuffe were the NYSF's 1999 productions. Winking at news headlines in the Age of Monica, the poster singles out the words "lust," "shrew" and "tart" in a degraded fluorescent red. "Lust! in Central Park" also needles Mayor Rudolph Guiliani's vision of a smut-free New York. (At the time the poster was made, Giuliani was conducting a crackdown on anything sex-related in New York City.)

56

DESIGN FIRM	Pentagram Design, New York, NY
ART DIRECTOR/ DESIGNER	Paula Scher
DESIGNER	Tina Chang
TYPEFACE	Garage Graphic
CLIENT	The Public Theater

57 CG. FALL PAPER EXPO POSTER / We needed to create a poster that would draw attendance to the Art Directors Club's "Paper Expo" show. We focused on the message through the message itself; tearing paper with the word "paper" exposes the word "expo." No other images or messages were needed.

57

DESIGN FIRM	Design Machine, New York, NY
ART DIRECTORS/ DESIGNERS	Alexander Gelman, Kaoru Sato
PROJECT MANAGER	Ari Bergen
TYPEFACE	Custom
TRIM SIZE	34 x 22 inches
PRINTER	Quebecor Specialty Group
PAPER	Gleneagle Dull Tint
CLIENT	The Art Directors Club

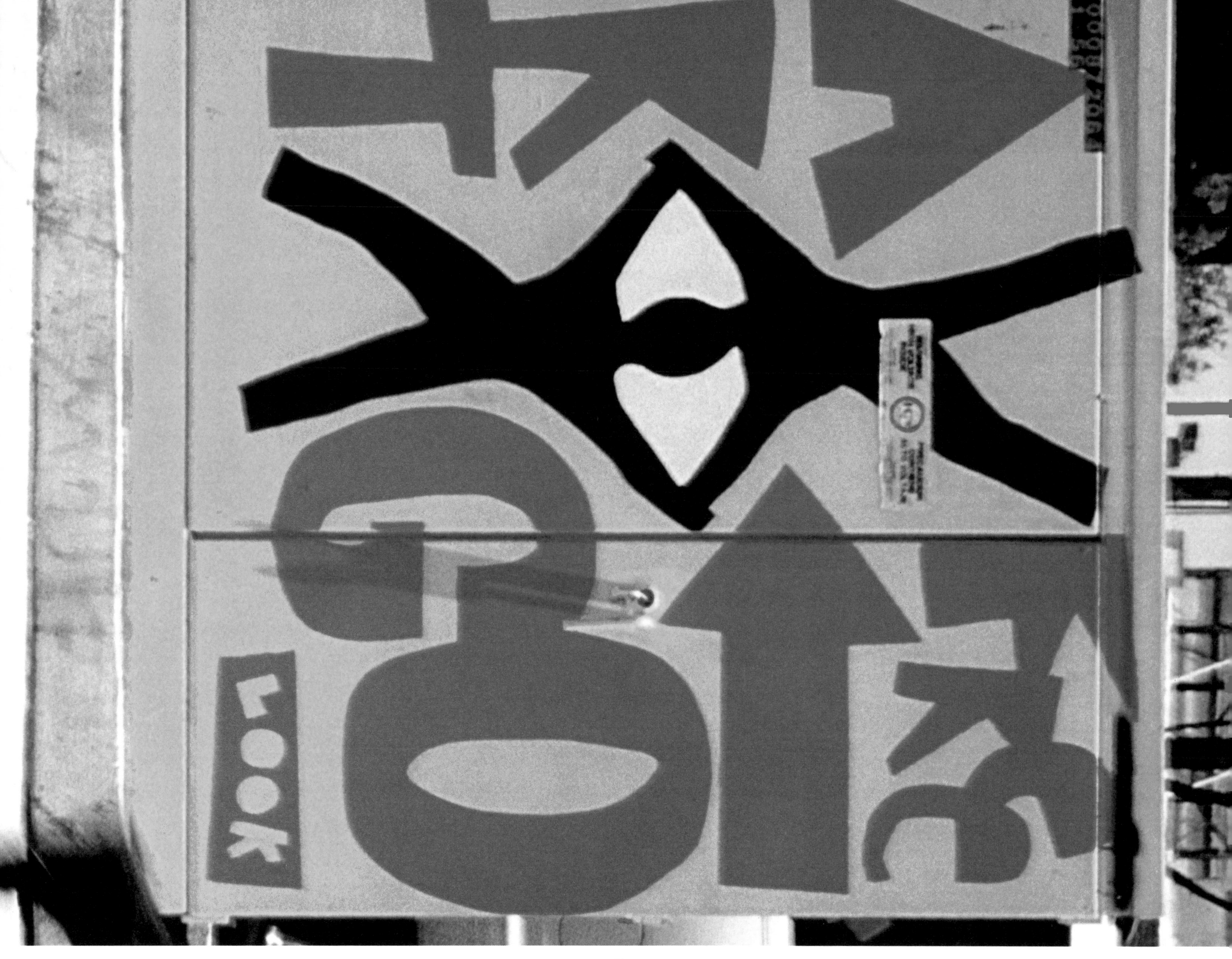

58

DESIGN FIRM	Studio Bustamante, San Diego, CA
CREATIVE DIRECTOR	Candace Lopez
DESIGNER/ ILLUSTRATOR	Gerald Bustamante
PROJECT MANAGER	Keith Lock
PHOTOGRAPHER	Dillon Kerekes
SIZE	Six-foot box (approximately)
CLIENT	The public, the City of San Diego Urban Art Trail Project

59 CG. COMPUSA STORE / Apple approached marchFIRST (formerly CKS) and Eight Inc. to develop a unique environment within the CompUSA San Francisco store. Apple secured a prominent space on the street level by repurposing a secluded storage area and exchange counter. The interior architecture and fixtures drew from new store-in-store components and Apple event vocabulary. The brand was expressed in a very simple manner blending genius banners with related items like a corporate manifesto, product packaging and the new rendered logo.

59

DESIGN FIRM	marchFIRST, San Francisco, CA
EXECUTIVE CREATIVE DIRECTOR	Andy Dreyfus
CREATIVE DIRECTOR	Patti Glover
ART DIRECTOR	Aki Shelton
ARCHITECTS	Various
DESIGNERS	Various
PRINTER	Graphics Unlimited
FABRICATOR	Eight Inc.
CLIENT	Apple Computer

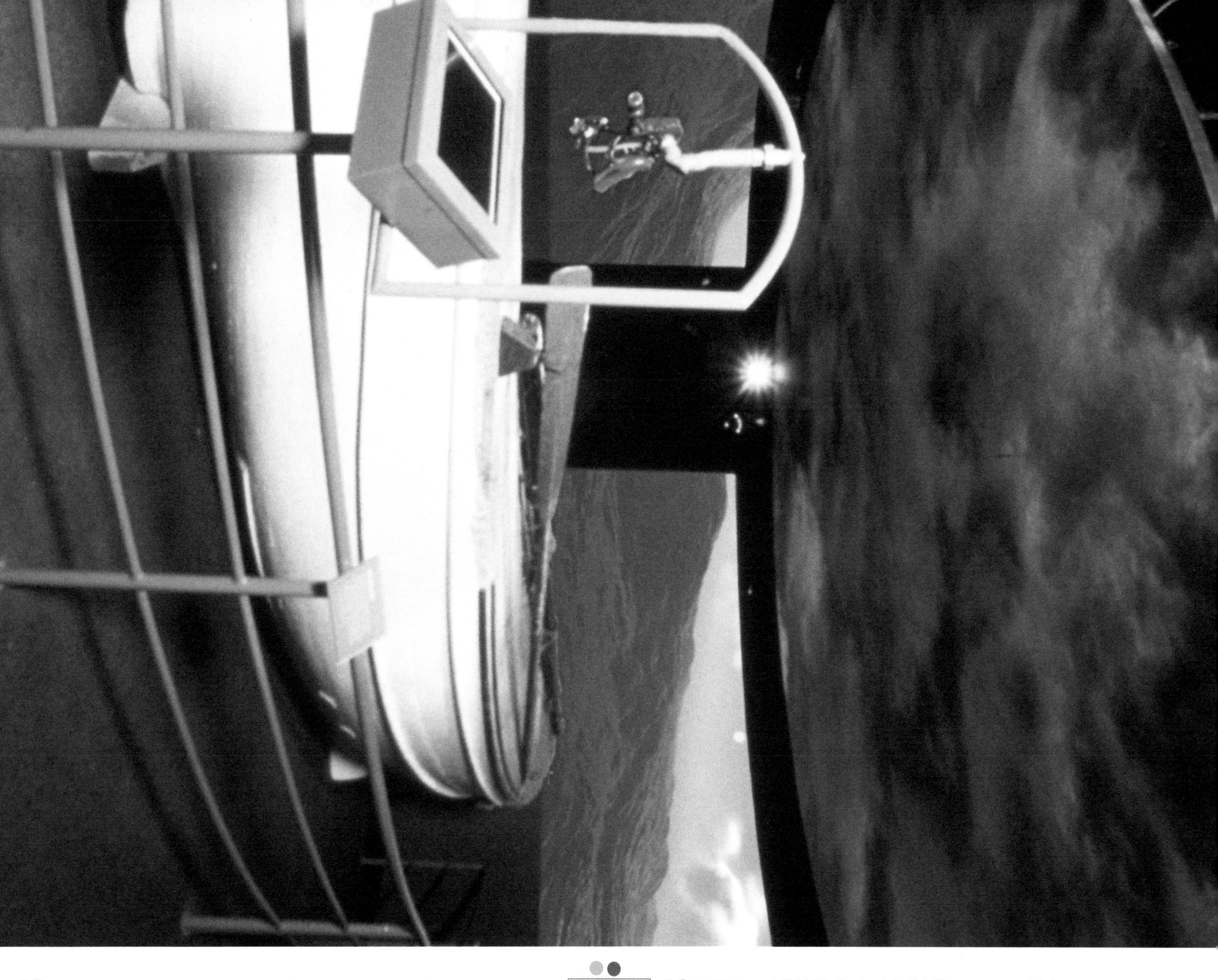

60 CG. SHACKLETON INTERACTIVE INSTALLATION / The centerpiece artifact of this AMNH installation was the actual boat that Shackleton and his men used. At the stern of the boat were two interactive stations, each featuring a real sextant fitted with sensors and microcontrollers and linked to a computer. Three screens with 50 feet of synchronized projections of an ominous Antarctic ocean surrounded this. At each station, visitors followed instructions that directed them to use the sextant to take a sight of the sun, visible only occasionally on the projection screens. The results of the visitor's navigational effort were displayed on the computer screen and compared to the route Shackleton and his crew actually took.

60

DESIGN FIRM	AMNH Exhibition Department, New York, NY
CREATIVE DIRECTOR	David Harvey
DESIGNERS	David Clinard, Paul dePass, Jayne Hertko, David McCormack, Frank Rasor, Stephanie Reyer, Kevin Walker
ANIMATOR	Molly Lenore
PROGRAMMER	Joseph Stein, D Dixon
EDITOR	Lauri Halderman
CLIENT	American Museum of Natural History

61 CG. YUM POSTER / When Apple followed up the success of the iMac with the introduction of five different colors, we were faced with the problem of launching it to the world. In an effort to simplify Apple's communications globally, we created a signature shot that could be used for everything from print to packaging to the web. The flower composition was the most unique and obvious way to show all five colors in one image. When it came to a tagline to express the luscious new colors, the natural choice was "Yum."

61

DESIGN FIRM	marchFIRST, San Francisco, CA
CREATIVE DIRECTORS	Andy Dreyfus, Hiroki Asai
ART DIRECTOR	Hiroki Asai
WRITER	David Begler
PHOTOGRAPHER	Hunter Freeman
PRINT PRODUCTION	Karen Emerson
TYPEFACE	Apple Garamond
CLIENT	Apple Computer

Yum.

e Architectural League of New York's 1999 Beaux Arts Ball at the Starrett-Lehigh Building, Satur

62 0G. LIGHT YEARS POSTER / "Light Years" was the theme of the 1999 annual gala held by the Architectural League of New York. The site, a Manhattan warehouse, was transformed for the evening by a variety of dramatic lighting effects. The poster took advantage of the coincidence of the matching number of letters in each word to create a "persistence of vision" effect reminiscent of a photogram. This graphic theme carried over into tickets, invitations and light installations at the actual event.

62

DESIGN FIRM	Pentagram Design, New York, NY
PARTNER/ DESIGNER	Michael Bierut
DESIGNER	Nicole Trice
TYPEFACE	Interstate Bold

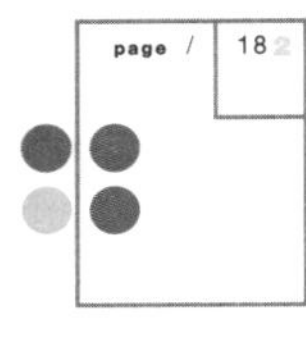

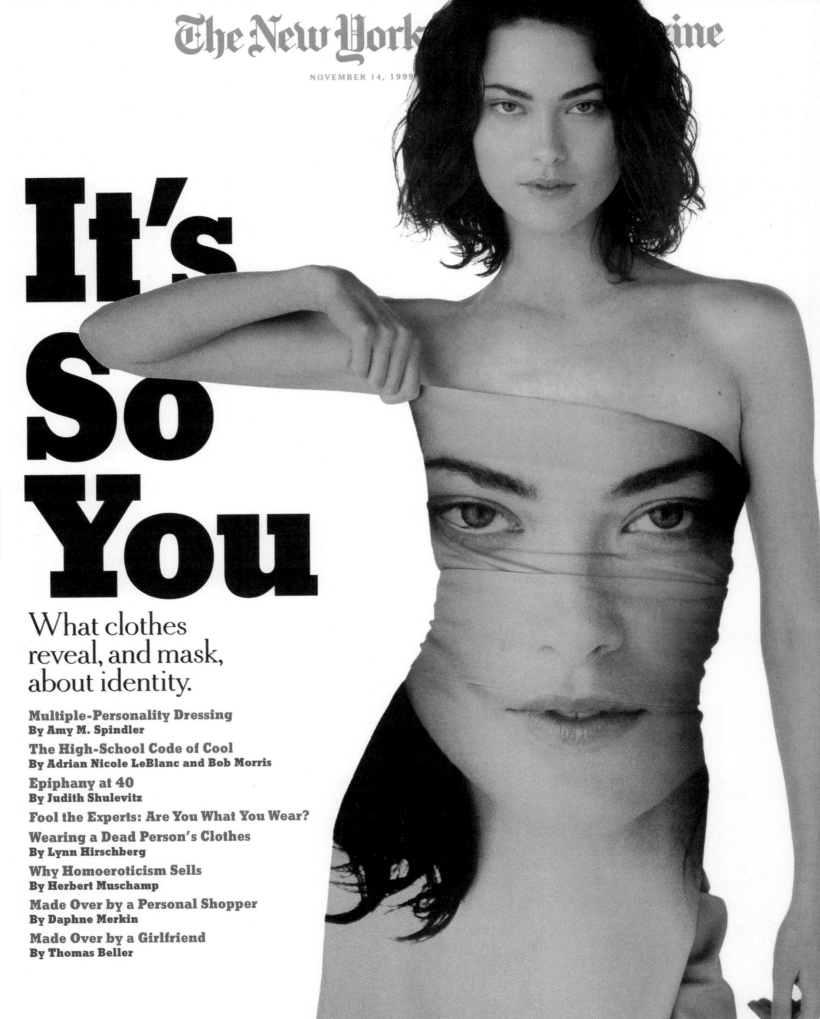

63 CG. "IT'S SO YOU" NEW YORK TIMES MAGAZINE COVER / This was a cover of a special issue of the magazine devoted to clothing and identity. Our mission was to create a stylish cover that would convey to the general reader that this was an intellectual inquiry into fashion and identity, but we had to do it without looking like a fashion magazine. We photographed the model Shalom Harlow in a plain muslin dress, and superimposed her face onto that dress. The double take prevents the image from reading like a fashion image, and forces the reader to consider the question "Are you what you wear?"

63

DESIGN FIRM	The New York Times Magazine, New York, NY
ART DIRECTOR	Janet Froelich
DESIGNER	Claude Martel
PHOTO EDITOR	Kathy Ryan
PHOTOGRAPHER	Andrew Elcues
TYPEFACES	Stymie Extra Bold, Cheltenham NYT extra light
PUBLISHER	The New York Times

The New York Times Magazine

NOVEMBER 14, 1999

It's So You

What clothes reveal, and mask, about identity.

Multiple-Personality Dressing
By Amy M. Spindler

The High-School Code of Cool
By Adrian Nicole LeBlanc and Bob Morris

Epiphany at 40
By Judith Shulevitz

Fool the Experts: Are You What You Wear?

Wearing a Dead Person's Clothes
By Lynn Hirschberg

Why Homoeroticism Sells
By Herbert Muschamp

Made Over by a Personal Shopper
By Daphne Merkin

Made Over by a Girlfriend
By Thomas Beller

64 CG. AIGA "COMPETITIONS & EXHIBITIONS" POSTER / The task was to design a one-off poster for AIGA's headquarter office to be placed in its competitions and exhibitions department. The concept was to express the variety and multitude of work entered and exhibited by using all the different names to describe the various design disciplines and categories. The intricate, overlapping letterforms and colored shapes was an idea that could not easily be sketched by hand—or even communicated to others—and is therefore a true computer design solution, directly created for the final Iris print process.

64 DESIGN FIRM Chermayeff & Geismar Inc., New York, NY

ART DIRECTOR/DESIGNER Steff Geissbuhler

PRINTER Pamplemousse

CLIENT AIGA

65 CG. ARLINGTON ROAD OPENING TITLES / This main title sequence questions those things many American citizens put their faith in: America, family, material culture. Suburban nightmares are suggested by discolored picket fences and distorted middle-American weekend iconography. The intent is to have the audience disturbed and curious. The images were shot in a guerilla filmmaking fashion on Velvia film, black-and-white high con, digital video, super 8, 16mm, 8mm and standard 35mm.

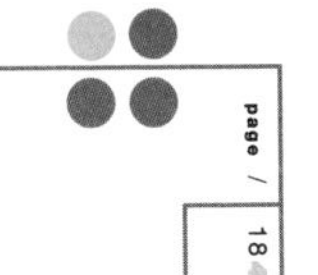

page / 184

65

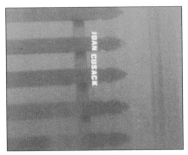

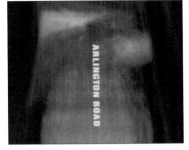

DESIGN FIRM	Imaginary Forces, Hollywood, CA
DIRECTORS	Mark Pellington, Kyle Cooper
DESIGNERS	Kyle Cooper, Michelle Dougherty
EXECUTIVE PRODUCERS	Peter Frankfurt, Kyle Cooper
HEAD OF PRODUCTION	Saffron Kenny
EDITOR	Lauren Giordano
INFERNO ARTIST	Lori Freitag-Hild
2-D ANIMATOR	Ben Lopez
COORDINATOR	Deidre Morrison

detail 01

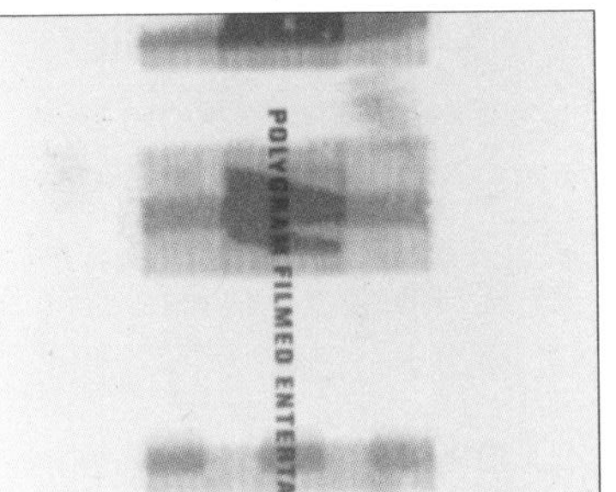

detail 02

detail 03

detail 04

detail 05

detail 06

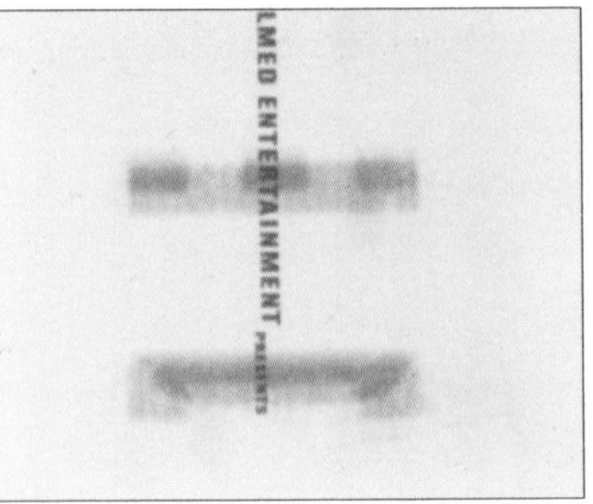

detail 07

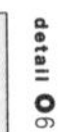

design firm. imaginary forces

communication graphics. | NO. 65

design firm. imaginary forces

communication graphics. | NO. 65

design firm. imaginary forces

communication graphics. | NO. 65

design firm. mtv networks

communication graphics. | NO. 66

design firm. mtv networks

communication graphics. | NO. 66

design firm. mtv networks

communication graphics. | NO. 66

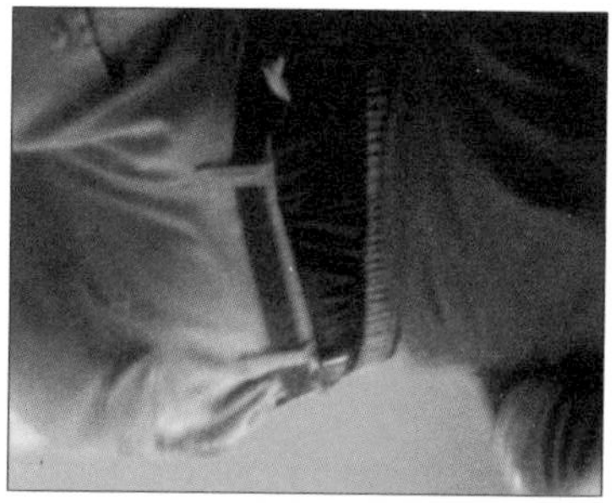
detail 01

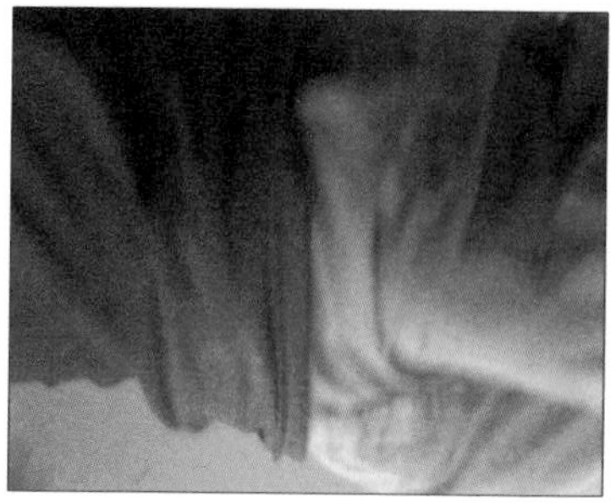
detail 02

detail 03

detail 04

detail 05

detail 06

detail 07

66 CG. HIP HOP WEEK SPOT /

66

DESIGN FIRM	MTV Networks, New York, NY
CREATIVE DIRECTOR	Jeffery Keyton
DESIGN DIRECTOR	Romy Mann
DESIGNER	Catherine Chesters
EXECUTIVE PRODUCER	Christina Norman
PRODUCER	Catherine Chesters
SOUND EDITOR	Finale/Rahzel (original score)
POST PRODUCTION	post millenium/National

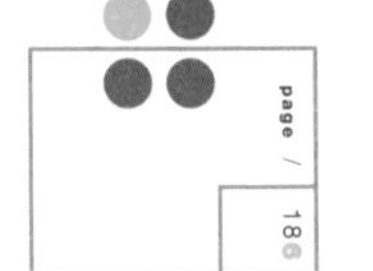

67 CG. SEGA "ANXIETY" SPOT / These spots were designed to represent the point of view of the new Sega Dreamcast console, a machine developed to be smart enough to analyze, predict and counter the player's every move. The triangular framing device is a reference to the triangular window on the game console that was designed to function as the Dreamcast's eye. The triangular device opens up at the start of the spots, which are numbered and color coded, creating visual and conceptual consistency.

67

DESIGN FIRM	Imaginary Forces, Hollywood, CA
AGENCY	Foote, Cone & Belding
DIRECTORS	Kyle Cooper, Mikon van Gastel
HEAD OF PRODUCTION	Saffron Kenny
PRODUCERS	Lisa Laubhan, Anna Frost, Robert Gondell
DESIGNERS	Mikon van Gastel, Matt Cullen, Sara Marandi
EDITOR	Philip Schtoll
INFERNO ARTIST	Phil Man
2-D ANIMATOR	Matt Cullen

detail O1

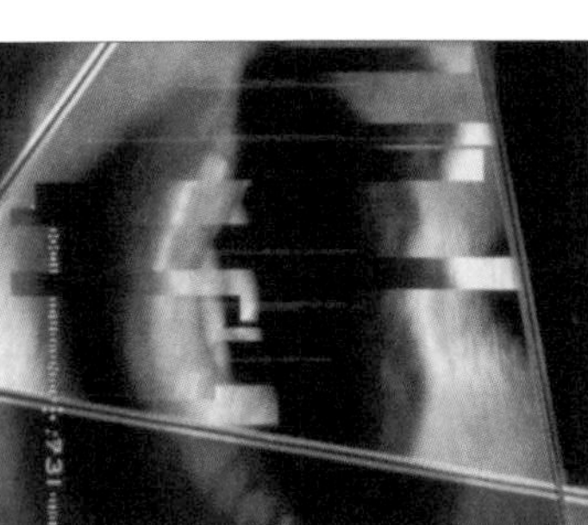

detail O2

detail O3

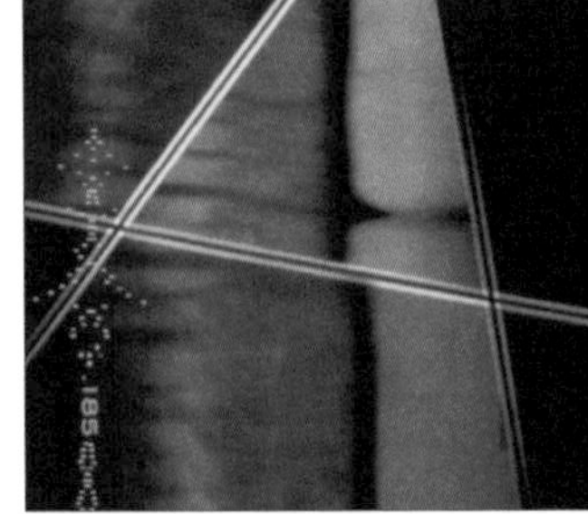

detail O4

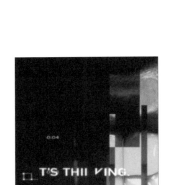

detail O5

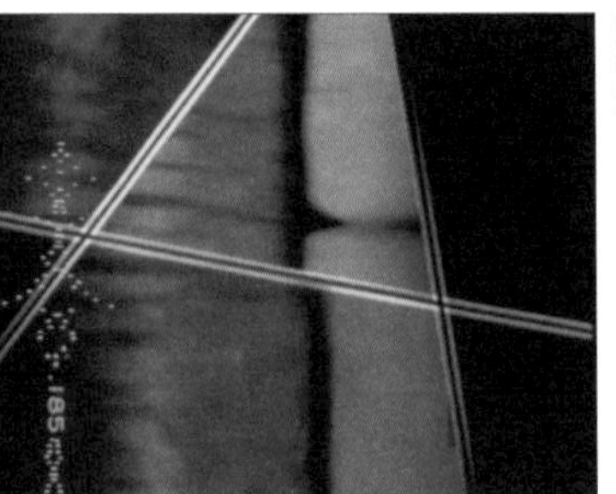

detail O6

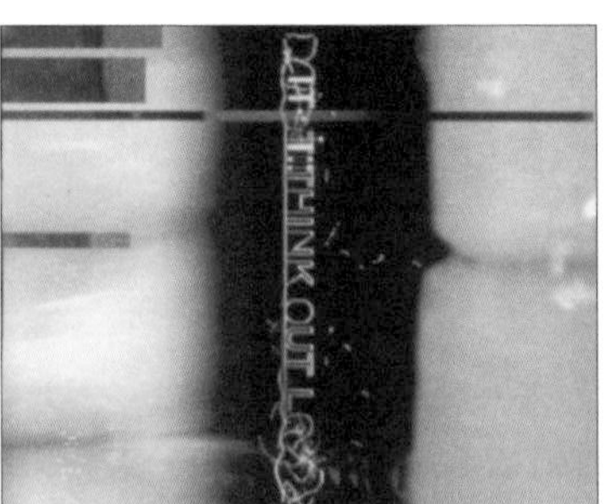

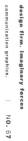

detail O7

design firm. imaginary forces
communication graphics. | NO. 67

design firm. imaginary forces
communication graphics. | NO. 67

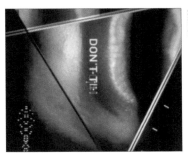

design firm. mtv networks
communication graphics. | NO. 68

design firm. mtv networks
communication graphics. | NO. 68

design firm. mtv networks
communication graphics. | NO. 68

detail 01

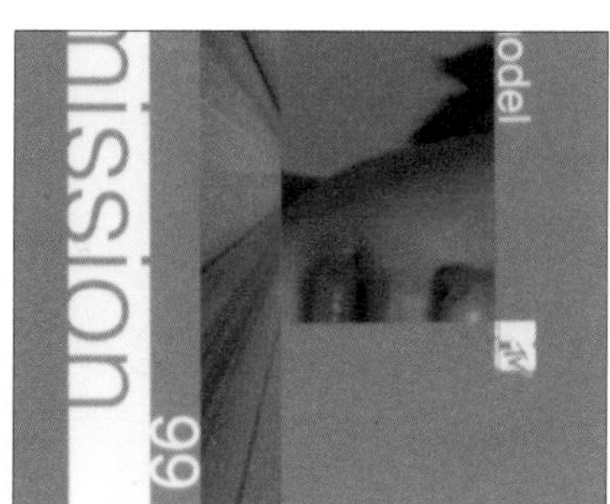

detail 02

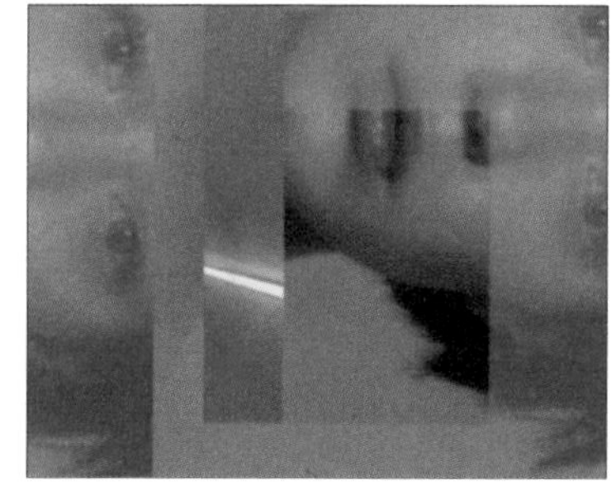

detail 03

detail 04

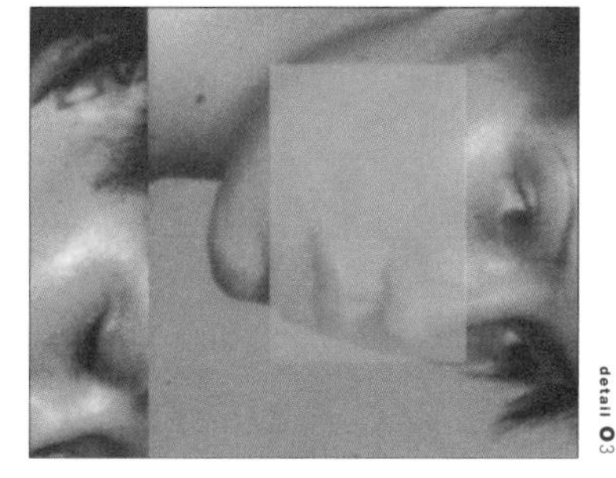

detail 05

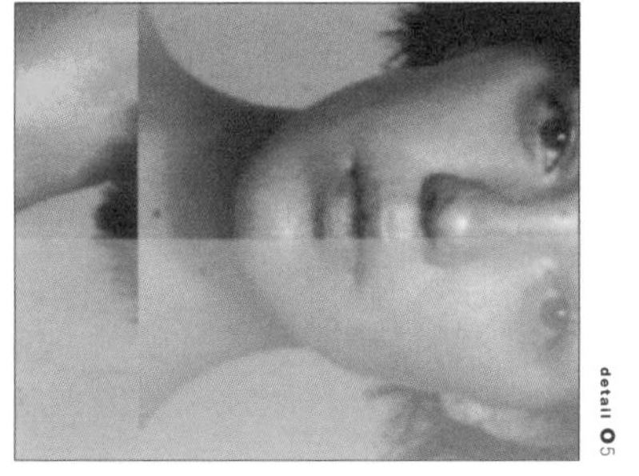

detail 06

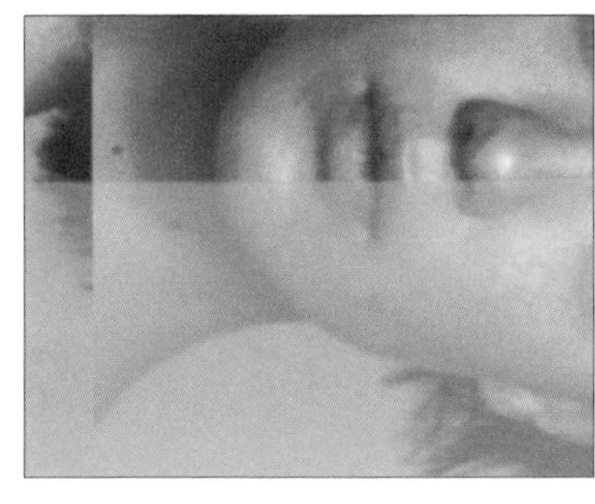

detail 07

68 CG. MODEL MISSION SPOT / We had to recycle footage and work with an existing logo. We decided to approach footage from a different angle perspective—one with more close-ups—and then added layers of transparent color and color in general.

68

DESIGN FIRM	MTV Networks, New York, NY
CREATIVE DIRECTOR	Jeffery Keyton
DESIGNER	Lara Hovanesian
PHOTOGRAPHER	Kenneth Willardt
TYPEFACE	Helvetica
DESIGN DIRECTOR	Romy Mann
EXECUTIVE PRODUCER	Christina Norman
EDITOR CONSULATE	Holle Singer

69 CG. TODAY'S MAN SPOT / We were approached to develop four 15-second commercial spots for the clothing store Today's Man. The budget was limited and the deadline was deadly. We set limitations for ourselves along the way, using one typeface and only those graphic elements that supported the message. We began by laying out the end frame of each spot that had text and working backwards. Throughout the process, we wanted to make sure the spots didn't feel like a movie trailer, so the animation to the movements of all the elements were kept subtle—no three-dimensional flying type or crazy texture blurs.

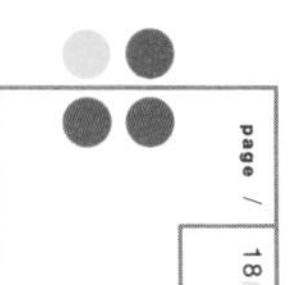

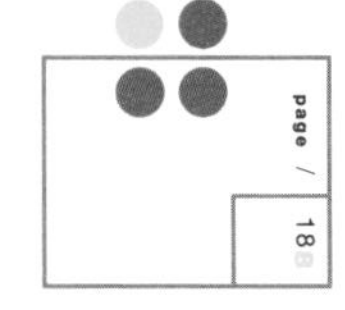

page / 188

69

DESIGN FIRM	44 phases, Hollywood, CA
ART DIRECTORS	Daniel Tsai, Daniel Garcia
DESIGNERS	Daniel Tsai, Daniel Garcia, Luis Jaime
TYPEFACE	Akzidenz Grotesk
EXECUTIVE PRODUCER	Konda Mason
ANIMATORS	Asa Hammond, Jeremiah Morehead
COMPOSER	Paula Gallitano
CLIENT	Today's Man, Arnell Brand Consulting (Peter Arnell)

detail 01

detail 02

detail 03

detail 04

detail 05

detail 06

detail 07

design firm. 44 phases
communication graphics. | NO. 69

design firm. 44 phases
communication graphics. | NO. 69

design firm. 44 phases
communication graphics. | NO. 69

design firm. imaginary forces

communication graphics. | NO. 70

design firm. imaginary forces

communication graphics. | NO. 70

design firm. imaginary forces

communication graphics. | NO. 70

detail O1

detail O2

detail O3

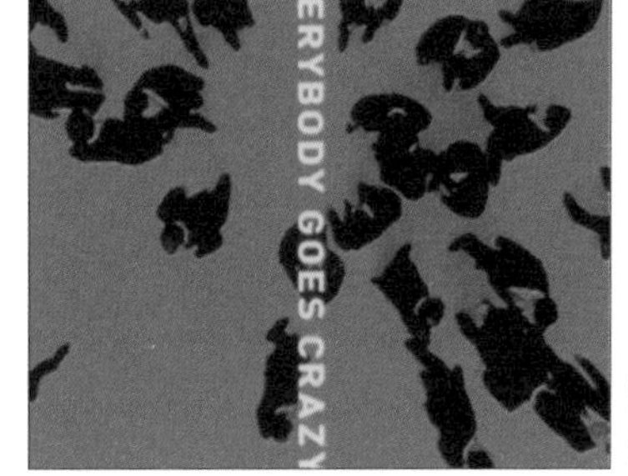

detail O4

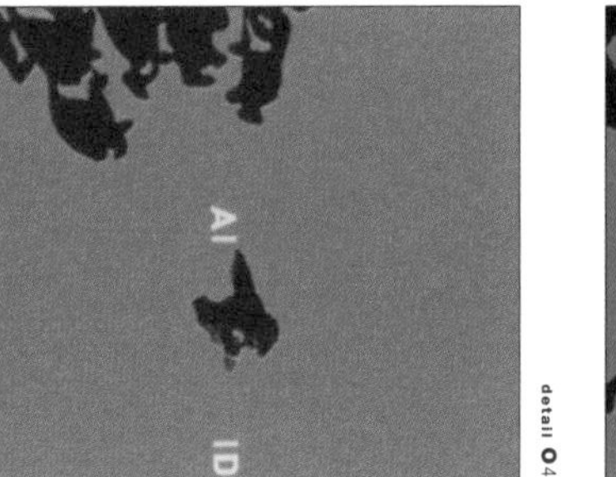

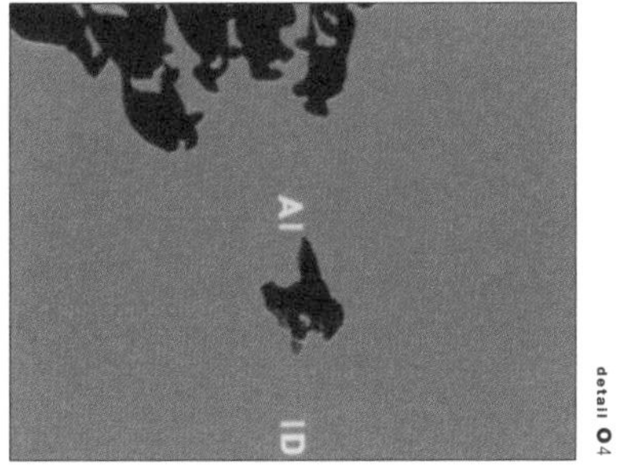

detail O5

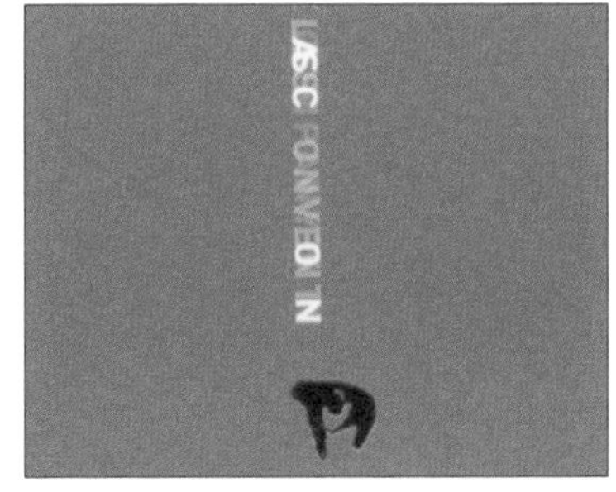

detail O6

70

DESIGN FIRM	Imaginary Forces, Hollywood, CA
AGENCY	Foote, Cone & Belding
DIRECTOR	Kyle Cooper
DESIGNERS	Kyle Cooper, Rafael Macho
HEAD OF PRODUCTION	Saffron Kenny
PRODUCERS	Lisa Laubhan, Robert Gondell
EDITORS	Jason Webb, Lauren Giordano
INFERNO ARTIST	Lori Freitag-Hild
2-D ANIMATOR	Rafael Macho
DIRECTOR	Tom Rosenfield

70 CG. JANUS "CONVENTION" SPOT / Janus is a mutual fund company that lends the impression of being extremely accessible and "user-friendly." We used simple metaphoric images to stand for the company, rather than submitting to the trend of inundating the viewer with a surge of tangentially related images. Each "Janus moment," however, represents more than mere simplicity. The commercials capitalize on events that the company is particularly proud of. The spots combine live action with animated typography, embodying Janus's reliability and persistence while still appealing visually to the masses.

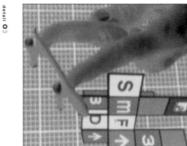

71 CG. SPORTS AND MUSIC FESTIVAL OPEN / We needed to create dynamic show packaging that would introduce various sports segments during MTV's annual "Sports and Music Festival," and incorporate the 3-D name into the design. We designed an identity that was the logo itself. In this case, the logo took on the shape of a halfpipe. Because we were working with a limited budget, the shooting of the "fingerboards" was done ourselves.

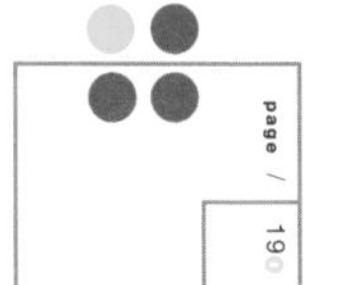
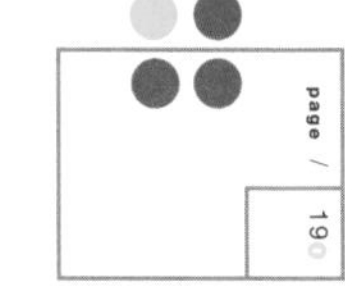
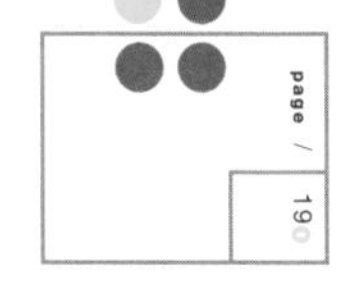
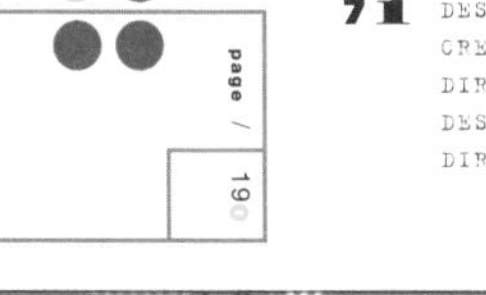

page / 190

71

DESIGN FIRM	MTV Networks, New York, NY
CREATIVE DIRECTOR	Jeffery Keyton
DESIGN DIRECTOR	Romy Mann
DESIGNER/PRODUCER	Todd St. John
TYPEFACE	Berthold Akzidenz Grotesk Extended
EXECUTIVE PRODUCER	Christina Norman
ANIMATOR	Sean Miller

details. / n 01 - 6 communication graphics. / NO. 71

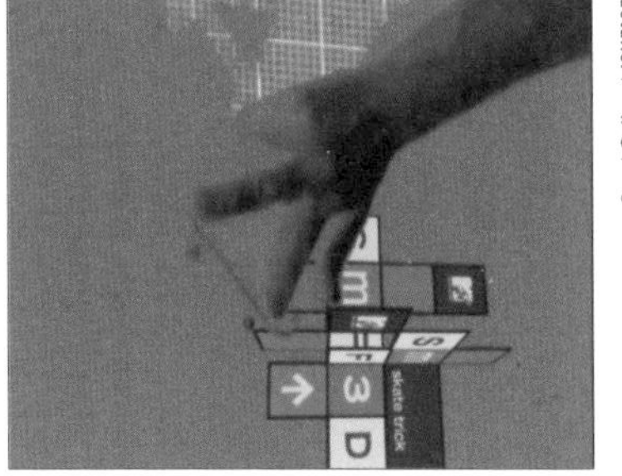

detail 01

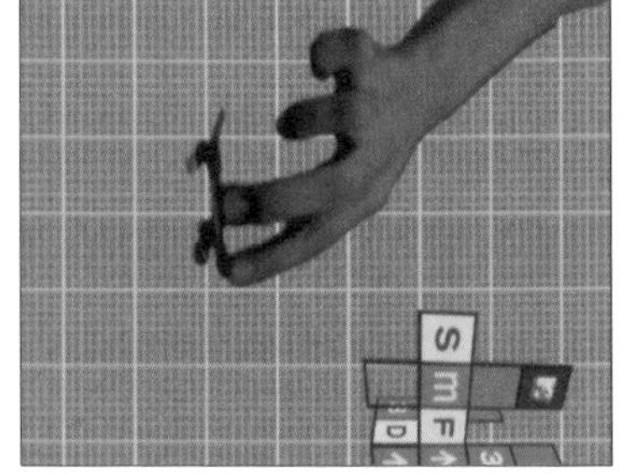

detail 02

detail 03

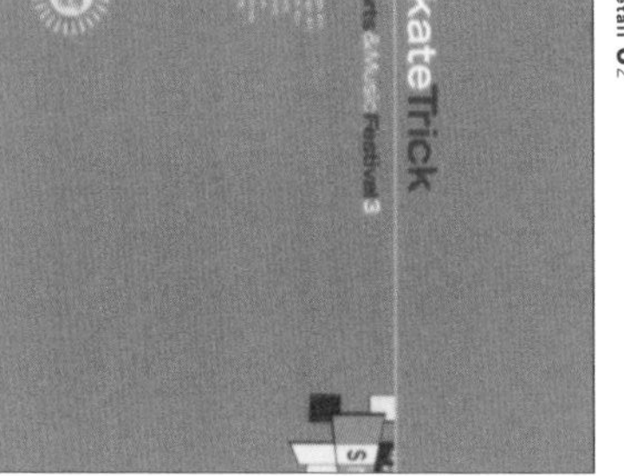

detail 04

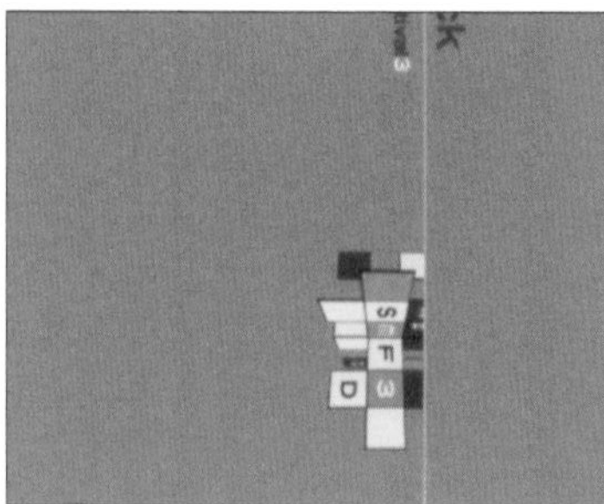

detail 05

detail 06

design firm. mtv networks

communication graphics. | NO. 71

design firm. mtv networks

communication graphics. | NO. 71

design firm. mtv networks

communication graphics. | NO. 71

design firm. the ink tank
communication graphics. | NO. 72

design firm. the ink tank
communication graphics. | NO. 72

design firm. the ink tank
communication graphics. | NO. 72

detail 01

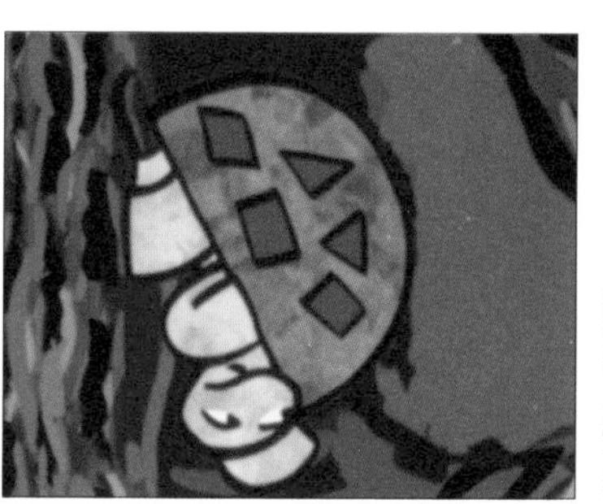

detail 02

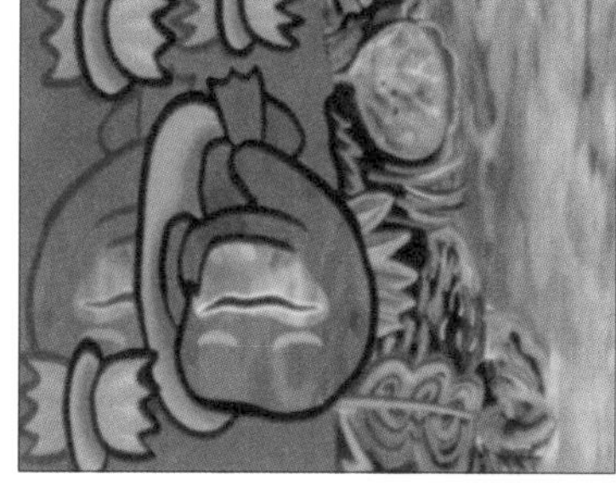

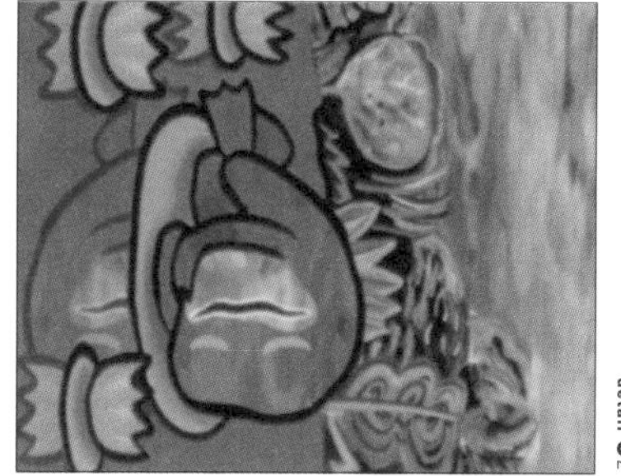

detail 03

detail 04

detail 05

detail 06

detail 07

72 CG. BRAHMS' LULLABY ANIMATION / Brahms' "Lullaby" is about nature going to sleep, so I decided to explore textures and their beautiful details. The biggest challenge was to make a 1:30 film in the relatively short period of six weeks. Fortunately, I had the right people help and we didn't overthink the project.

72

DESIGN FIRM	The Ink Tank, New York, NY
ART DIRECTOR	R. O. Blechman
ILLUSTRATOR	Maciek Albrecht
ANIMATORS	Maciek Albrecht, Todor Radoz
PRODUCTION DESIGNER	Maciek Albrecht
PROGRAMMER	Alexandra Reshanov
PRODUCERS	Brian O'Connell, Richard O'Connor
CLIENT	HBO producer/director Amy Schatz and the program "Goodnight Moon and Other Sleepytime Tales"

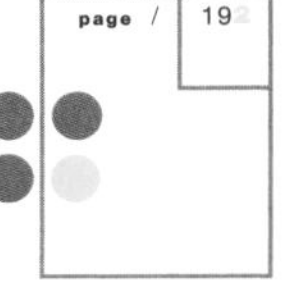

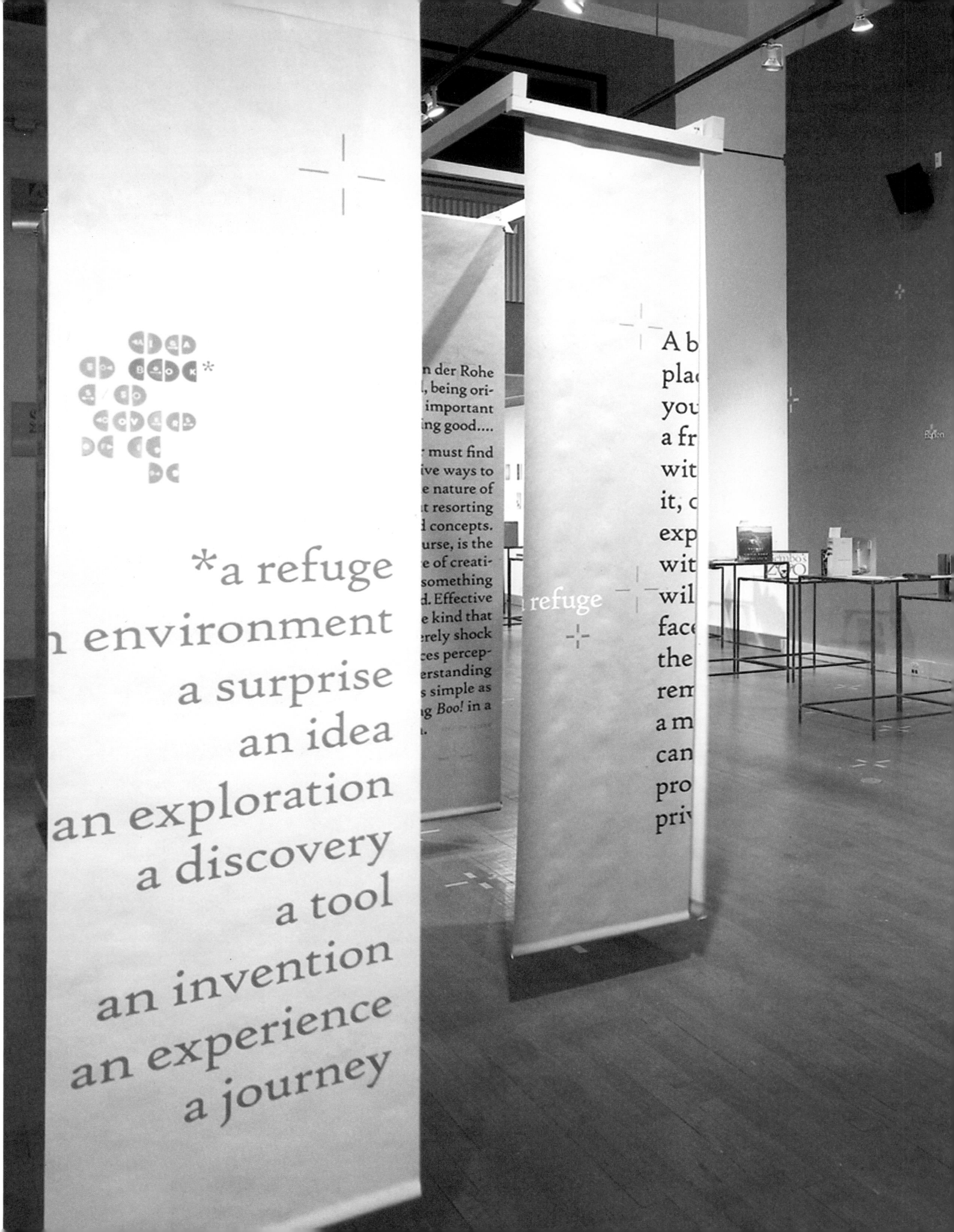

 Exhibition view of AIGA's "50 Books/50 Covers of 1999," designed by studio blue. Photograph © Jennifer Krogh.

50 books. 50 covers.

context essay. | 02

50 books. 50 covers.

context essay. | 02

50 books. 50 covers.

context essay. | 02

The Book: Rumors of its Death Are Greatly Exaggerated | **By Alice Twemlow**

¶01 Faced with the threat of redundancy—or at least charges of anachronism—in a culture increasingly skewed to the digital, book designers seem to be reinventing and repositioning themselves as editors, curators and shapers of content in an effort to validate their practice. When the designers of one of the winning entries in this year's "50 Books/50 Covers" contest were asked how the advent of electronic books would affect their work, their reply hinted at some kind of genetic evolution of the designer: "We will have to design smarter and better to make the books worth printing." It seems that many designers are already designing "smarter and better," and the result is a breed of books that is intelligent, beautiful and somehow more relevant and vital than ever.

¶02 The fundamental question of what a book really is and what the role of the book designer really is split this year's "50 Books/50 Covers" jury in two. One faction believed that a book is defined by its physical form and that a book designer is responsible for faithfully communicating an author's message to the reader using the specialized and recognizable conventions of book design. Rocky Stinehour, a printer who set up the acclaimed Stinehour Press in 1950, was an advocate for the book in its totality. "I'm a book maker," he said "and I see a book entirely differently from the book designers on this jury."

¶03 Both Stinehour and Mary Mendell, a veteran university press designer, expressed their concern that the traditional craft of book making was becoming a lost art. Throughout the two days of judging, Mendell argued resolutely that a book designer is a servant of content. "What good book design is about is trying to set up an architecture for the book that is typographically sound and that helps the reader find the information he wants. It's not about putting the designer's personality into it," she said. While Mendell, somewhat ironically, was voicing her desire that a designer's "voice" be inaudible, she was paying unconscious homage to typographer Beatrice Warde, who, in 1932, talked of the virtues of "transparent or invisible typography" and the designer's duty to engage in the practice of "thought transference."

¶04 The other camp, with studio blue's Cheryl Towler Weese at its vanguard, was not simply arguing for the designer's right to inject personality into his or her work, however. As one might expect, the debate over the state of American book typography in 1999 was more complex than the neat dichotomy of personal style versus neutrality outlined by Warde nearly 70 years ago. Former AIGA president Lucille Tenazas' remarks hint at how the conversation has developed since then: "I was trained in classical typography so I can appreciate the examples of straightforward good book design that we've chosen, but I'm also interested in a more considered use of typography—typography with feeling. It's an evolved sensibility."

¶05 This group, then, believed that a book is defined more by its purpose than its form and that, in this era of decentralized authorship, one of the roles of a book designer is to add his or her own critical take on the content. The whole jury trawled the 911 entries for examples of strong, elegant book design, but this contingent was also on the lookout for cases where the designer had shaped, edited or curated the author's material to enhance the reading experience.

¶06 Lorraine Wild, a former juror herself and one of this year's winners, echoes some of the jury's self-imposed criteria as she describes her own approach to book design in an interview with Eye magazine:

> I am often trying to make a very functional thing, but also to come up with a solution that possesses some sort of ineffable quality or "soul." This means devising a formal response to the content that comes out of a real appreciation for the subject, with some subtlety I hope. . . . I am always trying to create an overt visual narrative to pull the reader toward the content. To me, building those narratives is both an editing and a design process.

¶07 "Graceful," "restrained," "thoughtful," "simple" and "well-considered" were the adjectives the jury used to praise winning entries. They looked for examples where attention had been paid to small details, such as the positioning of footnotes or page numbers, the treatment of copyright information, chronologies, bibliographies and indices. "What we seemed to be consistently interested in were books whose forms were derived specifically from their content," notes Towler Weese, "books with individual and distinct personas, yet that retained a certain "bookishness" or sobriety about them, rather than adopting the slicker consumer language of much of the rest of graphic design production. Perhaps we felt that books still need to project a level of reticent dignity in our oversaturated media world."

¶08 Evidence of all of these qualities is found in a pair of unostentatious books designed by Michael Worthington documenting Uta Barth's photographs—nowhere near and and of time. Though on the surface, the books may appear minimally handled, they are, in fact, subtly complex. Worthington's sensitivity to the subject matter and his ability to capture its "essence" is apparent in all the various design elements: his choice of quiet yet contemporary typefaces (Gridnik for titles and Helvetica for text); his placement of the photographs on the page and his sequencing of those pages; his use of colors that spill out of the photographs and of a reversed-out box device for titles and footnotes that visually echoes the ubiquitous windowpanes in Barth's work. In Ed Ruscha: Editions 1959-1999, too, the designer's choice of an unobtrusive but strong organizational structure—the artist's graphic works are strung along a central horizontal axis that allows the reader to compare them through scale and chronology—adds to the content in a thoughtful way. And Sigmar Polke: Works on Paper 1963-1974 features double-spread dividers of pure color borrowed from the spectrum in the piece of work on the catalogue's cover; a ballpoint-pen blue that has been appropriated from Polke's pen drawings is used for the type and tiny layout maps are positioned near the captions to help the reader navigate the page.

¶09 These traces of considered minimalism tell a story about book design at the end of the millennium that supports Walker Art Center design director Andrew Blauvelt's theory that after the deconstructivist adventures of the 1990s there has been "a shift away from the simply complex towards a complex simplicity." "There are signs of different forms of design taking hold," Blauvelt wrote in an essay in EYE magazine last year, "projects and solutions that embrace reductive rather than additive working methods, explicit rather than implicit structures of organization, a preference for the literal over the ambiguous and where the ordinary and the quotidian . . . are sources of inspiration.

¶10 Michael Worthington's explanation of his design approach echoes just this: "I wanted to embrace the mundane," he says of his Uta Barth projects, "to refine a very limited number of design factors into a strategy that appears as if nothing much is going on, but on closer inspection has subtle relationships with the work and the idea of how we perceive change occurring over time."

¶11 AIGA's "50 Books/50 Covers" show acts as a microcosm—albeit a rarified one—for the larger arena of American book design. Trends in the treatment of type, image and form—glimpsed hazily through the windows of Barnes & Noble or amazon.com last year—are brought sharply into focus in the selections made by this jury. A curious fascination with book spines, for example, was evident in at least nine out of the 100 winning entries. Of particular note was Sagmeister Inc.'s innovative design solution for AMERICAN PHOTOGRAPHY 15, where a panoramic photograph of a quintessential American landscape reaches along the spine and the three edges of the annual. The image is sliced into 420 parts and printed as 1/8-inch bleeding frame on each of the 420 pages to mesmerizing effect as you flick through them. Some of the covers, such as that for ON BECOMING A NOVELIST, BEE SEASON and MADAME, play the postmodern game of either illustrating or photographically reproducing a book on a book cover, with simulated and real backbones of the books visually merging.

¶12 Marketing departments and booksellers can and do dictate their design preferences, and many attention-grabbing, clichéd visual tropes and gimmicks—including die cuts and embossed type—are perpetuated because of them. Some of the more tasteful and content-driven versions were picked by the jury: vellum jackets (HARD TO FORGET and NONZERO), specialty end papers and dividers (GOOD ENOUGH TO EAT), embossed type (SLACK JAW) and die cuts (EVERY OTHER SUNDAY and HOLY CLUES).

50 books. 50 covers.

context essay. | 02

¶13 One dominating trend in the paperback fiction world that thankfully didn't make it into the competition is the use of gold foil and now, increasingly, multicolored or shimmer-effect foil embossed type. A Danielle Steele novel ends up looking like some strange hybrid of a gilded manuscript and a cereal package. Perhaps we should blame Mr. Tinker, a critic for the NEW YORK TIMES, who, when speaking about the best designed trade books of 1940 at an AIGA book clinic, advised: "To get national sales you have to make an attractive package just as the breakfast-food manufacturer does."[4]

¶14 The fact that a significant proportion of books with luxury finishes, high production quality and lavish materials were picked by this year's jury is an indication of a more grassroots desire for tactility—a defiant gesture in the face of the inevitable onslaught of e-books. For even though we are living in an age of information overload and, increasingly, we receive our data and entertainment digitally—whether through PDAs, the Internet or e-books—the printed book still survives. The fact that $24 billion was spent on books in the U.S. last year shows that a technology invented in China in the 6th century isn't ready to be outmoded quite yet. In July 2000 the fourth Harry Potter book, published by Scholastic, was printed in an edition of 4 million, breaking all publishing records. Portable, accessible, cheap, tactile and user-friendly, books don't crash, and the only viruses they are subject to are the bookworms who read them. As Neil Gershenfeld, director of the MIT Media Laboratory's Things That Think consortium, has said, "If the book had been invented after the laptop, it would have been hailed as a great breakthrough." So while universal acceptance of the e-book is imminent, it will not completely preclude the printed book. What it does is to throw the role and relevance of the book and, by the same token, book design, into starker relief.

50 books. 50 covers.

context essay. | 02

¶15 SERGE LEBLON, a little book designed by Base, managed to provoke exactly this kind of examination. The designers have subverted the traditional structure of a book by turning it inside out, so that the white cloth-bound covers are found at the center of the volume, the exposed pages form the skin (sheathed in a white slip case for protection) and the stitching is revealed along one edge to form a fragile backbone. When David High of High Design saw it, he protested: "But it's not a book. It's a beautiful object or a game. A book should be a tool that conveys information."

¶16 Other jury members contended that the form of this "book" stems directly from the subject matter. The photographs are of the backs of peoples' heads and bodies, upsetting the normal photographic view of the human body, and Base's design decision to upset the normal view of a book can be seen to augment or intensify communication with the reader.

¶17 The book as a "tool" has a short life expectancy. Reference work such as encyclopedias, dictionaries, thesauruses and some children's books work very well when transmitted digitally, thanks to links and search functions. The book as "palpable and seductive experience," though, may stand a better chance of survival. For in addition to imparting information or stories, books are also artifacts that readers imbue with memories and emotions. They are smelled, eaten—who, in their infantile hunger for knowledge, hasn't attempted to consume a tome?—fondled, dog-eared, flicked or pored through, annotated, read aloud from, slept upon and loved. Books can be elements of interior design—bought by the yard for showroom suites, piled with calculated carelessness on coffee tables for WALLPAPER photo shoots or displayed like trophies to erudition and personal taste in our homes and workplaces. Books have a physicality that lingers in the memory often longer than the content. The fact that books are getting bigger—witness Helmut Newton's SUMO book, weighing in at 66 pounds and measuring 20 by 27-1/2-inches—more tactile and more intelligent is no coincidence. They are evolving into an elite subspecies of book—the "printed" book—and while they are still around, AIGA will continue to celebrate 100 of them every year.

50 books. 50 covers.

context essay. | 02

50 books. 50 covers.

context essay. | 02

50 books. 50 covers.

context essay. | 02

50 BOOKS.50 COVERS. CONTEXT ESSAY 02 / **left page** Exhibition view of AIGA's "50 Books/50 Covers of 1999," designed by studio blue. Photograph © Jennifer Krogh.

50 books. 50 covers.

eric madsen, chair. | juror 01

n 01

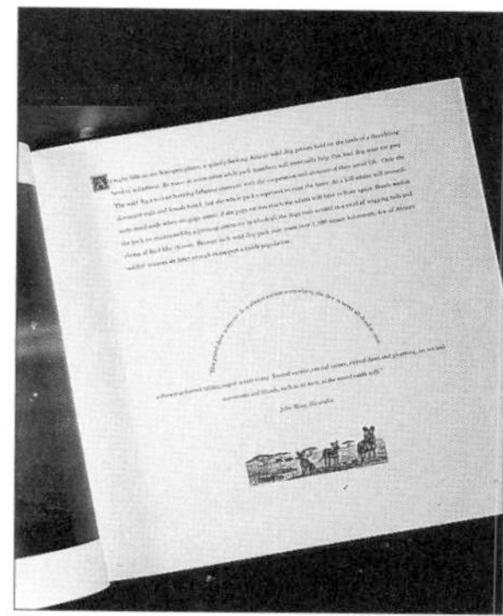

n 02

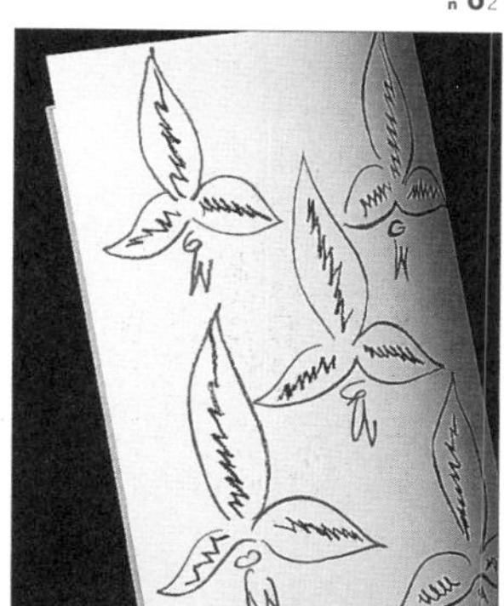

n 03

n 01, 02 and 04 Details from Wildlife as Canon Sees it (Book 2) for Canon, 1997.

n 04

n 05

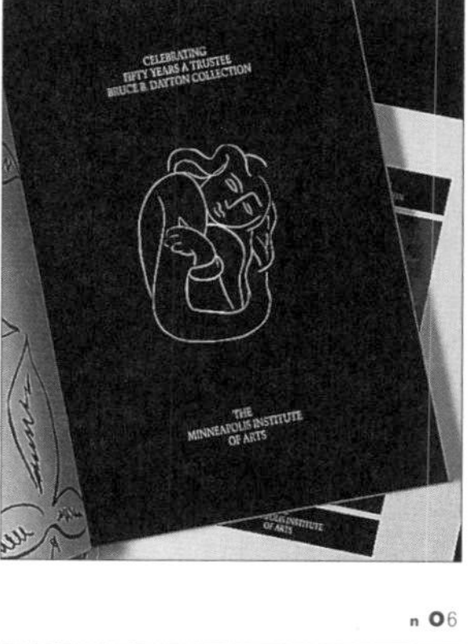

n 06

n 07

03, 06 and 07 Details from Celebrating Fifty Years A Trustee: Bruce B. Dayton Collection for Minneapolis Institute of Arts, 1992. 05 Eric Madsen.

01 50 BOOKS. 50 COVERS. ERIC MADSEN / Eric Madsen is president of the Office of Eric Madsen, a full-service graphic design firm located in Minneapolis. The firm specializes in all aspects of corporate identity and brand development, marketing and capability materials, magazines and book design for clients in the United States, Europe and Japan. Madsen's work has been recognized nationally and internationally by such organizations and publications as AIGA, Applied Arts (Canada), the Society of Typographic Arts, the Society of Publication Designers, Communication Arts, Idea (Japan), Graphis, Print and the Art Directors Clubs of New York, Dallas, Houston, Los Angeles and Minneapolis. Madsen currently serves on AIGA's national board of directors and on the board of trustees of the College of Visual Arts, St. Paul. He is a past vice president and founding board member of AIGA's Minnesota chapter and has served as chairman of the organization's national nominating committee. Madsen has also been a board member of the Minnesota Center for Book Arts.

50 books. 50 covers.

david saylor. | juror 02

02 50 BOOKS.50 COVERS. DAVID SAYLOR / David Saylor's first job in New York was for Lettering Directions, a photo-lettering type house. After working in the production and manufacturing departments at Marcel Dekker, Random House and Farrar, Straus and Giroux, he studied design at Parsons and switched careers in 1987. He has since worked as an art director for HarperCollins Publishers, Ticknor and Fields Books for Young Readers and Houghton Mifflin Children's Books. Saylor is currently creative director for the Book Group at Scholastic Inc., where he is responsible for the art and design of trade hardcover and paperback book publishing. As it turned out, his background in history and English at Pomona College served as grounding for all his work in publishing. In 1999, Saylor received the LMP Award honoring excellence in graphic design for his work in children's books.

n 01

n 02

n 03

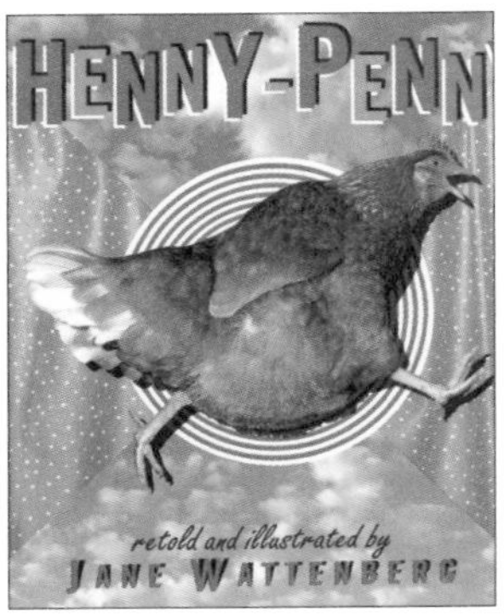

n 04

n 05

n 06

n 07

n 08

n 01, 02, 05 and 07 Details from Harlem, illustrated by Christopher Myers for Scholastic, 1997. 03 David Saylor. 04 Cover from Henny-Penny, illustrated by Jane Wattenberg for Scholastic, 2000.

06 Cover from Harry Potter and the Prisoner of Azkaban, illustrated by Mary GrandPré for Scholastic, 1999. 08 Cover from Harry Potter and the Chamber of Secrets, illustrated by Mary GrandPré for Scholastic, 1999.

50 books. 50 covers.

david high. | juror 03

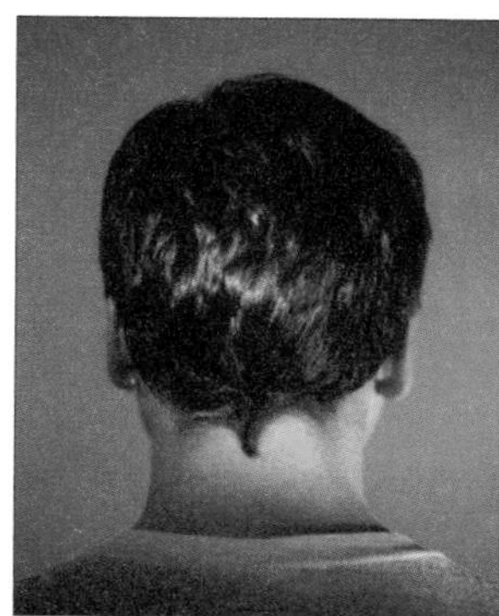

n O1

n O2

n O1 David High. Photograph © Ralph C. Del Pozzo. O2-O4 Details from a trade show booth created to publicize ETV's Style network, 1998-99.

n O3

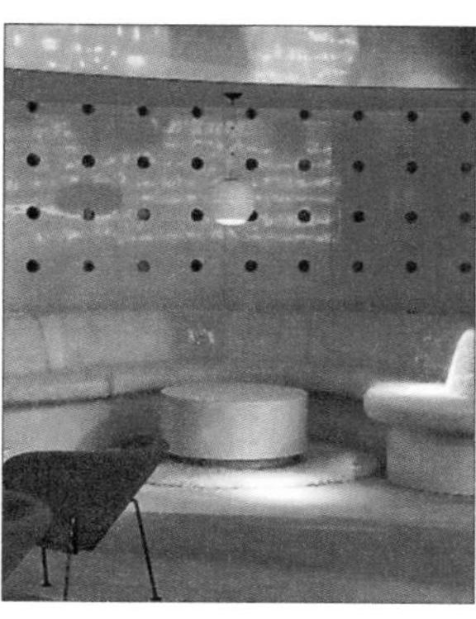

n O4

n O5

O5 David High's hand. Photograph © Ralph C. Del Pozzo. O6 Cover for The House of Sleep for Vintage, 1999. O7 Cover for The Confirmation for Knopf, 2000.

n O6

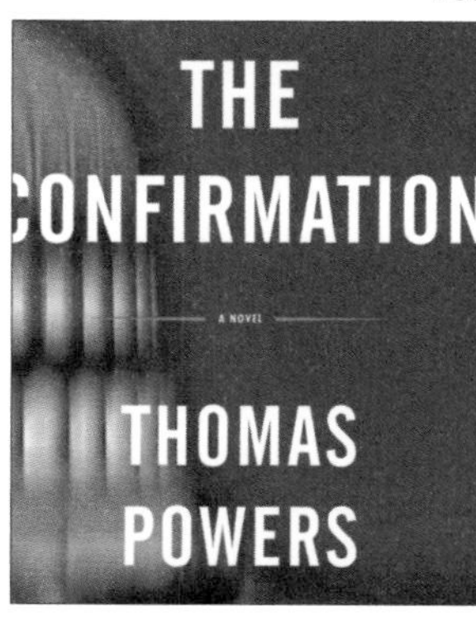

n O7

O3 50 BOOKS. 50 COVERS. DAVID HIGH / A native of Miami, David High has been designing for most of his life. While earning his BFA, High art directed two monthly magazines, which taught him about the intricacies of directing photo shoots as well as the perilous relationship between designer and typesetter (pre-Mac). Career limitations and constant sunburn drove him to New York, where he freelanced for numerous design firms before establishing iT design with a partner. In 1993, High ventured on his own as High Design and in 1998 joined forces with his life partner, photographer and artist Ralph Del Pozzo.

High's work has been featured in the AIGA annual, I.D. magazine, Type Directors Club, Broadcast Design Association, Print, How, Step-By-Step Electronic Design and Step-By-Step Japan. With over 100 book jackets designed a year, High Design's publishing clients are ever increasing. The studio also works in the entertainment industry and is responsible for launching the looks of MSNBC, USA/Sci-Fi and, most recently, ETV's Style network.

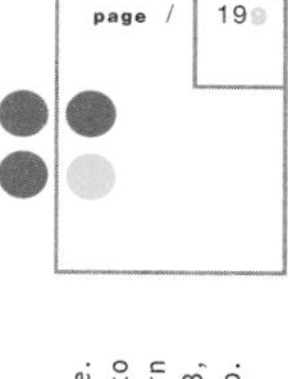

n 01

n 02

50 books. 50 covers.

roderick stinehour. | juror 04

n 03

n 01 and 03 Details from Iso Papo: Drawings & Watercolors for the Boston Public Library, 2000.
02, 04 and 06 Roderick Stinehour outside the Stinehour Press in Lunenburg, Vermont.

n 04

n 05

05 and 07 Details from Printing a Book at Verona in 1622 for Fondation Custodia, 1993.

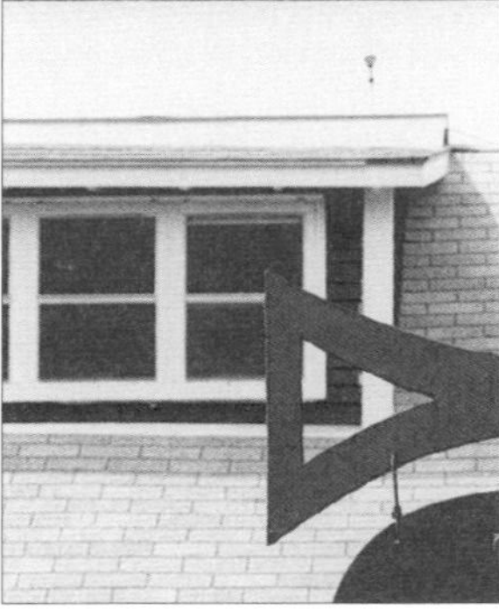

n 06

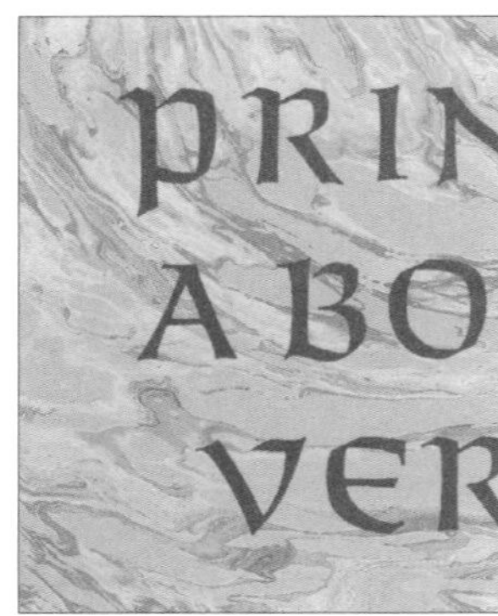

n 07

04 50 BOOKS. 50 COVERS. RODERICK STINEHOUR / Roderick (Rocky) Stinehour studied design and printmaking with Ray Nash at Dartmouth College. After graduation in 1950, he established the Stinehour Press in Lunenburg, Vermont, where he soon earned an international reputation in book design and in the printing of scholarly books for publishers in the arts and humanities. In 1981, Stinehour was awarded an honorary degree at Dartmouth for his accomplishments. He has also been presented with the Goudy Award by the Rochester Institute of Technology and the Laureate Award by the American Printing Historical Society. Stinehour is a fellow of the American Academy of Arts and Sciences and is currently involved with a book arts program he established at Dartmouth College in 1989.

50 books. 50 covers.

cheryl towler weese. | juror 05

n 01

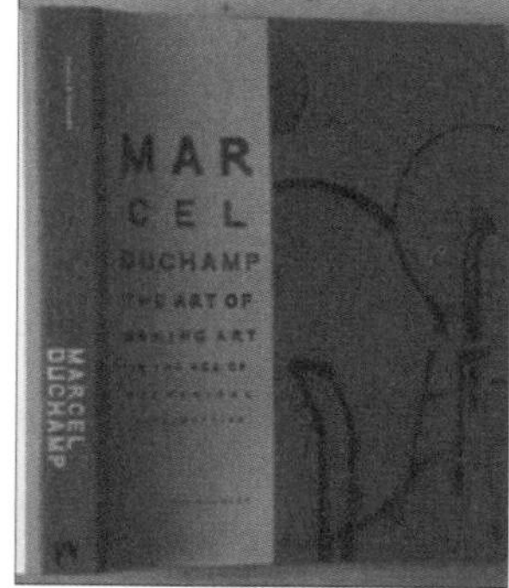

n 02

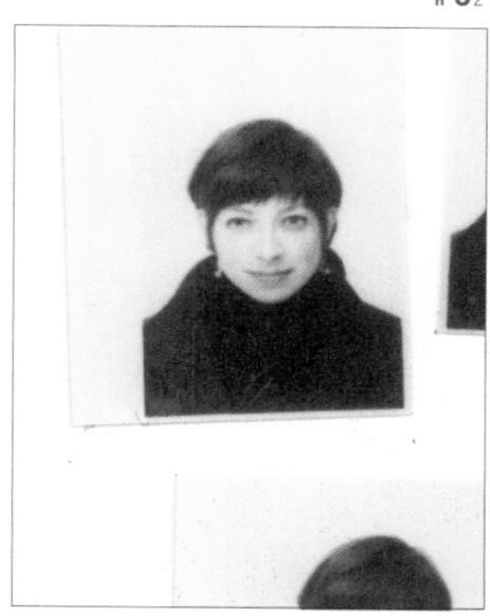

n 03

n 04

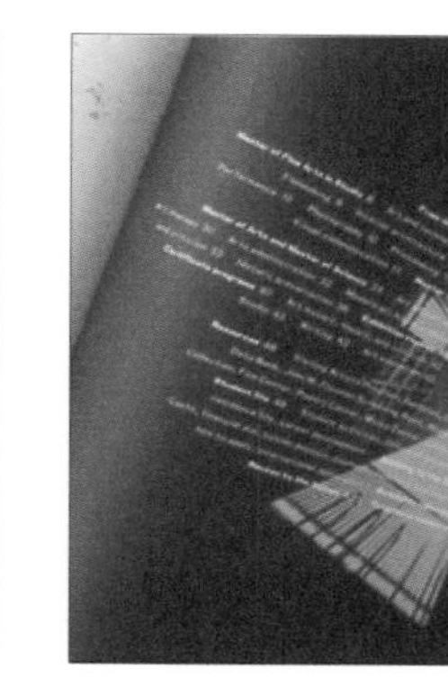

n 05

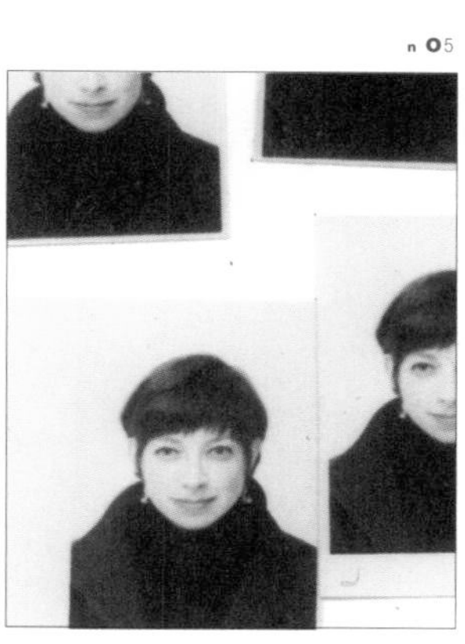

n 06

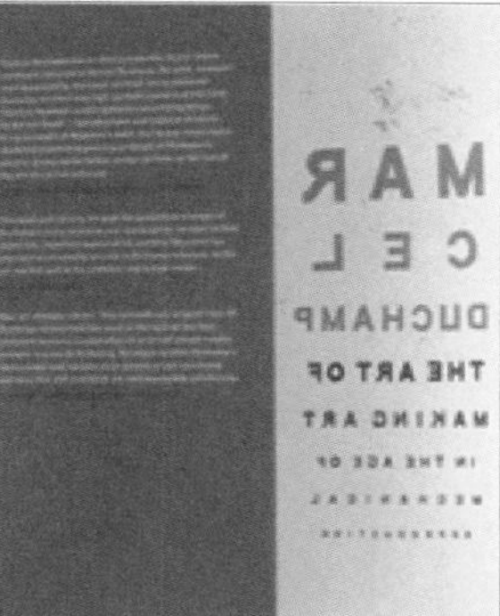

n 07

n 01 and 04 Details from Regarding Beauty catalogue for Hirschhorn Museum, 1999. 02 and 07 Details from the front and back cover of Marcel Duchamp: The Art of Making Art in the Age of Mechanical Reproduction for Ludion Press and Harry N. Abrams, 1999.

03 and 06 Cheryl Towler Weese. 05 Detail from view book for School of the Art Institute of Chicago, 1998.

05 50 BOOKS. 50 COVERS. CHERYL TOWLER WEESE / Cheryl Towler Weese—along with partner Kathy Fredrickson—runs studio blue, a firm that develops, designs and produces diverse forms of visual communication, including books, environmental design, websites and a range of printed matter. The studio works with museums, publishers, universities and other institutions, focusing on projects that involve close collaboration between client and designer and afford the opportunity to develop content and innovative ways of communicating with the public. The work of studio blue has been recognized by AIGA as well as the American Center for Design, the American Association of Museums, the Art Library Society, the Stiftung Buchkunst, the Carl Hertzog Foundation and Print. Towler Weese received her BA from Wesleyan University and her MFA from Yale.

06 50 BOOKS. 50 COVERS. MARY MENDELL / Mary Mendell has been the design and production manager at Duke University Press for the past 15 years and is a regular participant in the book shows and other design activities of the American Association of University Presses. Mendell's career in publishing began in 1971, when she was hired for an entry-level position in the marketing department at Beacon Press in Boston. Some months later she was dispatched to Beacon's design and production department, where she learned that books are designed and discovered the existence of typefaces and the basics of production. Mendell's education in typography and book design continued while working as a textbook designer at Houghton Mifflin. During this period, Mendell saw an exhibit of university press books and was attracted to them, both for their content and the care with which they were designed and produced. In 1975, she went to work as design and production manager for the University of Massachusetts Press in Amherst, where she remained until moving to North Carolina in 1984.

n 01

5 TERMINAL RESISTANCE/ CYBORG ACCEPTANCE

n 02

The Story of a Dance

Deborah Hay

n 03

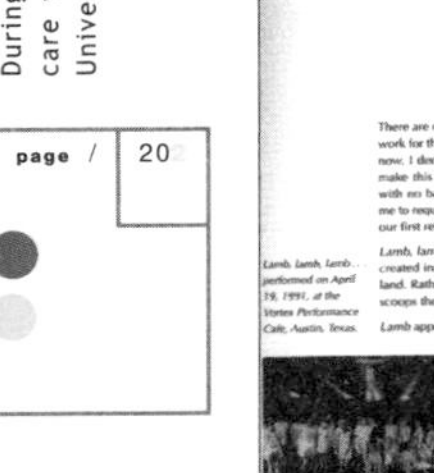

Lamb at the Altar / the story of a dance

n 04

n 05

n 06

n 07

50 books. 50 covers.

mary mendell. | juror 06

n 01 Detail from cover of HER HUSBAND for Duke University Press, 2000. 02 and 06 Details from interior and cover of TERMINAL IDENTITY: THE VIRTUAL SUBJECT IN POSTMODERN SCIENCE FICTION for Duke University Press, 1993.

03 and 04 Details from cover and interior of LAMB AT THE ALTAR: THE STORY OF A DANCE for Duke University Press, 1994. 05 Mary Mendell. 07 Detail from cover of LASZLO MOHOLY-NAGY: BIOGRAPHICAL WRITINGS for Duke University Press, 1995.

50 books. 50 covers.

lucille tenazas. | juror 07

n 01

n 02

n 03

n 01 and 02 Details from a postcard announcing architecture lecture series for the AIGA and SFMOMA, 1998. 03 and 07 Details from a poster for California College of Arts and Craft graduate program, 1999.

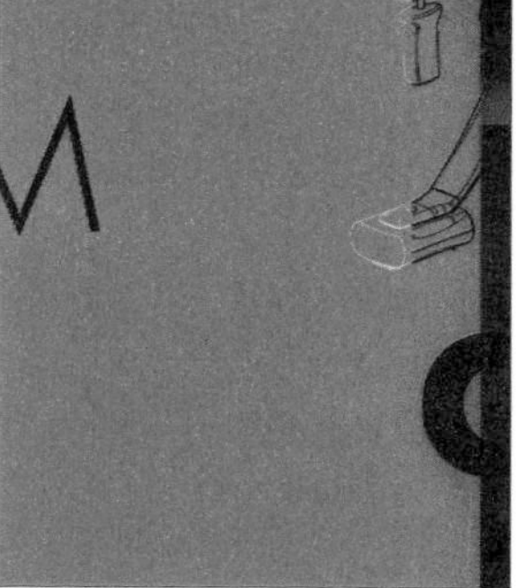

n 04

n 05

n 06

n 07

04 and 06 Details from a change of address card for the Moto Development Group, 1998. 05 Lucille Tenazas.

07 50 BOOKS. 50 COVERS. LUCILLE TENAZAS / Lucille Tenazas is principal of Tenazas Design, a multidisciplinary communications design firm in San Francisco that reflects an interest in the complexity of language and the overlapping relationship of meaning, form and content. Tenazas Design's clients represent a wide range of public, nonprofit and private institutions, including Rizzoli International, the Stanford University Art Museum, Southwest Parks and Monuments and the National Endowment for the Arts, as well as several design and architecture firms. Raised in Manila, the Philippines, Tenazas studied at the California College of Arts and Crafts (CCAC) and received her MFA from Cranbrook Academy of Art. She is currently the chair of the newly established MFA program in design at CCAC and is responsible for shaping its three-pronged curriculum in the areas of form-giving, teaching and leadership. Tenazas is active in AIGA and has served for seven years on the board of the San Francisco chapter. From 1996 to 1998, she also served as president of AIGA's National Board—the first presidential appointment made outside of New York in the organization's 80-year history.

01 50 BOOKS.50 COVERS. ATTENTION'S LOOP: A SCULPTOR'S REVERIE ON THE COEXISTENCE OF SUBSTANCE AND SPIRIT / The biggest challenge was having to pair conceptual text with a very specific visual "story." I decided to use changes in scale as a way to relate the text to the photographs.

01

DESIGN FIRM	Harry N. Abrams, Inc., New York, NY	PRINTER	Dai Nippon
DESIGNER	Judith Hudson	PAPER	Shiraoi Matte 157 gram
PHOTOGRAPHER	Katherine Wetzel	AUTHOR	Elizabeth King
TRIM SIZE	7 3/4 x 10 inches	PUBLISHER	Harry N. Abrams, Inc.
PAGES	88		
TYPEFACE	Gill Sans		

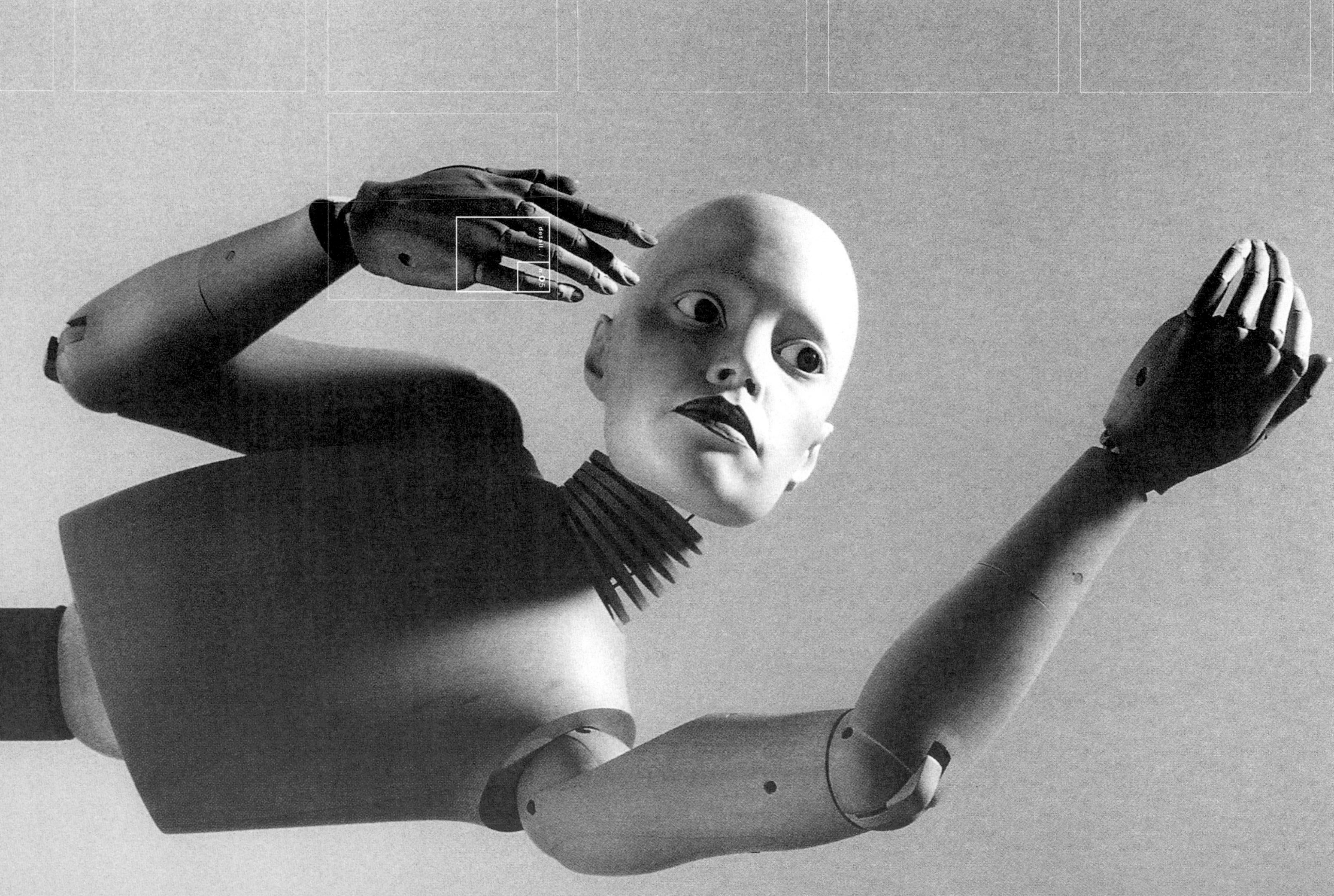

design firm. harry n. abrams, inc.

50 books. 50 covers. | NO. 01

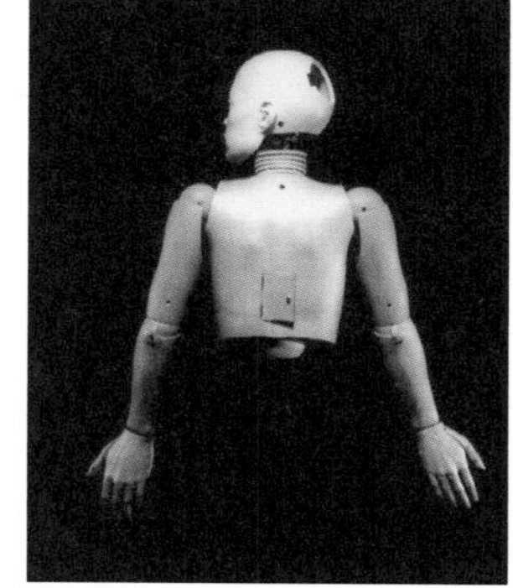

detail O1

ATTENTION'S LOOP

detail O2

detail O3

design firm. harry n. abrams, inc.

50 books. 50 covers. | NO. 01

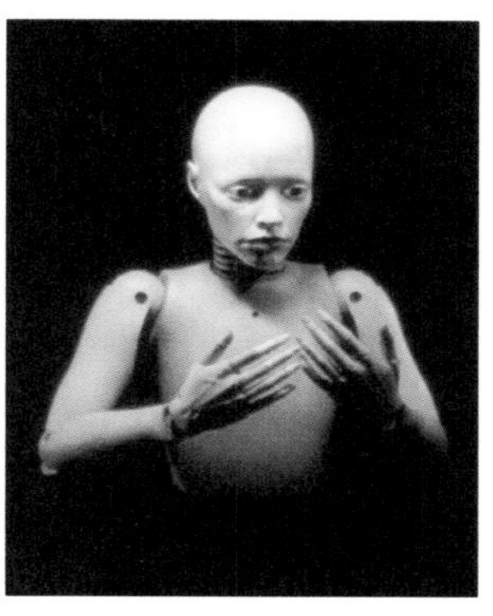

detail O4

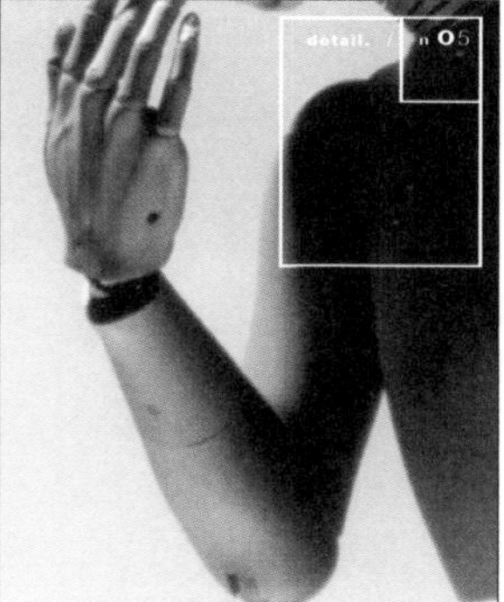

detail O5

design firm. harry n. abrams, inc.

50 books. 50 covers. | NO. 01

Bridge

One may dream
sensations. The
able to push or
The sensation o
of pressure. The
unable to take a
sensations of be
thing, perhaps s
of control, like a

detail O6

detail O7

02 50 BOOKS.50 COVERS. PETER HALLEY: MAINTAIN SPEED / Peter Halley is an artist, writer, publisher and lecturer. To grasp the multiplicity of his production, we began with 1,600 images and edited these down to 550 images, which we then assembled into multiple, but related, stories. In tackling this process, we took our cue from Halley, whose own raw materials consist of conduits, cells and links. We provided a kind of compass in the form of an information bar that runs along the bottom of each page and facilitates linkages within and outside of the book and sparks interpretation by presenting views of Halley's paintings in different contexts, quotations, documentation of events and details about the plates.

page / 20

02

DESIGN FIRM	COMA, Brooklyn, NY, and Amsterdam, The Netherlands
ART DIRECTORS	Cornelia Blatter, Marcel Hermans
TRIM SIZE	8 1/2 x 10 1/4 inches
PAGES	228
TYPEFACE	The Sans
PRINTER	Veenman Drukkers
PAPER	Libra Matte 150 gram, Pop Five Pearlescent 120 gram, Canson Transparant 95 gram
PUBLISHER	Distributed Art Publishers

I decided to take the fact of geometry's omnipresence in the social landscape as a given. 1988

design firm. coma

50 books. 50 covers. | NO. 02

peterhalley
maintain speed

detail O1

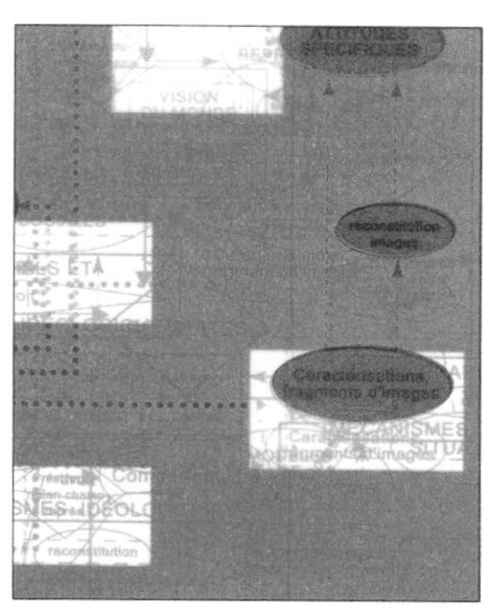

detail O2

design firm. coma

50 books. 50 covers. | NO. 02

detail O3

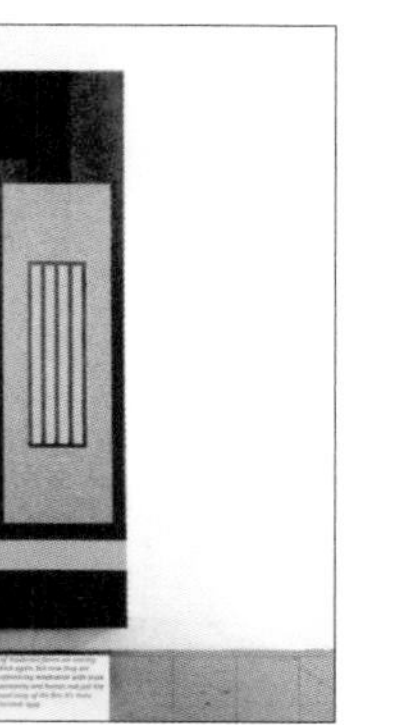

detail O4

detail O5

design firm. coma

50 books. 50 covers. | NO. 02

detail O6

detail O7

03 50 BOOKS.50 COVERS. WALKER EVANS / There was the classic and timeless challenge of convincing a non-visual, traditional publisher that biography illustrations are not limited to a signature of photographs on coated paper collected and inserted mid-book. This is a book of words; pictures are secondary but important. To get maximum quality from halftones and one black on uncoated paper, we worked with the pre-press house and did some tests. Best results came from a modest screen of 150 percent and with extremely "open negatives."

03

DESIGN FIRM	John Hill, Bethany, CT
ART DIRECTOR	John Hill
ILLUSTRATOR	Jane Sargeant
TRIM SIZE	6 1/2 x 9 1/8 inches
PAGES	656
TYPEFACES	Adobe Caslon, Big Caslon, Italics Caslon 40
PRINTER	R.R. Donnelley
JACKET PRINTER	Coral Graphics
AUTHOR	James R. Mellow
PUBLISHER	Basic Books, Perseus Books Group

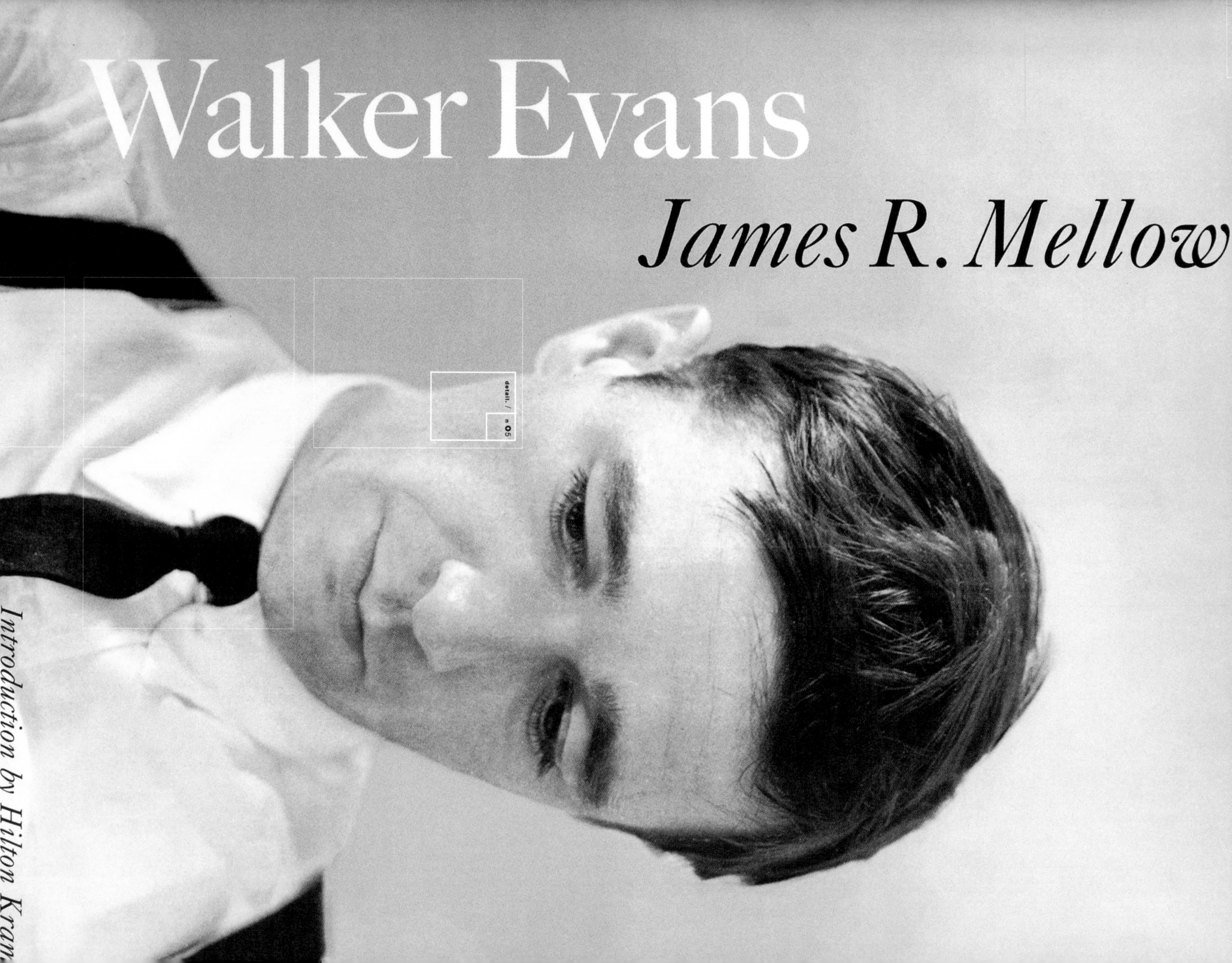

design firm. john hill

50 books. 50 covers. | NO. 03

Walker Evans

Jam

detail O1

detail O2

design firm. john hill

50 books. 50 covers. | NO. 03

496 "My girl (section 2)"; WE to JES, "Sunday Evening;" [Au
WEA/MMA.
497 "But the *noise!* the *people!*"; Ibid.
497 "Well Gee Zuss: what a landscape"; WE to JES, "Wednes
20, 1947, MMA.
497 "Does anybody know why tourists are so repulsive?"; Ibid.
497 "Well I swan and great Scott"; WE to JES, "Thursday" A
WEA/MMA.
498 "So I looked at a poor but large Dali on the wall"; Ibid.
498 "...be sure oval silver links are in it"; Ibid.
499 "you gotta not feel so bad, please miss"; Ibid.
499 "But listen you got no business feeling"; WE to JES, "We
[August, n.d., 1947], WEA/MMA.
499 "in sin"; WE to JES, August 22, [1947], WEA/MMA.
499 "portrait hacking or something"; WE to JES, August 21, [
499 "She's a good egg and quite bright"; WE to JES, "Monday
9, [1947]; s/b perhaps September 8 or Tuesday, September
499 "It is of course spectacular"; WE to JES, August 21, [1947]
499 "quite good"; Ibid.
499–500 "Want to set down those memory quick sight sketches"; I
472 "I just lay (sic) in the sun"; WE to JES, August 22, 1947.
502 "For good reason, for at almost nine"; Ibid.

detail O3

detail O4

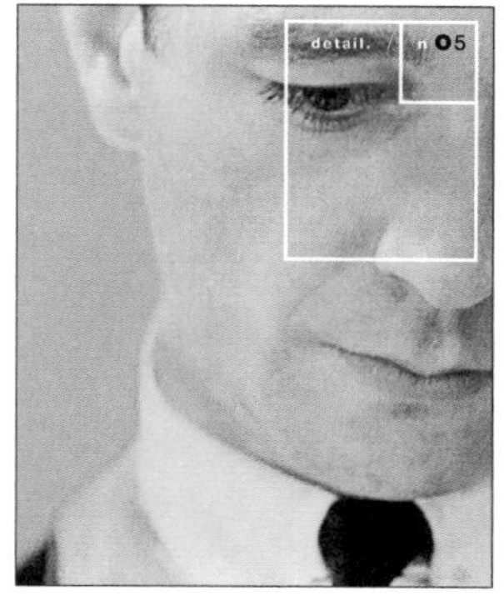

detail O5

design firm. john hill

50 books. 50 covers. | NO. 03

detail O6

detail O7

 SIGMAR POLKE: WORKS ON PAPER 1963–1974 / Sigmar Polke's boundless creativity, infectious good humor, far-reaching knowledge of art historical and contemporary issues and provocative combinations of text and image challenge our assumptions about what painting and drawing should be. Our design strategy was, above all, to highlight the drawings, their subject matter and their materiality. We wanted readers to see the drawings first before turning to the book's details or character. By developing a classic layout, choosing bright white uncoated paper and silhouetting individual works of art we kept our design in the background, allowing Polke's imagination and exuberance to come to the fore.

page / 21

04

DESIGN FIRM COMA, New York, NY, and Amsterdam, The Netherlands
ART DIRECTORS Cornelia Blatter, Marcel Hermans
TRIM SIZE 8 3/8 x 10 3/8 inches
PAGES 200
TYPEFACE News Gothic
PRINTER Stamperia Valdonega
PAPER Biancoflash 140 gram
AUTHORS Margit Rowell, Michael Semff, Bice Curiger
PUBLISHER The Museum of Modern Art

detail. / n 08

Giess einen auf die Lampe

2 *B-Man • B-Mann.* 1963.
Poster paint, 38 15/16 x 29 5/16" (99 x 74.5 cm)

design firm. coma

50 books. 50 covers. | NO. 04

design firm. coma

50 books. 50 covers. | NO. 04

design firm. coma

50 books. 50 covers. | NO. 04

detail O1

detail O2

detail O3

detail O4

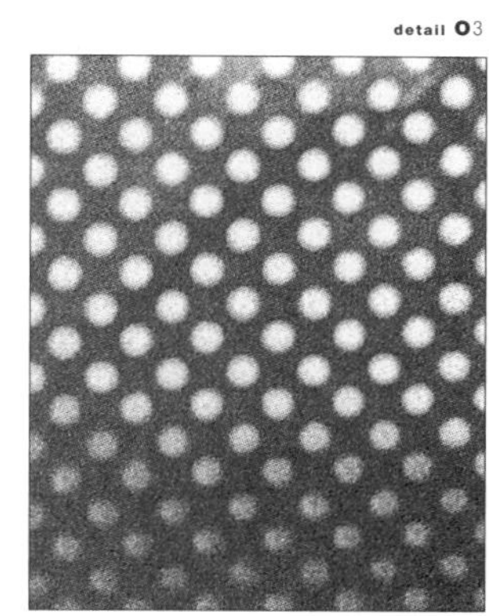

detail O5

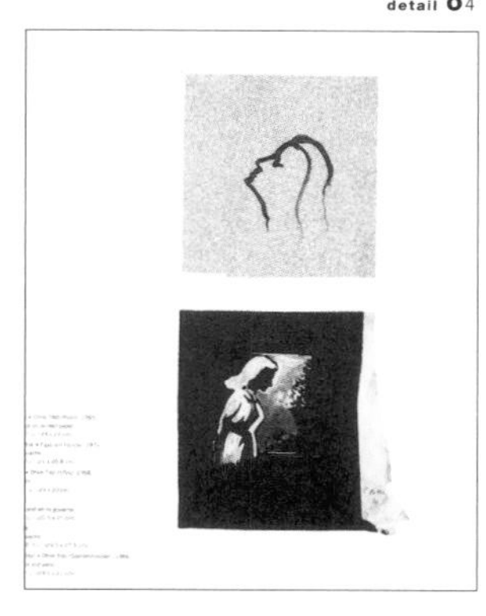

detail O6

detail O7

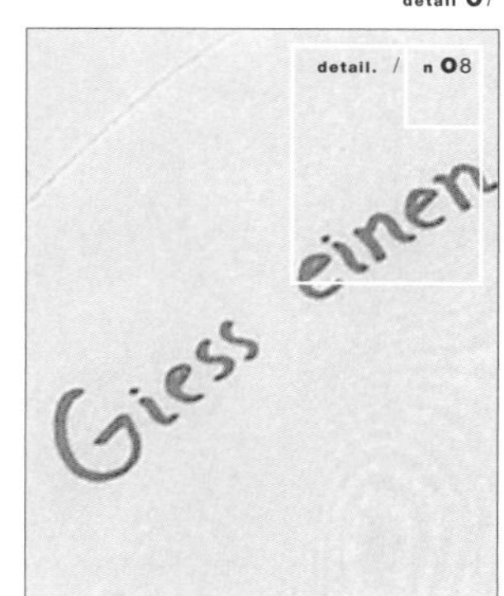

detail O8

05 50 BOOKS.50 COVERS. RAY JOHNSON: CORRESPONDENCES / Ray Johnson maneuvered around traditional distribution systems through his invention of mail art, making work that resists categorization and often plays off previous pieces and miscommunications. I wanted to "write" with Johnson, so I used some of his hand-drawn elements typographically; a series of tiny bunny heads indicate the end of an essay, while three dots on a line separate sections in the bibliography and checklist. I also used a monospaced version of The Sans to indicate Johnson's quotes throughout the book that refer to his type-written flyers.

DESIGN FIRM	Heavy Meta, New York, NY
CREATIVE DIRECTOR	Barbara Glauber
DESIGNERS	Barbara Glauber, Beverly Joel
TRIM SIZE	8 1/16 x 10 5/8 inches
PAGES	224
TYPEFACES	Various
PRINTER	Pollina
EDITORS	Donna De Salvo, Catherine Gudis
PUBLISHER	Wexner Center for the Arts, Flammarion

detail. / n 01

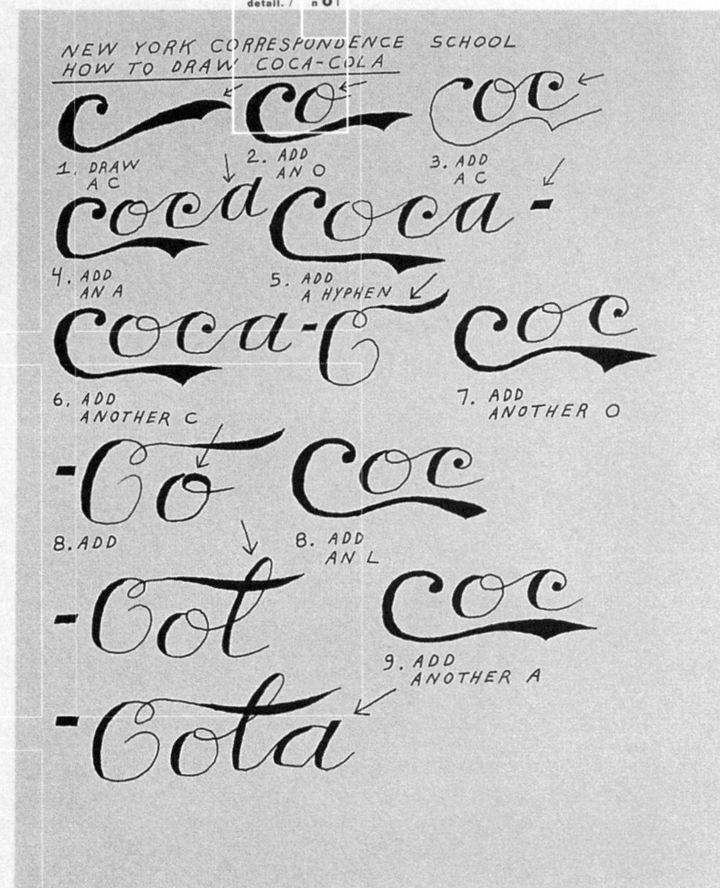

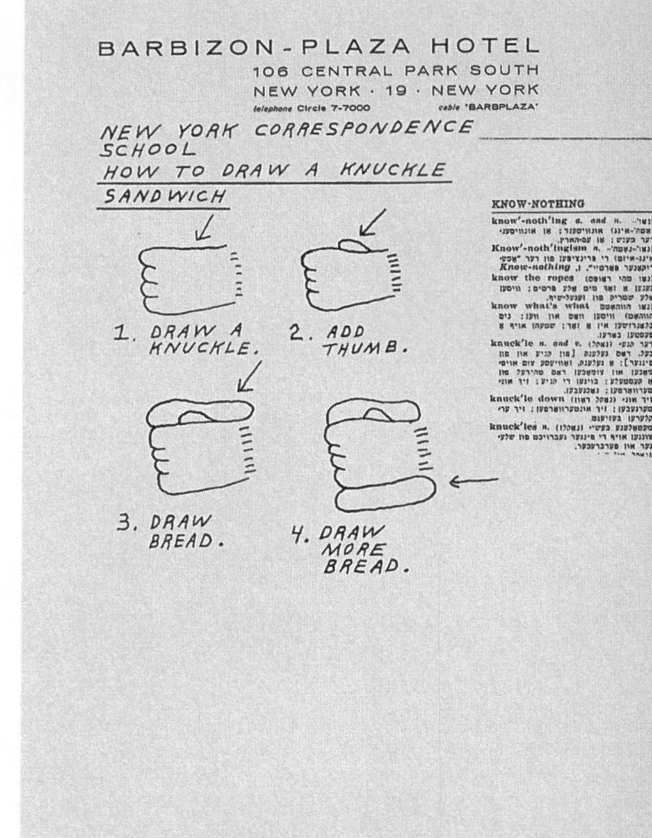

5. ADD A HYPHEN

BARBIZON-PLAZA HOTEL
106 CENTRAL PARK SOUTH
NEW YORK · 19 · NEW YORK
telephone Circle 7-7000
cable 'BARBPLAZA'
NEW YORK CORRESPONDENCE SCHOOL
HOW TO DRAW COCA-COLA
HOW TO DRAW A KNUCKLE SANDWICH
1. DRAW A KNUCKLE.
2. ADD THUMB.
3. DRAW BREAD.
4. DRAW MORE BREAD.
KNOW-NOTHING

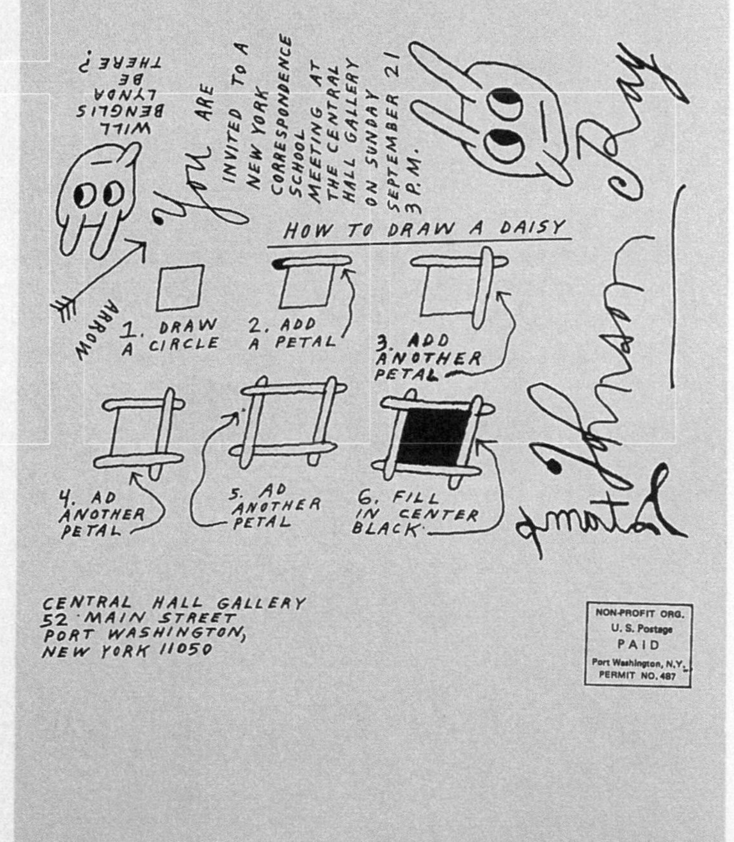

WILL BENGLIS LYNDA BE THERE?
YOU ARE INVITED TO A NEW YORK CORRESPONDENCE SCHOOL MEETING AT THE CENTRAL HALL GALLERY ON SUNDAY SEPTEMBER 21 3 P.M.
Ray Johnson
HOW TO DRAW A DAISY
ARROW
HOW TO DRAW A TENDER BUTTON
1. DRAW A CIRCLE
2. DRAW A CIRCLE WITHIN FIRST CIRCLE
3. DRAW VERY SMALL CIRCLE
4. DRAW ANOTHER SMALL CIRCLE
5. DRAW ANOTHER SMALL CIRCLE
6. DRAW ANOTHE SMALL CIRCLE
7. FILL IN BLACK
2. ADD A PETAL
3. ADD ANOTHER PETAL
4. AD ANOTHER PETAL
5. AD ANOTHER PETAL
6. FILL IN CENTER BLACK
CENTRAL HALL GALLERY
52 MAIN STREET
PORT WASHINGTON,
NEW YORK 11050
NON-PROFIT ORG.
U. S. Postage
PAID
Port Washington, N.Y.
PERMIT NO. 487

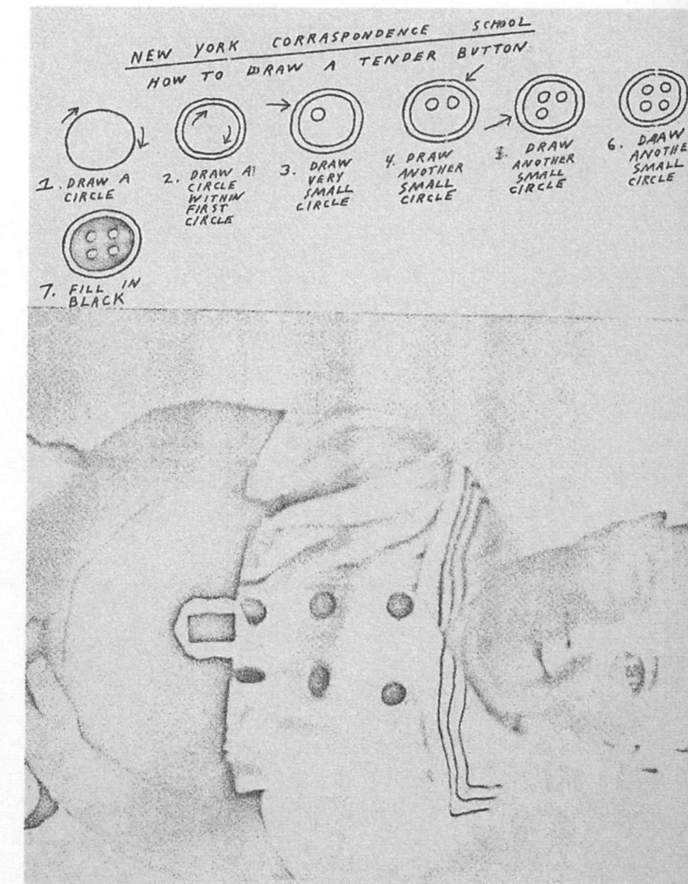

Mailings, ca. 1980s

design firm. heavy meta

50 books. 50 covers. | NO. 05

detail O1

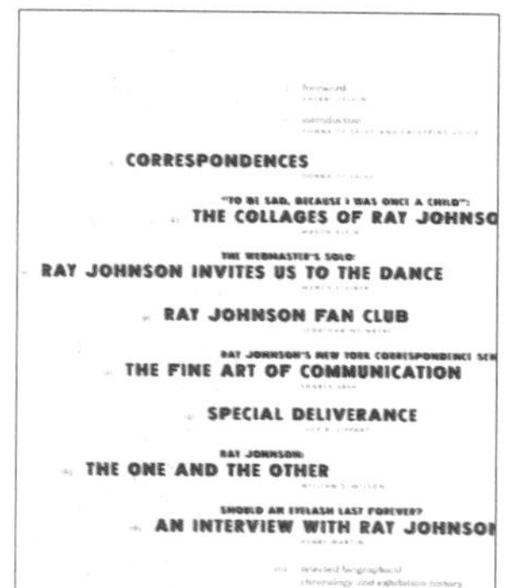

detail O2

design firm. heavy meta

50 books. 50 covers. | NO. 05

detail O3

detail O4

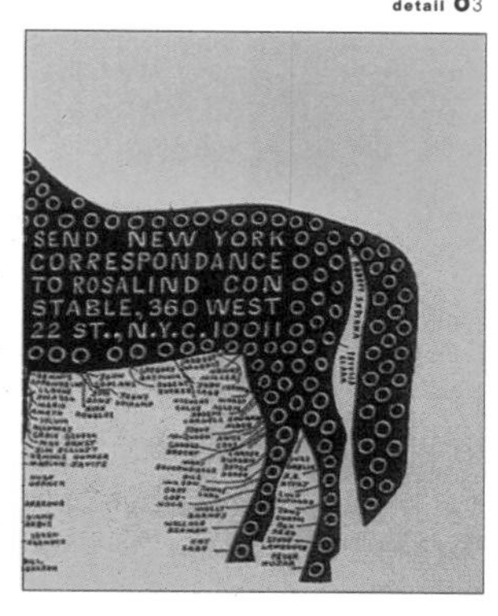

detail O5

design firm. heavy meta

50 books. 50 covers. | NO. 05

detail O6

detail O7

detail O8

06 50 BOOKS.50 COVERS. SERGE LEBLON / Our special challenge was to make a classic book with a twist. Our design solution was to question the structure of a book by turning it inside out.

06

DESIGN FIRM	Base, New York, NY
CREATIVE DIRECTOR/ DESIGNER/ PHOTOGRAPHER	Base
TRIM SIZE	8 1/4 x 9 5/6 inches
PAGES	68
TYPEFACES	Dot Matrix, Base Matrix
PRINTER	Salto
PUBLISHERS	Serge Leblon, Base

detail. /

design firm. base

50 books. 50 covers. | NO. 06

design firm. base

50 books. 50 covers. | NO. 06

design firm. base

50 books. 50 covers. | NO. 06

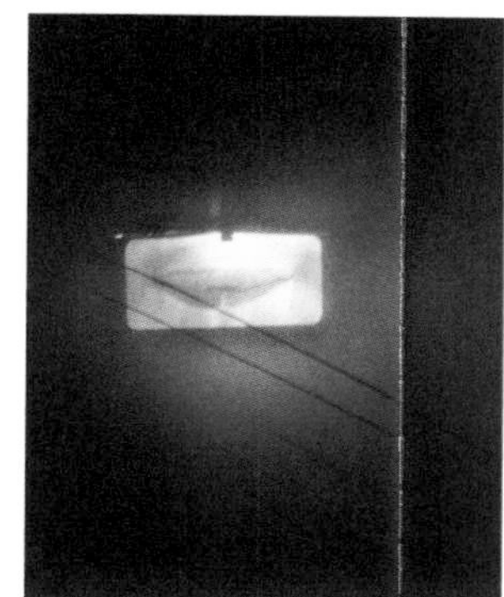

detail O1

detail O2

detail O3

detail O4

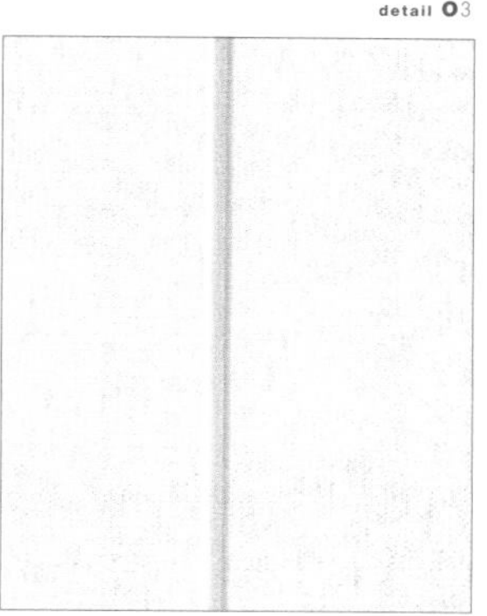

detail O5

!!ñÜ ä UÅ Ü Œ
ü ØÅÓ Œ \\\\\\\\\\\\
////////// Œ Â=Â=Â="= Îÿò
.104 ¤(c) Û,Ø ~~ Û/ /"
=JÛÅÏ Œ Â=Â=Â="= Î Å
YYÅÁ Œ ÂÂÅ " ¤ß J==d"
¤ ã jñ, Û Œ Å %.Œ Â
e SHGDG DSFHHD SDFGHÛ
gland Û,ü LL11 111111222222
= Îúí Ï (ÿ////// ã jÅ
o = Å¥

detail O6

detail O7

07 50 BOOKS.50 COVERS. ADULTERY / This book is a memoir and a cultural study, a literary exploration and a survivor's memoir. I used a very limited palette of typographic elements due to the book's trim size, and I wanted to avoid any ornamentation. This left type as the only design element. Adultery seemed to be such a French thing, so I ended up choosing the typeface Fournier. It is compact enough to be used in a small book, and its italic has a beautiful, crawling, slightly sick slant. To convey the idea of multiplicity, I repeated the book's title and part numbers several times.

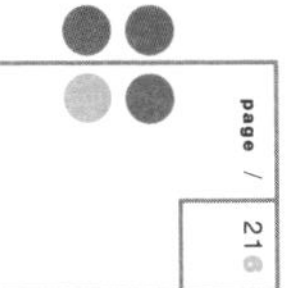

07

DESIGN FIRM	Beacon Press, Boston, MA
DESIGNER/ COMPOSITOR	Julia Sedykh
TRIM SIZE	4 1/2 x 7 inches
PAGES	176
TYPEFACE	Fournier
PRINTER	Maple-Vail
PAPER	Glatfelter Sebago 55 pound
JACKET DESIGNER	Paul Sahre
JACKET PRINTER	Coral Graphics
AUTHOR	Louise A. DeSalvo
PUBLISHER	Beacon Press

detail. / n 04

detail. / n 06

Adultery
Adultery
Adultery
Adultery
Adultery
Louise DeSalvo

design firm. beacon press

50 books. 50 covers. | NO. 07

One

detail 01

Unless you consciously (or unconsciously) want to jet-propel yourself into committing adultery, reading about it isn't such a good idea. Because reading about it, I can assure you, will almost certainly result in your thinking about doing it, and perhaps even in your doing it.

(Dante believed this too. For in the *Inferno* of his *Divine Comedy*, he recounts the story of the beginning of the adulterous affair between Paolo and Francesca. Francesca explains to Dante that one day, while she and Paolo are reading about Lancelot and Guinevere, their erotic desire becomes so uncontrollable that they drop the book and yield to impulse. Francesca explains: "He kissed my mouth all trembling: / A Galeotto was the book, and he who wrote it; / That day we read no further."

detail 02

design firm. beacon press

50 books. 50 covers. | NO. 07

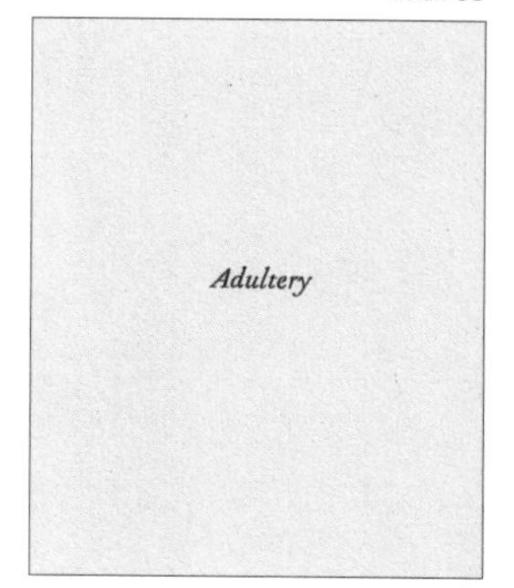

detail 03

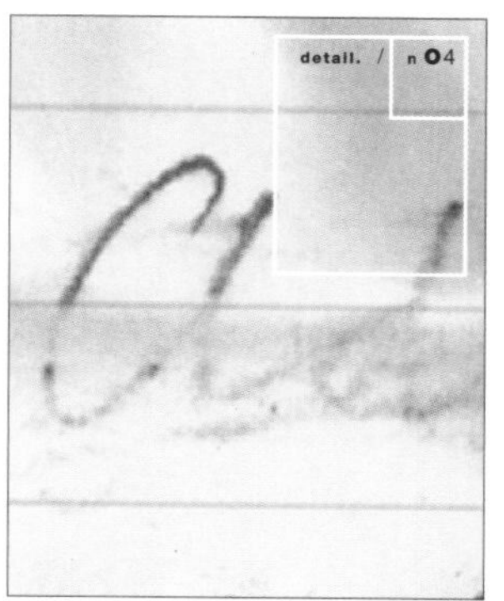

detail 04

n your thinking abou
your doing it.
(Dante believed th
Divine Comedy, he re
ning of the adulterou
Francesca. Francesca
while she and Paolo a
Guinevere, their erot

detail 05

design firm. beacon press

50 books. 50 covers. | NO. 07

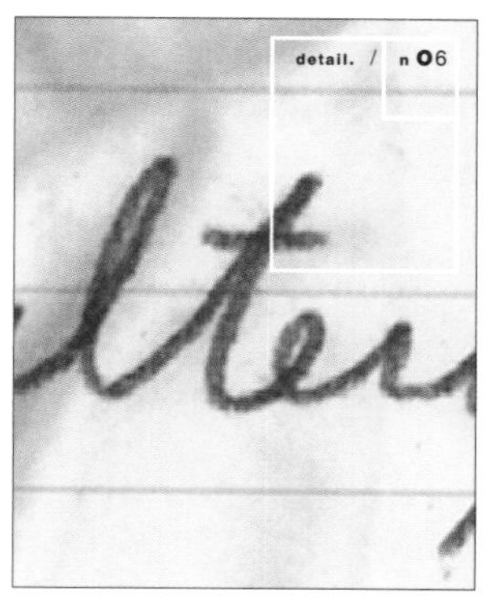

detail 06

Unless you con
to jet-propel your
ing about it isn't s
about it, I can ass
in your thinking a

detail 07

08 50 BOOKS. 50 COVERS. GOOD ENOUGH TO EAT / This book was a personal cookbook given to the author's best friends. The writing, the recipes and the illustrations all had a personal meaning to the author and her friends. With care, collaboration and a lot of meals with the author, we were able to fuse them all together by the use of color, paper and differently designed sections of the book.

DESIGN FIRM	AdamsMorioka, Inc., Beverly Hills, CA
ART DIRECTORS	Sean Adams, Noreen Morioka
DESIGNER	Noreen Morioka
ILLUSTRATOR	Daniel Samakow
TRIM SIZE	7 1/4 x 11 inches
PAGES	124
PAPER	Appleton Utopia One Balanced White with special Japanese papers
ENDPAPERS	Japanese Washi papers
AUTHOR	Carol Doumani
PUBLISHER	Wave Publishing

detail. / no2

"A good meal ought to begin with hunger."

— FRENCH PROVERB

design firm. adamsmorioka, inc.

50 books. 50 covers. | NO. 08

My mother taught me to make this dish. I love her version, but sometimes I substitute brown rice for the traditional white rice, to give the stuffing a nutty flavor and texture. I also cut back on the amount of oil, which makes the *yalanchi* a little drier (not a bad thing) and lower in calories.

Makes about 150 *Yalanchi*

onions, **finely chopped**
3 cups cooked brown rice (about 1 cup uncooked)
½ cup vegetable oil
8 ounces tomato sauce, or pureed tomatoes
1 cup water
1 teaspoon salt
½ teaspoon pepper
½ teaspoon allspice
½ teaspoon ground cinnamon
Juice of one lemon (about 2 tablespoons)
1 bunch parsley, **finely chopped**
1 ounce (about ¼ cup) pine nuts (optional)
2 large jars (20-ounce) grape leaves packed in brine

detail O1

detail O2

1. Saute onions in oil until transparent. Add rice, tomato sauce, water, salt, pepper, allspice, cinnamon, and lemon juice. Coo[k] slowly, stirring occasionally, until most of the liquid is gone, about 20 minutes.

2. Remove from heat and stir in parsley and pine nuts, if desired.

3. Rinse the grape leaves and set aside any that are torn. Lay 12 leaves at a time flat on a counter with the leaf vein facing up. Put a tablespoon of the rice mixture onto the center of each leaf, and roll cigar style, tucking in the end as you roll. Continue until all of the whole leaves have been used.

4. Place tough or torn leaves on the bottom of a 2-quart stovetop casserole dish and arrange grape leaf rolls closely together aroun[d] the bottom, then layer until all grape leaf rolls are used. Place dish on top of the rolls to keep them from unrolling.

5. Pour enough boiling water over the rolls to barely cover (if you used puréed tomatoes instead of tomato sauce in the rice mixture, you can add a little more of the purée to the boiling water to give the *yalanchi* more flavor).

6. Cover the casserole and bring to a boil over medium heat. Reduce heat to low and simmer for approximately 1 hour. Whe[n] *yalanchi* are cooked through, pour more lemon juice over them an[d] cool completely.

7. Serve *yalanchi* at room temperature. They can be kept in the refrigerator 5 or 6 days. Unfortunately, they do not freeze well.

detail O3

design firm. adamsmorioka, inc.

50 books. 50 covers. | NO. 08

Wild Rice and Black Bean Salad

Makes 12 luncheon entrées

This is my favorite salad to serve at a luncheon. Not only can it be prepared ahead, but since it is served at room temperature, it can even be put on the platter and set out long before serving time. It is healthy, versatile, and somewhat unusual, a vegetarian dish that will satisfy even diehard sandwich-eaters.

1. In a large bowl, combine cooked black beans, wild rice, and brown rice.
2. Add pecans, dried cherries or raisins, mint, green onion, orange, roasted pepper, artichoke hearts, and water chestnuts.
3. In a small bowl, combine olive oil and orange juice, and add salt and pepper to taste. Pour dressing over salad mixture and toss thoroughly. Cover and refrigerate. Let stand at room temperature for two hours before serving.

detail O4

detail O5

design firm. adamsmorioka, inc.

50 books. 50 covers. | NO. 08

1. For the Pastry Shells: In a medium mixing bowl, combine flour, butter, salt, Parmesan cheese, and egg. With your hands, work the ingredients together until they form a dough. Turn the dough out onto a lightly floured surface and knead for a few seconds until it holds together nicely. Wrap the dough in plastic wrap and chill for one hour.

2. Preheat the oven to 450 degrees. Grease 36 miniature muffin cups.

3. Pinch off a piece of dough the size of a large hazelnut and roll in[to] a ball. With your thumb, press the ball into a miniature muffin cup, gently press the dough into the corners so it covers the sides and Do not let dough extend above the edge of the cup, as it will [make] tartlets more difficult to remove from the tin. Repeat procedu[re] remaining dough.

4. Bake pastry shells for 5 minutes. Reduce oven tempera[ture] to 400 degrees, and bake an additional 8 to 10 minutes. on a wire rack, then remove from the muffin tins, using tip of a sharp knife to carefully pry them out. (If you using the shells immediately, they can be frozen in an plastic bag and kept almost indefinitely.)

5. For the Filling: In a large skillet, break up the sa[usage] and cook over medium heat until no longer pink.

6. Stir in the salsa. Combine the cheeses, and reser[ve] ⅓ cup (about 1 ounce) for topping. Add remaining ⅔ cup (3 ounces) cheese and green chilies, and sim[mer] until the mixture thickens, about 5 minutes. Cool.

7. Preheat the oven to 350 degrees. Put 1 teaspoon the sausage mixture into each of the cooked pastry sprinkle with reserved cheeses, and bake until the mix hot and the cheese is melted, about 10 minutes.

detail O6

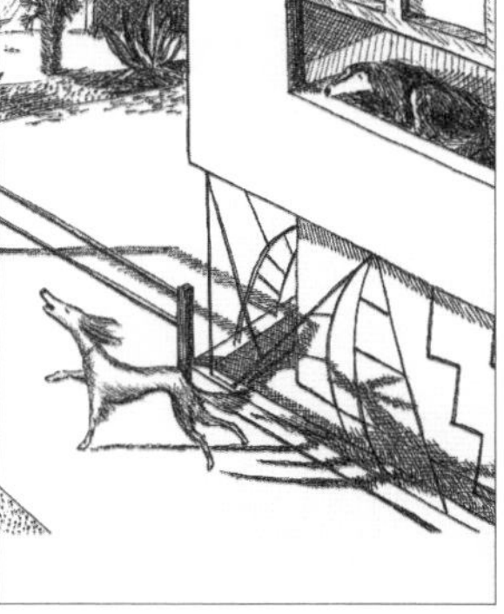

detail O7

09 50 BOOKS.50 COVERS. AMERICAN PHOTOGRAPHY 15 / We could not decide on a single image among all the photos in this book to use for the cover, so we ended up showing them all. The striped, almost abstract pattern on the cover features tightly compressed versions of all photographs in the book. By slicing an image into 420 parts and printing it as a bleeding frame on all pages, the book features a panoramic photograph of a quintessential American landscape all around the spine and edges of the book.

09

DESIGN FIRM	Sagmeister Inc., New York, NY
CREATIVE DIRECTOR	Stefan Sagmeister
DESIGNER	Hjalti Karlsson
PHOTOGRAPHER	Jury selected
TRIM SIZE	9 1/4 x 12 1/4 inches
PAGES	340
TYPEFACE	Syntax
PRINTER	Dai Nippon
PAPER	Biberist 135 gram
PUBLISHER	Amilus Inc.

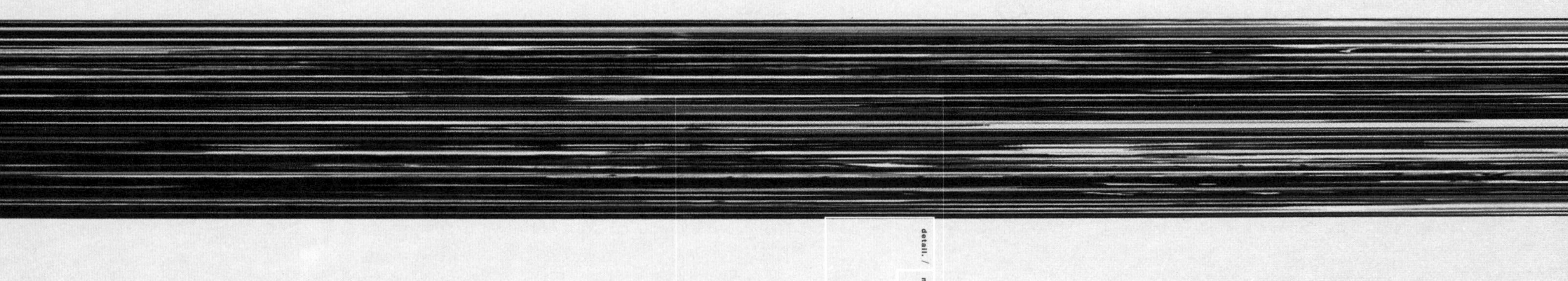

American Photography 15

detail. / n01

detail. / n 01

design firm. sagmeister inc.

50 books. 50 covers. | NO. 09

detail 01

detail 02

design firm. sagmeister inc.

50 books. 50 covers. | NO. 09

detail 03

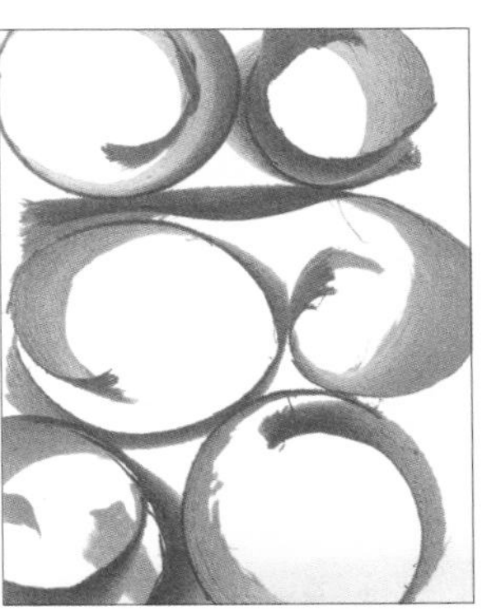

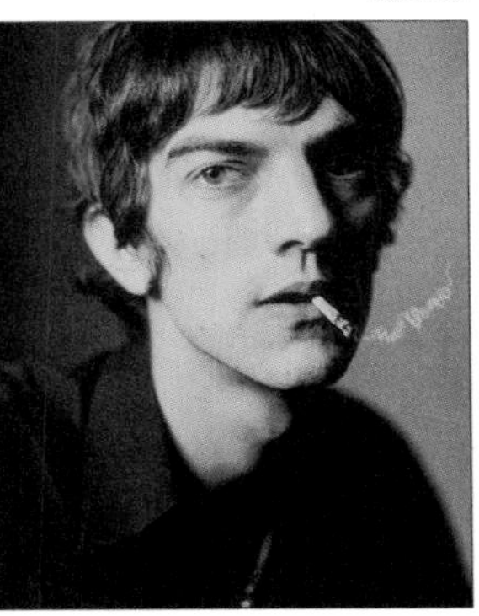

detail 04

detail 05

design firm. sagmeister inc.

50 books. 50 covers. | NO. 09

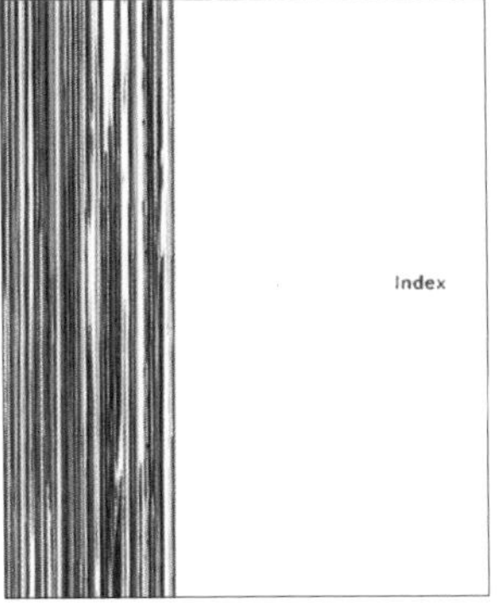

detail 06

detail 07

10 50 BOOKS.50 COVERS. SEARCHLIGHT: CONSCIOUSNESS AT THE MILLENNIUM / We wanted our design to reflect the book's content as much as possible. Consciousness is, of course, the most ubiquitous and elusive condition of existence. After reviewing much of the artwork in the show, we conducted our own visual experiments using materials that are normally "invisible." Combining plastic, acetate, tape and thread with type led to many of the book's techniques. In the reprint section, we worked with the idea of "similar differences." The typography changes subtly from page to page, column to column.

10

DESIGN FIRM	Appetite Engineers, San Francisco, CA
ART DIRECTOR	Martin Venezky
DESIGNERS	Martin Venezky, Geoff Kaplan
PHOTOGRAPHER	Cesar Rubio
TRIM SIZE	9 x 11 inches
PAGES	196
TYPEFACES	Folio, Century Schoolbook
PRINTER	Artegrafica
AUTHOR	Lawrence Rinder
PUBLISHERS	Thames & Hudson, CCAC Institute

detail. / n01

design firm. appetite engineers

50 books. 50 covers. | NO. 10

design firm. appetite engineers

50 books. 50 covers. | NO. 10

design firm. appetite engineers

50 books. 50 covers. | NO. 10

detail. / nO1

detail O1

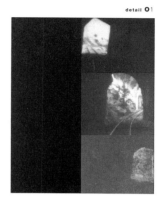

proust / douglas / edison:
"...something dark indeed..."

detail O2

detail O3

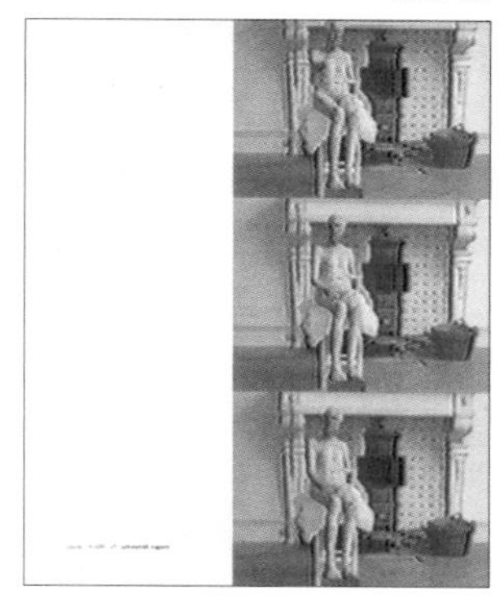

detail O4

detail O5

detail O6

Gilles Deleuze

detail O7

11 50 BOOKS.50 COVERS. LUIS GONZÁLEZ PALMA: POEMS OF SORROW / The main challenge was to ensure that the reproductions showed the integrity of Luis González Palma's original artwork, and were encased in something rich to convey his use of multimedia. We decided to use a rich, warm, matte coated paper and colors like red and umber. Our image sequencing flowed from full bleeds to crossovers to pages with white space, and we used elegant, unobtrusive text. Finally, the wrap-around dust jacket showcases the diptych image to maximum effect and the red ribbon is an element that the artist uses a lot in his work.

11

DESIGN FIRM	Arena Editions, San Francisco, CA
ART DIRECTOR/ DESIGNER	Elsa Kendall
PHOTOGRAPHER	Luis González Palma
TRIM SIZE	10 x 10 inches
PAGES	152
TYPEFACE	Adobe Caslon
PRINTER	EBS
PUBLISHER	Arena Editions

Y nosotros.
¿Hasta cuándo habremos de estar
¿Hasta cuándo habremos de sufrir este
Pájaros que vuelan por última vez somos.
Pájaros que vuelan en busca del olvido
y la sombra.
detail.
n 06

design firm. arena editions

50 books. 50 covers. | NO. 11

No hay espacio más ancho
que el dolor, / no hay universo
aquél que sangra.

Pablo Neruda

detail 01

detail 02

detail 03

design firm. arena editions

50 books. 50 covers. | NO. 11

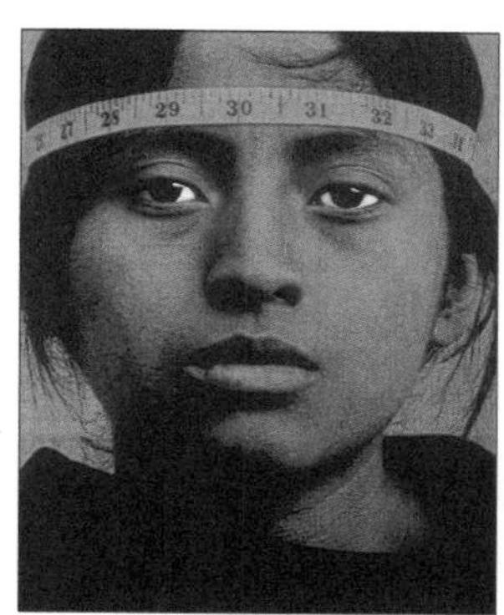

detail 04

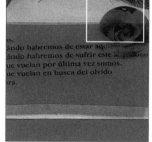

KODAK 5062

detail 05

design firm. arena editions

50 books. 50 covers. | NO. 11

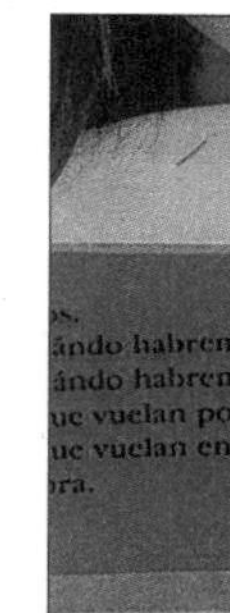
detail. / n 06
ándo habremos de estar aq
ándo habremos de sufrir este
ue vuelan por última vez somos.
ue vuelan en busca del olvido
ra.

detail 06

detail 07

12 50 BOOKS.50 COVERS. JUAN MUÑOZ / The artist's installations simulated streetscapes into which the audience was drawn to engage and interact with various scenes. Our challenge was to translate this movement into the flow of a book. We echoed the sequence of interactions with black-and-white images that slowly filtered into color, with its opposite counterpart in the second half of the book going from color to black and white. The text part, which separates the two image-parts of the book, works with the theatricality of the exhibitions.

12

DESIGN FIRM	Dia Center for the Arts, New York, NY
ART DIRECTOR	Karen Kelly
DESIGNER	Filiep Tacq
ILLUSTRATOR	Juan Muñoz
PHOTOGRAPHER	Various
TRIM SIZE	7 1/2 x 11 inches
PAGES	124
TYPEFACE	Bodoni
PRINTER	Ediciones El Viso
PAPER	Maco Matte 170 gram
AUTHOR	Lynne Cooke
PUBLISHER	Dia Center for the Arts

detail.

design firm. dia center for the arts

50 books. 50 covers. | NO. 12

design firm. dia center for the arts

50 books. 50 covers. | NO. 12

design firm. dia center for the arts

50 books. 50 covers. | NO. 12

Juan Muñoz

Text by Lynne Cooke

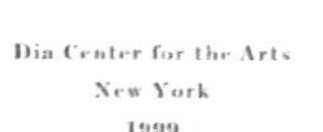
Dia Center for the Arts
New York
1999

detail 01

detail 02

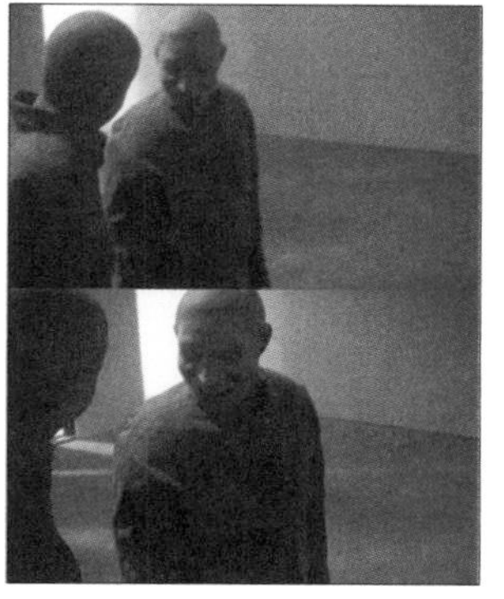

detail 03

detail 04

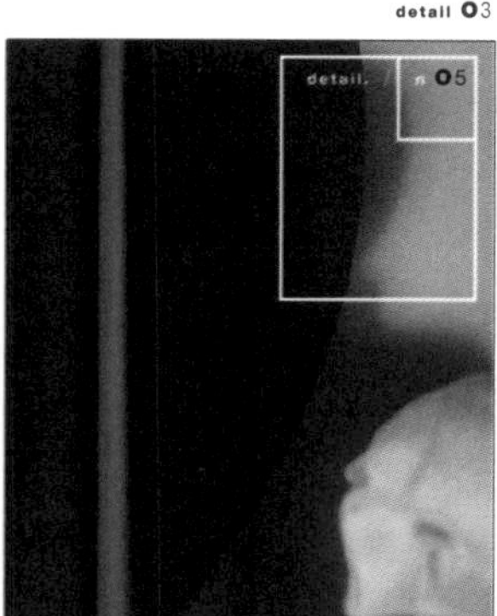

detail 05

detail 06

detail 07

detail 08

13 50 BOOKS.50 COVERS. VIENNESE TYPES: PHOTOGRAPHS C. 1910 BY DR. EMIL MAYER / There were no special challenges in this project. I just wanted to make the book worthy of the subject matter in attitude and scale—and avoid breaking the publisher's pocketbook.

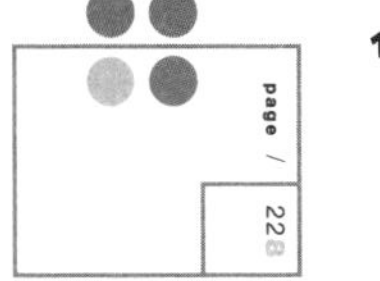

13

DESIGN FIRM	Carl Zahn Graphics, Sarasota, FL
CREATIVE DIRECTOR	Edward Rosser
DESIGNER	Carl Zahn
TRIM SIZE	7 1/4 x 10 1/4 inches
PAGES	76
TYPEFACE	Minion
PRINTER	Stamperia Valdonega
PAPER	Custom-made paper from Cartiere Magnani
AUTHOR	Edward Rosser
PUBLISHER	Blind River Editions

detail. / n05

design firm. carl zahn graphics

50 books. 50 covers. | NO. 13

:VIENNESE TY
[WIENER TYPE

detail O1

detail O2

design firm. carl zahn graphics

50 books. 50 covers. | NO. 13

:VIEN
[WIE

detail O3

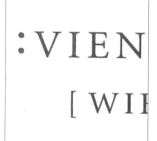

:VIENNESE
[WIENER T
PHOTOGRAPHS
DR. EMIL M
(1871–19

detail O4

detail O5

design firm. carl zahn graphics

50 books. 50 covers. | NO. 13

An In

ONE BASIC social differen
countries in the centuries si
of the middle classes. It is t
Kleinstadt, the small town.
one of spirit.

In cities the leading mind
games of political strategy, t
Kleinstadt, the resonance of
newspaper, which in the m
together with a bottle of milk

detail O6

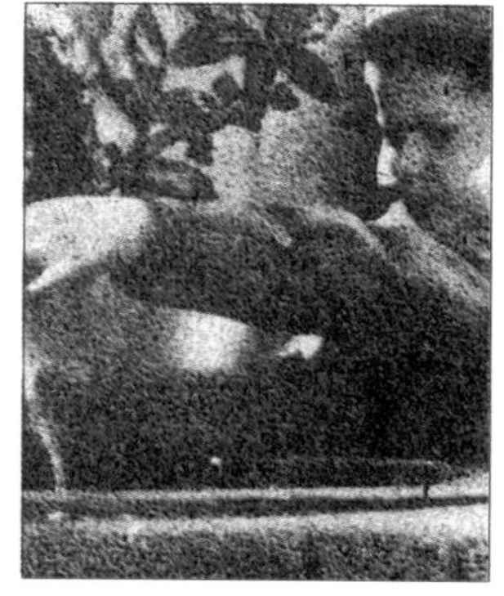

detail O7

The editor and baseball savant Dan Okrent, who is also an excellent cook,[2] once brought a ham larded with pistachios, garlic, and raisins to a potluck lunch. The cookbook editor Judith Jones, who happened to be a guest, enjoyed it so much that she asked Dan for the recipe, which he provided verbatim from a book by James Beard. ("I thought she wanted to *cook* it," he explained later. "Not *publish* it.") When *American Food*, by Judith's husband, Evan Jones, appeared a few years later, there, on page 224,

---

1. Ecclesiastes 1:9: "The thing that hath been, it is that which shall be . . . and there is no new thing under the sun." Cf. Jean de La Bruyère, *Les Caractères* (1688): "We come too late to say anything which has not been said already." La Bruyère probably stole his line from Robert Burton's *Anatomy of Melancholy* (1621): "We can say nothing but what hath been said." Burton probably stole *his* line from Terence's *Eunuchus* (161 B.C.): "Nothing is said that has not been said before." I stole the idea of comparing these four lines from a footnote in *Bartlett's Familiar Quotations*.

2. Actually, I've never eaten anything Dan Okrent has cooked, but my friend Kathy Holub went to a dinner party at his home in 1994 and gave the pork loin high marks. I later found out that it had been cooked by Dan's wife, Becky. However, several people have assured me that Dan *could* have cooked it.

14 50 BOOKS.50 COVERS. EX LIBRIS: CONFESSIONS OF A COMMON READER / This book is a collection of essays about reading, and I wanted the feel of the book to reflect the joy of reading and a life surrounded with books. With its subject matter, the book needed to be classic in style. Even with the smaller trim size, I wanted to create a book with a very gracious and open page. I find the display face, Mrs. Eaves, and the text face, Walbaum, very satisfying and clear, and I think they convey a pleasant, bookish look.

page / 230

14 DESIGN FIRM Farrar, Straus and Giroux, New York, NY
ART DIRECTOR Susan Mitchell
DESIGNER Jonathan D. Lippincott
TRIM SIZE 5 x 7 1/2 inches
PAGES 176
TYPEFACES Various
PRINTER R.R. Donnelley
PAPER Various
JACKET PRINTER Phoenix Color
AUTHOR Anne Fadiman
PUBLISHER Farrar, Straus and Giroux

design firm. farrar, straus and giroux

50 books. 50 covers. | NO. 14

Ex L

detail 01

design firm. farrar, straus and giroux

50 books. 50 covers. | NO. 14

EX LIBR

CONFESSIONS OF A COMMO

ANNE FADIM

detail 02

detail. / n 03

INSET A CARROT

prooflistening for mistakes in
He figured that if he char
would become a rich man. H
h light of morning, however,
he software company, the n
nd would therefore not wish
owned up to a dark chapter
h. When I was twenty-three

detail 03

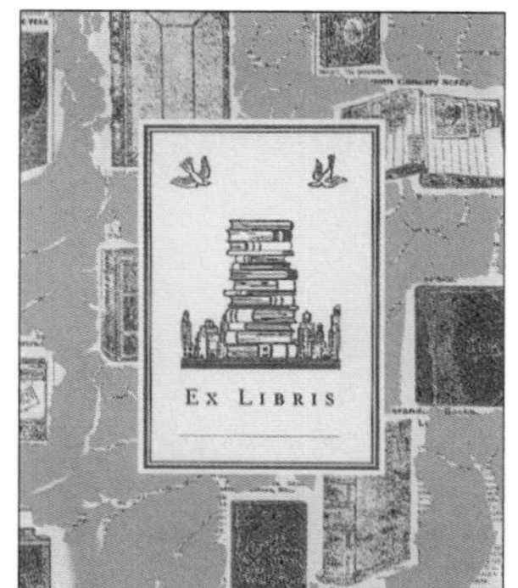

detail 04

design firm. farrar, straus and giroux

50 books. 50 covers. | NO. 14

CONTE

Preface *ix*

Marrying Libraries
The Joy of Sesquip
My Odd Shelf 21

detail 05

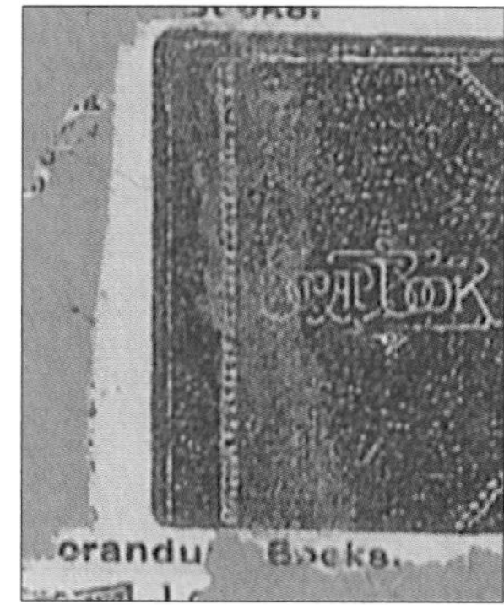

detail 06

15 50 BOOKS.50 COVERS. ANSICHTS SACHEN/VIEWING MATTERS / One challenge of the book was to recontextualize an exhibiton by the conceptual artist Hans Haacke, who had arranged in thematic groupings the collection under storage at the Boijmans van Beuningen Museum in Rotterdam. The design solution was to do a walk-through of the art installation using the conceit of a book to represent space. We designed and arranged the book based on the themes established by the author. Each of these chapters had its own particular design treatment.

15

DESIGN FIRM	Design/Writing/Research, New York, NY
CREATIVE DIRECTOR	J. Abbott Miller
ART DIRECTOR	Paul Carlos
TRIM SIZE	8 7/8 x 11 1/4 inches
PAGES	200
TYPEFACE	FF Balance
PAPER	White wood-free Hello matte coated 150 gram
PRINTER	Heinrich Winterscheidt GmbH
AUTHOR	Hans Haacke
PUBLISHER	Richter Verlag

detail. / n04

design firm. design/writing/research

50 books. 50 covers. | NO. 15

Roger Tallon; Thompson
Téléavia
1963

Ennio Brion &
Gino Fornasini
Television Set Top 1
1986

detail O1

design firm. design/writing/research

50 books. 50 covers. | NO. 15

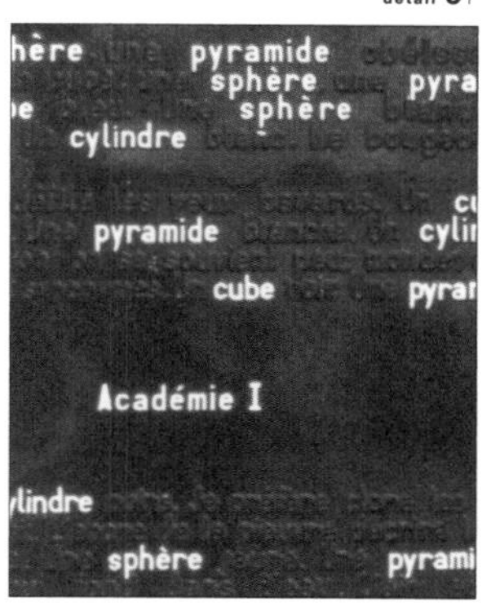

detail O2

detail O3

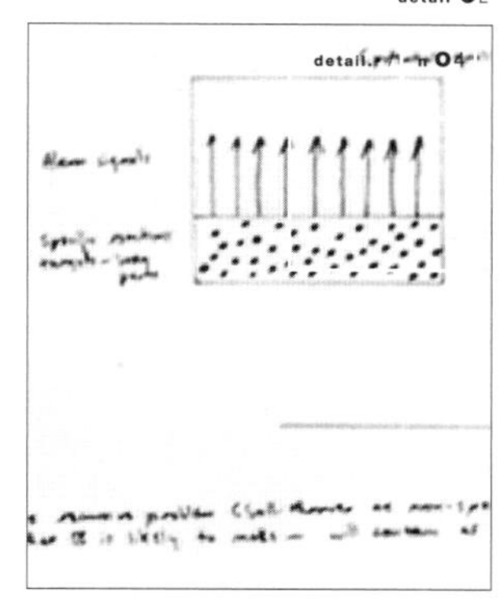

detail O4

design firm. design/writing/research

50 books. 50 covers. | NO. 15

detail O5

Philips Concern Industrial
Design Centre
Philips GTC 2100/00R
1980

Stig Lindberg
(Wega Radio Gmb
Wegavision 2000
1963

detail O6

detail O7

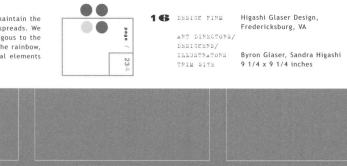

16 50 BOOKS.50 COVERS. ROUND THE GARDEN / To honor the simplistic beauty of the poem and maintain the fluidity of the text, we devoted entire spreads to the type, placing it in rhythmic sequence with the illustration spreads. We used icons on the type spreads to foreshadow the illustrations, and to suggest a continual unfolding that is analogous to the growth cycle. As the book opens, the color palette begins with yellow and circles through the entire spectrum of the rainbow, eventually returning again to yellow. We also incorporated scientific diagrams such as cloud types and the natural elements required in the growth process.

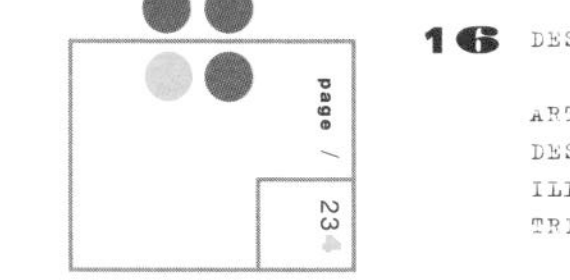
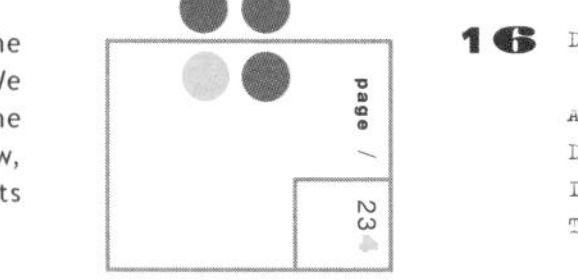
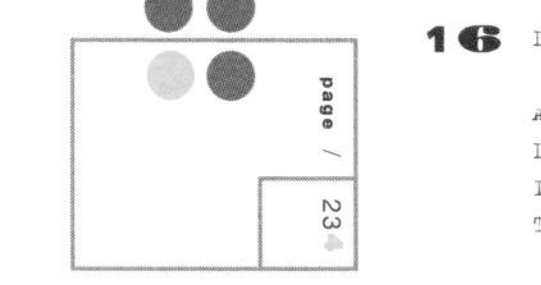
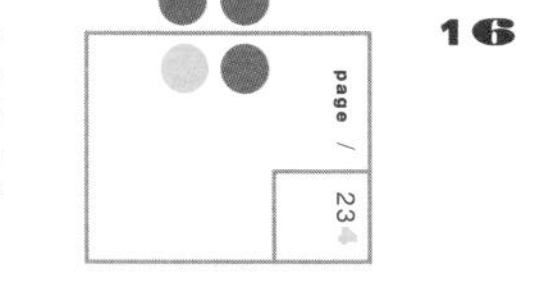
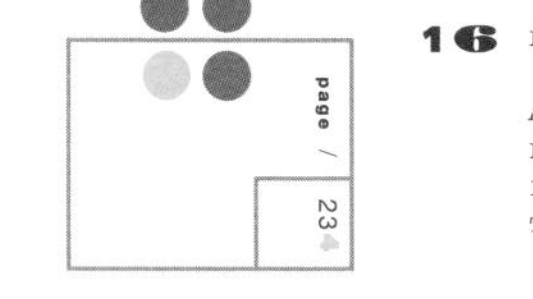

16

DESIGN FIRM	Higashi Glaser Design, Fredericksburg, VA
ART DIRECTORS/ DESIGNERS/ ILLUSTRATORS	Byron Glaser, Sandra Higashi
TRIM SIZE	9 1/4 x 9 1/4 inches
PAGES	34
TYPEFACES	Nobel and Monoline
PRINTER	C&C Offset Printing Co., Ltd.
PAPER	Japanese Matte Coated 157 gram
AUTHOR	Omri Glaser
PUBLISHER	Harry N. Abrams, Inc.

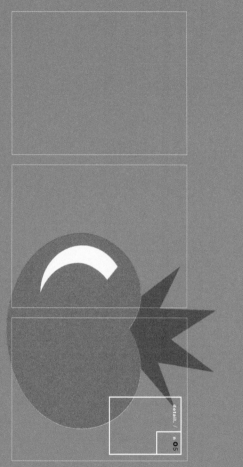

design firm. higashi glaser design

50 books. 50 covers. | NO. 16

This is the tear

detail O1

detail O2

design firm. higashi glaser design

50 books. 50 covers. | NO. 16

detail O3

detail O4

design firm. higashi glaser design

50 books. 50 covers. | NO. 16

detail O5

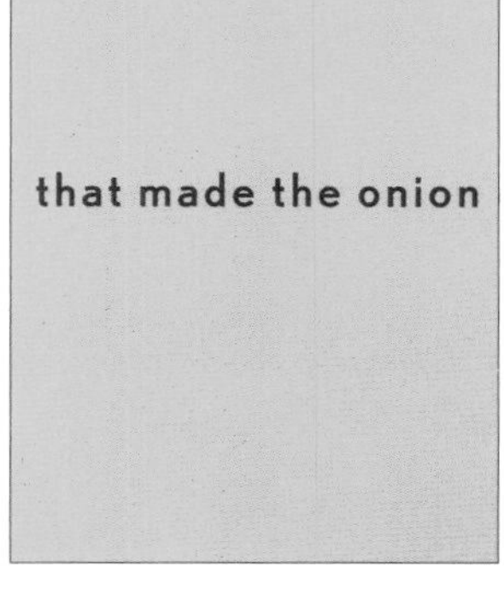

detail O6

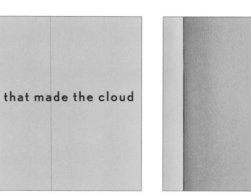

17 50 BOOKS.50 COVERS. BEMBO'S ZOO / It was my daughter's first Christmas and I wanted to make something for her. Every night I read to her in Portuguese and English, so I decided to create an alphabet book that I could read in both languages. I decided to create a whole menagerie out of one single weight of a family font—Bembo Roman. The animals had to be constructed with the letters of its own name. There were no common animals in Portuguese and English for the letters N, O, X and W, so ultimately I had to drop the bilingual aspect of the project.

17

DESIGN FIRM	RVC Design, New York, NY
ART DIRECTOR/ DESIGNER/ ILLUSTRATOR	Roberto de Vicq de Cumptich
TRIM SIZE	8 1/4 x 13 inches
PAGES	32
TYPEFACE	Bembo Roman Monotype
PRINTER	Hong Kong Graphics and Printing
PAPER	Matte Art Paper 135 gram
AUTHOR	Roberto de Vicq de Cumptich
PUBLISHER	Henry Holt and Company

detail. /

design firm. rvc design

50 books. 50 covers. | NO. 17

detail O1

detail O2

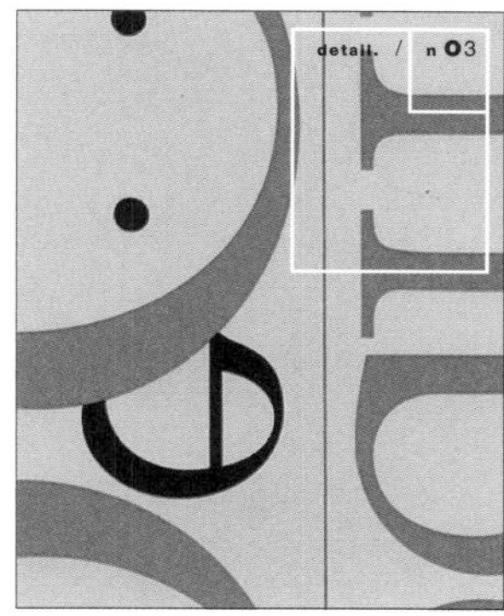

detail O3

detail O4

detail O5

design firm. rvc design

50 books. 50 covers. | NO. 17

detail O6

design firm. rvc design

50 books. 50 covers. | NO. 17

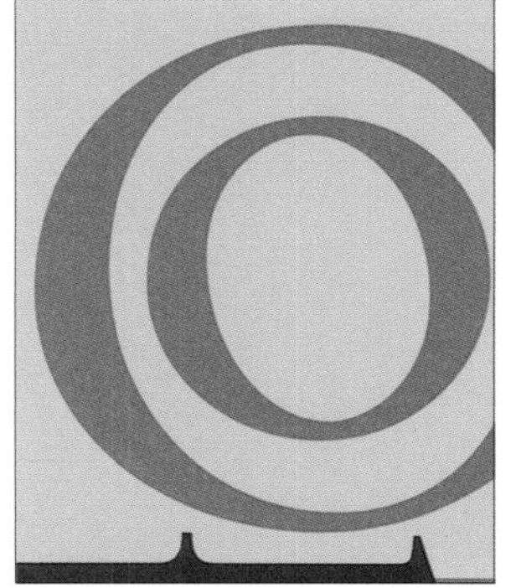

detail O7

18 50 BOOKS.50 COVERS. DUGONG, MANATEE, SEA COW / The manatee and its relatives are cuddly looking creatures, but humankind's treatment of them has been anything but cuddly. The mandate of the poem was that there be no cuteness to the portrayal in the typography and illustration. The book's design was born out of the language and content of the poem, which is written in a peculiar 19th-century style. The design steals aspects of late-19th-century maps—line numbers undulating like latitude lines, a cordoned text block tucked low and toward the spine like a legend, pages lettered in circles rather than numbered.

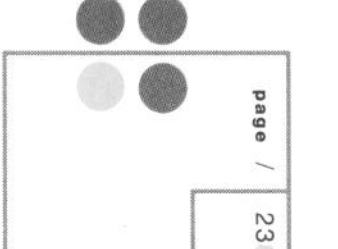

18

DESIGN FIRM	[sic], New York, NY
ART DIRECTOR/ DESIGNER/ ILLUSTRATOR	Charles Nix
	Stefano Arcella
TRIM SIZE	9 x 9 1/4 inches
PAGES	32
TYPEFACES	Various
PRINTER	Oddi Printing
PAPER	Munken Pure 150 gram
AUTHOR	Arnold Klein
PUBLISHER	Tsimmes Editions

DUGONG,

Manatee,

SEA COW.

detail. / n 05

detail. / n 02

ARNOLD KLEIN

design firm. [sic]

50 books. 50 covers. | NO. 18

detail 01

detail. / n 02

SEA COW

ARNOLD

detail 02

DELUSION, to be sure. 096
n; and pursue it
d the Senegal,
hemmed round with dangers
for some believe it
atee was followed as a business 101

om the bank, 105
aplings,
e is eating, his great bulk,
e dark, 108
eavy night, displaces them,
the heavy spear 110
anatee in pools, 111
g waters to the central river, 112
vel falling fast,
114

detail 03

design firm. [sic]

50 books. 50 covers. | NO. 18

detail 04

detail. / n 05

DUGONG,

Manate

SEA COW.

detail 05

DELUSION, to be sure. 096
n; and pursue it
d the Senegal,
hemmed round with dangers
for some believe it
atee was followed as a business 101

om the bank, 105
aplings,
e is eating, his great bulk,
e dark, 108
eavy night, displaces them,
the heavy spear. 110

detail 06

design firm. [sic]

50 books. 50 covers. | NO. 18

detail 07

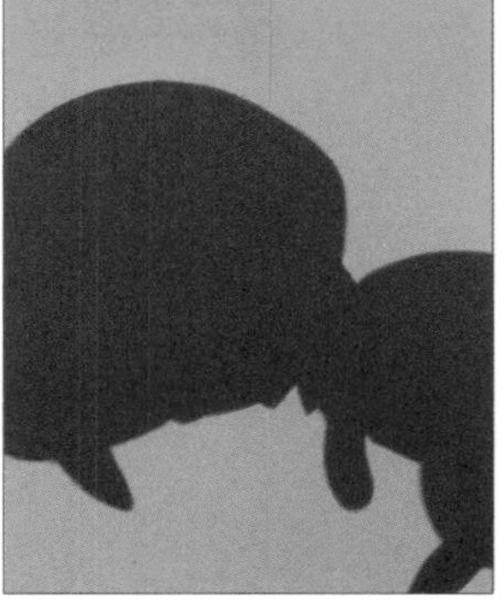

detail 08

Road-side Dog

19 50 BOOKS.50 COVERS. ROAD-SIDE DOG / The most important task was to keep the design literary and classic. I chose a classic, literary type solution.

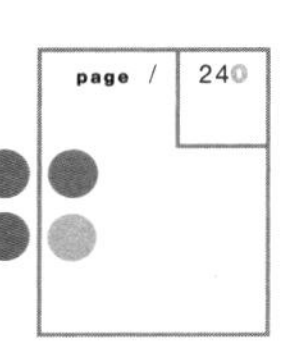

19

DESIGN FIRM	Farrar, Straus and Giroux, New York, NY
ART DIRECTOR/ DESIGNER	Abby Kagan
ILLUSTRATOR	Brian Cronin
TRIM SIZE	5 1/2 x 6 1/2 inches
PAGES	224
PRINTER	Berryville Graphics
PAPER	Glatfelter B-18 cream
JACKET PRINTER	Phoenix Color
AUTHOR	Czeslaw Milosz
PUBLISHER	Farrar, Straus and Giroux

design firm. farrar, straus and giroux

50 books. 50 covers. | NO. 19

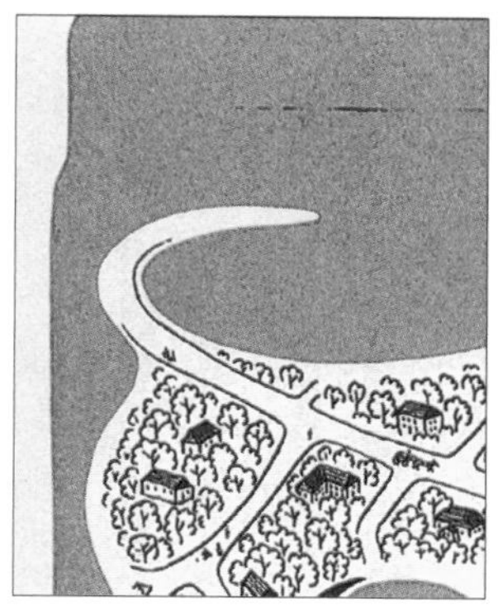

detail 01

detail 02

design firm. farrar, straus and giroux

50 books. 50 covers. | NO. 19

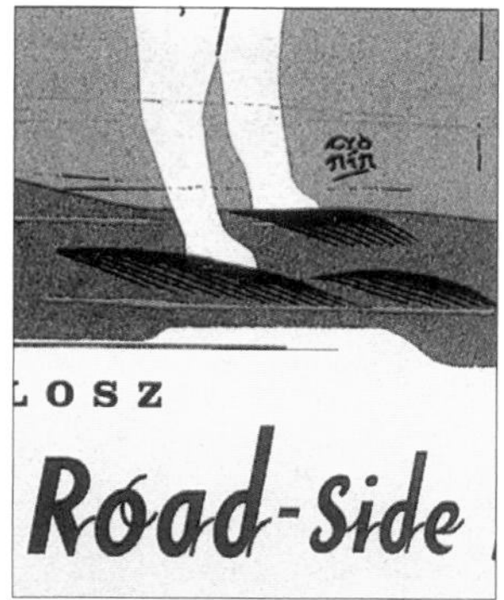

detail 03

U.S.A. $22.00

Canada $35.00

I went on a jour
myself with my
wagon with a lo
bucket rattling i
been thinking n

detail 04

design firm. farrar, straus and giroux

50 books. 50 covers. | NO. 19

detail 05

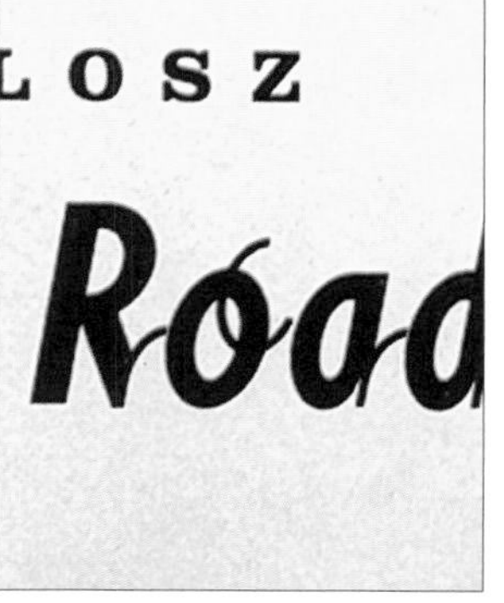

detail 06

20 50 BOOKS.50 COVERS. BUSY BUSY CITY STREET / The real challenge in designing this book was to give visual form to what was essentially an auditory experience. I used handlettering throughout, which gave me lots of options for matching letterforms to the sounds, and I incorporated letterforms into the images to give them roles as important as the people, vehicles and cityscapes. I made the words actual characters in the book and presented finished artwork in the form of watercolor paintings, with all lettering as part of the art.

20

DESIGN FIRM	Guarnaccia, New York, NY
ART DIRECTOR	Nina Putignano
DESIGNER/ ILLUSTRATOR	Steven Guarnaccia
TRIM SIZE	11 1/4 x 9 1/4 inches
PAGES	26
TYPEFACES	Handlettered
AUTHOR	Cari Meister
PUBLISHER	Viking/Penguin Group

detail. /

design firm. guarnaccia

50 books. 50 covers. | NO. 20

detail 01

detail 02

detail 03

design firm. guarnaccia

50 books. 50 covers. | NO. 20

detail 04

detail 05

design firm. guarnaccia

50 books. 50 covers. | NO. 20

detail 06

detail 07

21 50 BOOKS.50 COVERS. TENOCHE ME RONDA / The author had written the narrative in such a manner that each page had to start and conclude with a pre-determined word in the text. This strongly limited the typography of each text box and pages, and consequently the complete book as text could not freely flow from one text box to the next. Fortunately, this resulted in a fascinating process in which both author and designer intensively worked together to make the text fit within the structure of the grid either by adjusting the typography or editing the text. "Messing" with kerning was never an option.

21

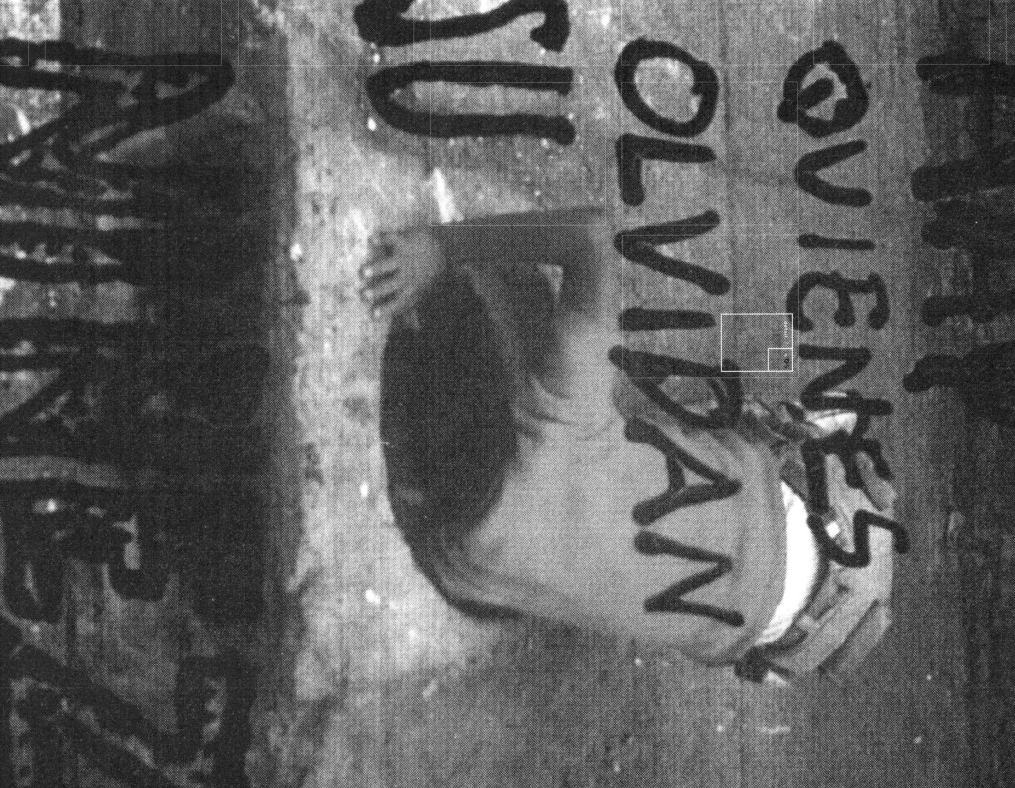

DESIGN FIRM	Henk van Assen Design, New York, NY
CREATIVE DIRECTOR	Henk van Assen
DESIGNERS	Henk van Assen, Héctor Olea
TRIM SIZE	8 x 8 inches
PAGES	278
TYPEFACES	Trinité, Scala Sans, Bureau Grotesque
PRINTER	Kestrel Printing
PAPER	Cougar Opaque
AUTHOR	Héctor Olea
PUBLISHER	Whichever Press

design firm. henk van assen design

50 books. 50 covers. | NO. 21

TENOCHE
ME HECTOR OLEA
RONDA
(desenredo poetografítico...)

detail O1

(tierra...)

detail O2

Para los suyos, la fam

En Marcha, Zacateos
ya. Niños, ¡hay qu
en su sitio...! Marc
distancia. ¡No se r

detail O3

design firm. henk van assen design

50 books. 50 covers. | NO. 21

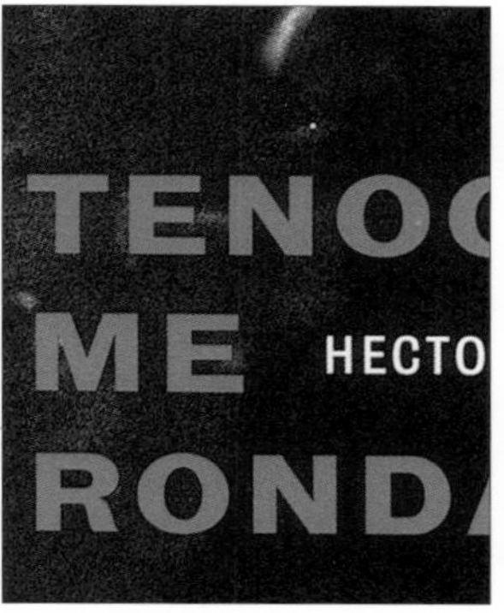

TENOC
ME HECTO
RONDA

detail O4

detail O5

design firm. henk van assen design

50 books. 50 covers. | NO. 21

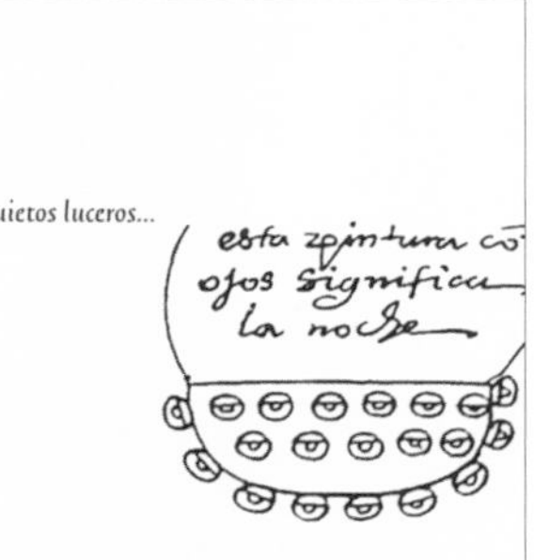
uietos luceros...
e... Triste. Bastará la significación del debuj
, Delector Suave– lo sepa poner más al nat

detail O6

Palabras en Reposo

detail O7

22 50 BOOKS.50 COVERS. CANADA POST: THE MILLENNIUM COLLECTION / This project was created to mark the millennium with a unique collection of 68 stamps that distinguishes itself from the traditional yearly album published by Canada Post, and to develop an approach that adds value to collectors. The fold-out hardcover case and flexible binding system provide flexibility in assembling the book. Stamps designed by approximately 50 designers and five photographers from across Canada were printed on actual perforated stamp paper. In short, each element in the album is unique and orchestrated to create emotion, spirit and an enjoyable visual experience.

22

DESIGN FIRM	Gottschalk+Ash International, Montreal, Canada
CREATIVE DIRECTORS	Peter Steiner, Alain Leduc
DESIGNERS	Hélène L'Heureux, Ian Drolet, Geneviève Caron
PHOTOGRAPHERS	Various
TRIM SIZE	11 x 10 1/4 inches
PAGES	96 pages
PRINTERS	The Lowe-Martin Group, Ashton Potter
PUBLISHER	Canada Post Corporation

design firm. gottschalk+ash international

50 books. 50 covers. | NO. 22

detail O1

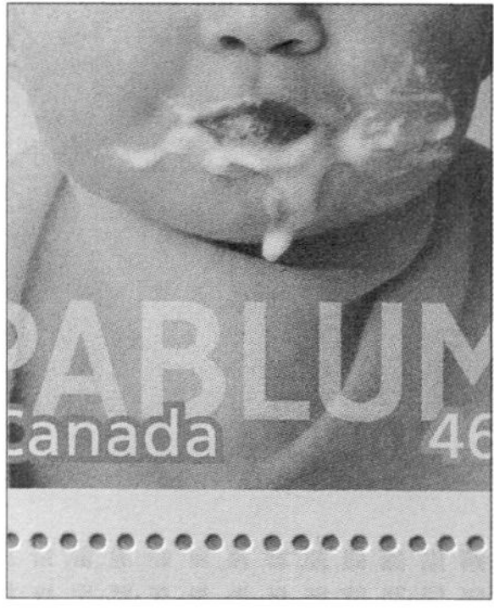

detail O2

design firm. gottschalk+ash international

50 books. 50 covers. | NO. 22

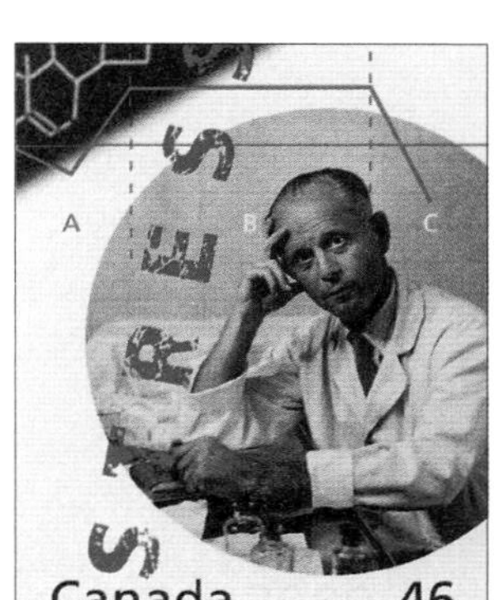

detail O3

detail O4

design firm. gottschalk+ash international

50 books. 50 covers. | NO. 22

detail O5

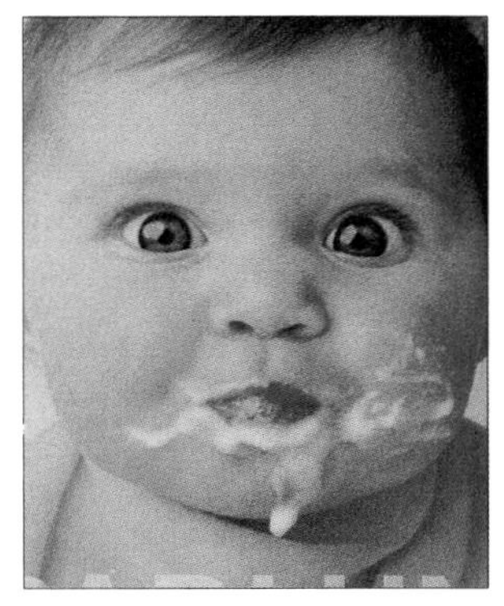

detail O6

23

DESIGN FIRM	Knopf Publishing Group, New York, NY
ART DIRECTOR/ DESIGNER	Peter Andersen
JACKET DESIGNER	Carol Devine Carson
PHOTOGRAPHER	Lynn Davis
TRIM SIZE	10 1/4 x 10 1/4 inches
PAGES	288
TYPEFACE	Adobe Garamond
PRINTER	R.R. Donnelley
AUTHOR	Henry Louis Gates, Jr.
PUBLISHER	Alfred A. Knopf

23 50 BOOKS.50 COVERS. WONDERS OF THE AFRICAN WORLD /

design firm. knopf publishing group

50 books. 50 covers. | NO. 23

detail 01

design firm. knopf publishing group

50 books. 50 covers. | NO. 23

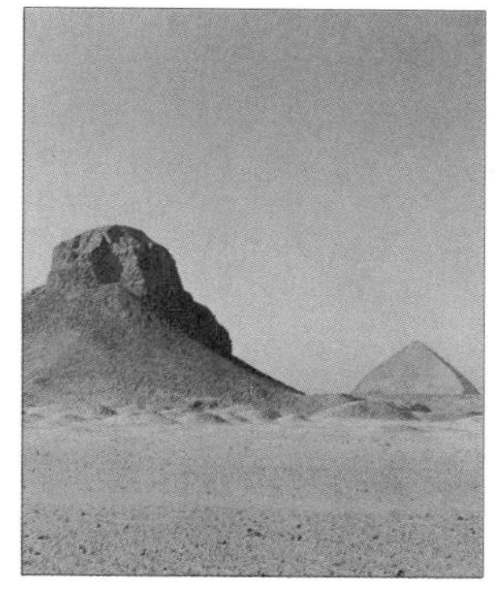

detail 02

detail. / n 03

detail 03

2

NUBIA

BLACK GODS A

As between the Egyptians and the Ethiopians, I should not l

It is curious withal, that the earliest known civilization was,
a negro civilization. The original Egyptians are inferred, f
have been a negro race: it was from negroes, therefore, that t
and to the records and traditions of these negroes did the Gr
career resort (I do not say with much fruit) as a treasury of r

detail 04

design firm. knopf publishing group

50 books. 50 covers. | NO. 23

detail 05

detail 06

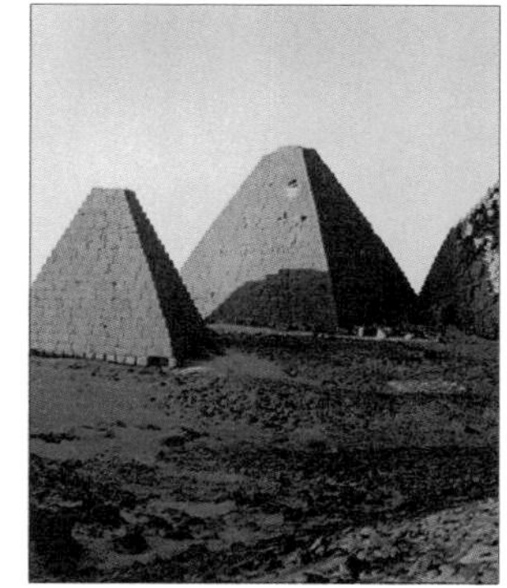

detail 07

24 50 BOOKS.50 COVERS. NOWHERE NEAR/...AND OF TIME / Designing an environment that was physically and emotionally sympathetic to the artist's photographs was the biggest challenge. I decided to embrace the mundane. I did this by refining a very limited number of design factors into a strategy that appears as if nothing much is going on, but on closer inspection has subtle relationships with the work and the idea of how we perceive change occurring over time.

24

DESIGN FIRM	Michael Worthington, Los Angeles, CA
DESIGNER	Michael Worthington
PHOTOGRAPHER	Uta Barth
TRIM SIZE	8 1/2 x 9 1/4 inches
PAGES	40/56 (total 96)
TYPEFACES	Gridnik, Helvetica
PRINTER	Typecraft/Delta Graphics
PAPER	Lustro, Pegasus
AUTHORS	Jan Tumlir, Timothy Martin
PUBLISHER	Uta Barth

detail. /

design firm. michael worthington

50 books. 50 covers. | NO. 24

detail O1

detail O2

design firm. michael worthington

50 books. 50 covers. | NO. 24

detail O3

detail O4

detail O5

design firm. michael worthington

50 books. 50 covers. | NO. 24

detail O6

detail O7

BYZANTIUM 9: A LITERARY ANNUAL / The biggest challenge was working with a tight budget, limited colors and paper availability. I created a classical-looking book with a modern flair, respecting the Byzantine Era.

DESIGN FIRM	Lisa Hoffman Design, New York, NY
ART DIRECTOR/DESIGNER	Lisa Hoffman
TRIM SIZE	6 1/2 x 9 inches
PAGES	165
TYPEFACES	Various
PRINTER	Poor Richard's Press
PAPER	Various
EDITORS	Amanda Burt, Summer Oram

a dancer, a plastic surgeon and a psychiatrist."

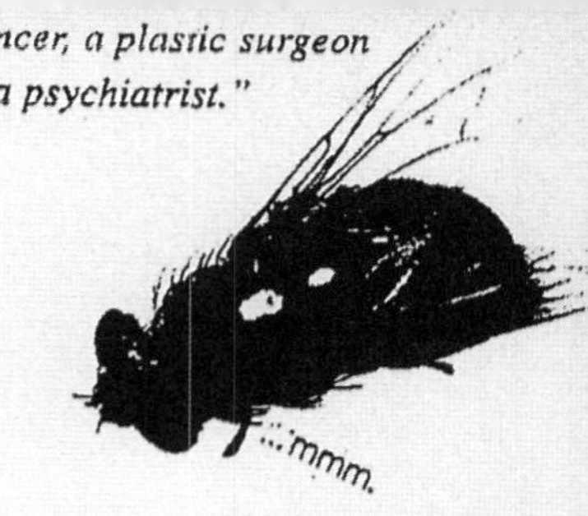

YOUR World. god spirit faith life (choose one)

has BEEN kidnapped

don't PLAY HERO

PaY THE RANSom

simply call 1.800.333.9463.

detail. / n 02

GOD It is what it is. A popcorn machine, a cotton candy PUZZLE adrenaline rush A eulogy for the cerebral soldie

Stomach-in-the-throat thrills a self-imposed exile sweaty palms solitary and conspicuous que

INDELIBLY DIVINE

REMEMBER THIS

You will be tested later.

TELL THE WHOLE STORY revere the weird *know where you're going* fight for SINFUL PLEASURES

HAVE A LIFE Travel *unfamiliar roads* with A MORAL COMPASS *look for the next landmark.*

Be SUSPICIOUS OF GOVERNMENT DANGEROUS *technology* DON'T BEHAVE YOURSELF reveal the sug plums that dan in your hea

develop as mentally and emotionally sound individuals.

Or be PATRIOTIC

BELIEVE IN THE POWER OF THE MIND separate FICTION FROM FACT TAKE ON DIMENSION

HAVE God ON SPEED DIAL always look your best

ITS probably a test designed to concentrate attention through pain and fear

looking up, he said, "This cow's been mutilated." A WARM MEMORY OF OUR OWN CHILDHOOD. THERE IS THE SIMPLE SWEETNESS OF LIFE, THE QUIET MAGIC OF THE EVERYDAY, Despised by fringe groups and spurned by the centrists, This is why God probably wants you to vote

There was no blood or footprints on the muddy ground, nor any visible mortal wound, in every state the long arm of the law reaches into the bedr

WHAT YOU NEED TO KNOW ABOUT THIS

sublime absurd. R EVOLUTION

47% believe that homosexuality is learned

Elvis will be the dark-horse presidential candidate in the year 2000?

49% believe that war is immoral

32% believe humankind is basically evil

your neurological receptor is going into overdrive

SURGEON GENERAL'S WARNING:

THE EMPEROR HAS NO CLOTHES THE PARTY'S OVER

design firm. lisa hoffman design

50 books. 50 covers. | NO. 25

MUSTANG D

UILDING SUITE 226

CAL POLY STATE UNIVERSITY

Editorial # 756.1

Advertising # 756

Fax # 756.6784

www.mustangdaily.c

detail O1

detail. / nO2

nply call 1.800.333.9463.

e rush A eulogy for the cere

solitary and conspicuo

detail O2

design firm. lisa hoffman design

50 books. 50 covers. | NO. 25

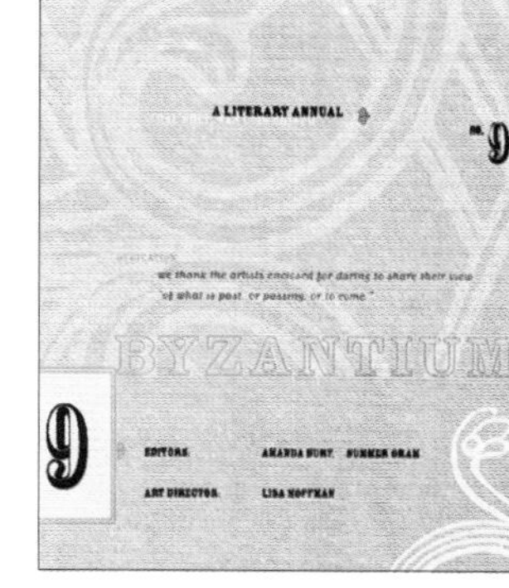

detail O3

AMANDA HUNT

detail O4

detail. / nO5

no blood or footprints on the muddy

WHAT Y

47% believe

homosexuality is le

32

your neurol

detail O5

design firm. lisa hoffman design

50 books. 50 covers. | NO. 25

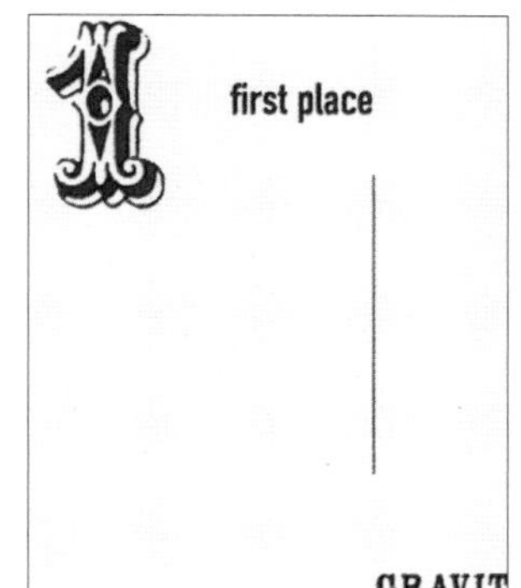

detail O6

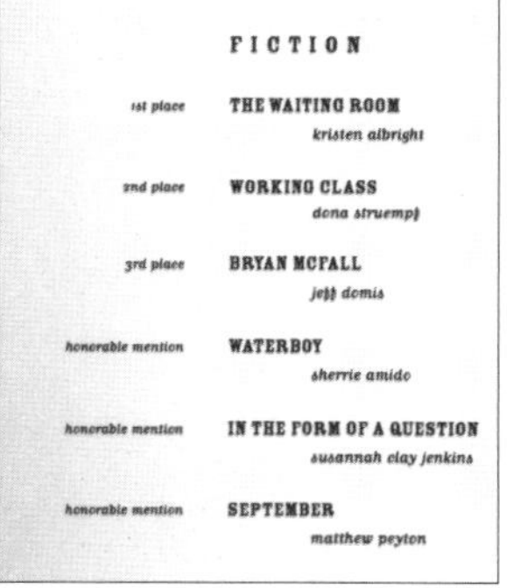

detail O7

…OKS.50 COVERS. ELEANOR ANTIN / Since Antin's work is narrative, we wanted to present the work in a …s that—almost a cinematic look. We decided to make the book read in a strong horizontal manner.

26

DESIGN FIRM	Los Angeles County Museum of Art, Los Angeles, CA	PAGES	262
ART DIRECTOR	Jim Drobka	TYPEFACE	Minion
DESIGNERS	Lausten + Cossutta Design	PRINTER	C&C Offse…
PHOTOGRAPHER	Supervised by Steve Oliver	PAPER	Multiart …
TRIM SIZE	6 1/2 x 9 1/2 inches	AUTHOR	Howard N…

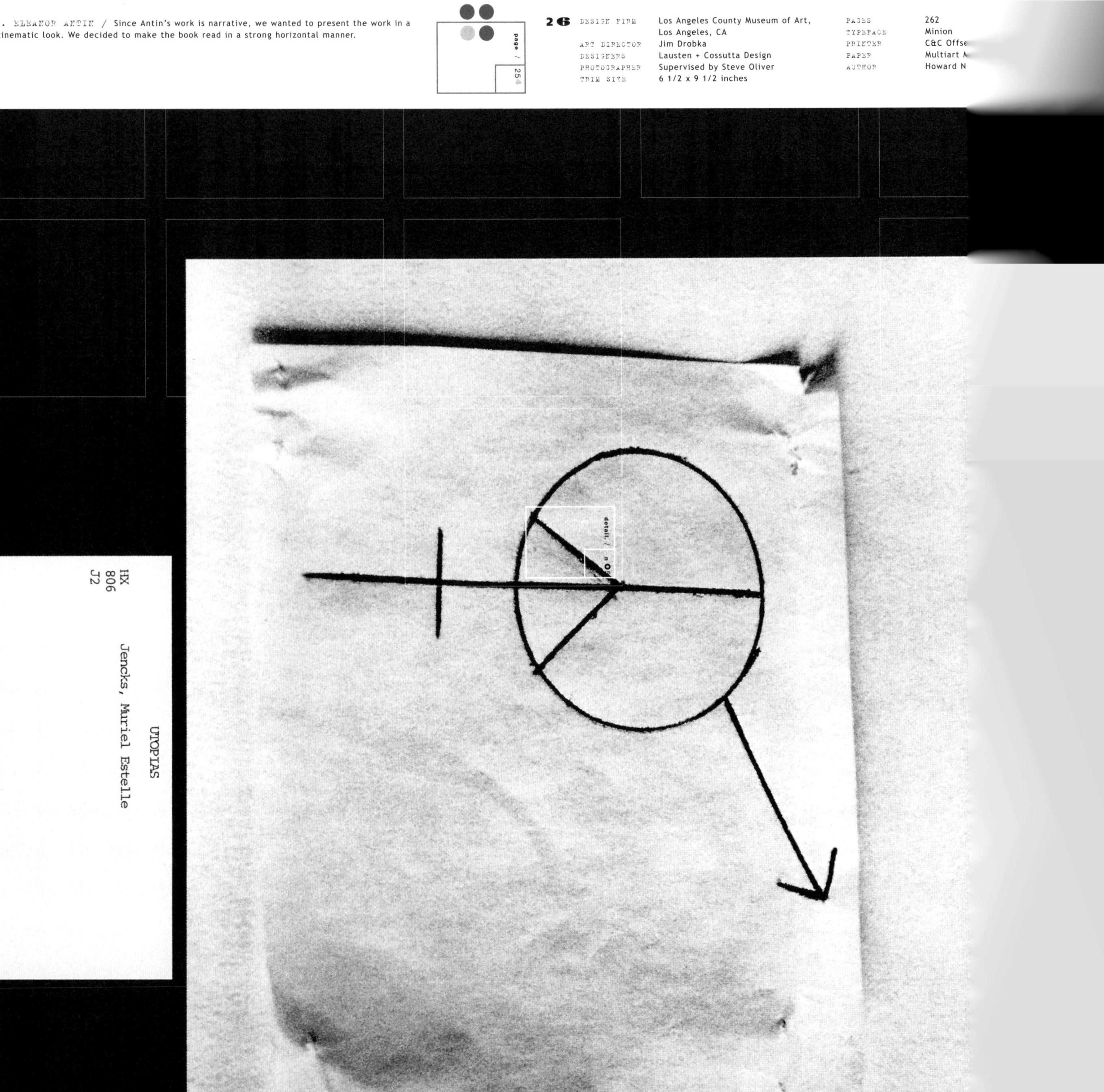

design firm. los angeles county museum of art

50 books. 50 covers. | NO. 26

detail 01

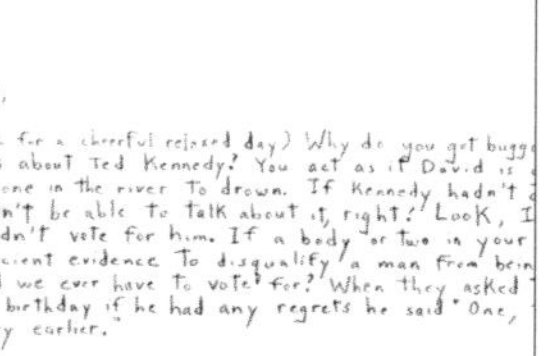

detail 02

design firm. los angeles county museum of art

50 books. 50 covers. | NO. 26

detail 03

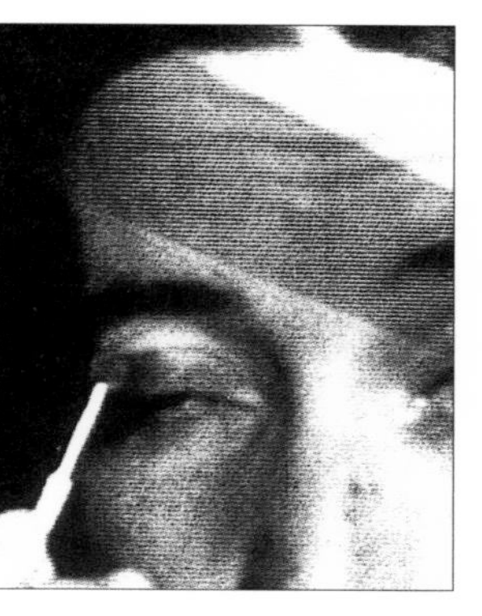

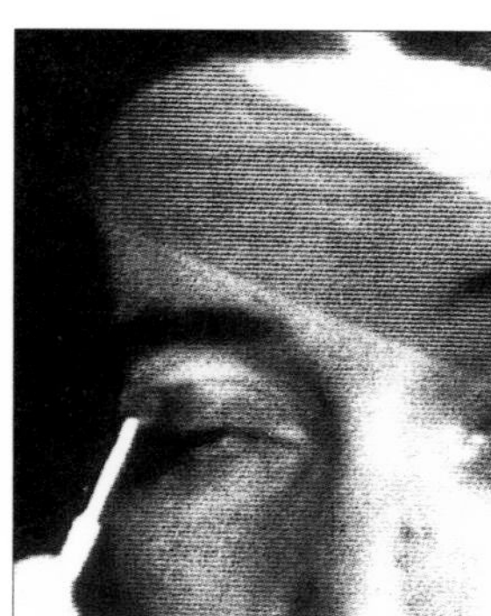

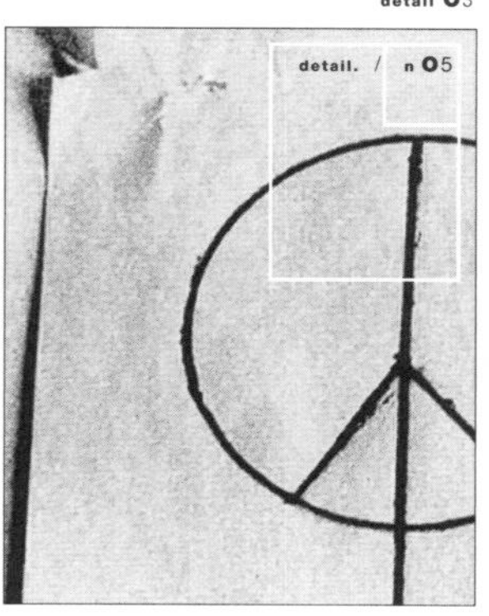

detail 04

detail 05

design firm. los angeles county museum of art

50 books. 50 covers. | NO. 26

detail 06

detail 07

27 50 BOOKS.50 COVERS. DEEP DESIGN: NINE LITTLE HISTORIES / In nine observant, quirky and irreverently spirited essays, critic Libby Lumpkin suggests that what appear to be deep theoretical problems of art are merely simple problems of design. Subjects include art histories of the Smiley Face and the Prohibition Symbol. Rather than using a traditional means of laying out text with illustrations, the pictures are instead placed at the front and back of the book, encapsulated within 12-page, four-color signatures. The frontis to each essay is a visually rhythmic, typographic interpretation of one specific quote chosen to accompany each essay.

27

DESIGN FIRM	Shiffman Design, Santa Monica, CA
ART DIRECTOR/ DESIGNER	Tracey Shiffman
ILLUSTRATOR	Cover from a painting by Ingrid Calame
TRIM SIZE	6 x 9 inches
PAGES	128 plus 24-page color insert
TYPEFACES	Janson with heads in Linoscript
PRINTER	Sinclair Printing Company
AUTHOR	Libby Lumpkin

detail. / n05

Deep Design

Nine
Little Art Histories

LIBBY LUMPKIN

design firm. shiffman design

50 books. 50 covers. | NO. 27

detail 01

detail 02

design firm. shiffman design

50 books. 50 covers. | NO. 27

detail 03

detail 04

detail. / n 05

Deep D

detail 05

design firm. shiffman design

50 books. 50 covers. | NO. 27

detail 06

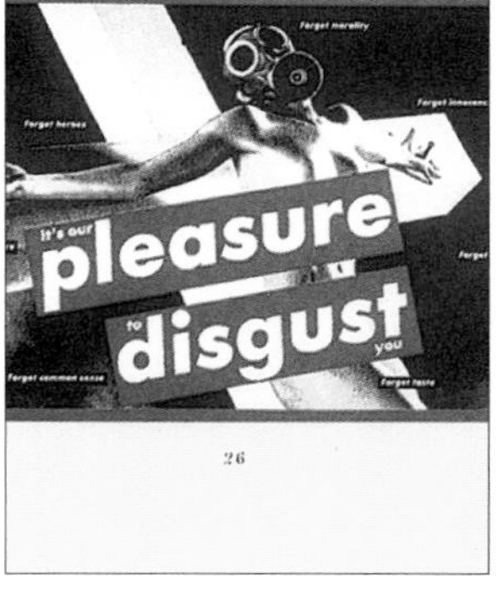

detail 07

28 50 BOOKS.50 COVERS. BLACKLETTER: TYPE AND NATIONAL IDENTITY / We had to recreate the experience of the accompanying exhibition in printed form. Each case in the exhibition was devoted to a single theme. Each theme either became a single page or a double-page spread. The look and feel (including the large lowercase N's) of the installation, the entire text and over half the images were all transferred to the catalogue. The large N is a visual key to the different themes, highlighting stylistic differences and allowing the reader to navigate the catalogue by typographic form.

28

DESIGN FIRMS	Peter Bain Design and Paul Shaw/ Letter Design, New York, NY
DESIGNERS/ COMPOSITORS	Peter Bain, Paul Shaw
TRIM SIZE	7 1/2 x 10 1/2 inches
PAGES	80
TYPEFACES	Various
PRINTER	The Stinehour Press
PAPER	Mohawk Superfine text and cover
AUTHORS	Peter Bain, Paul Shaw
PUBLISHER	American Printing History Association

8.

Fette kleine Canon Antiqua.

Paris, Stockholm, Wien

Minimum 20 Ct. pr. Ct. 1/12 Rk.

4.

Ausstellung
24.9.–2.11.1986
detail. / n 05
Galerie am Fischmarkt
»Haus zum Roten Ochsen« · Erfurt
Geöffnet:
Mittwoch – Sonntag 10 – 18 Uhr
Verband Bildender Künstler der DDR
Ministerium für Kultur
DIE 100 BESTEN
1985
PLAKATE

Bibelen

eller

den Heliga Skrift

innehållande

Gamla och Nya Testamentets

Canoniska Böcker.

New York:
Amerikanska Bibel-Sällskapet;
Upprättadt år 1816.
1909.

[Swedish, Brevier 12mo.]

Blackletter:
Type and National Identity

A catalogue of the exhibition

March 3 to May 2, 1998

The Herb Lubalin Study Center
of Design and Typography,
School of Art,
The Cooper Union for the
Advancement of Science and Art

Curated by
Peter Bain and Paul Shaw

detail 01

detail 02

design firm. peter bain design and paul shaw/letter design

50 books. 50 covers. | NO. 28

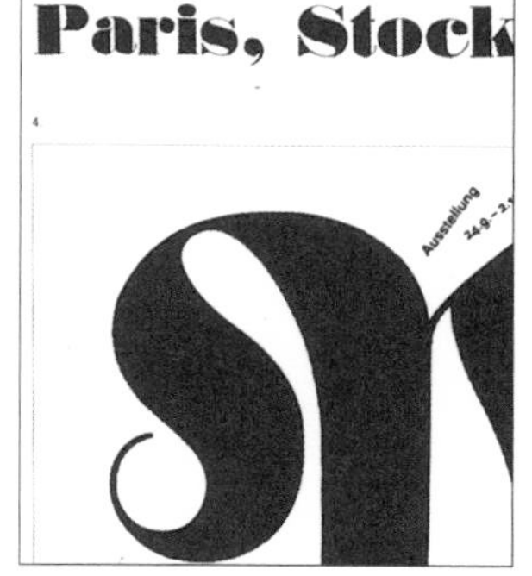

detail 03

design firm. peter bain design and paul shaw/letter design

50 books. 50 covers. | NO. 28

ABCDEFGHIJK
LMNOPQRSTU
VWXYZ
abcdefghijklmn
opqrsſtuvwxyz
chck 1234567890

detail 04

Galerie am Fischmarkt
»Haus zum Roten Ochsen« · Erfurt
Geöffnet:
Mittwoch – Sonntag 10 – 18 Uhr

detail 05

design firm. peter bain design and paul shaw/letter design

50 books. 50 covers. | NO. 28

detail 06

detail 07

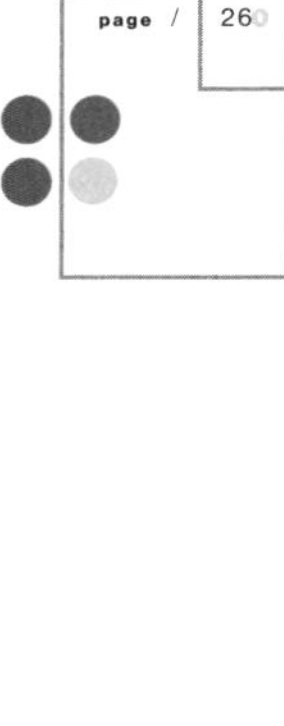

graph

A graph plots data in a gridded space, whose axes represent variables such as time, temperature, or quantity. Many **graphs** depict change over time with a linear mark, as in a sine curve or a "fever" chart. The **graph** belongs to the category of signs called the **index**, which has a causal relationship to its referent. For example, a photograph, a footprint, or a shadow is an index, because it results from physical contact with an object. An arrow is an index, because its meaning in any given instance depends on its proximity to an object. Indexical signs appear throughout the textbooks of Klee, Kandinsky, and Moholy-Nagy; they serve as potential characters in a universal script that would have a direct link to the physical or spiritual world.

Figure 5

Figure 4

Figure 3

24

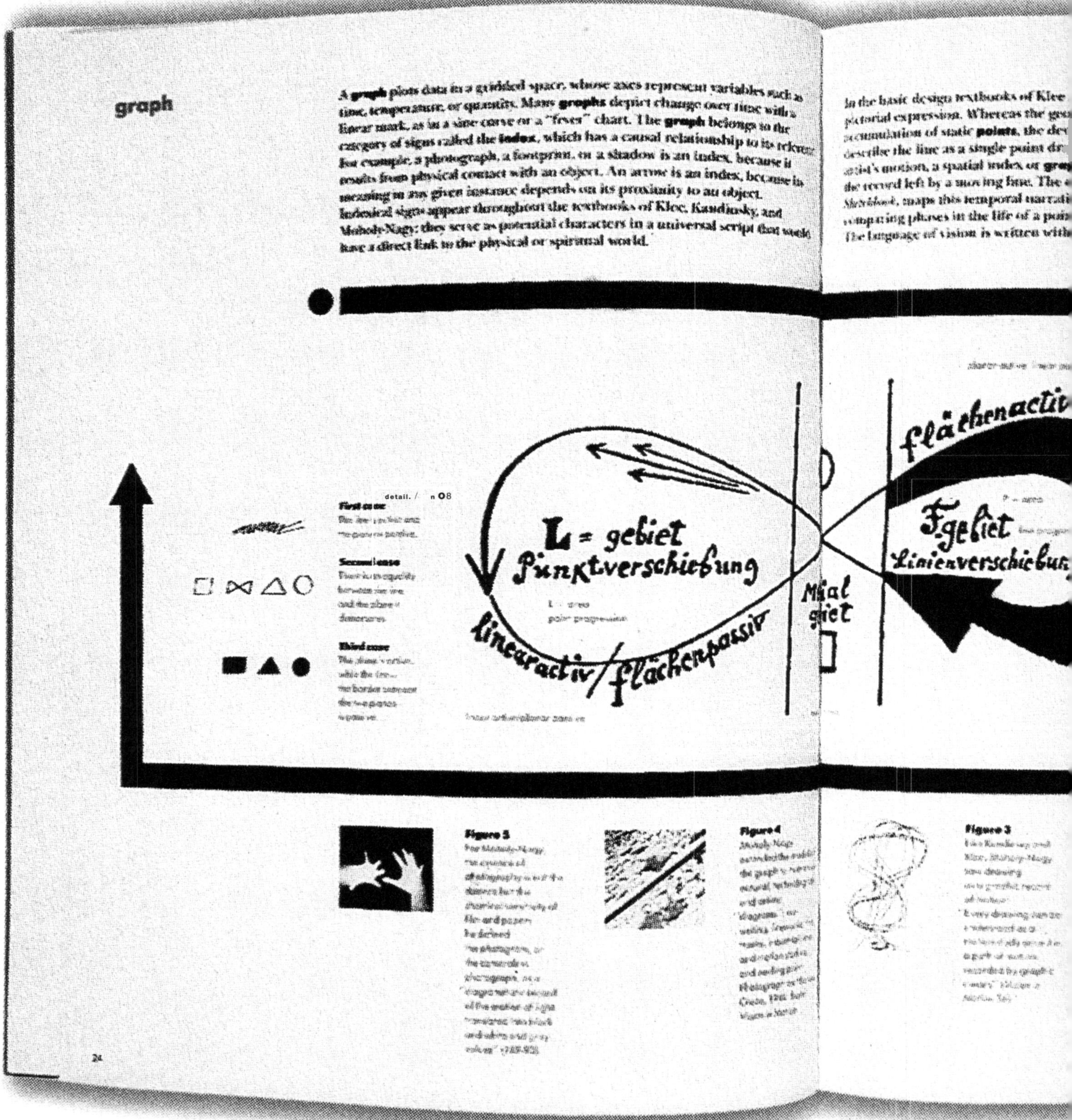

The ABCs of ▲■●: The Bauhaus an

design firm. pentagram design

50 books. 50 covers. | NO. 29

a retrospective of winners

DaimlerChrysler
DESIGN AWARDS
1993–1999

detail 01

detail 02

design firm. pentagram design

50 books. 50 covers. | NO. 29

detail 03

MATTHEW·CARTER'S
MANTINIA
A·NEW·DESIGN
WITH·CAPITALS
TALL·CAPITALS
ALTERNATIVES
SUPERIORS·&
LIGATURES

detail 04

detail 05

design firm. pentagram design

50 books. 50 covers. | NO. 29

detail 06

detail 07

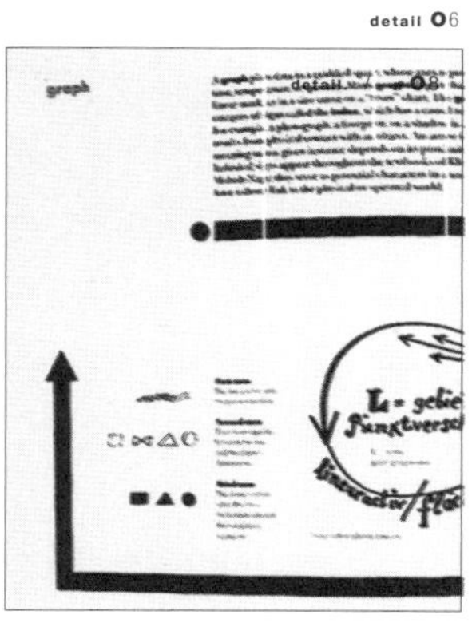

detail 08

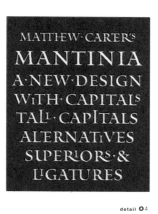

30 50 BOOKS.50 COVERS. WILLIAM MORRIS: MYTH, OBJECT AND THE ANIMAL / Some of the artwork in this book was shot after we designed the pages, and the flow of the exhibit—for which this serves as catalogue—heavily influenced the narrative of the book as a whole. In designing books about art, I think it is important for the viewer to experience the work as if they were there in person. Cropping, focus on details and juxtaposition of type and color can help frame and highlight those aspects of the artwork that are missing in a more traditional art book layout.

30

DESIGN FIRM	The Traver Company (now Methodologie), Seattle, WA
ART DIRECTOR	Anne Traver
DESIGNER	Margo Sepanski
PHOTOGRAPHERS	Robert Vinnedge, Russell Johnson
TRIM SIZE	9 5/8 x 10 1/2 inches
PAGES	64
TYPEFACES	Serifa, Adobe Caslon
PRINTER	C&C Offset Printing Co., Ltd.
AUTHOR	Holle Simmons
PUBLISHER	William Morris Studio

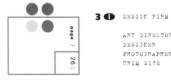

MYTH, OBJECT, AND THE ANIMAL

detail. / n 05

detail. / n 02

William Morris

Glass Installations

design firm. the traver company

50 books. 50 covers. | NO. 30

detail O1

detail O2

design firm. the traver company

50 books. 50 covers. | NO. 30

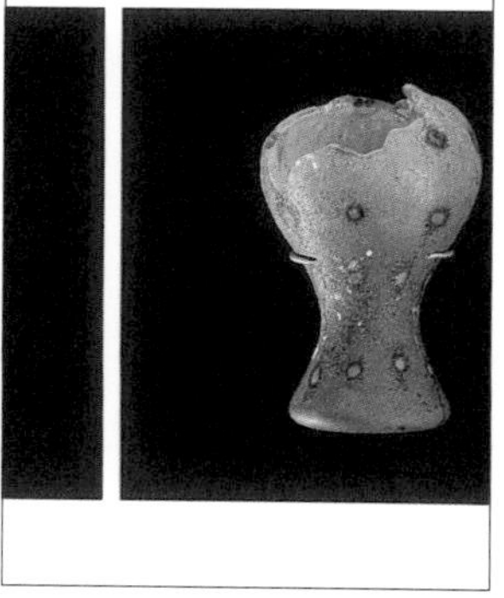

detail O3

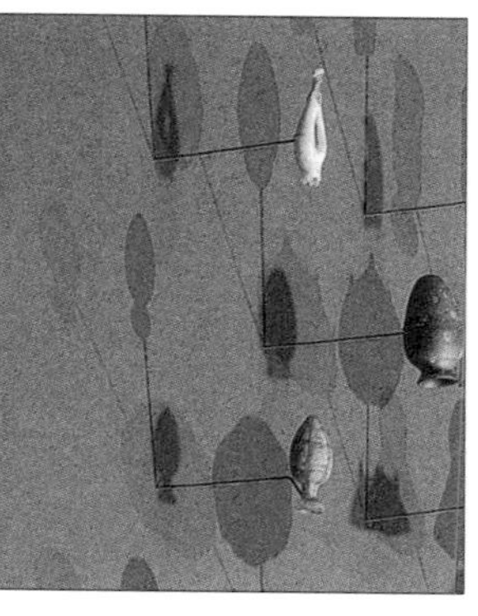

detail O4

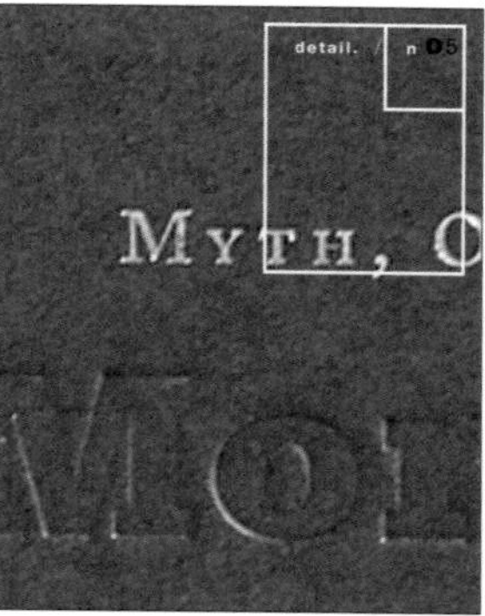

detail O5

design firm. the traver company

50 books. 50 covers. | NO. 30

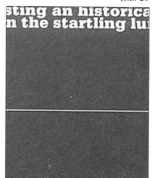

detail O6

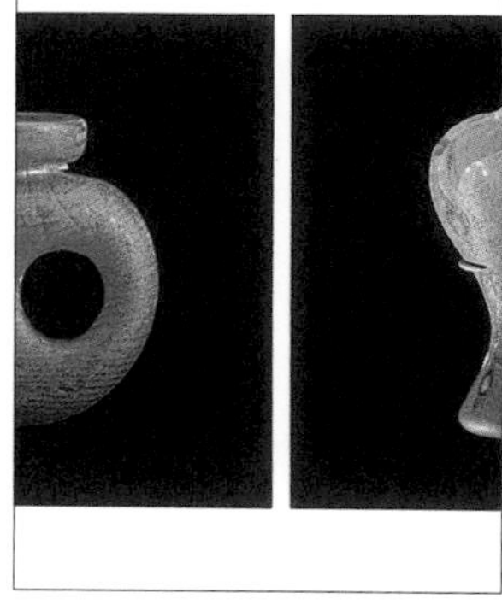

detail O7

31

DESIGN FIRM	Light Work, Syracuse, NY
ART DIRECTORS	Jeffrey Hoone, Gary Schneider, Carrie Mae Weems, Jerry Kelly
DESIGNER	Jeffrey Hoone
PHOTOGRAPHER	Gary Schneider
TRIM SIZE	10 x 8 inches
PAGES	64
TYPEFACE	Bembo
PRINTER	The Stinehour Press
PAPER	Mohawk Dulcet
PUBLISHER	Light Work

detail. / n 03

GARY SCHNEIDER

genetic self-portrait

design firm. light work

50 books. 50 covers. | NO. 31

design firm. light work

50 books. 50 covers. | NO. 31

design firm. light work

50 books. 50 covers. | NO. 31

50 books. 50 covers. / NO. 31

details. / n 01 - 7

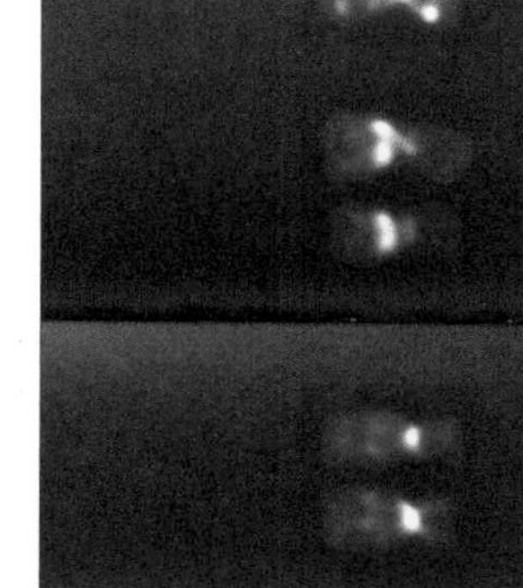

detail 01

detail 02

detail. / n 03

GARY

detail 03

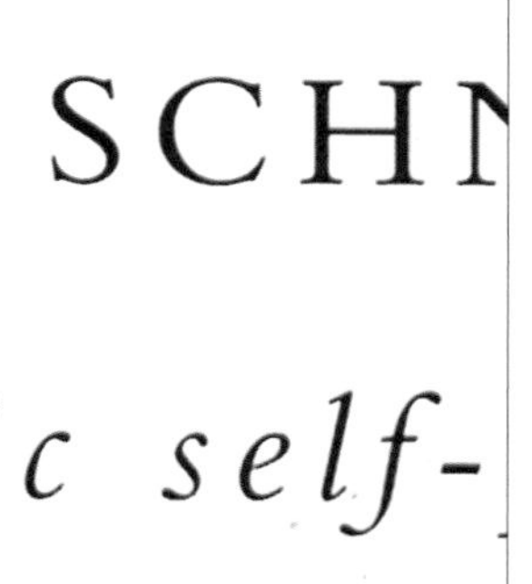

detail 04

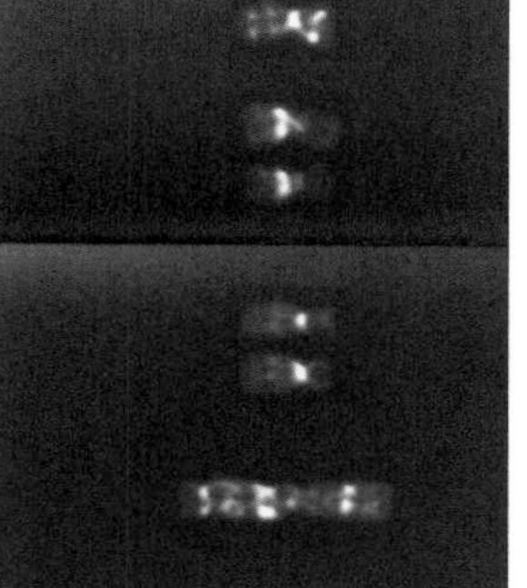

detail 05

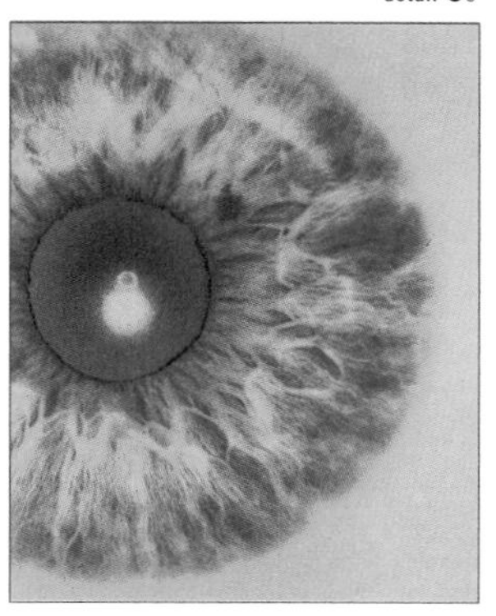

detail 06

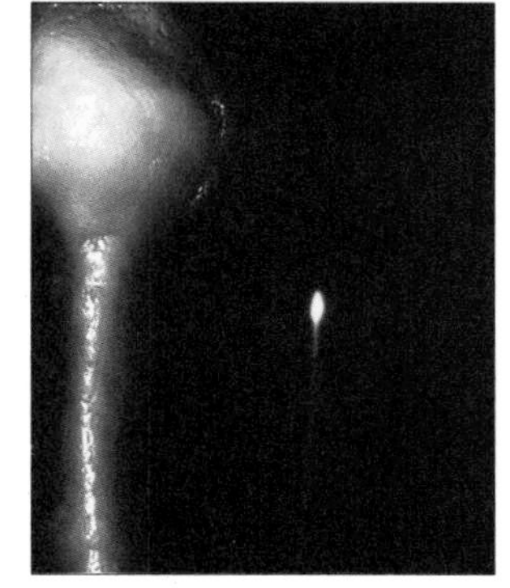

detail 07

32 50 BOOKS.50 COVERS. FRAGMENTED DEVOTION: MEDIEVAL OBJECTS FROM THE SCHNÜTGEN MUSEUM COLOGNE / The exhibition "Fragmented Devotion" explored modes of collecting, displaying and interpreting fragments of medieval devotional art using objects from the collection of Alexander Schnütgen, a 19th-century Catholic priest and collector in Cologne. The concept of the exhibition is conveyed through the use of three distinct typefaces—blackletter, 19th-century German typeface and sans serif. The idea of fragmentation is reflected in the exhibition's logo, in the subtle reference to a crucifix on the title page and on the part openers and in the "incomplete cross" appearing between the duotone images.

32

DESIGN FIRM	Julia Sedykh Design, Somerville, MA
ART DIRECTORS	Julia Sedykh, David Williams
DESIGNER	Julia Sedykh
TRIM SIZE	8 x 11 inches
PAGES	176
TYPEFACES	Berthold Walbaum, Thesis-The Sans, Goudy Text
PRINTER	Meridian Printing
PAPER	Mohawk Superfine, Potlatch McCoy
PUBLISHER	McMullen Museum of Art, Boston College

detail. / n03

FRAGMENTED devotion

detail. / n06

MEDIEVAL OBJECTS FROM THE SCHNÜTGEN MUSEUM COLOGNE

Edited by

NANCY NETZER

VIRGINIA REINBURG

McMullen Museum of Art

BOSTON COLLEGE

FRAGMENTED
devotion
MEDIEVAL OBJECTS FROM
THE SCHNUTGEN MUSEUM
COLOGNE

NANCY NETZER
VIRGINIA REINBURG

BOSTON COLLEGE

detail 01

detail 02

design firm. julia sedykh design

50 books. 50 covers. | NO. 32

detail 03

re significant, though, will be the
d the art a post-Holocaust cultu
rt fashions from matter and spi
the teaching of reverence for th
y and soul. And perhaps somec
ption of Mary will come to be u
ation of that integrity: the heave

detail 04

detail 05

design firm. julia sedykh design

50 books. 50 covers. | NO. 32

design firm. julia sedykh design

50 books. 50 covers. | NO. 32

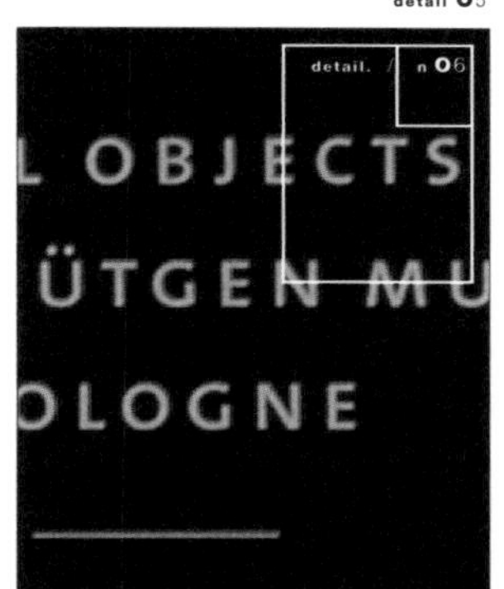

detail 06

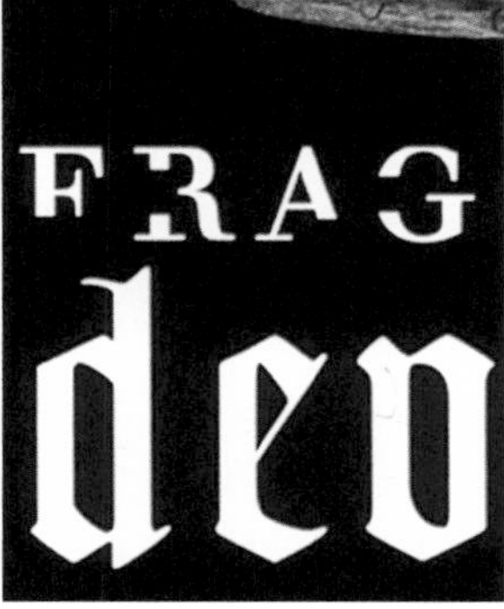

detail 07

33 50 BOOKS.50 COVERS. CITY SECRETS: ROME / Accepting the realities imposed by the small size of this guidebook presented a big challenge, as did designing intricate and detailed maps in this page size, with one color. I chose to use the personality of the book's unique content as a guide. A reader can use this book to quickly locate an additional spot of interest nearby or to study an area of the city for the next day's experience. Further cross-reference features allow a reader to look up a specific place or the full comments of a specific contributor.

33

DESIGN FIRM	Red Canoe, Deer Lodge, TN
CREATIVE DIRECTOR	Deb Koch
DESIGNER/ ILLUSTRATOR/ MAP DESIGNS	Caroline Kavanagh
PHOTOGRAPHY	Fototeca Unione, American Academy in Rome
TRIM SIZE	4 x 7 inches
PAGES	288
PRINTER/BINDER	South China Printing
PUBLISHER	The Little Bookroom

detail. / n 06

9

8

design firm. red canoe

50 books. 50 covers. | NO. 33

detail 01

ITINERARY

a Capitoline Museum, Room of the Dying Gaul

b Capitoline Museum, middle *salone*

c Church of the Cappuccini (Santa Maria della Concezione), via Vittorio Veneto

d Tarpeian Rock

Read *The Marble Fa*
go to the Dying Gaul,
here proceed through
to the great, middle s
Hawthorne's Marble
hard to track down as
in the room. (Georgin
Hawthorne's faun in t
Dying Gaul, but, to m
there nor in the Sala
the large *salone* is m
with Hawthorne's des
fully and you will find
the words of Hawtho
animal, yet no monste
both races meet on fr
"if the spectator broo
the statue, he will be

design firm. red canoe

50 books. 50 covers. | NO. 33

detail 02

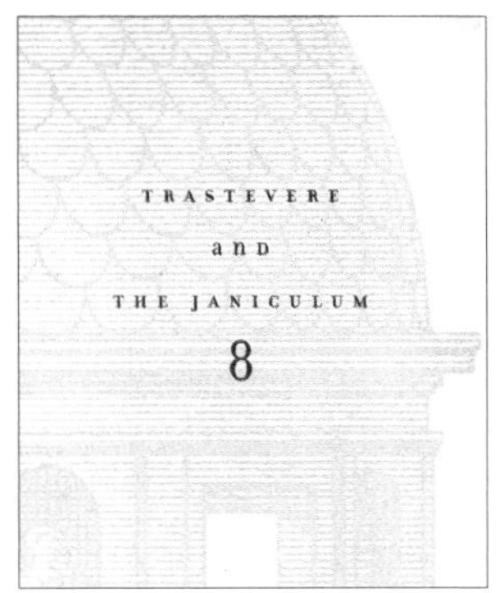

detail 03

detail 04

design firm. red canoe

50 books. 50 covers. | NO. 33

guide

detail 05

detail 06

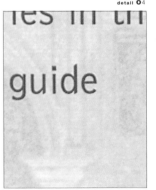

34 50 BOOKS.50 COVERS. WINE / There were no special challenges with this book. It was a project where the book was conceived in total in my mind and then I just created the final digital files based on that vision. The design solution was a very formal, straightforward presentation of things related to wine such as wine-tasting terminology, facts, symbolism, graphic ephemera, etc. This book obviously just touches briefly on these subjects and was meant to provide some basic information to the attendees of a wine-tasting event.

34

DESIGN FIRM	Polite Design, Philadelphia, PA
DESIGNER/ ILLUSTRATOR/ PHOTOGRAPHER	Kerry Polite
TRIM SIZE	4 1/2 x 6 3/4 inches
PAGES	48
TYPEFACE	Trade Gothic Regular
PRINTER	Pearl Pressman Liberty
PAPER	Mohawk Superfine
PUBLISHER	AIGA Philadelphia

design firm. polite design

50 books. 50 covers. | NO. 34

detail O1

DEEP/ DEPTH
THIS WINE IS WORTH TASTING
THERE IS MORE TO IT TH
IMPRESSION; IT FILLS YOU
DEVELOPING FLAVORS. DEE
MEANS HARD TO SEE

FIRM
FLAVOR THAT STRIKES THE PA
WITH HIGH ACIDITY OR TANN
GIVING THE IMPRESSION THA
YOUTHFUL VIGOR AND WILL
THINGS. AN EXCELLENT QUA
FLAVORED FOODS, AND AL
POSITIVE.

detail O2

design firm. polite design

50 books. 50 covers. | NO. 34

W I N E

detail O3

detail O4

design firm. polite design

50 books. 50 covers. | NO. 34

TAKE COUNSEL
IN WINE
BUT RESOLVE
AFTERWARDS
IN WATER.
BENJAMIN FRANKLIN

detail O5

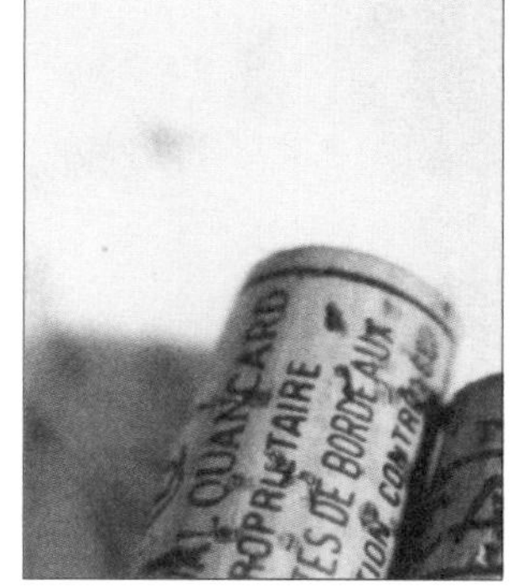

detail O6

35 50 BOOKS.50 COVERS. MEMORY, MATTER AND MODERN ROMANCE: BRUCE AND NORMAN YONEMOTO /
Since 1976, the brothers Bruce and Norman Yonemoto have created an extensive body of film, single-channel video installations and objects that explore the creation of meaning through filmic representation and analyze mass media's hold on our perceptions of personal identity. This book engages the viewer's imagination in an exploration of their cinematic works within the parameters inherent to the opaque, static surface of the print medium. Strategically captured frame sequences have been synchronized with the essays as sound to film. In this format the stories unfold in fragments, encouraging the possibility for a creative narrative interpretation.

35

DESIGN FIRM	Shiffman Design, Santa Monica, CA
ART DIRECTOR	Tracey Shiffman
PHOTOGRAPHERS	Bruce and Norman Yonemoto
TRIM SIZE	11 1/4 x 9 1/4 inches
PAGES	104
COMPOSITOR	Shiffman Design
TYPEFACES	Frutiger and Mrs. Eaves
PRINTER	Delta Graphics
PAPER	Starwhite Vicksburg, Mountie Matte
CURATOR	Karin Higa
PUBLISHER	Japanese American National Museum, Fellows of Contemporary Art

design firm. shiffman design

50 books. 50 covers. | NO. 35

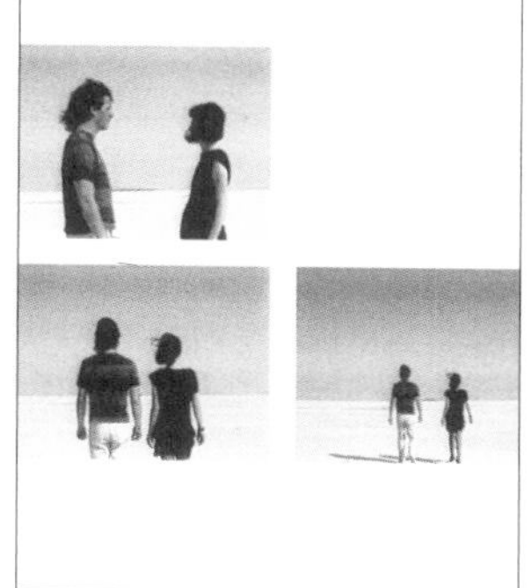

detail 01

detail 02

design firm. shiffman design

50 books. 50 covers. | NO. 35

detail 03

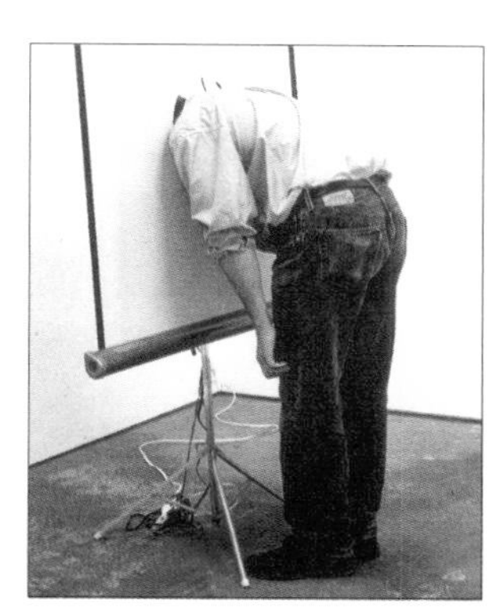

detail 04

memory
matter and
modern ROMANCE

detail. n 05

Bruce and Norman Yonemoto

detail 05

design firm. shiffman design

50 books. 50 covers. | NO. 35

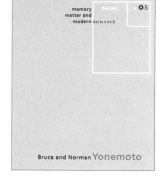

detail 06

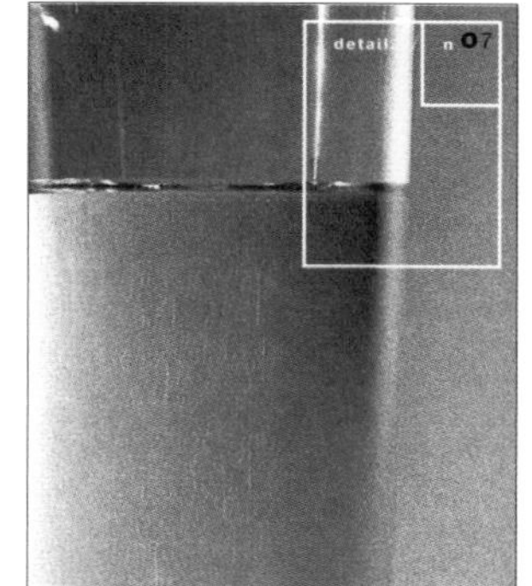

detail 07

FOR GIGI

detail. / no2

Richard Wiley

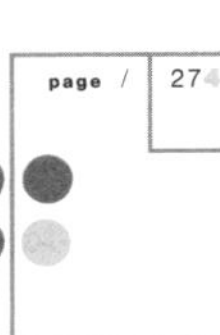

3G DESIGN FIRM The Perishable Press Limited, Mount Horeb, WI

CREATIVE DIRECTOR/DESIGNER/COMPOSITOR Walter Hamady

ILLUSTRATOR Jim Lee

TRIM SIZE 9 3/4 x 6 7/8 inches

PAGES 32

TYPEFACE Gill Sans

PRINTER/BINDER Walter Hamady

PUBLISHER The Perishable Press Limited

design firm. the perishable press limited

50 books. 50 covers. | NO. 36

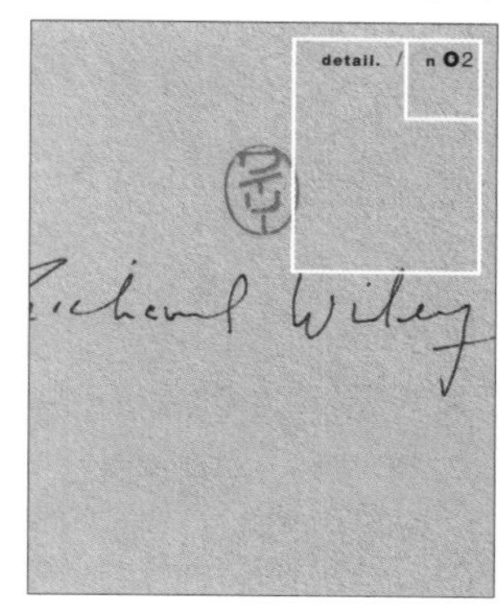

detail 01

detail 02

design firm. the perishable press limited

50 books. 50 covers. | NO. 36

MANJIRO HAD NOT TOLD A
chocolates, but on an extraordinary v
and gave them to Fumiko's sister, Tsu
early the next day.
Manjiro had met this sister twice be
Einosuke and Fumiko's wedding, and
cherry blossom viewing excursion to K
at the wedding, but in Kyoto they sat
wooden walkway that bordered th
Temple, while Einosuke sketched the g
his replica. Tsune held the infant, Mas
younger than her sister by some doz
was clear she would become the tru
exquisite of face and form, but in pos

detail 03

detail 04

detail 05

design firm. the perishable press limited

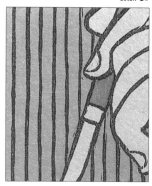

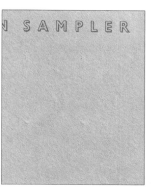

50 books. 50 covers. | NO. 36

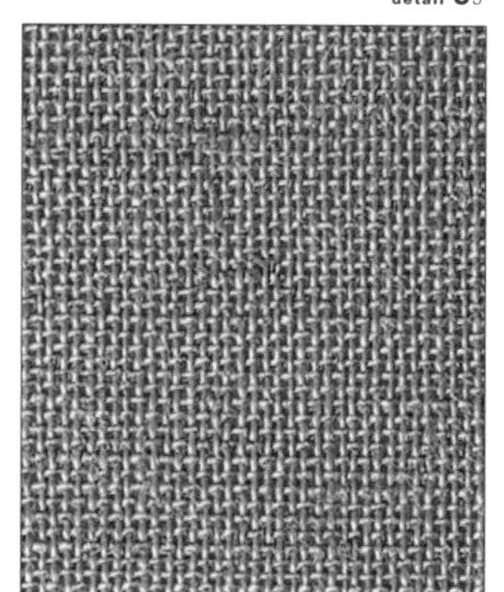

detail 06

detail 07

37 50 BOOKS.50 COVERS. SAVION! MY LIFE IN TAP / The greatest challenge was to transmit the spirit of Savion Glover's artistic approach to a young audience. I reflected this by developing a fairly traditional editorial/book format and inserting large-scale elements throughout the book that serve to animate the page or provide a place to rest. I created a visual vocabulary by emphasizing type size, weight and color to communicate Glover's particular creative process, which entails a collaboration with others in a sort of "scat" dialogue wherein he sounds out various taps to the floor.

37

DESIGN FIRM	Paula Kelly Design, New York, NY
ART DIRECTORS	Paula Kelly, Barbara Fitzimmons
DESIGNER	Paula Kelly
PHOTOGRAPHER	Various
TRIM SIZE	7 1/4 x 9 inches
PAGES	80
TYPEFACES	Eurostyle and Clarendon
PRINTER	Quebecor Hawkins
AUTHORS	Savion Glover, Bruce Weber
PUBLISHER	William Morrow and Company, Inc.

design firm. paula kelly design

50 books. 50 covers. | NO. 37

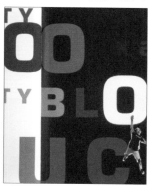

detail O1

detail O2

detail O3

design firm. paula kelly design

50 books. 50 covers. | NO. 37

detail O4

detail O5

design firm. paula kelly design

50 books. 50 covers. | NO. 37

detail O6

detail O7

38 50 BOOKS.50 COVERS. THE AUTOBIOGRAPHY OF MICHEL DE MONTAIGNE / I decided we ought to go out in style and make this edition an especially elegant one, classical and generous in its proportions, printed inside and out on especially nice textured papers. I made my first text typeface especially for this great classic, though it appeared in a number of titles published before this one. It is called Montaigne Sabon, inspired in part by some drawings for a never-realized foundry version of Jan Tschichold's famous Sabon types. The result is a very restrained design of generous proportions intended for long-haul reading.

38

DESIGN FIRM	The Philidor Company, Jamaica Plain, MA
ART DIRECTOR/ DESIGNER/ COMPOSITOR	Scott-Martin Kosofsky
TRIM SIZE	5 1/2 x 8 1/4 inches
PAGES	384
TYPEFACES	Montaigne Sabon, Duc de Berry, Mantinia
PRINTER/BINDER	Daamen Printing
PAPER	Glatfelter laid 55 pound
AUTHOR	Michel de Montaigne
PUBLISHER	David R. Godine Inc.

detail. / n 06

THE AUTOBIOGRAPHY OF

Michel de Montaign

design firm. the philidor company

50 books. 50 covers. | NO. 38

·MI

MO

detail 01

Contents

n and His World

arvin Lowenthal

detail 02

design firm. the philidor company

50 books. 50 covers. | NO. 38

THE AU

Michel

COMPRISIN

MAN OF HIS

YOUTH, AND

detail 03

detail 04

MO

TRA

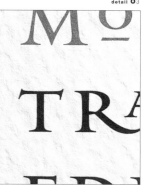

detail 05

design firm. the philidor company

50 books. 50 covers. | NO. 38

detail. / n 06

THE

Mich

detail 06

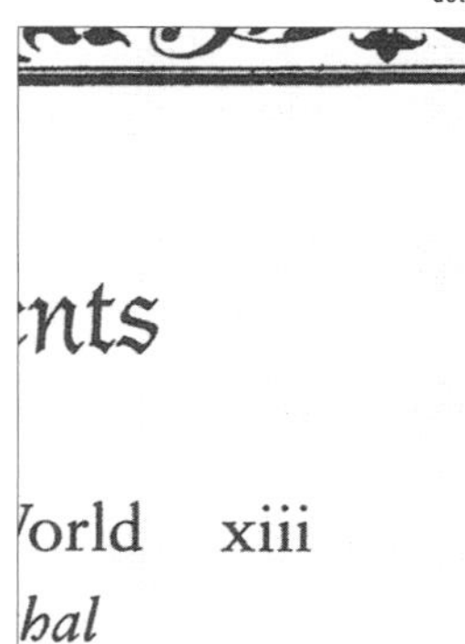

detail 07

39 50 BOOKS.50 COVERS. ADAM'S SKETCHBOOK / This book grew out of an assignment to my graphic design class at the University of Illinois at Chicago. I gave them a print of Dürer's Adam and Eve in the Garden of Eden and asked them to use the inherent symbolism but bring it up to date by altering the image or context. I was also fascinated by the amount of information compressed into the first three chapters of Genesis, so I decided to decompress it using Adam as a device to express my ideas about art, politics, science and nature.

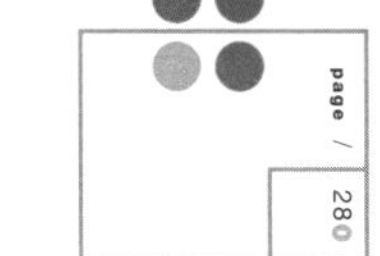
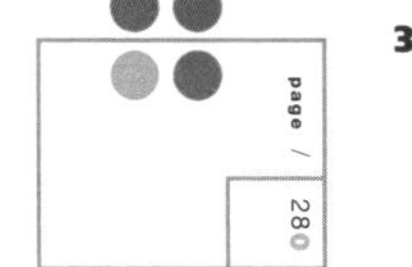

39

DESIGN FIRM	Greiner Design Associates, Chicago, IL
ART DIRECTOR/ DESIGNER/ ILLUSTRATOR	John Greiner
PHOTOGRAPHERS	Kenneth Short, David Bentley
TRIM SIZE	8 x 8 inches
PAGES	80
TYPEFACES	Gill Sans, ITC Novarese
PRINTER	Arla Graphics
PAPER	Crane's Crest Natural 10016
AUTHOR	John Greiner
PUBLISHER	Ravenswood Editions

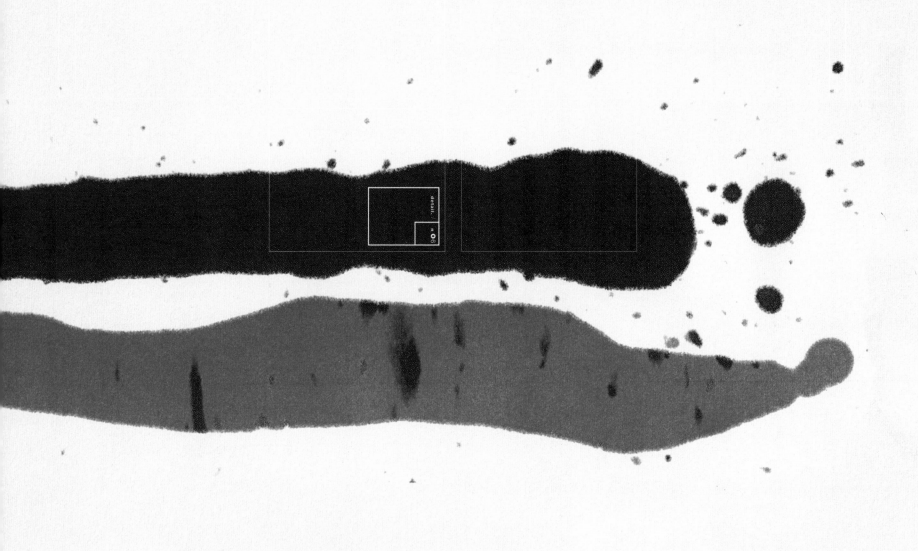

detail. / n 06

Adam's Sketchbook
A Fable on Cre
John Greiner
Ravenswood

detail O1

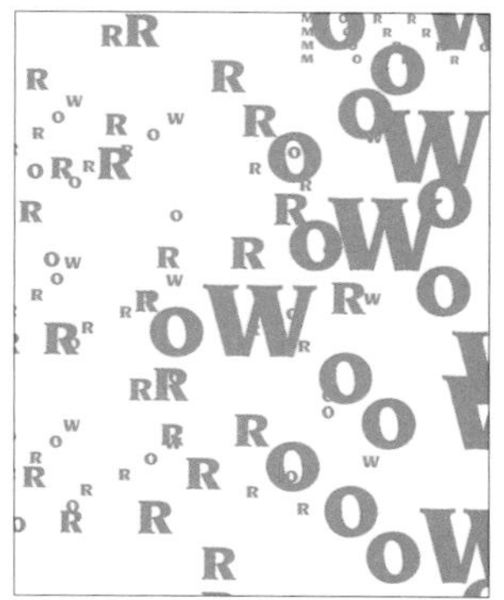

detail O2

design firm. greiner design associates

50 books. 50 covers. | NO. 39

trage gripppe
hag riss
magen abritt
verlag kurios
flag trial
again reprieve
rage crime
daggar brittle
agitar amarillo
agua motrida
cagamelos corriz
guagua retorica
agaru amari
hagaki naritatsu
ehagaki tori
okage buriki
aglio zarina
adagio tugurio
passaggio risorsa
maga marinare

detail O3

design firm. greiner design associates

50 books. 50 covers. | NO. 39

yclopedia of facts.
a thousand forests
is in one acorn,
and Egypt, Greece, Ro
y in the first man.

would be a man
must be a non conformist.

Ralph Waldo Emerson

detail O4

detail O5

design firm. greiner design associates

50 books. 50 covers. | NO. 39

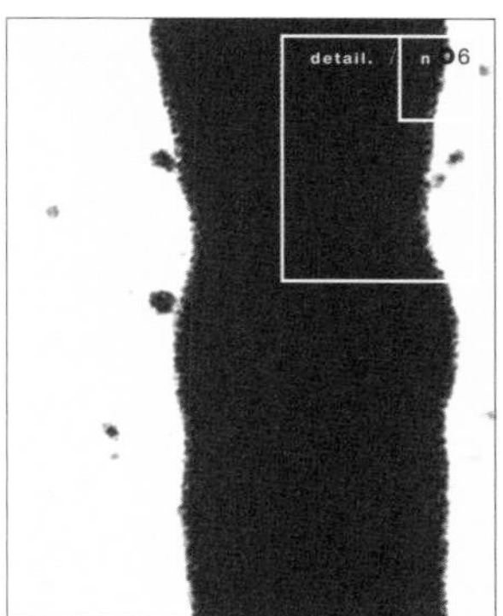

detail O6

detail O7

40 50 BOOKS.50 COVERS. ALVAR NÚÑEZ CABEZA DE VACA / This account of Cabeza de Vaca's voyage across California in the 16th century appears in the original Spanish with a parallel translation in English. Extensive notes accompany the text in both languages and entries vary considerably in length. The basic design problem was to relate so many variables while retaining some feeling of an historically appropriate typography. A fairly complex manuscript like this is actually easier to design than a novel or biography, because its problems are readily identifiable and point toward their own resolution.

40

DESIGN FIRM	University of Nebraska Press, Lincoln, NE
DESIGNER	Richard Eckersley
TRIM SIZE	7 1/2 x 10 1/2 inches
PAGES	1,412 (three volumes)
TYPEFACE	Adobe Minion
PRINTER/BINDER	Edwards Brothers, Inc.
PAPER	Glatfelter Offset B16 55 pound
PUBLISHER	University of Nebraska Press

detail. / n 03

[f48r]

design firm. university of nebraska press

50 books. 50 covers. | NO. 40

b. Suárez] Z: Gutiérrez

there went about
make mention
are named here:
Enríquez [as] co
inspector of min
Suárez[b] went as
with him. We arr
forty-five days st
more than one h
remain there bec
made to them.
a port on the isl
there, the govern
it occurred that

detail O1

a. long] V: long, merino, like an Hibernian cape.

b. over] V: over all

c.] Z: *om.* V: Chapter nineteen: Of how the Indians separated us.

Cows sometimes ra
them. And it seems
have small horns li
brown and others b
of it than those fro
make robes to cove
they make shoes a
through the land to
more than four hu
the valleys through
down and sustain th
quantity of hides.[5]
[c]When the six m
to put into effect th
pears, which is from
leagues.[6] And when
us fought amongst
and struck one ano
And with the great

detail O2

design firm. university of nebraska press

50 books. 50 covers. | NO. 40

detail. / n O3

[f48r]

detail O3

b. over] V: over all

detail O4

[f1r]

a. The account . . . company] V: The account and commentaries of Governor Álvar Núñez Cabeza de Vaca, of what occurred on the two journeys he made to the Indies. By royal authorization. Valuated by the lords of the Council [of Castile] at eighty-five *maravedís*.

The account that Álvar Núñez Cabeza de Va
Indies on the expedition of which Pánfilo
from the year [15]27 to [15]36, when he
members of his company.[a]

detail O5

design firm. university of nebraska press

50 books. 50 covers. | NO. 40

[f34r]

a. long] V: long, merino, like an Hibernian cape.

detail O6

our authori
Two leagues
for the peop
the Indians
mountains.
bade us fare
to their hon

detail O7

41 50 BOOKS.50 COVERS. EDWARD RUSCHA: EDITIONS 1959–1999 / As a catalogue raisonné that documents the complete body of graphic editions by this Los Angeles-based artist, the challenge was to organize the extensive amount of information associated with Ruscha's vast array of works. The book was split into two parts: volume 1 contains the images that document all of the editioned works; volume 2 contains the words that comprise the essays. Volume 1 was structured on a consistent horizontal line that organizes the works in chronological order and shows them in proportional scale to each other.

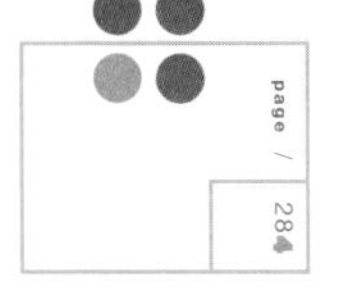

41

DESIGN FIRM	Walker Art Center Design Department, Minneapolis, MN
DESIGN DIRECTOR	Andrew Blauvelt
DESIGNER/ COMPOSITOR	Conny Purtill
PHOTOGRAPHER	Dan Dennehy
TRIM SIZE	10 x 12 1/4 inches
PAGES	160 (volume one), 128 (volume 2)
PRINTER/BINDER	Dr. Cantz'sche Druckerei
PAPER	BVS matte 150 gram
PUBLISHER	Walker Art Center

detail. / n05

Catalogue Raisonné, Volume

PRINTS
BOOKS
MISC.

design firm. walker art center

50 books. 50 covers. | NO. 41

detail O1

detail O2

detail O3

design firm. walker art center

50 books. 50 covers. | NO. 41

detail O4

detail O5

detail O6

design firm. walker art center

50 books. 50 covers. | NO. 41

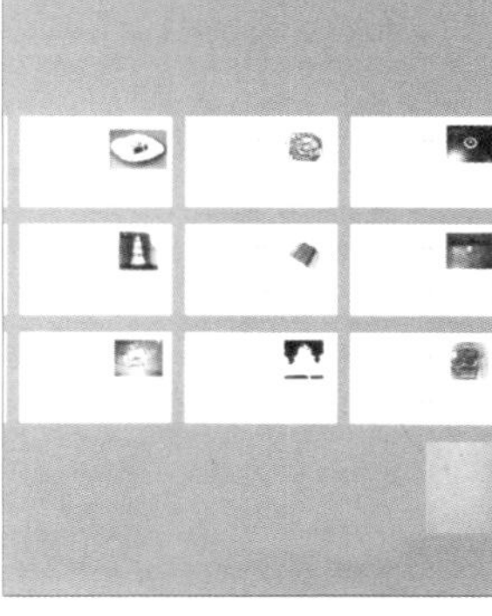

detail O7

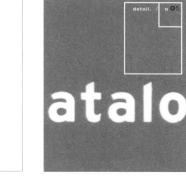

42 50 BOOKS.50 COVERS. MORPHOSIS: BUILDINGS AND PROJECTS 1993–1997 / The architecture firm Morphosis has gone completely "digital," so the only conventional images to work with were preliminary sketches and photographs of a few study models and completed buildings. We wanted to create a process that would allow the architects a way to visually explicate the projects. The first 256 pages of the book were initially conceived of as a continuous "accordion" drawing created by the architects in a variety of CAD programs that were then imported into Quark, where the designers added typographic information.

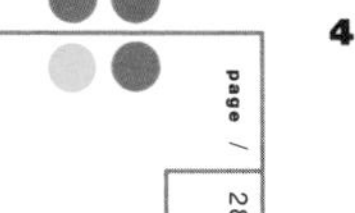

42

DESIGN FIRM	Lorraine Wild Design, Los Angeles, CA
CREATIVE DIRECTORS	Lorraine Wild, Thom Mayne
DESIGNERS	Lorraine Wild and Thom Mayne with Bele Cucke, Scott Lee, Ana Llorent-Thurik, Robyn Sambo
ILLUSTRATOR	Various
PHOTOGRAPHER	Various
TRIM SIZE	8 1/2 x 11 inches
PRINTER/BINDER	Sfera Srl
PUBLISHER	Rizzoli International Publications

1996

1997

detail. / a 04

Buildings

design firm. lorraine wild design

50 books. 50 covers. | NO. 42

detail 01

detail 02

design firm. lorraine wild design

50 books. 50 covers. | NO. 42

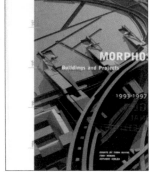

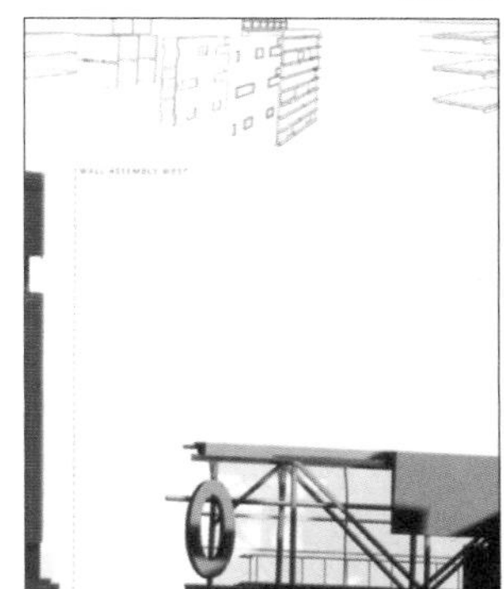

detail 03

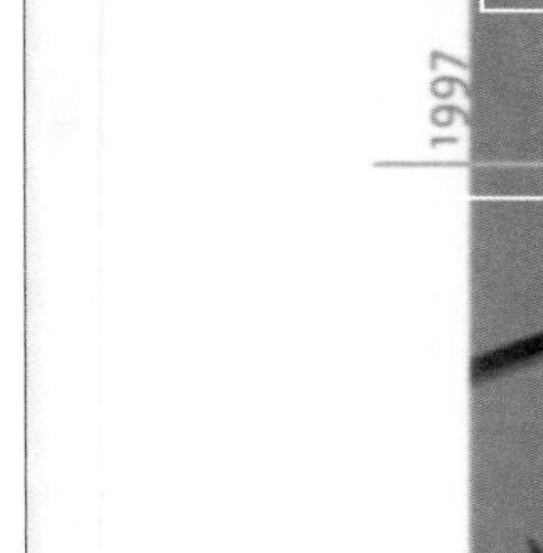

detail 04

detail 05

design firm. lorraine wild design

50 books. 50 covers. | NO. 42

detail 06

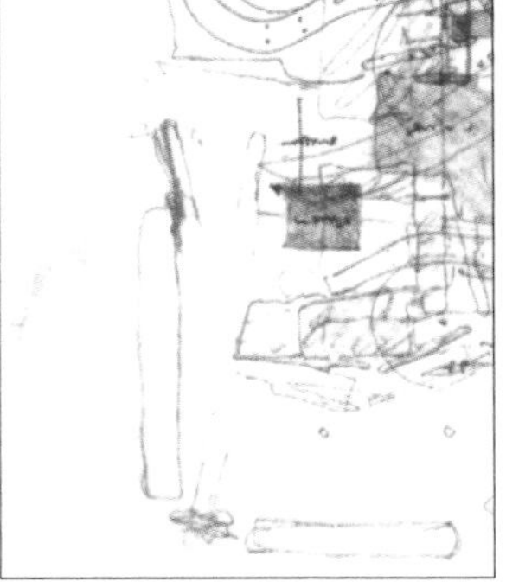

detail 07

 / By keeping all the poems to one page, the book keeps to a consistent rhythm of image on left, poem on right. I made the book an engaging visual balance of word and picture by being sensitive to spacing on the page. In reference to the historical nature of the book's content (17th-century Elizabethan bestiaries) and the medium of illustration (pen-and-ink drawings), the book was printed in black ink with red titling. Also, the cover and the spine were letterpress printed by hand with metal type to add to the tactile nature of the book.

43

DESIGN FIRM Horse & Buggy Press, Raleigh, NC
ART DIRECTOR/DESIGNER Dave Wofford
ILLUSTRATOR Ippy Patterson
PHOTOGRAPHER M.J. Sharp
TRIM SIZE 8 x 11 inches

PAGES 92
TYPEFACES Jenson, Goudy Lombardic Capitals
PRINTER A.D.S. Printing (offset), Horse & Buggy Press (letterpress)
PUBLISHER Horse & Buggy Press

Shape changers
appearing, vanishing at will.
Seeing all when abroad.
Removing their eyes when home.

With beautiful kind love
bewitching
men
only
to feed on them.

Breasts large,
desirous.
No other voice but as
the dragon's hiss.

With cumbrous male stones
filthy
smelling of sea calves.

With a goat's back parts
a bear's forelegs
a woman's upper parts.

Scaled
like a dragon.

THE *Lamia*

detail. /

design firm. horse & buggy press

50 books. 50 covers. | NO. 43

An Elizabethan

detail O1

Bestiary: Retold

Poems
Jeffery Beam

Illustrations
Ippy Patterson

Photographs
M. J. Sharp

detail O2

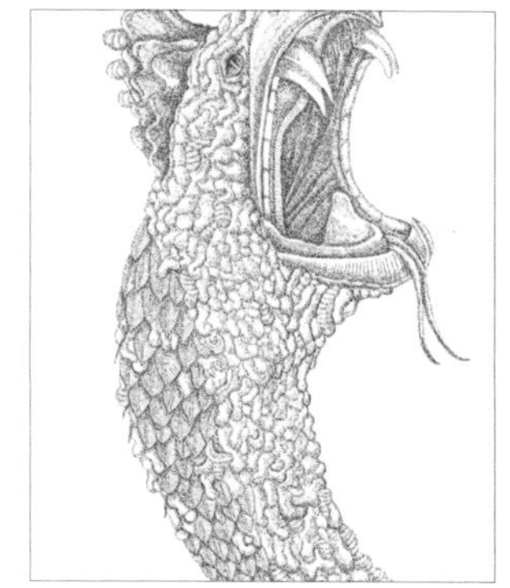

detail O3

design firm. horse & buggy press

50 books. 50 covers. | NO. 43

detail. / n O4

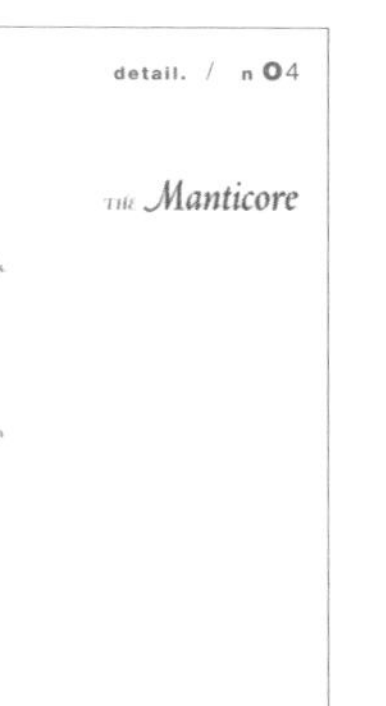

Three rows of teeth
A lion's feet.
A man's face and ears.
Gray-eyed, red
Tail armed
with sharp
castable quills.

A voice
trumpet-like.

Devourer.
Relisher of
man
flesh.

THE Manticore

detail O4

ETHAN

Retold

detail O5

design firm. horse & buggy press

50 books. 50 covers. | NO. 43

detail O6

detail O7

detail. / n 05

THE HISTORIOGRAPHY OF MODERN ARCHITECTURE

PANAYOTIS TOURNIKIOTIS

41 DESIGN FIRM MIT Press Design Department, Cambridge, MA
ART DIRECTOR/DESIGNER Jim McWethy
TRIM SIZE 7 x 9 inches
PAGES 360

TYPEFACES Garamond 3, Symbol Greek, Times Roman
PRINTER/BINDER Edwards Brothers, Inc.
PAPER Utopia 3 matte
AUTHOR Panayotis Tournikiotis
PUBLISHER The MIT Press

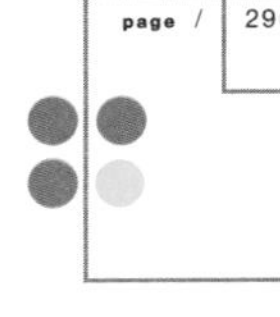

design firm. mit press design department

50 books. 50 covers. | NO. 44

THE
HISTORIOG
OF
MODER
ARCHITEC

detail 01

RAPHY
RN
TURE

detail 02

detail 03

design firm. mit press design department

50 books. 50 covers. | NO. 44

detail 04

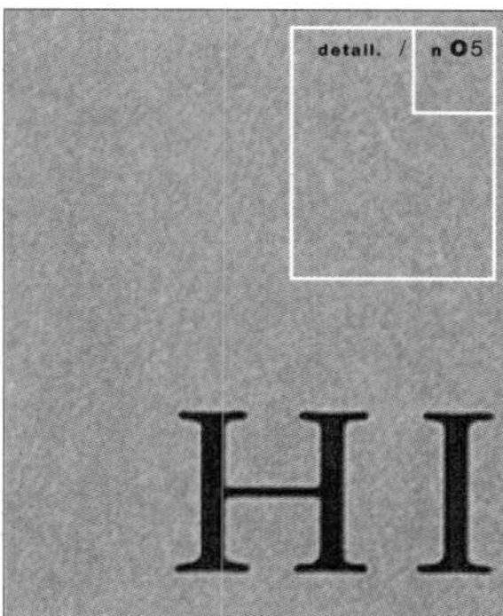

detail 05

design firm. mit press design department

50 books. 50 covers. | NO. 44

52 "Doric, for [Cho
previous ages. '.
new types, more

53 "Gothic . . . was
the culmination
ised being whose
traditional mod

detail 06

FIGURE 2.2
The spiral evolution of the history of archi
in Bruno Zevi, *Storia dell'architettura mo*
(Turin: Einaudi, 1950), p. 552

detail 07

45 50 BOOKS.50 COVERS. THE SUNDAY LECTIONARY, YEAR B / This three-volume lectionary is designed to grace the large rooms where Mass is celebrated. The design objective was to display the three Scripture readings per Sunday with utmost clarity and dignity while eliminating disruptive page-turnings. Primary factors determined the structural proportions and typography, the size of the book, reading distance, traditional line breaks and the rhythm of reading. The use of vermilion and of generous margins allow the coordinated and consistent presentation of emphasized, secondary and reference texts. Foils of different colors replace the imbedded jewels that traditionally served as ornament.

45

DESIGN FIRM	Liturgy Training Publications, Chicago, IL
DESIGNERS	Katharine Weingart-Wolff, Kerry Ishizaki, Anna Manhart
ILLUSTRATOR	Linda Ekstrom
TRIM SIZE	9 5/8 x 13 1/2 inches
PAGES	480
TYPEFACES	Goudy Oldstyle, Syntax Italic
PRINTER	Thiessen Printing and Graphics Corporation
PAPER	Mohawk Satin
PUBLISHER	Liturgy Training Publications

design firm. liturgy training publications

50 books. 50 covers. | NO. 45

detail O1

detail O2

design firm. liturgy training publications

50 books. 50 covers. | NO. 45

detail O3

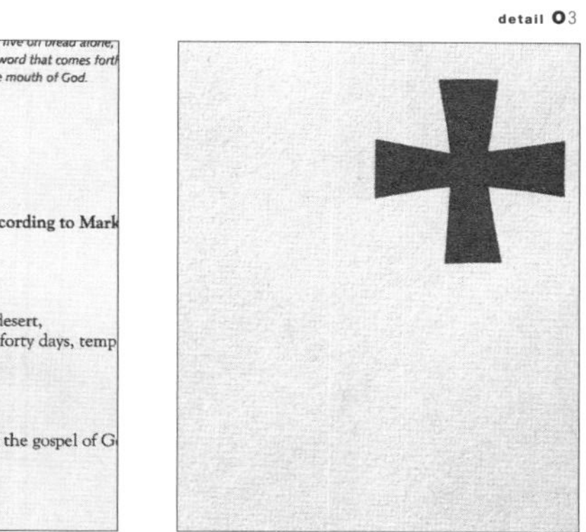

detail O4

detail O5

design firm. liturgy training publications

50 books. 50 covers. | NO. 45

detail. / n O6

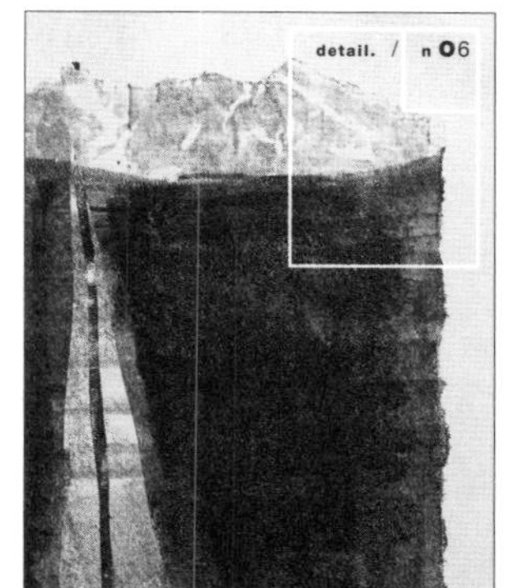

detail O6

detail O7

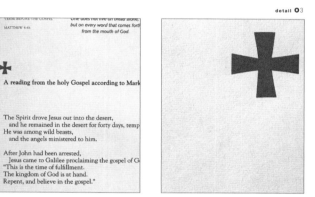

46

DESIGN FIRM	Lorraine Wild Design, Los Angeles, CA
ART DIRECTOR	Lorraine Wild
DESIGNERS	Lorraine Wild, Andrea Tinnes
PHOTOGRAPHER	Pat Pollard Studio
TRIM SIZE	14 1/4 x 11 3/8 inches
PAGES	392
TYPEFACE	Quadraat, Nobel, calligraphy by Midori Kono Thiel
PRINTER	Quebecor MI+L
PAPER	Parilux gloss text 115 pound
PUBLISHER	Cotsen Occasional Press

detail / n 03

design firm. lorraine wild design

50 books. 50 covers. | NO. 46

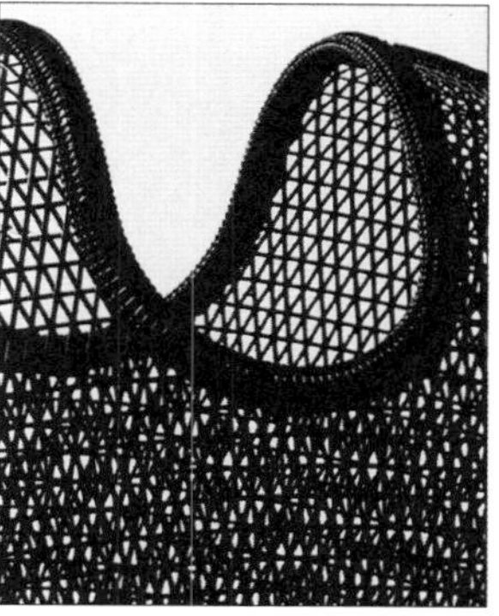

detail O1

design firm. lorraine wild design

50 books. 50 covers. | NO. 46

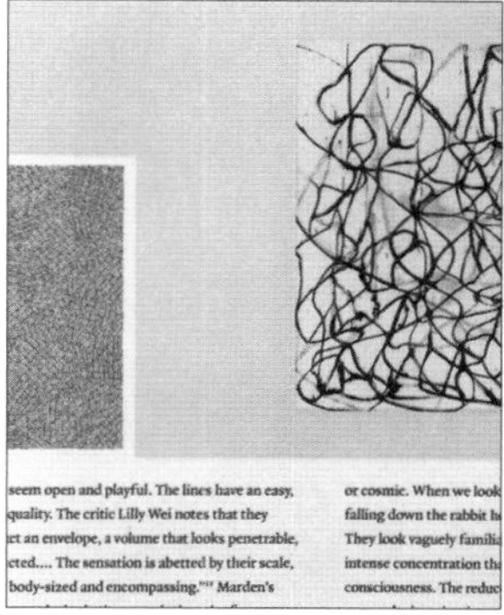

seem open and playful. The lines have an easy,
quality. The critic Lilly Wei notes that they
ct an envelope, a volume that looks penetrable,
cted.... The sensation is abetted by their scale,
body-sized and encompassing."[11] Marden's

or cosmic. When we look
falling down the rabbit h
They look vaguely famili
intense concentration th
consciousness. The reduc

detail O2

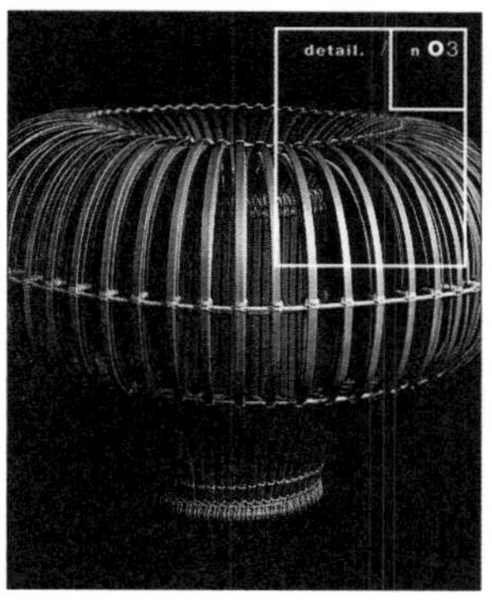

detail O3

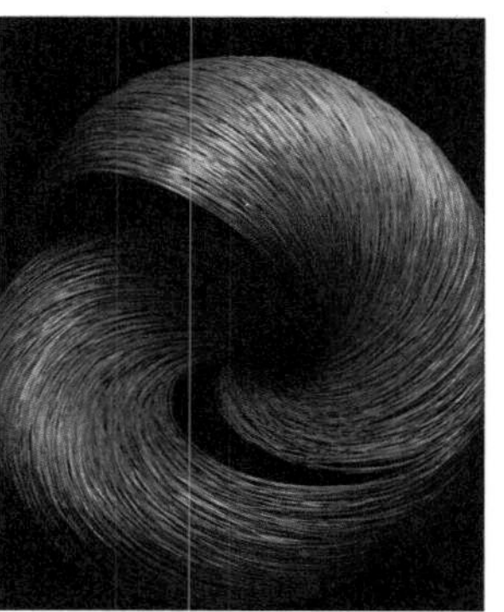

detail O4

design firm. lorraine wild design

50 books. 50 covers. | NO. 46

LIBRARY OF CONGRESS CATALOG CARD NUMB

its
of baskets in the collection are by Pat Pollard,
o, Taos, N.M., except for details of signatures
by Dennis Nervig, Second Wind Productions.

ll other artworks are courtesy of the owner
noted otherwise:
otsen
tography Studio, Los Angeles County

alerie Jaudon/licensed by VAGA, New York, NY
1998 by Brice Marden/ARS, New York;
ouglas M. Parker Studio
tograph © Sarah Wells 1995
tograph by Geoffrey Clements
13, fig. 4; p. 115, fig. 7; p. 119,
nal Museum of Modern Art, Tokyo
97 Kou Chifusa/Photonica

Type set in Quadraat and Nobel by Lorraine Wil

A note on the typefaces
Quadraat was designed in 1961 by Fred Smeijer
The Netherlands; and Nobel was designed in 19
in Amsterdam, The Netherlands, and then digit
by Tobias Frere-Jones, USA.

Calligraphy by Midori Kono Thiel, Seattle, Was
The calligraphy on page 121 is in the cursive (g

Separations and electronic retouching by Digita
Offset printing by Quebecor MIL, Toronto, Onta
Binding by Anstey Book Binding, Inc., Toronto

detail O5

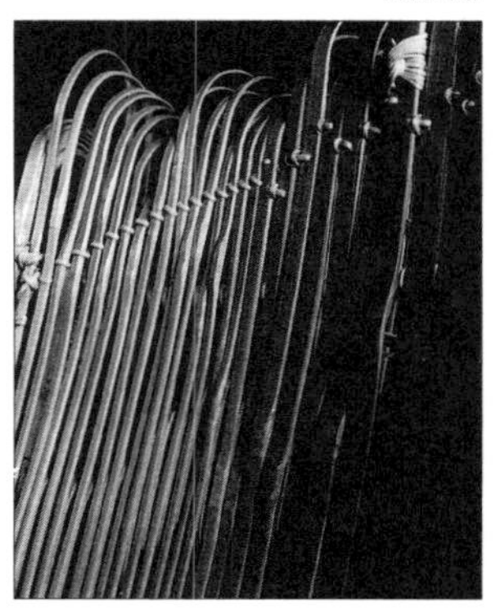

detail O6

47 50 BOOKS.50 COVERS. OF THE FABRIC OF THE HUMAN BODY, BOOK II: THE LIGAMENTS AND MUSCLES / The original text (published in Latin in 1543) consisted of seven books contained in one large folio, approximately 10 x 16 inches. Our challenge was to preserve the integrity and beauty of the text while maintaining a format that was accessible and informative. The size of the text required that the work be split into several volumes. We decided on a 9 x 12 trim size that would allow almost all of the illustrations to be printed at full size. We picked a readily available text stock that was similar in appearance and feel to works published in the 16th century.

47

DESIGN FIRM	Norman Publishing, San Anselmo, CA
DESIGNER	Steve Renick
TRIM SIZE	9 x 12 inches
PAGES	492
TYPEFACES	Bembo, Centaur
PRINTER/BINDER	Thomson-Shore, Inc.
PAPER	Mohawk Superfine Softwhite Eggshell
AUTHOR	Andreas Vesalius
PUBLISHER	Norman Publishing

detail / no3

ANDREAS VESALIUS

THE FABRIC OF HUMAN BODY

A Translation of

umani Corporis Fabrica Libri Septem

BOOK II

The Ligaments and Muscles

ANDREAE VESALII
BRVXELLENSIS, SCHOLAE
medicorum Patauinae professoris, de
Humani corporis fabrica
Libri septem.

detail O1

design firm. norman publishing

50 books. 50 covers. | NO. 47

ON THE FABRIC OF THE HUMAN

Translator's Notes

MUSCLES MOVING THE THIGH

VESALIUS	MUSCLE TABLES											
	I	II	III	IV	V	VI	VII	VIII	IX	X	XI	XII
First		u		v					Π	κ		
Second		y		μ	ς				o	Σ	δ	
Third						ν					Σ	t
Fourth										β	Φ	u
Fifth: largest in body		ε ζ		ϕ	ω	ς	β	Φ c	x	ρ	Ω	Ξ Σ Π

detail O2

design firm. norman publishing

50 books. 50 covers. | NO. 47

detail. / n O3

OF

MA

detail O3

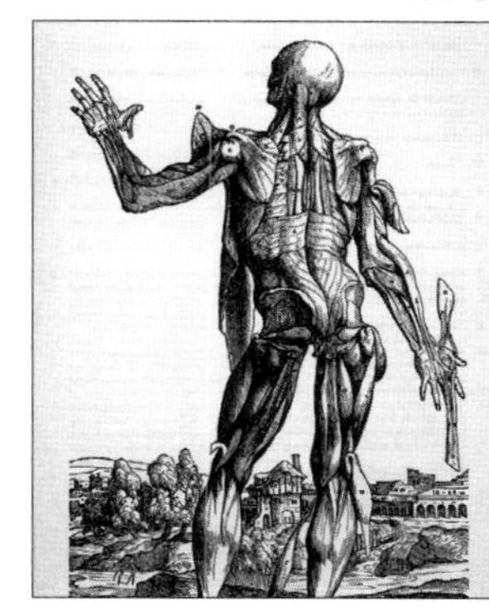

detail O4

design firm. norman publishing

50 books. 50 covers. | NO. 47

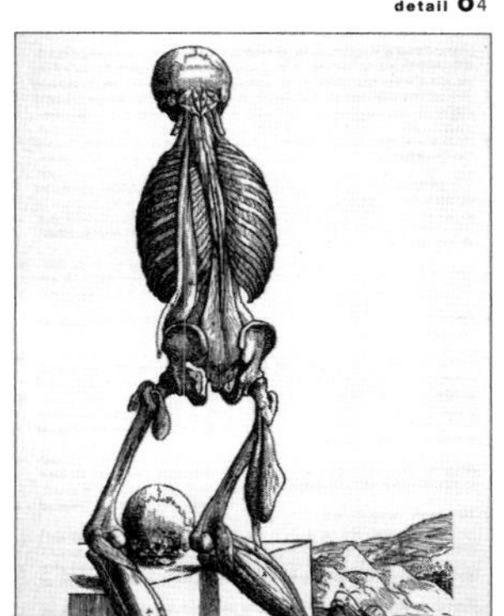

detail O5

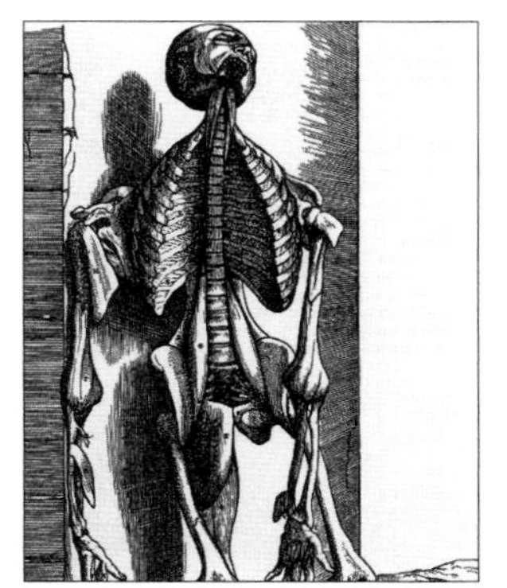

detail O6

Aristotle (References are to the stan
of the original text, then to page
translation.)
Study
517b 28 14
517b 32 14
Parts
653b 19ff 14
672b 13ff 29
Galen
Bones (References are to chapter
nal work, then to page of this
8 32
10–11 42
17 35
Doctrines of Hippocrates and Plato (
to book and chapter of the ori
then to volume and page of D

detail O7

48

DESIGN FIRM	Silvio Design, Inc., Chicago, IL
ART DIRECTOR	Sam Silvio
TRIM SIZE	9 1/2 x 12 inches
PAGES	200
TYPEFACE	Grotesque
PRINTER	Meridian Printing
AUTHOR	Sylvia Wolf
PUBLISHER	The Art Institute of Chicago

detail. / n 03

Fig. 1

design firm. silvio design, inc.

50 books. 50 covers. | NO. 48

Kenneth Josephson: A Retrosp

Sylvia Wolf

with an essay by Andy Gru

and a chronology and interview by Stephanie Lipscomb

The Art Institute of Chicag

detail 01

detail 02

design firm. silvio design, inc.

50 books. 50 covers. | NO. 48

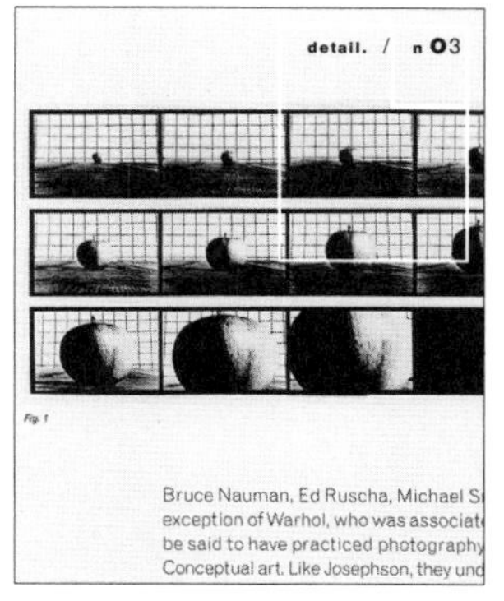

detail 03

detail 04

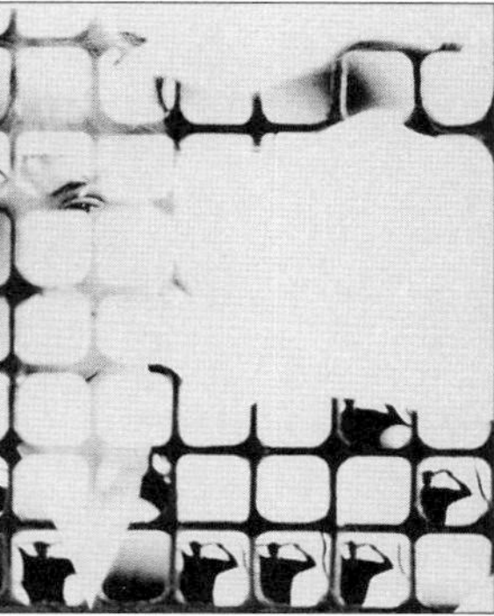

detail 05

design firm. silvio design, inc.

50 books. 50 covers. | NO. 48

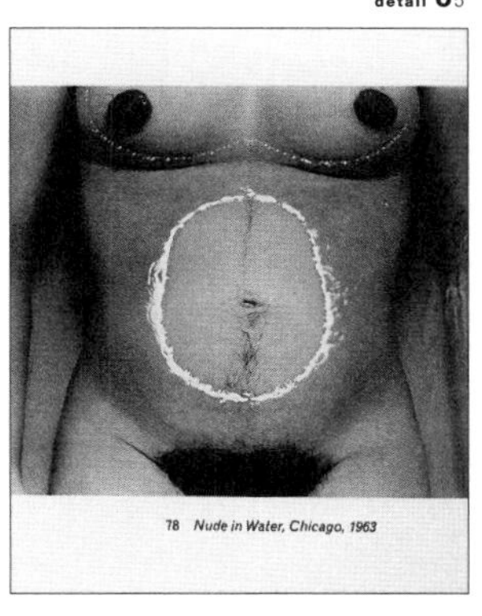

78 *Nude in Water, Chicago, 1963*

detail 06

detail 07

49

DESIGN FIRM	Twin Palms Publishers, Santa Fe, NM	PRINTER	Stamperia Valdonega
DESIGNER	Jack Woody	PAPER	Tritone
PHOTOGRAPHER	Stephen Barker	AUTHOR	Stephen Barker
TRIM SIZE	9 x 13 inches	PUBLISHER	Twin Palms Publishers
PAGES	96		
TYPEFACE	Minion		

detail. / nº04

design firm. twin palms publishers

50 books. 50 covers. | NO. 49

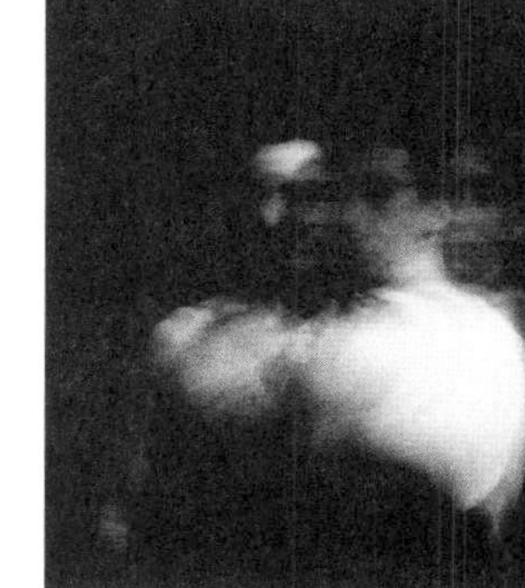

detail 01

detail 02

design firm. twin palms publishers

50 books. 50 covers. | NO. 49

detail 03

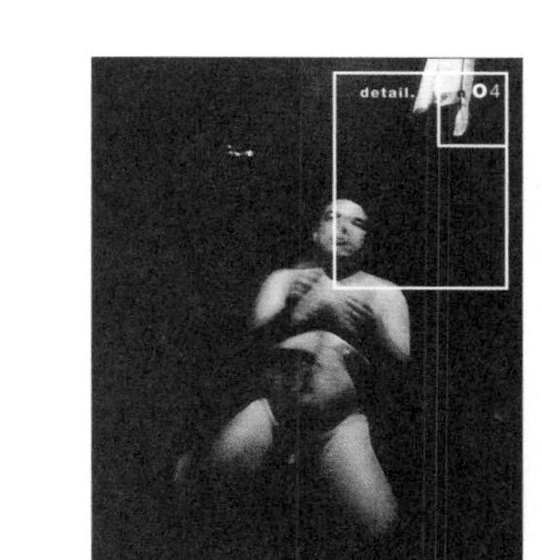

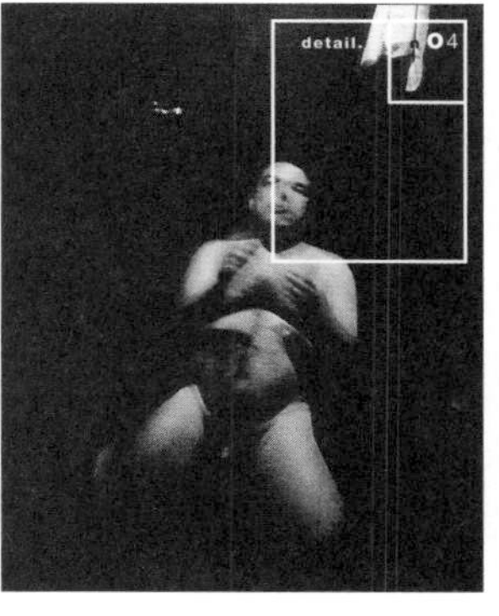

detail 04

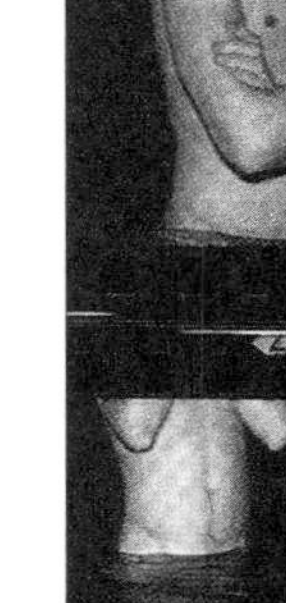

detail 05

design firm. twin palms publishers

50 books. 50 covers. | NO. 49

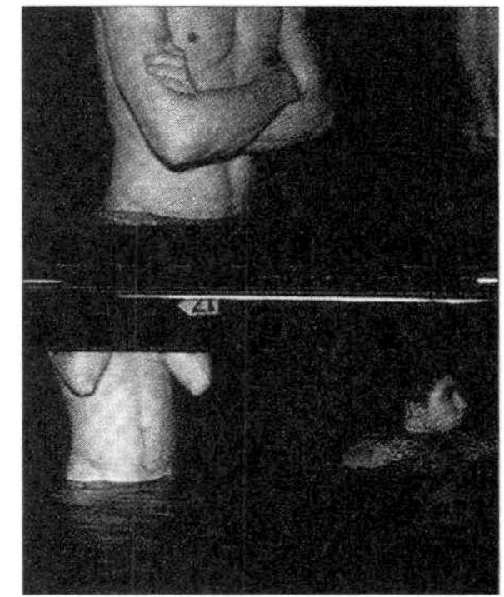

detail 06

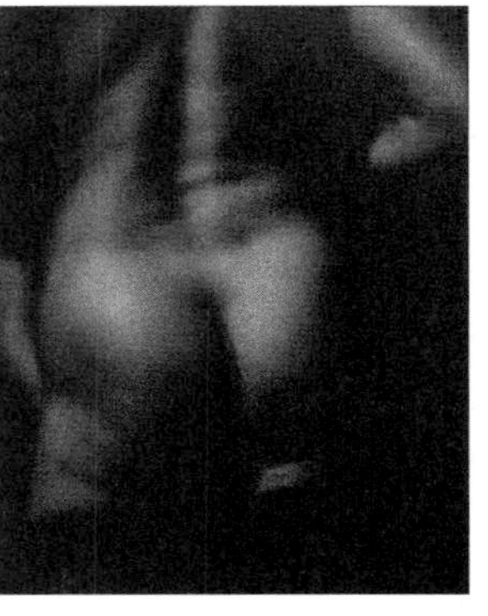

detail 07

Years ago

sent me a fax saying that she must aga

nited States because she had something

be said in person. The following week sh

ter arrived with a family friend. When w

neal, she told the story of how she had fir

fe to the practice of *seiki jutsu*. At that tin

shrine of an ancestor and was given a pie

detail. / n 07

50 50 BOOKS.50 COVERS. IKUKO OSUMI: JAPANESE MASTER OF SEIKI JUTSU ("PROFILES OF HEALING" SERIES) / This book is the second in a series of more than 10 books. The challenge is to maintain the series format that Davidson Design established with the first book while seeking innovative responses to each individual book. I created a format derived from the subject's traditions. A diverse range of artwork had to be incorporated while maintaining a sensitivity to Japanese culture.

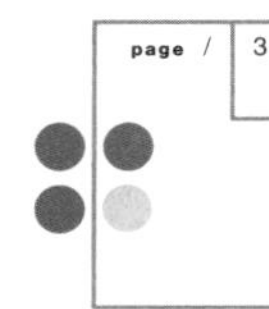

50

DESIGN FIRM	Davidson Design, Inc., New York, NY
CREATIVE DIRECTOR/ DESIGNER	Karen Davidson
PHOTOGRAPHY	Kern L. Nickerson, Naoki Ohara, Shogoro Yano, archival images
TRIM SIZE	7 x 10 inches
PAGES	96 pages, audio CD, CD envelope
TYPEFACES	Trajan, Centaur, Gill Sans
PRINTER/BINDER	Asia Pacific Offset
PUBLISHER	Ringing Rocks Press, Leete's Island Books

design firm. davidson design, inc.

50 books. 50 covers. | NO. 50

IKU Japan

detail 01

detail 02

design firm. davidson design, inc.

50 books. 50 covers. | NO. 50

detail 03

detail 04

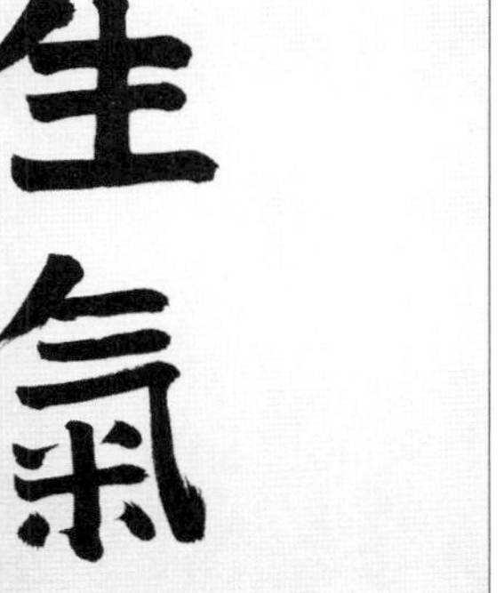

detail 05

design firm. davidson design, inc.

50 books. 50 covers. | NO. 50

detail 06

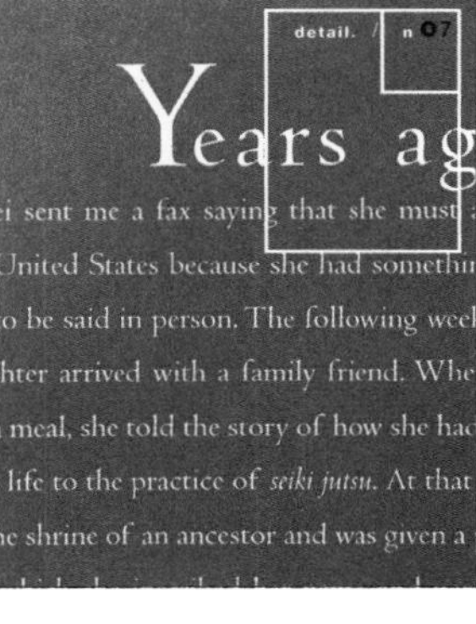

detail 07

01 50 BOOKS.50 COVERS. MADAME / I (fortunately) had to give up on the first design because we were unable to get permission for a Picasso drawing the author wanted to use. Once I had the idea for the painting, everything went along smoothly. I saw a book of René Gruau illustrations and I thought their look and feel perfectly illustrated the main character's obsession with this sparkling, elegant, yet elusive young French teacher. I did a few comps using Gruau's work, but they showcased the clothes the models were wearing too much. So I decided to paint it myself.

01

DESIGN FIRM	Farrar, Straus and Giroux, New York, NY
ART DIRECTOR	Susan Mitchell
DESIGNER/ ILLUSTRATOR	Lynn Buckley
TRIM SIZE	5 1/2 x 8 1/4 inches
TYPEFACE	Opti Bodoni
PRINTER/BINDER	R.R. Donnelley
PAPER	Glatfelter B-18 cream
JACKET PRINTER	Jaguar Advanced Graphics
AUTHOR	Antoni Libera
PUBLISHER	Farrar, Straus and Giroux

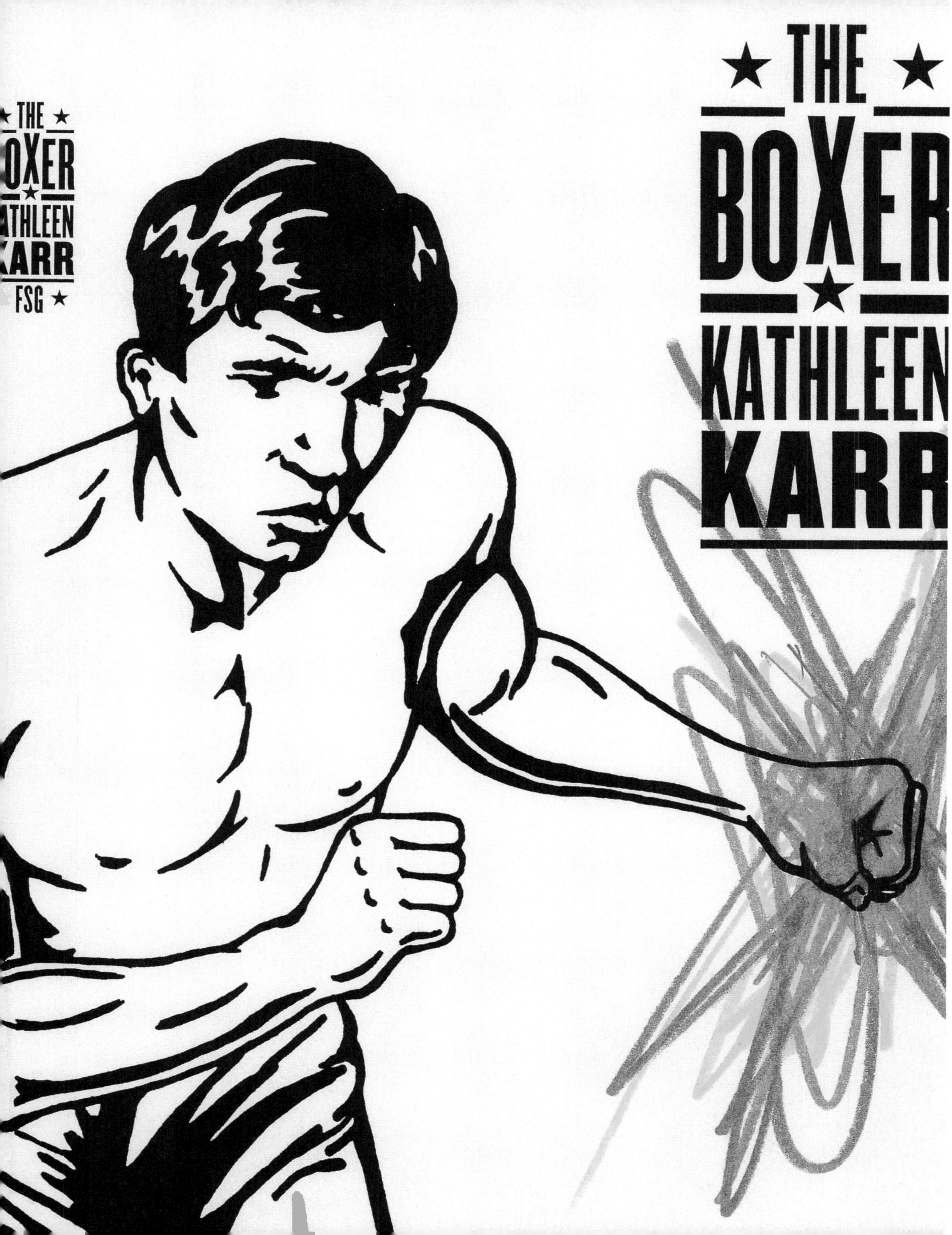

★ THE ★
BOXER
★
KATHLEEN
KARR
FSG ★

★ THE ★
BOXER
★
KATHLEEN
KARR

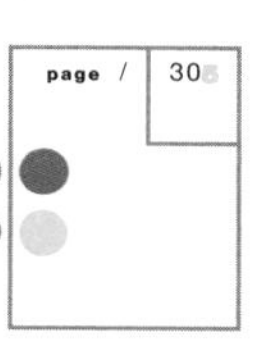

02 DESIGN FIRM Farrar, Straus and Giroux, New York, NY
ART DIRECTOR/ DESIGNER Rodrigo Corral
TRIM SIZE 5 1/2 x 8 1/4 inches
JACKET PRINTER Phoenix Color

AUTHOR Kathleen Karr
PUBLISHER Farrar, Straus and Giroux

03 50 BOOKS.50 COVERS. PERIOD / Trying to integrate the photos and type to the book so the reader would get the feel of a diary proved to be a challenge. I decided to integrate rough handwriting and a photo on a deckled, edged paper.

03

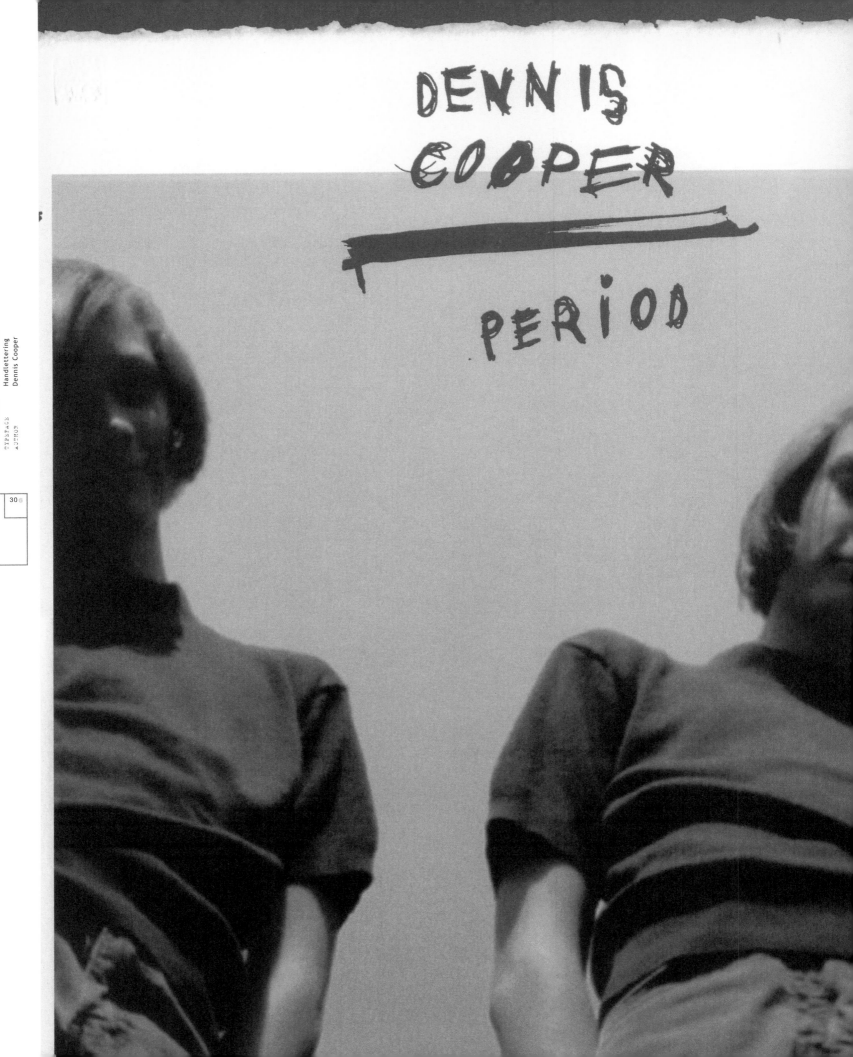

DESIGN FIRM	Stanislav Grinapol, Brooklyn, NY
ART DIRECTOR	Charles Woods
DESIGNER	Stanislav Grinapol
PHOTOGRAPHER	Joel Westendorf
TYPEFACE	Handlettering
AUTHOR	Dennis Cooper
PUBLISHER	Grove Press

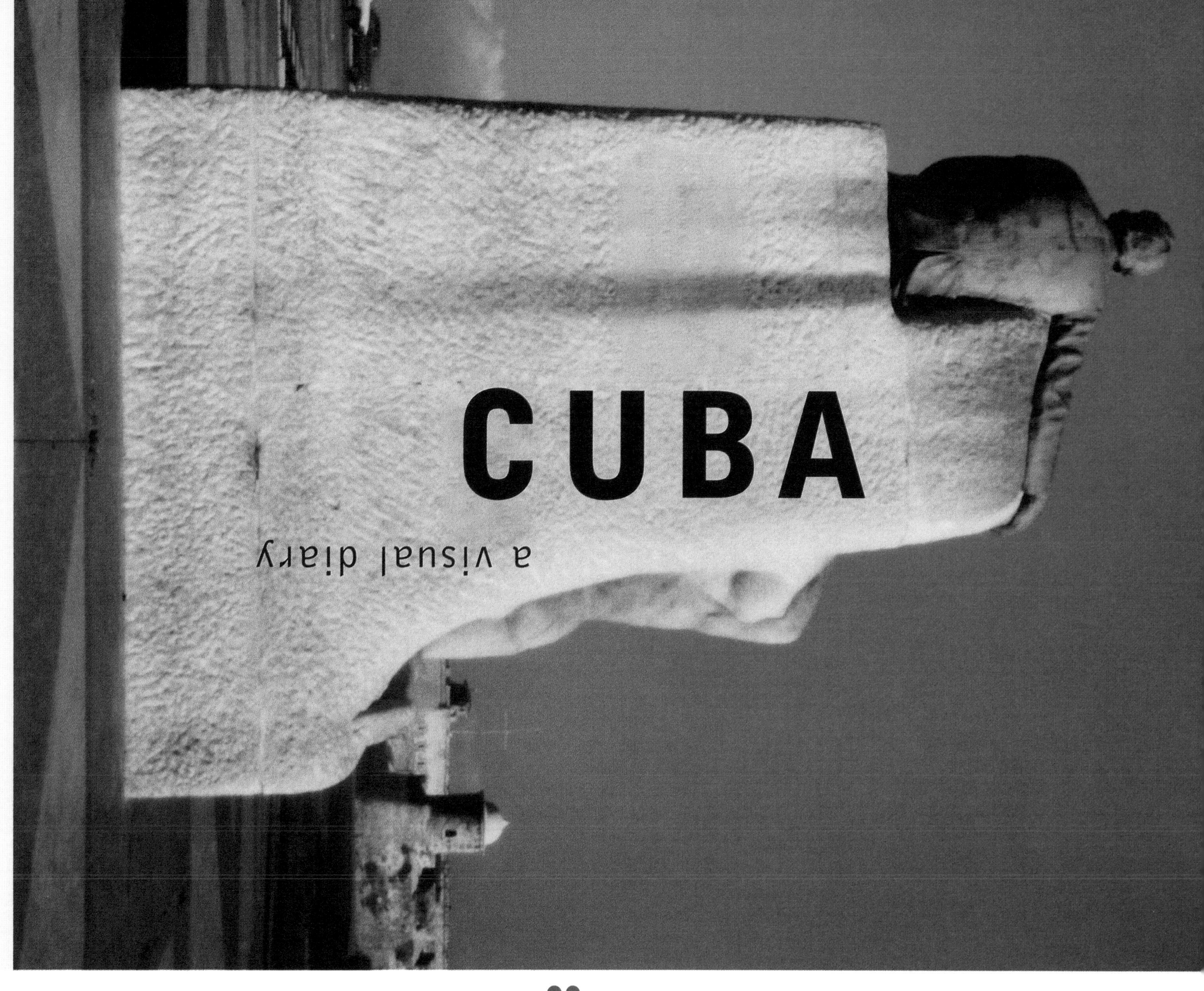

04 50 BOOKS.50 COVERS. CUBA: A VISUAL DIARY / I was approached by the photographer Evan Dion, who had gone to Cuba for two weeks and came back with great film he wanted to translate into a book. To make sense of all the intense, strong images, it was important to identify some themes, and the overriding one was "gesture." The "hugging statue" sums up the spirit of the book and the photographer's vision. I decided to simply let the photographs create a narrative. The use of type and white space is meant to accentuate the elements that make the cover photograph work.

04

DESIGN FIRM	Teikna Graphic Design Inc., Toronto, Canada
ART DIRECTOR/ DESIGNER	Claudia Neri
PHOTOGRAPHER	Evan Dion
TRIM SIZE	5 1/2 x 8 inches
TYPEFACES	Bell Gothic, Clarendon
PRINTER	CJ Graphics
PAPER	Mead Signature Gloss 80 pound Cover
PUBLISHER	Evan Dion

05

DESIGN FIRM	Doubleday/Random House, New York, NY
ART DIRECTORS	Timothy Hsu, Mario Pulice
PRODUCTION COORDINATOR	Lusia Francavilla
DESIGNER	Timothy Hsu
TRIM SIZE	6 1/4 x 9 1/2 inches
JACKET PRINTER	Brady-Palmer
AUTHOR	Richard Steinberg
PUBLISHER	Doubleday/Random House

THE 4 phase MAN

DOUBLEDAY

RICHARD STEINBERG

4PHASEMAN

RICHARD STEINBERG

THE FOUR PHASE MAN

RICHARD STEINBERG

THE 4 phase MAN

A NOVEL BY

RICHARD STEINBERG

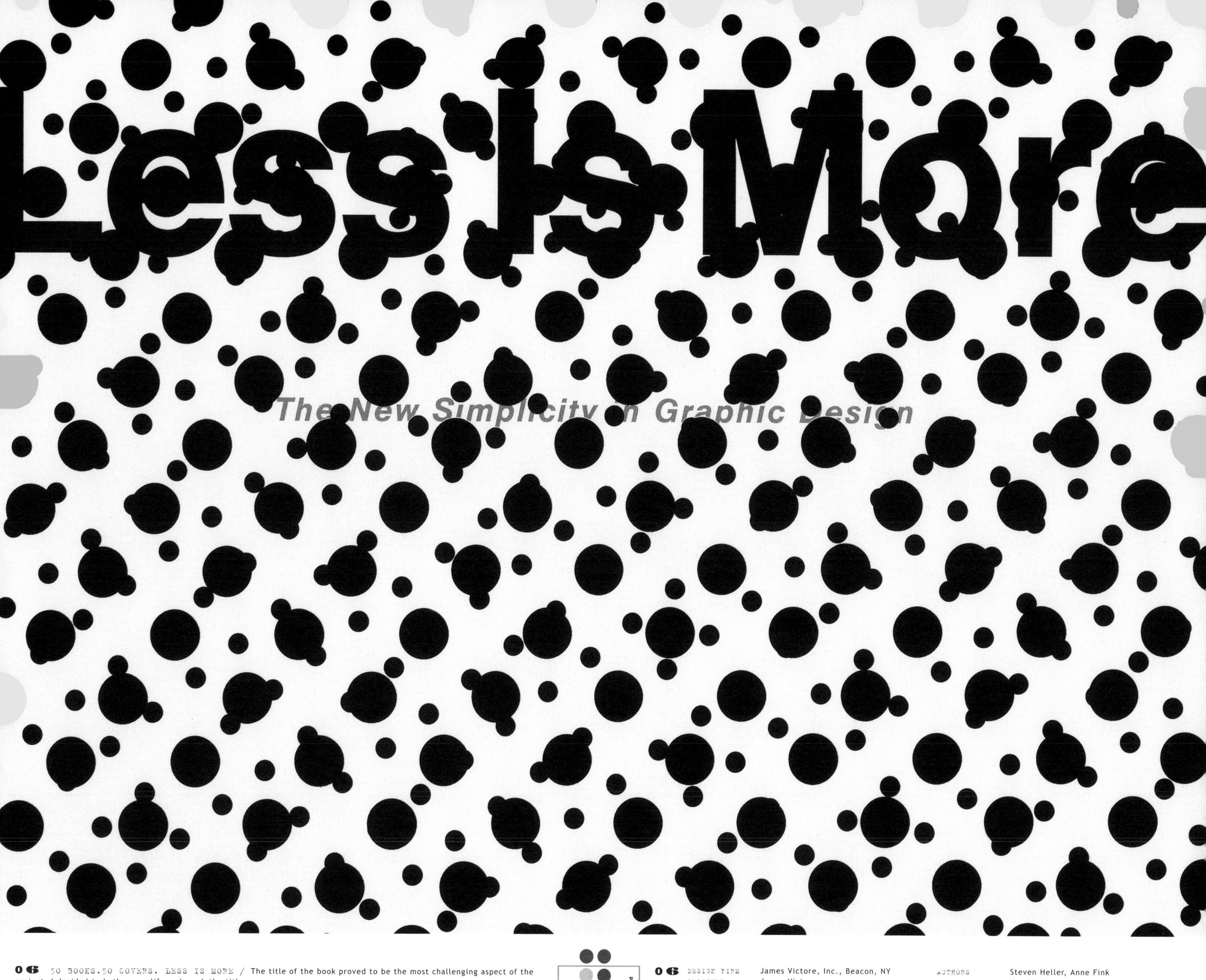

06 50 BOOKS.50 COVERS. LESS IS MORE / The title of the book proved to be the most challenging aspect of the project. I decided to both exemplify and mock the title.

06

DESIGN FIRM	James Victore, Inc., Beacon, NY
DESIGNER	James Victore
PRODUCTION COORDINATOR	Lynn Haller
TRIM SIZE	9 1/2 x 12 1/4 inches
TYPEFACE	Helvetica
AUTHORS	Steven Heller, Anne Fink
PUBLISHER	Northlight

07

DESIGN FIRM	Farrar, Straus and Giroux, New York, NY
ART DIRECTOR	Susan Mitchell
DESIGNER	Rodrigo Corral
PHOTOGRAPHER	Frederick S. Schmitt
PRODUCTION COORDINATOR	Harvey Hoffman
TRIM SIZE	5 3/4 x 8 1/4 inches
JACKET PRINTER	Phoenix Color
AUTHOR	Adam Zagajewski
PUBLISHER	Farrar, Straus and Giroux

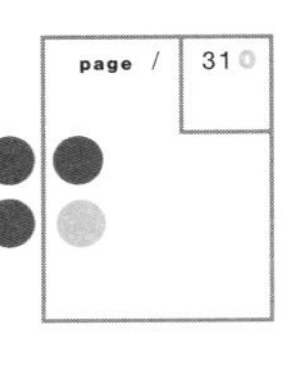

dam Zagajewski
nslated from the Polish
Clare Cavanagh

Mysticism
for Beginne

Poems

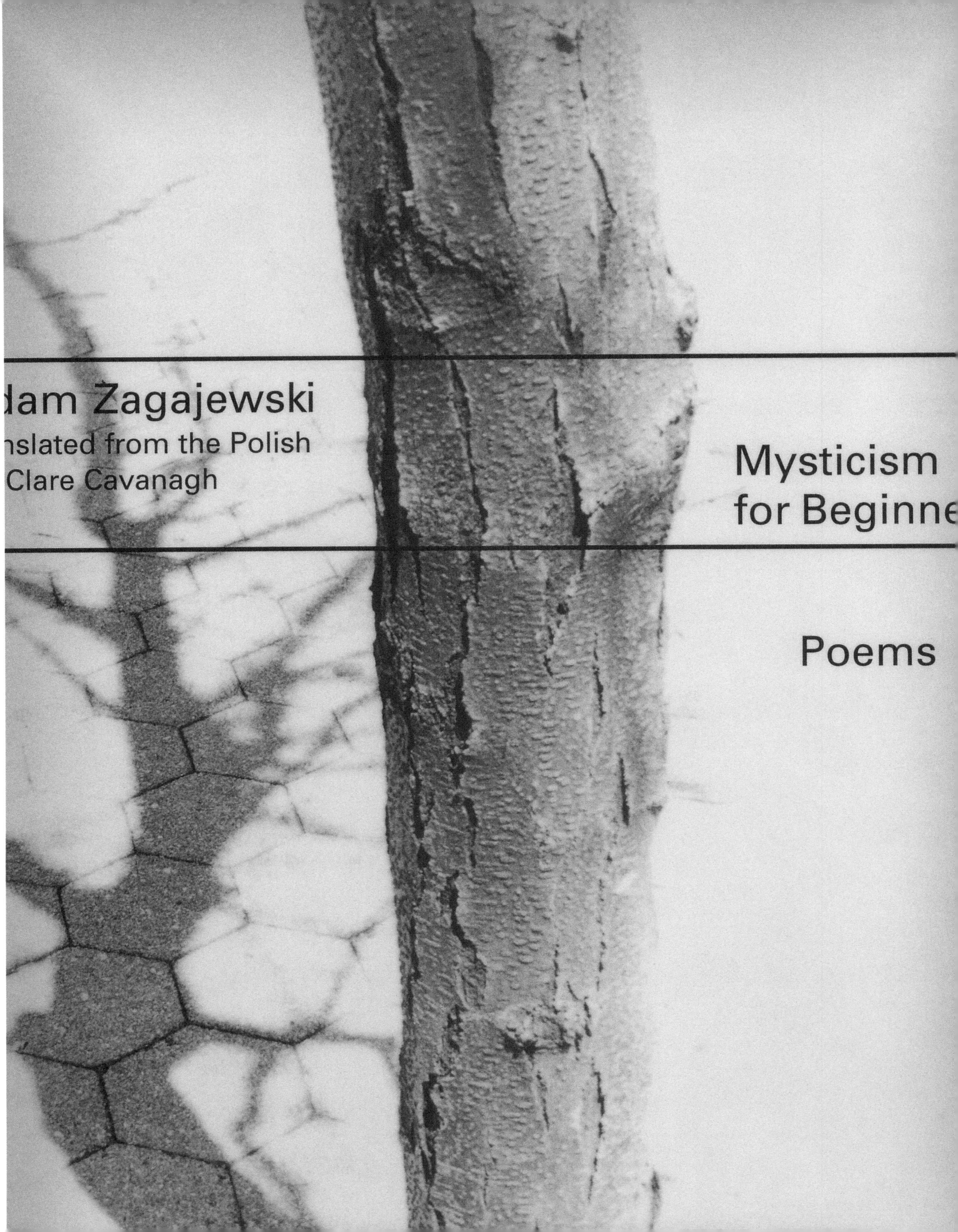

08 50 BOOKS.50 COVERS. MOTHERLESS BROOKLYN / The biggest challenge was trying not to make the book look too noirish or dark. The design solution is all in the photograph; I did extensive research.

DESIGN FIRM	Bantam Doubleday Dell, Inc., New York, NY
ART DIRECTOR/DESIGNER	Amy C. King
PHOTOGRAPHER	Eugene Richards
TYPEFACE	Franklin Gothic Extra Condensed
AUTHOR	Jonathan Lethem
PUBLISHER	Doubleday/Random House

09 50 BOOKS.50 COVERS. NONZERO: THE LOGIC OF HUMAN DESTINY / The title refers to the concept of the "nonzero-sum," which comes from game theory. The author describes how only through different levels of cooperation (or nonzero-sum relationships) have we been able to evolve from Stone Age Man to who we are today. The two pieces of this package—the case and jacket—visualize this concept since they are only successful if they work together.

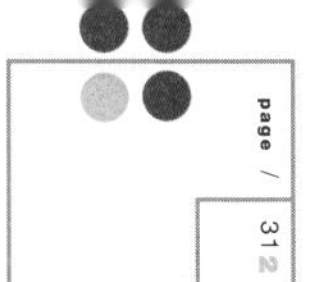

09

DESIGN FIRM	Pantheon Books, New York, NY
DESIGNER	Eric Fuentecilla
TYPEFACE	Rotis Semi Serif
AUTHOR	Robert Wright
PUBLISHER	Pantheon Books

NON
ZERØ

THE LOGIC OF
HUMAN DESTINY

ROBERT
WRIGHT

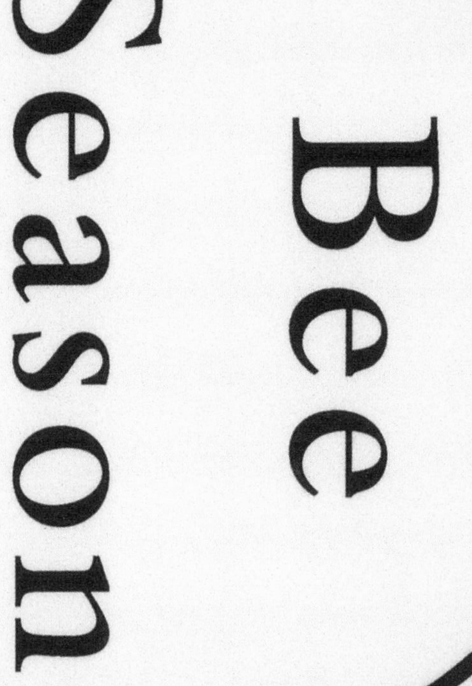

10 50 BOOKS.50 COVERS. BEE SEASON / This was a book by a first-time author, so it needed a mass, genderless appeal. I also wanted to make a statement with the design in marketing the book. I picked up on the main character's obsession with words and her love of this dictionary in her father's library. There were many rejected solutions, but this one seemed to answer and skirt a lot of issues in selling this book. Ultimately, we wanted a package that people would want to pick up—even if they didn't know why.

10

DESIGN FIRM	Bantam Doubleday Dell, Inc., New York, NY
ART DIRECTOR/ DESIGNER	Amy C. King
PHOTOGRAPHER	Barry Marcus
TYPEFACE	Bembo
AUTHOR	Myla Goldberg
PUBLISHER	Doubleday/Random House

The Spell

Alan Hollinghurst

A novel by the author of *The Swimming-Pool Library*

11 50 BOOKS. 50 COVERS. THE SPELL / The challenge in designing this cover was acknowledging its content—a soap opera starring sharp-tongued gay men set in the English countryside—in a manner appropriate to the literary stature of the author. The title refers to the spell of love, of hallucinogenic drugs and the brief but intense time the characters spent together. This led me to the original concept, depicting Danny—the book's coveted young stud—with his face covered in droplets of sweat and overlaid with techno-inspired patterns. After repeated revisions, the patterns were removed and the sweat edited out.

11

ART DIRECTOR	Paul Buckley
DESIGNER	Evan Gaffney
PHOTOGRAPHER	Marc Yankus
TRIM SIZE	6 1/8 x 9 1/4 inches
TYPEFACE	Helvetica
JACKET PRINTER	Coral Graphics
JACKET PAPER	Potlatch Northwest White
AUTHOR	Alan Hollinghurst
PUBLISHER	Viking

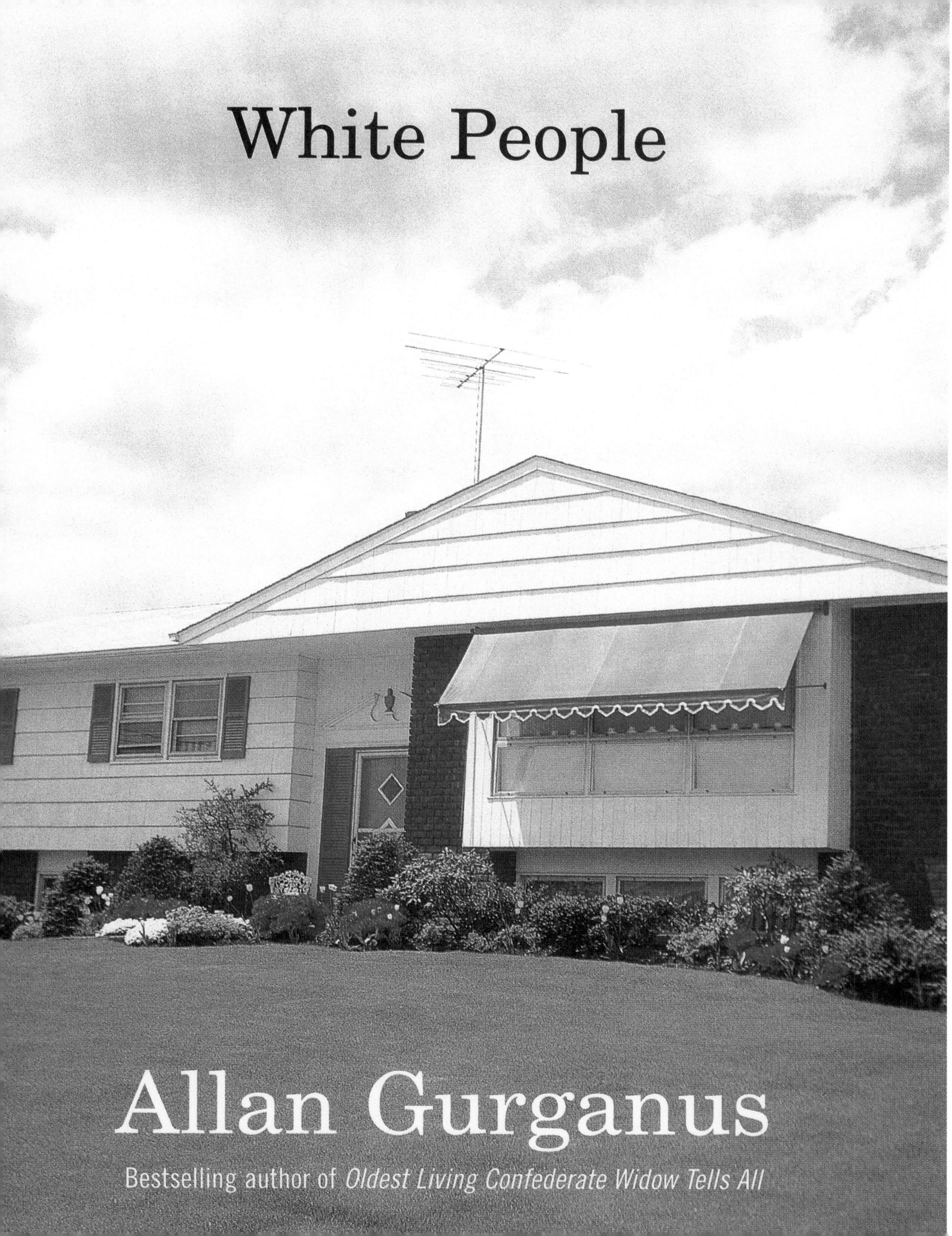

White People

Allan Gurganus

Bestselling author of *Oldest Living Confederate Widow Tells All*

12 50 BOOKS.50 COVERS. WHITE PEOPLE / With a title this loaded it was necessary to diffuse it with a bit of humor—especially since the stories within are of a warmly satirical nature and are not necessarily even about white people.

12

DESIGN FIRM	Vintage Books, New York, NY
DESIGNER	John Gall
PHOTOGRAPHER	FPG
TRIM SIZE	5 3/16 x 8 1/4 inches
TYPEFACE	Century Schoolbook
PRINTER	Coral Graphics

AUTHOR	Allan Gurganus
PUBLISHER	Vintage Books

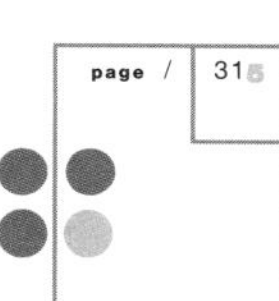

13 50 BOOKS.50 COVERS. DANISH CHAIRS / With over 150 examples of Danish chair design by 66 premier designers, this book surveys the innovative and prolific output of Denmark's design elite. Intended for designers and furniture enthusiasts, the book showcases the beauty of the Danish chair's functional design, strong yet spare architecture and elegant, organic curves. The book's cover uses schematic line drawings and the bold palette of the Danish flag to highlight the sculptural quality of Arne Jacobsen's Laminated Chair No. 4130.

13

DESIGN FIRM	Character, San Francisco, CA
DESIGNER	Patricia Evangelista
ILLUSTRATOR	Noritsugu Oda
PHOTOGRAPHER	Yoshio Hayashi
TRIM SIZE	8 3/42 x 11 15/162 inches
TYPEFACES	Gill Sans, Trade Gothic
PRINTER	Toppan
PAPER	Bon Ivory 310 gram
AUTHOR	Noritsugu Oda
PUBLISHER	Chronicle Books

DANISH

CHAIRS

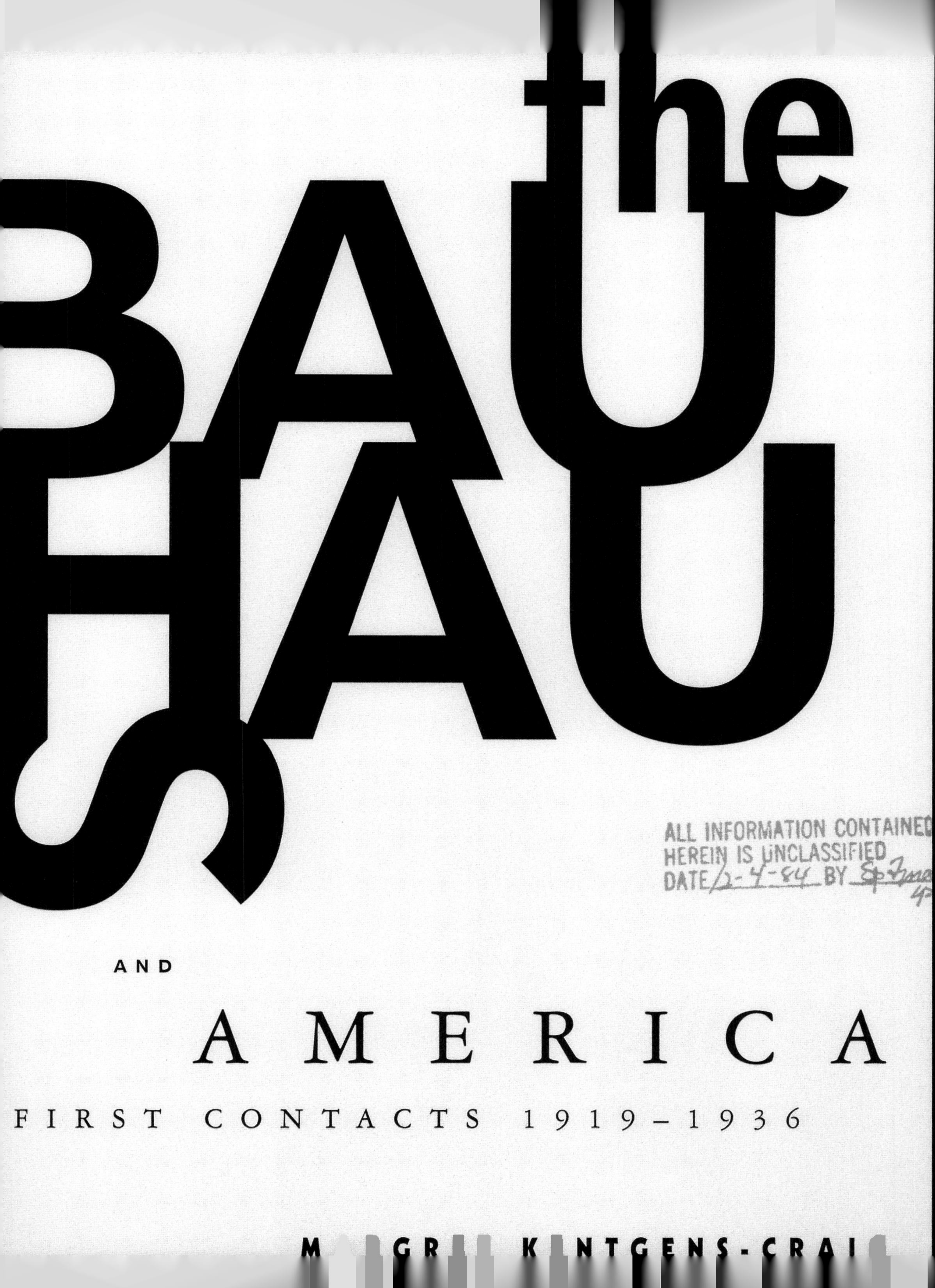

the BAUHAUS

AND

AMERICA

FIRST CONTACTS 1919–1936

MARGRET KENTGENS-CRAIG

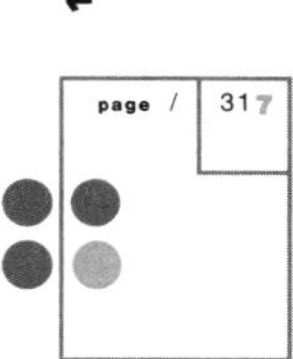

11

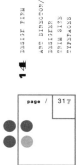

DESIGN FIRM	MIT Press Design Department, Cambridge, MA
ART DIRECTOR/DESIGNER	Jim McWethy
TRIM SIZE	7 x 9 inches
TYPEFACES	Garamond 3, Geometric BT, Universal News
PRINTER	Maple Press
PAPER	New Life satin 70 pound
JACKET PRINTER	Henry Sawyer Company
AUTHOR	Margret Kentgens-Craig
PUBLISHER	The MIT Press

15 50 BOOKS.50 COVERS. ON BECOMING A NOVELIST / It is always a challenge when you have to design a cover for a book about writing. The options for imagery are somewhat limited and tired: a typewriter, a fancy-looking pen, a fancy-looking typewriter. Not that reproducing a book on a bookcover isn't a cliché, but I've always wanted to get a spine on the front of a book.

15

DESIGN FIRM	John Gall Graphic Design, Hoboken, NJ
ART DIRECTOR	Ingsu Liu
DESIGNER/ PHOTOGRAPHER	John Gall
TRIM SIZE	5 3/16 x 8 1/4
TYPEFACES	Alternate Gothic, Granjon
AUTHOR	John Gardner
PUBLISHER	W.W. Norton

ON BECOMING A NOVELIST

JOHN GARDNER

Foreword by RAYMOND CARVER

16 50 BOOKS.50 COVERS. HIROSHI SUGIMOTO: PORTRAITS / This book was designed to accompany a traveling exhibition sponsored by the Guggenheim and showing at the Deutsche Guggenheim in Berlin, then moving onto the Guggenheim in Bilbao and New York. The exhibition features a series of photographs of life-sized wax figures and the catalogue covers derived directly from one part of the show exhibiting six close-up pictures of the wives of Henry VIII. Each series of six covers shows one of Henry VIII's wives on the front cover with his image on the back cover.

16

DESIGN FIRM	Matsumoto Incorporated, New York, NY
ART DIRECTOR	Takaaki Matsumoto
PHOTOGRAPHER	Hiroshi Sugimoto
PRODUCTION COORDINATOR	Beth Levy (Guggenheim Museum)
TRIM SIZE	11 x 12 inches
TYPEFACES	Futura family
PRINTER	Eurografica S.P.A.
PAPER	Phoenix Imperial Gloss 170 gram
PUBLISHER	Guggenheim Museum Publications

17 50 BOOKS.50 COVERS. SCREAMING WITH JOY: THE LIFE OF ALLEN GINSBERG / This was the first-ever illustrated book on Allen Ginsberg. I decided to give the book a contemporary look using archival material.

17

DESIGN FIRM RVC Design, New York, NY
ART DIRECTOR Roberto de Vicq de Cumptich
PHOTOGRAPHER Timothy Greenfield-Sanders
TYPEFACES Texas Hero, Engraver's Gothic Bitstream
PAPER Coated one-side 80 pound

JACKET PRINTER Jaguar Advanced Graphics
AUTHOR Graham Caveney
PUBLISHER Broadway Books

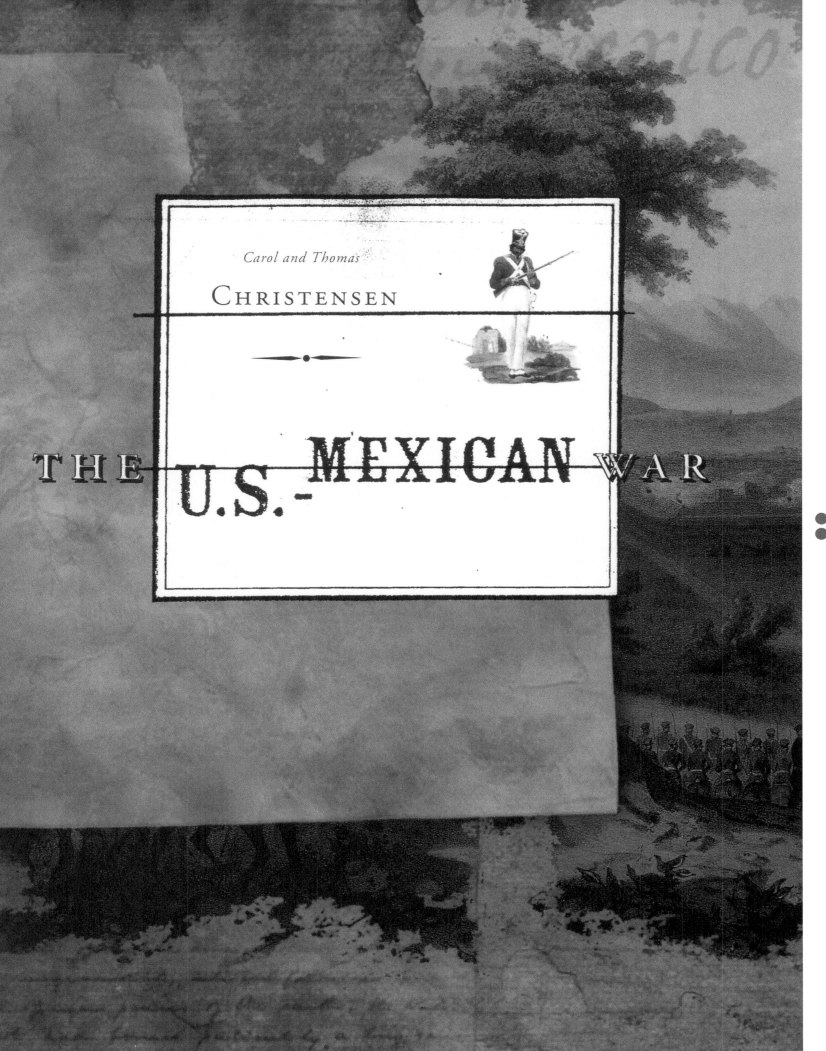

Carol and Thomas
CHRISTENSEN

THE U.S.-MEXICAN WAR

18 50 BOOKS.50 COVERS. THE U.S.-MEXICAN WAR / I needed to create a cover that was evocative and provocative, combining historical images with a modern sensibility. Collaging significant images of the past in a layered fashion implied a depth of content.

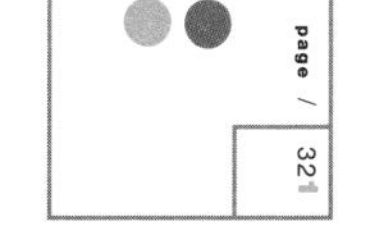

18

DESIGN FIRM	Cabra Diseño, San Francisco, CA
ART DIRECTOR	Raul Cabra
DESIGNERS	Tom Sieu, Patrick Vallé
ILLUSTRATOR	Carl Nebel
TRIM SIZE	9 x 11 inches
PRINTER/BINDER	Asia Pacific Offset
PAPER	Japanese Kinmari 80 pound gloss with matte lamination
JACKET PRINTER	APO
AUTHOR	Carol and Thomas Christensen
PUBLISHER	Bay Books

19
DESIGN FIRM St. Martin's Press, New York, NY
ART DIRECTOR/ DESIGNER Henry Sene Yee
PHOTOGRAPHER Steve Vaccariello/Nonstock
TRIM SIZE 5 5/8 x 8 1/2 inches
JACKET PRINTER Phoenix Color
AUTHOR Caroline Kettlewell
PUBLISHER St. Martin's Press

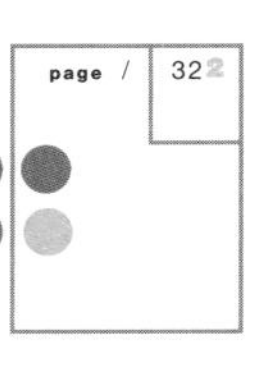

Caroline Kettlewell SKIN GAME

ST. MARTIN'S PRESS

a cutter's memoir

SKIN GAME

CAROLINE KETTLEWELL

The 1999 AAUP Book, Jacket, and Journal Show

20 50 BOOKS.50 COVERS. THE 1999 AAUP BOOK, JACKET AND JOURNAL SHOW / Probably the biggest challenge was having free rein—there was no input from anyone else. I'm not used to that, but I got to like it very quickly. Some of the book-show winners are sticking out of a paper bag (electronically accomplished) as if they were being brought home to be consumed.

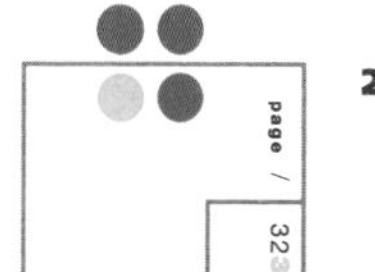

20

DESIGN FIRM	Yale University Press Design Department, New Haven, CT
DESIGNER	Nancy Ovedovitz
PHOTOGRAPHER	PhotoDisc with alterations by Luft/Leone Design
TRIM SIZE	8 x 9 inches
TYPEFACES	The Sans 5 and 6
JACKET PRINTER	Jaguar Advanced Graphics
PUBLISHER	Association of American University Presses

21 50 BOOKS.50 COVERS. EVERY OTHER SUNDAY / This book was produced as a commemorative item for fanatical sports historians and civil rights researchers, and tells the story of Alabama's Birmingham Black Barons, one of the most successful baseball teams in the Negro League history. From 1920 until its breakup in the early '60s, the Barons' home games at Rickwood Field were scheduled on Sunday afternoons to alternate with major league teams. The die-cut calendar numbers are the actual three months of Sundays that the 1948 Black Barons played. Starting center fielder was a 16-year-old rookie named Willie Mays.

21

DESIGN FIRM	Slaughter Hanson, Birmingham, AL
CREATIVE DIRECTOR	Marion English Powers
PHOTOGRAPHER	Kansas City Negro League Museum
TRIM SIZE	5 3/4 x 8 3/4 inches
TYPEFACES	Industrial, Alternate Gothic, Bell Gothic
PRINTER	Ad Shop
PAPER	Sappi Strobe Dull
AUTHOR	Christopher D. Fullerton
PUBLISHER	R. Boozer Press

13 27 11

25 8 22

EVERY OTHER SUNDAY

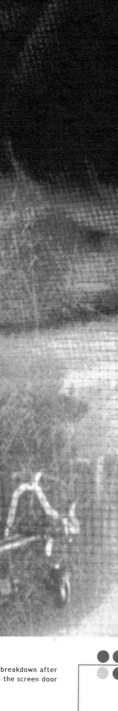

Blameless Lisa

Blameless

A NOVEL

LISA REARDON

22 50 BOOKS.50 COVERS. BLAMELESS / This is a story of a strong, fearless woman who suffers a breakdown after finding the body of a young child, a daily passenger on her school bus route. The brooding face peering through the screen door and the breakup of the title into black and white underscore the themes of guilt and moral responsibility.

22

DESIGN FIRM	Random House, Inc., New York, NY
ART DIRECTOR	Robbin Schiff
PHOTO	
ILLUSTRATOR	Debra Liss
TYPEFACES	Bauer Bodoni, Trade Gothic
JACKET PRINTER	Coral Graphics
AUTHOR	Lisa Reardon
PUBLISHER	Random House, Inc.

23 50 BOOKS.50 COVERS. SHAKESPEARE AFTER THEORY / I wanted the jacket to feel both historical and modern in sensibility, to allude to the act of writing without being too literal and to use actual words from Shakespeare's plays so that the viewing experience would be more emotional and immediate. My solution was to create a sensual, simple image using stacks of deckled 100 percent rag cotton paper (16th-century style) and to layer text from HAMLET and MACBETH in a somewhat unexpected, graphic way.

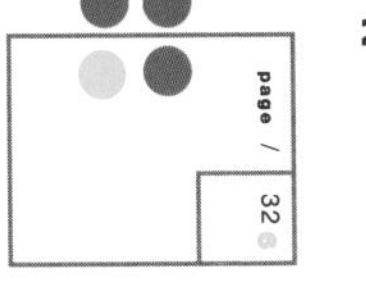

23

DESIGN FIRM	Weinstock Design, New York, NY
DESIGNER/ PHOTOGRAPHER	Ann Weinstock
PRODUCTION COORDINATOR	Liana Fredley
TRIM SIZE	6 x 9 inches
TYPEFACES	Aquiline, Galliard, Poetica, Ehrhardt
PAPER	Coated one-side Domtar
JACKET PRINTER	Jaguar Advanced Graphics
AUTHOR	David Scott Kastan
PUBLISHER	Routledge

Shakespeare after Theory

speak no more!
t mine eyes into my very soul,
see such black and grained spots
leave their tinct.

live
sweat of an enseamed bed,
rruption, honeying and making love
asty sty!

me no more!
s like daggers enter in mine ears.
weet Hamlet!

Macbeth.
Whence is that knocki
How is't with me whe
What hands are here?
Will all great Neptune
Clean from my hand?
The multitudinous sea
Making the green one

Enter Lady Macbeth.

Lady.
My hands are of your
To wear a heart so wh
A little water clears us
How easy is it then! Y
Hath left you unatten
Get on your nightgow
And show us to be wa
So poorly in your tho

Macbeth.

SLACK JAW

"YOU BETTER START LEARNING BRAILLE NOW"

JIM KNIPFEL

24 DESIGN FIRM Chip Kidd, New York, NY
PHOTOGRAPHER Marc Yankus
AUTHOR Jim Knipfel
PUBLISHER Tarcher/Putnam

25 50 BOOKS.50 COVERS. WILLIAM SHAKESPEARE: THE MAN BEHIND THE GENIUS / Most Shakespeare bios tend to resort to very expected cover solutions. I wanted to avoid all the obvious clichés—the redundant old scripty type, the quill. Given the title of the book, I thought that since Shakespeare was a recognizable face there was no real need to state the obvious by repeating his name on the cover. The subtitle could easily be placed on the spine. Laurie Rosenwald was chosen for her ability to capture a likeness and for her beautiful informal line quality. Add some orange, yellow, a little silver foil and voilà!

25

DESIGN FIRM	Little, Brown and Company, New York, NY
ART DIRECTOR	Michael Ian Kaye
DESIGNER	Rymn Massand
ILLUSTRATOR	Laurie Rosenwald
TRIM SIZE	6 x 9 1/4 inches
AUTHOR	Anthony Holden
PUBLISHER	Little, Brown and Company

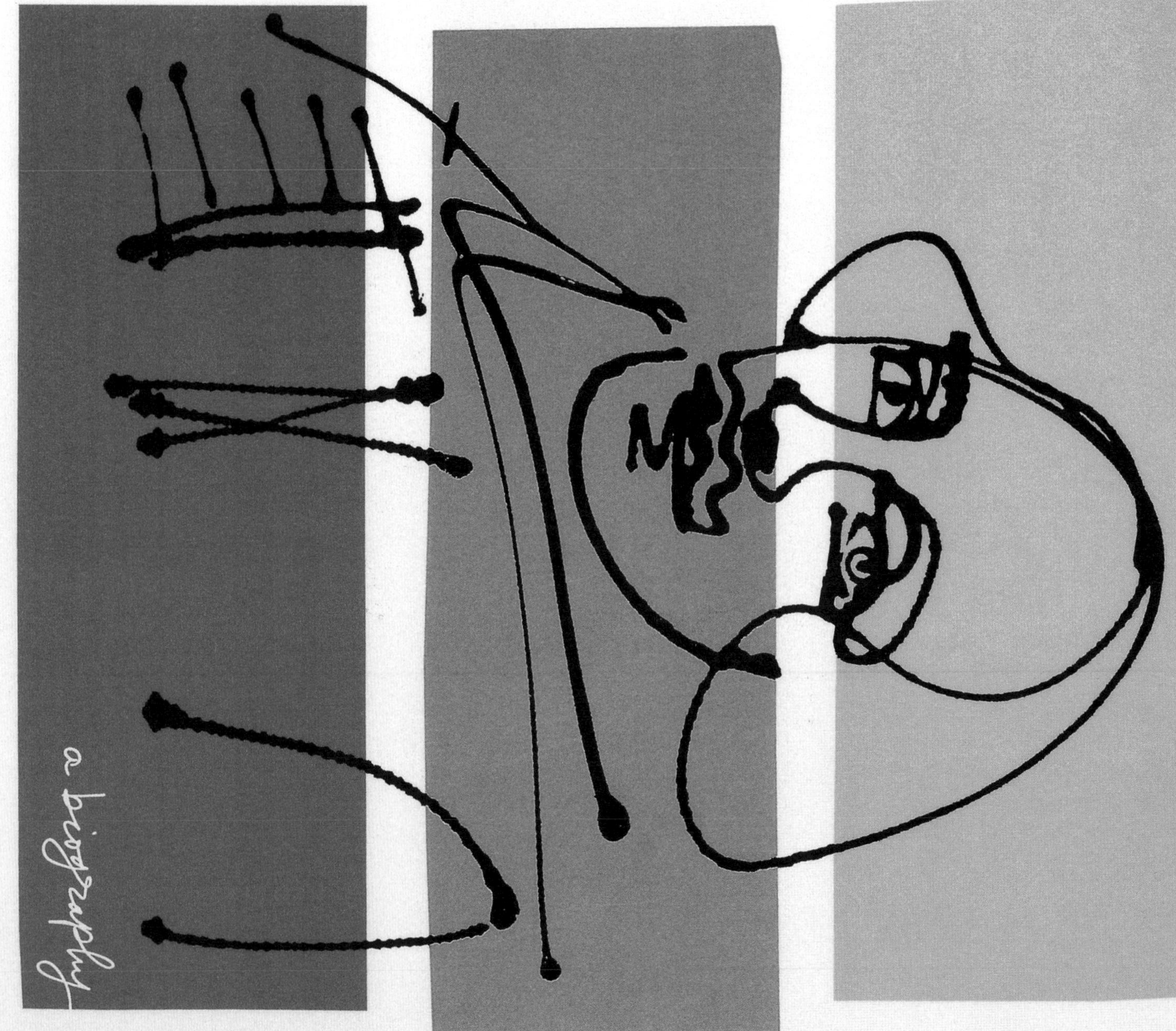

DAVID TREUER THE HIAWATHA

ADOR

USA

THE HIAWATHA

DAVID TREUER

a novel

26

DESIGN FIRM	St. Martin's Press, New York, NY
ART DIRECTOR/ DESIGNER	Henry Sene Yee
TRIM SIZE	5 5/8 x 8 1/2 inches
TYPEFACES	Opti Futura Display, Magneto-super Bold Extended
PAPER	Foil
JACKET PRINTER	Brady-Palmer
AUTHOR	David Treuer
PUBLISHER	Picador USA

Lieutenant-Colonel de Maumort

ROGER MARTIN DU GARD

KNOPF

Lieutenant-Colonel de Maumort

a novel

ROGER MARTIN DU GARD

WINNER OF THE NOBEL PRIZE

27

DESIGN FIRM Alfred A. Knopf, New York, NY
ART DIRECTOR/DESIGNER Carol Devine Carson
PHOTOGRAPHER Marc Yankus
TRIM SIZE 6 3/8 x 9 7/16 inches
TYPEFACE Adobe Garamond
PRINTER Quebecor Fairfield
JACKET PRINTER Coral Graphics
AUTHOR Roger Martin Du Gard
PUBLISHER Alfred A. Knopf

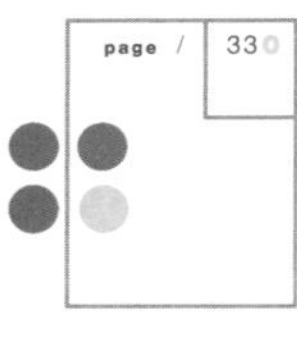

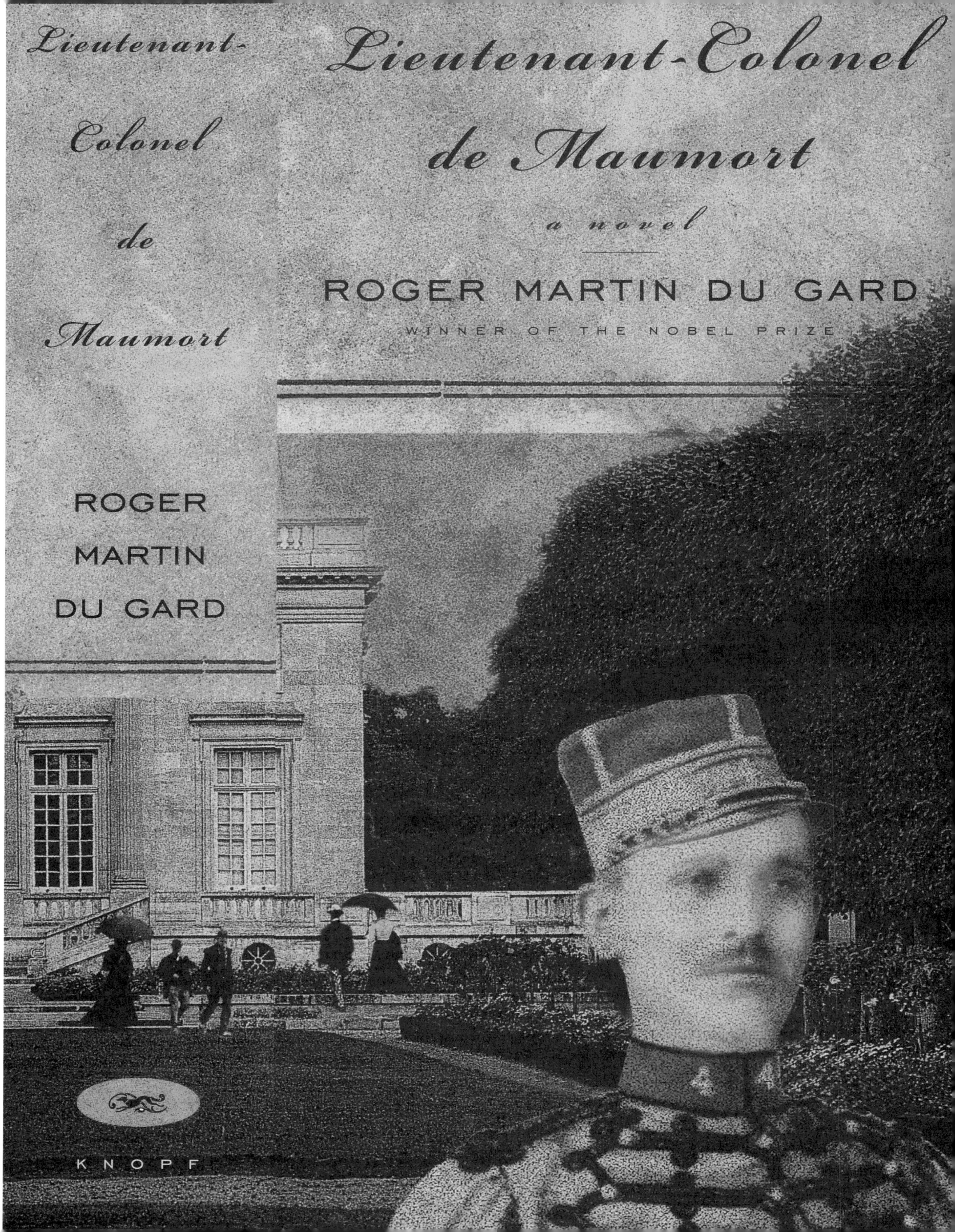

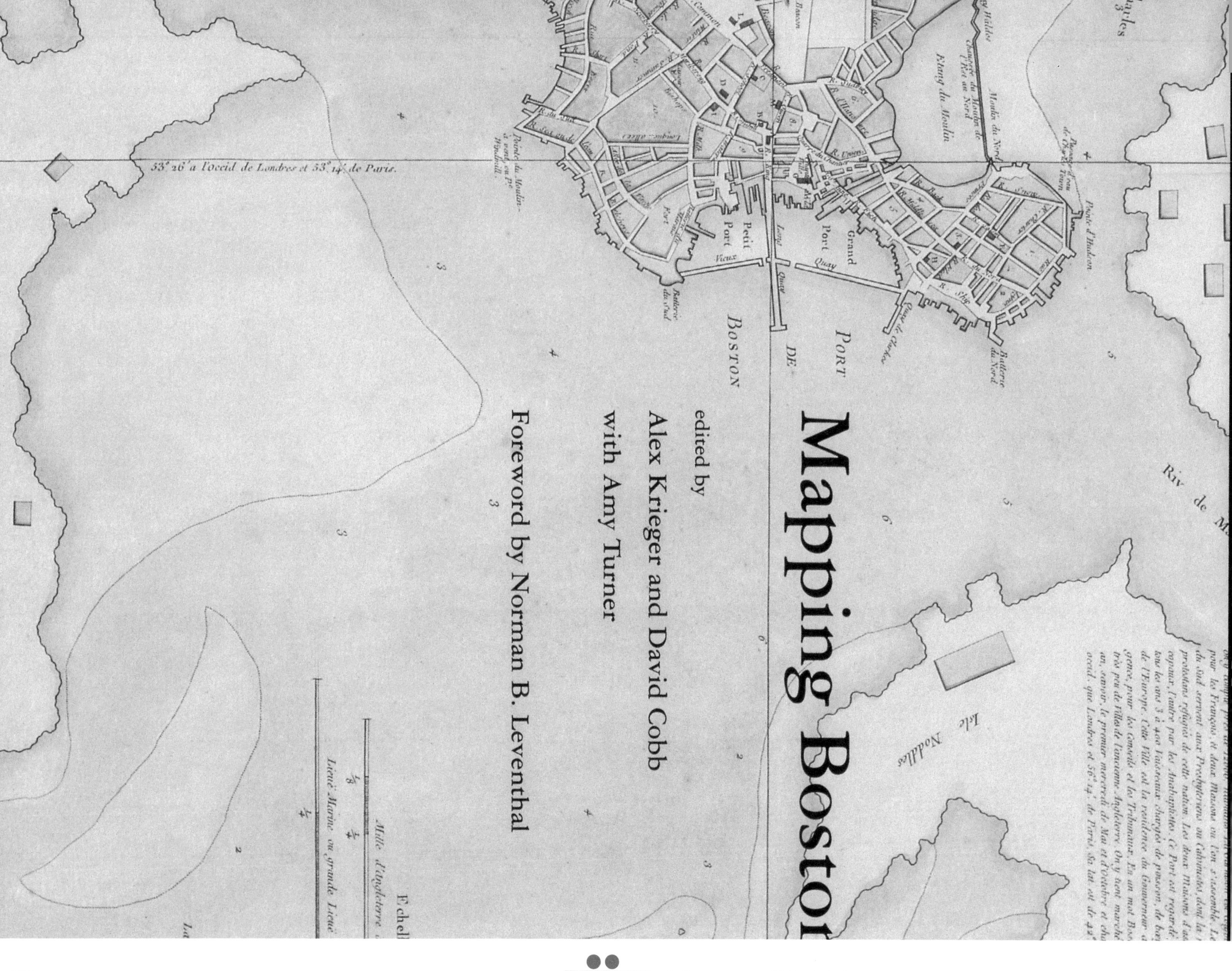

28 50 BOOKS.50 COVERS. MAPPING BOSTON / It was a definite challenge to select cover art from an array of wonderful maps. The colors and feel of the cover reflect those found on old maps.

28

DESIGN FIRM	MIT Press Design Department, Cambridge, MA
ART DIRECTOR	Yasuyo Iguchi
ILLUSTRATORS	Jacques Nicolas Bellin, Captain John Smith
PHOTOGRAPHER	Alex MacLean, various
TRIM SIZE	12 x 11 1/2 inches
TYPEFACES	Garamond 3, Snell Roundhand
PRINTER	Meridian Printing
PAPER	Pheno Star 80 pound
PUBLISHER	The MIT Press

29 50 BOOKS.50 COVERS. A DANGEROUS FRIEND / This novel takes place in Vietnam during the early 1960s before U.S. military involvement. The jacket needed to convey that colonial period, as well as appeal to women. I tried to convey the steamy heat of Vietnam through color, and the cover's graduated bands and shadows evoke a time of ceiling fans and louvered blinds. I also wanted to show that the "Dangerous Friend" in question was a Westerner—not an Asian—by the panama hat, which plays a role in the book.

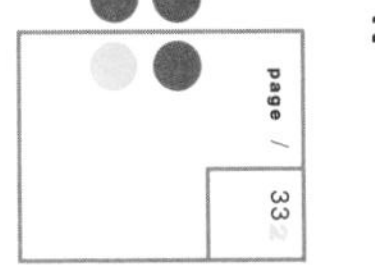

29

DESIGN FIRM	Houghton Mifflin Company, New York, NY
ART DIRECTOR/ ILLUSTRATOR	Michaela Sullivan
PHOTOGRAPHER	Corbis, Photonica
TRIM SIZE	5 5/8 x 8 1/2 inches
TYPEFACE	Perpetua
PRINTER/BINDER	Quebecor Martinsburg
PAPER	Quebecor Liberty Antique 50 pound
JACKET PRINTER	Henry Sawyer Company
AUTHOR	Ward Just
PUBLISHER	Houghton Mifflin Company

A DANGEROUS FRIEND WARD JUST

HOUGHTON MIFFLIN

A DANGEROUS FRIEND

WARD JUST

A NOVEL BY THE AUTHOR OF ECHO HOUSE

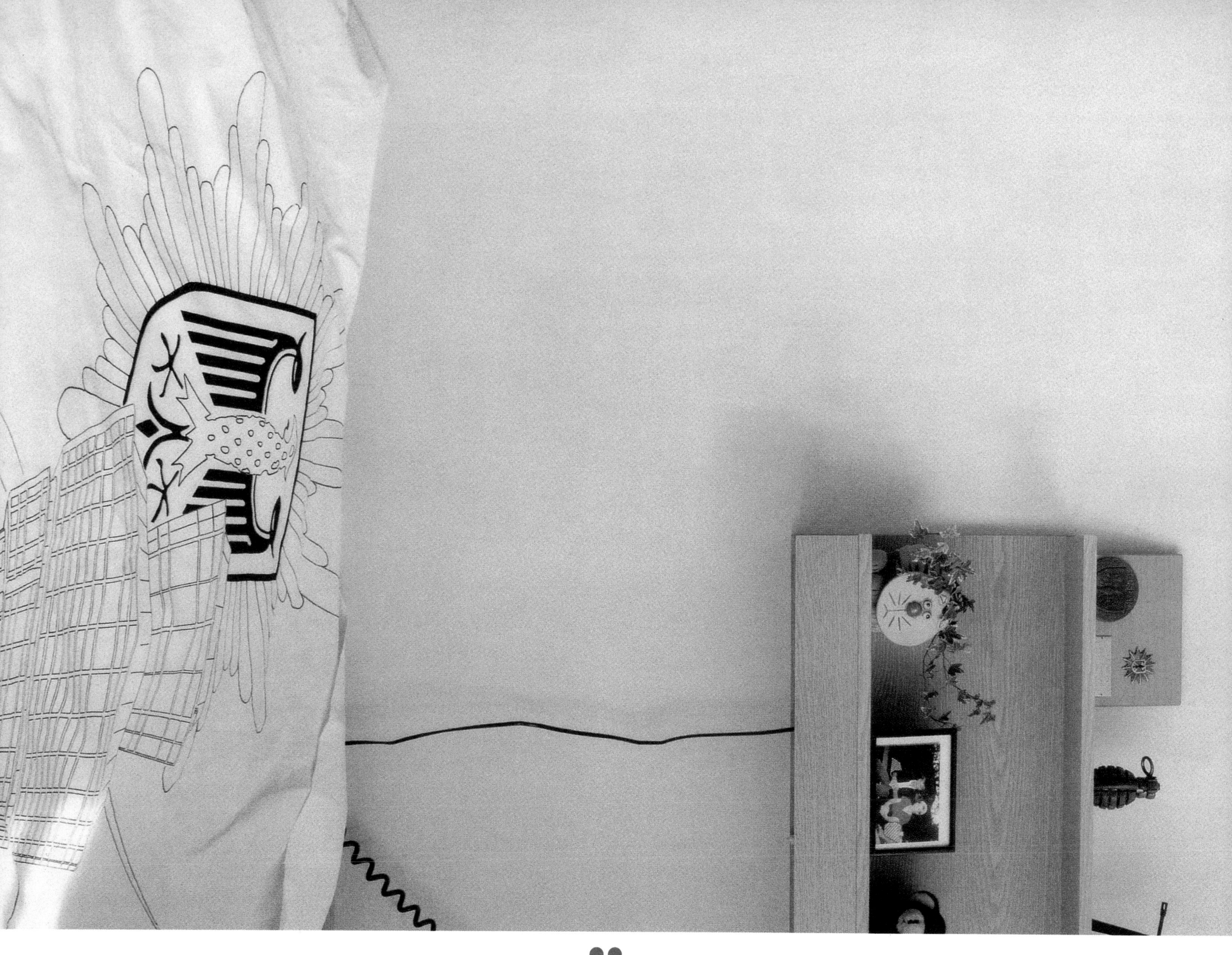

30 50 BOOKS.50 COVERS. VID INGELEVICS: ALLTAGSGESCHICHTEN (SOME HISTORIES OF EVERYDAY LIFE) / There was a budget for only 28 pages when the content determined 48 pages, which made things quite challenging. I chose to immerse the reader immediately into the photographer's work, then follow up with essays and explanations. In effect, I created a bound snapshot of the artist's travels.

30

DESIGN FIRM	Bhandari & Plater Inc., Toronto, Canada
ART DIRECTORS	Sunil Bhandari, Laurie Plater
DESIGNER	Laurie Plater
PHOTOGRAPHER	Vid Ingelevics
PRODUCTION COORDINATORS	Stella Kyriakakis, Maureen McEvoy
TRIM SIZE	8 x 8 inches

31 50 BOOKS.50 COVERS. *WEREWOLVES IN THEIR YOUTH* / Keeping things simple for this particular book of short stories was the challenge. To attract the youthful audience the book speaks to, I wanted to create an original typeface that was modern yet uncommon. Since the book was a collection of short stories, I wanted the type to evoke several different moods. With the various elements of type design at play—spacing, placement, color and texture—I believe I achieved that mood while keeping it visually simple.

31

DESIGN FIRM	Random House, Inc., New York, NY
ART DIRECTOR	Andy Carpenter
DESIGNER	Kapo Ng
TRIM SIZE	5 3/4 x 9 1/2 inches
AUTHOR	Michael Chabon
PUBLISHER	Random House, Inc.

MICHAEL CHABON WEREWOLVES IN THEIR YOUTH

MICHAEL
CHABON
WEREWOLVES
IN THEIR
YOUTH STORIES

PARTS AND PLACES

THE STRUCTURES OF SPATIAL REPRESENTATION

ROBERTO CASATI AND ACHILLE C. VARZI

32 50 BOOKS.50 COVERS. PARTS AND PLACES: THE STRUCTURES OF SPATIAL REPRESENTATION / This book discusses fundamental issues in the philosophy of spatial representation, and includes an analysis of the interplay between mereology (the study of part/whole relations), topology (the study of spatial continuity and compactness) and the theory of spatial location proper. It was a lot of fun creating this cover image of handcut paper typography. The low budget couldn't accommodate a professional photograph, but thanks to PhotoShop my own amateur shoot was sufficient after some retouching.

32

DESIGN FIRM	MIT Press Design Department, Cambridge, MA
DESIGNER	Ori Kometani
PRODUCTION COORDINATOR	Bill McCormick
TRIM SIZE	6 x 9 inches
AUTHORS	Roberto Casati, Achille C. Varzi
PUBLISHER	The MIT Press

33 50 BOOKS.50 COVERS. NOISE WATER MEAT: A HISTORY OF SOUND IN THE ARTS / The title is derived from modern performance art and the recorded sounds and noises that accompany it like water dripping, screams and bestial cries. The biggest challenge was to translate sound into visual language. The man's mouth is manipulated to look like ripples in water. It also gives the illusion of a cacophony of vibrating noises.

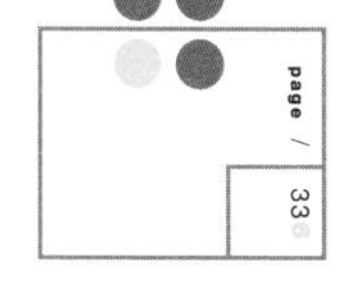

page / 33

33

DESIGN FIRM	MIT Press Design Department
DESIGNER	Jean Wilcox
PHOTOGRAPHER	PhotoDisc
TRIM SIZE	7 x 9 inches
TYPEFACES	Bell Gothic, Officina
JACKET PRINTER	Phoenix Color
AUTHOR	Douglas Kahn
PUBLISHER	The MIT Press

DOUGLAS KAHN

NOISE WATER MEAT

A HISTORY OF SOUND IN THE ARTS

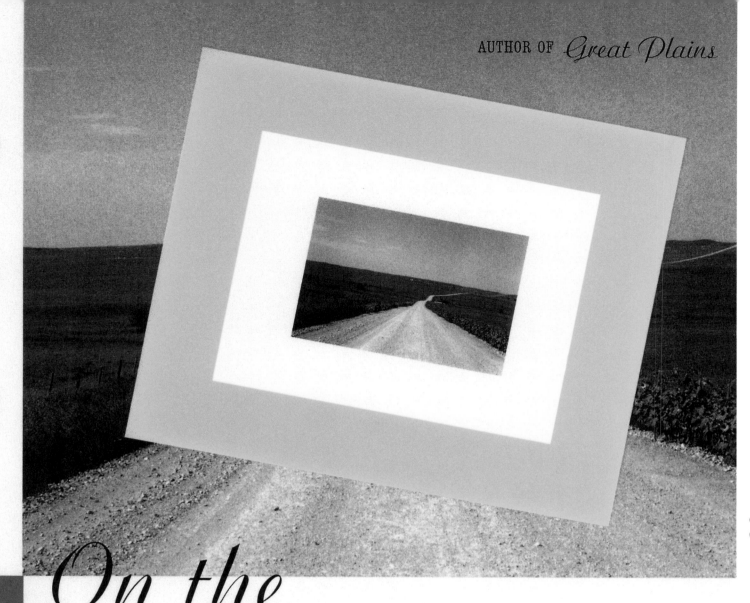

AUTHOR OF *Great Plains*

On the REZ

IAN FRAZIER

On the Rez

FRAZIER

FSG

34

DESIGN FIRM	Farrar, Straus and Giroux, New York, NY
ART DIRECTOR	Susan Mitchell
DESIGNER	Rodrigo Corral
PHOTOGRAPHER	Ian Frazier
PRODUCTION COORDINATOR	Peter Richardson
TRIM SIZE	6 1/2 x 9 1/2 inches
JACKET PRINTER	Phoenix Color
AUTHOR	Ian Frazier
PUBLISHER	Farrar, Straus and Giroux

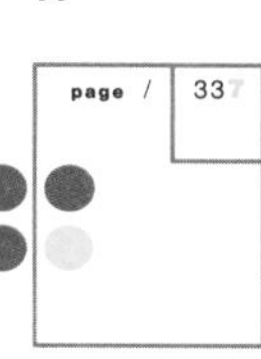

35 50 BOOKS.50 COVERS. THE STORIES OF JOHN CHEEVER / I was very aware that a cover representing an author's lifetime of writing shouldn't impose itself on the content. On the other hand, it shouldn't be a lifeless cover. I decided to keep the cover monochromatic and to use various shades of red, but layered the reds to create a wider range of hues.

35

DESIGN FIRM	Doyle Partners, New York, NY
ART DIRECTOR	Stephen Doyle
DESIGNER	Vivian Ghazarian
TRIM SIZE	5 3/16 x 8 inches
TYPEFACE	Bembo
AUTHOR	John Cheever
PUBLISHER	Vintage Books

the stories of John Cheever

c o m m u n i c a t i o n

EDITED BY MARC D. HAUSER AND MARK KONISHI

36 50 BOOKS.50 COVERS. THE DESIGN OF ANIMAL COMMUNICATION / This book looks at diverse communication systems in the animal world from the four perspectives of mechanisms, ontogeny, function and phylogeny. The comparative cases exemplified include chimps, bees, frogs and songbirds.

36

DESIGN FIRM	MIT Press Design Department, Cambridge, MA
DESIGNER	Ori Kometani
PRODUCTION COORDINATOR	Mary Ann Farren
TRIM SIZE	8 x 9 inches
PUBLISHER	The MIT Press

37 DESIGN FIRM Henry Holt and Company, New York, NY
CREATIVE DIRECTOR Raquel Jaramillo
DESIGNER Darlene Barbaria
TYPEFACE Mrs. Eaves Roman
PRODUCTION COORDINATOR Eva Diaz
TRIM SIZE 6 x 9 inches
JACKET PRINTER Phoenix Color
AUTHOR Jerome M. Segal
PUBLISHER Henry Holt and Company

37 50 BOOKS.50 COVERS. GRACEFUL SIMPLICITY: TOWARD A PHILOSOPHY AND POLITICS OF SIMPLE LIVING / I really wanted to keep it very simple and spare yet visually interesting. I guess this is an instance where less is more. The nautilus shell on a white background was used to signify beauty and grace within a simple, natural form. The art was "feathered" to keep the edges soft. The colors used were earth tones.

GRACEFUL SIMPLICITY

JEROME M. SEGAL

HENRY HOLT

GRACEFUL SIMPLICITY

Toward a Philosophy and Politics of Simple Living

JEROME M. SEGAL

the white bone

A NOVEL

38 50 BOOKS.50 COVERS. THE WHITE BONE / I really wanted to prevent the cover from getting "cute." (It was about a baby elephant, after all.) I ended up choosing monotone colors that kept it from looking like a nature book.

38

DESIGN FIRM	Henry Holt and Company, New York, NY
CREATIVE DIRECTOR	Raquel Jaramillo
PHOTOGRAPHER	PhotoShop-enhanced, royalty-free image
TYPEFACE	Beowolf
TRIM SIZE	5 x 8 inches
JACKET PRINTER	Phoenix Color
AUTHOR	Barbara Gowdy
PUBLISHER	Metropolitan Books

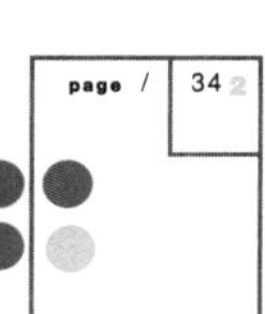

DESIGN FIRM Random House, Inc., New York, NY
ART DIRECTOR Robbin Schiff
DESIGNER Chin-Yee Lai
PHOTOGRAPHER Jane Yeomans
AUTHOR Charles P. Pierce
PUBLISHER Random House, Inc.

HARDTOFORGET

ANALZHEIMER'SSTORY

CHARLESP.PIERCE

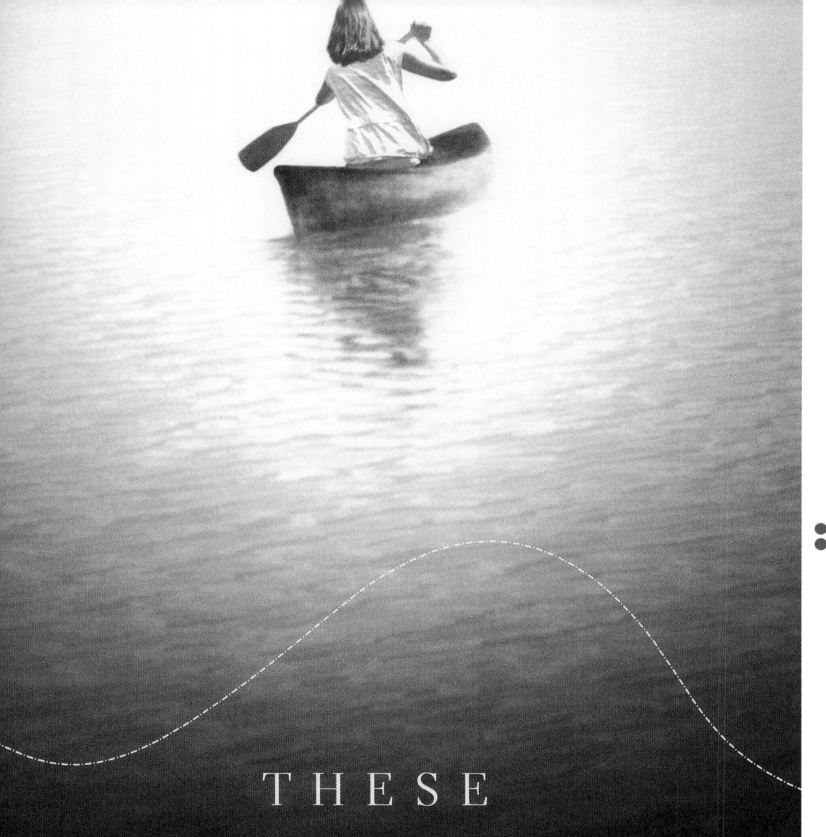

40 50 BOOKS.50 COVERS. THESE GRANITE ISLANDS / Everyone liked the direction from the start, but they wanted the woman on the front to have a different head. Solving the type of head (hair color, style, hat, etc.) took months, but the final image summarizes many feelings of the story. A woman afraid of the water canoes out to be a lookout while her best friend meets her lover. The woman is against her friend's infidelity, but understands the power of love and helps her. Capturing this moment and adding the layering of stitching/island shapes made the package emotional, pretty and complex.

40

DESIGN FIRM	Little, Brown and Company, New York, NY
ART DIRECTOR	Michael Ian Kaye
DESIGNER	John Fulbrook III
PHOTOGRAPHER	Deborah Lill
TRIM SIZE	5 1/2 X 9 1/4 inches
TYPEFACES	Electra, Univers
AUTHOR	Sarah Stonich
PUBLISHER	Little, Brown and Company

Joël Dor

The Clinical Lacan

41 50 BOOKS.50 COVERS. THE CLINICAL LACAN / The biggest concern was how to give a feel for Lacanian psychoanalysis without using an image of Lacan. I decided to use Freud's image in a warm, empty space with a couch.

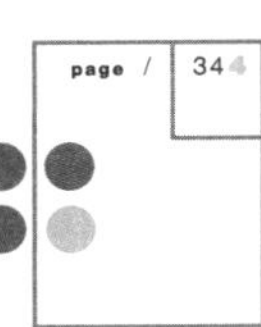

41

DESIGN FIRM	Terry Berkowitz, New York, NY
DESIGNER	Terry Berkowitz
ILLUSTRATOR	Danny Juchtmans
TRIM SIZE	5 3/8 x 8 1/4 inches
TYPEFACES	Electra Bold Display, Futura family
PAPER	Jenn Book Offset 55 pound
JACKET PRINTER	Boyd Printing
AUTHOR	Joël Dor
PUBLISHER	Other Press LC

42

DESIGN FIRM	Kathleen DiGrado Design, New York, NY
ART DIRECTOR	Robbin Schiff
TYPEFACE	Meta Plus Bold
JACKET PRINTER	Phoenix Color
AUTHOR	Lauren Slater
PUBLISHER	Random House

43 50 BOOKS.50 COVERS. CAPITAL CRIMES / This book examines the sources of crime and attributes them to greed fueled by global capitalism. Instead of taking an aggressive and gritty approach, I designed a very sleek and seductive cover that demonstrates the book's premise. The shiny, metallic cover and its bright yellow band is used to attract attention. On closer examination, it becomes clear that the yellow band is the tape used to fence off crime scenes. In this case, it surrounds a less obvious scene of crime: an office tower that symbolizes the elite economic interests that determine criminal activity.

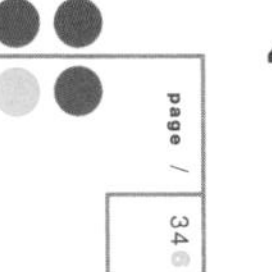

43

DESIGN FIRM	Carey George Dean Martin Inc., Toronto, Canada
CREATIVE DIRECTOR	Dean Martin
DESIGNER	Gilbert Li
PHOTOGRAPHER	Kim Steele/PhotoDisc
TRIM SIZE	6 x 9 inches
TYPEFACE	ITC Franklin Gothic
PRINTER	Best Book Manufacturers
AUTHOR	George Winslow
PUBLISHER	Monthly Review Press

CAPITAL CRIMES

A globe-spanning account of the violence of power and money—from street crime to corporate crime.

GEORGE WINSLOW

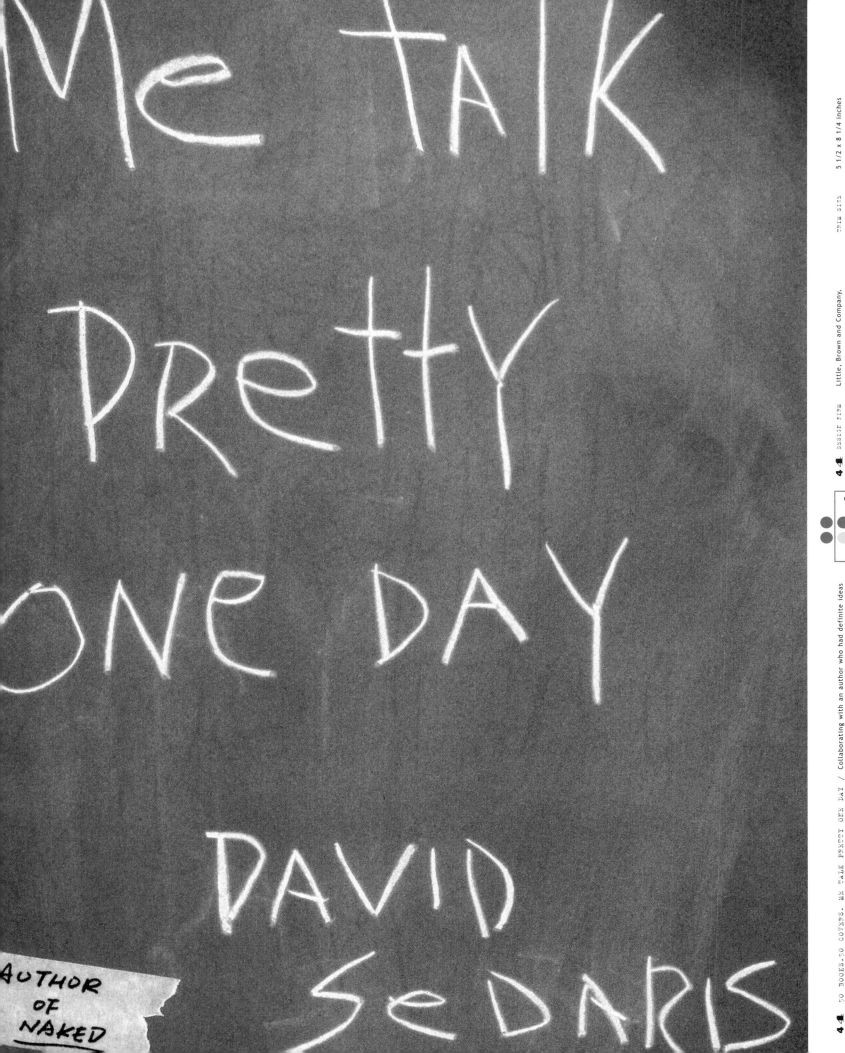

44 50 BOOKS.50 COVERS. ME TALK PRETTY ONE DAY / Collaborating with an author who had definite ideas about what he did and didn't want was a major challenge. I ended up writing the title and author's name on a chalkboard as if it were a classroom exercise.

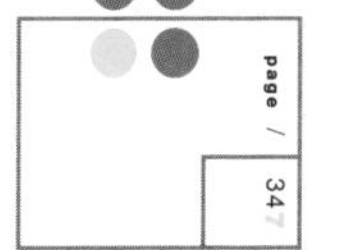

44

DESIGN FIRM	Little, Brown and Company, New York, NY
ART DIRECTOR	Michael Ian Kaye
DESIGNERS	Michael Ian Kaye, Melissa Hayden
PRODUCTION COORDINATOR	Antoinette Marotta

TRIM SIZE	5 1/2 x 8 1/4 inches
PRINTER	Phoenix Color
PAPER	House stock 80 pound
AUTHOR	David Sedaris
PUBLISHER	Little, Brown and Company

45 50 BOOKS.50 COVERS. INTO AND OUT OF DISLOCATION / This piece of writing was highly personal, cerebral and very abstract and seemed to be written in a manner that purposely left it fluid and uncategorizable. It also jumped freely between the past and present. It was a challenge to reflect this quality in a two-dimensional way that gave some clues as to the book's content. I chose to lay it out in a way that would keep it vague yet intriguing, using old photos with a modern design that gave a sense of the cold northern territories and African American history.

45

DESIGN FIRM	Paul Buckley Design, New York, NY
ART DIRECTOR	Susan Mitchell
DESIGNER	Paul Buckley
PHOTOGRAPHER	British Columbia Archives, Katherine E. Wright
TRIM SIZE	5 1/2 x 8 1/4 inches
TYPEFACE	Tarzana
JACKET PRINTER	Phoenix Color
AUTHOR	C.S. Giscombe
PUBLISHER	Farrar, Straus and Giroux/ North Point Press

A **NEW YORK TIMES** NOTABLE BOOK

(A LOVE STORY)

two cities

OHN EDGAR WIDEMAN

unrelenting power comes from its savvy exploration of love, loss, [and] forgiveness." — ESSENCE

46 50 BOOKS.50 COVERS. TWO CITIES: A LOVE STORY / As the subtitle implies, this is a love story, and I was asked to design a cover with a romantic sensibility. The book itself, however, is challenging, rhythmic and haunting at the same time—anything but a conventional love story. I decided on a very cinematic or film poster-like approach in order to highlight the book's narrative quality. The relationships in the story are represented very simply by the photographs.

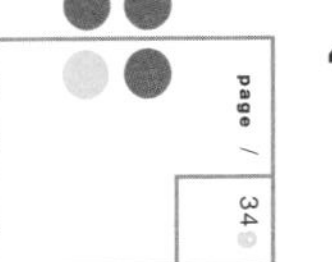

46

DESIGN FIRM	Houghton Mifflin Company, New York, NY
DESIGNER	Christopher Moisan
PHOTOGRAPHER	Jason Homa/The Image Bank, Steve Nilsson/Swanstock
TRIM SIZE	5 1/2 X 8 1/4 inches
JACKET PRINTER	Henry Sawyer Company
AUTHOR	John Edgar Wideman
PUBLISHER	Mariner Books

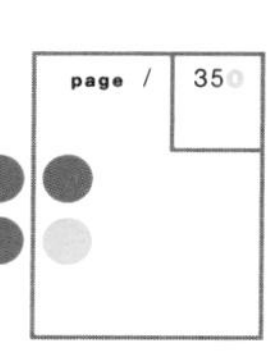

47

DESIGN FIRM	Kathleen DiGrado Design, New York, NY
ART DIRECTOR	Marjorie Anderson
DESIGNER	Kathleen DiGrado
PHOTOGRAPHER	Corbis/Bettmann
TYPEFACES	Democratica Bold, CG Gothic No.3
PRINTER	Coral Graphics
AUTHOR	Stephen Kendrick
PUBLISHER	Pantheon Books

HOLY CLUES

The Gospel According to Sherlock Holmes

STEPHEN KENDRICK

48 50 BOOKS.50 COVERS. TOWER: FAITH, VERTIGO, AND AMATEUR CONSTRUCTION / The most difficult thing was to avoid what I deemed to be the expected photographic nonfiction approach to unusual subject matter. Guy Billout, the illustrator of the book, set the tone by making the author's relationship to his tower a metaphysical experience. I let his palette and message guide me to my solution—the midnight background tones lead the eye deeper into the piece. My use of the right-hand vertical panel hinting at the building's siding further increases the depth, and a touch of moonlight in the type color completes the effect.

48

DESIGN FIRM	Farrar, Straus and Giroux, New York, NY
ART DIRECTOR/ DESIGNER	Susan Mitchell
ILLUSTRATOR	Guy Billout
TRIM SIZE	5 x 7 1/2 inches
TYPEFACES	Meta, Willow
PRINTER	R.R. Donnelley
JACKET PRINTER	Phoenix Color
AUTHOR	Bill Henderson
PUBLISHER	Farrar, Straus and Giroux

49 50 BOOKS.50 COVERS. THE INFORMATION RESOURCES POLICY HANDBOOK: RESEARCH FOR THE INFORMATION AGE / This book is based on the concept of information as a resource, such as computers, telecommunications, the mass media, financial services and so on. It discusses factors underlying digital technologies as well as the resulting public and strategic policy issues.

49

DESIGN FIRM	MIT Press Design Department, Cambridge, MA
DESIGNER	Ori Kometani
PRODUCTION COORDINATOR	Claude Lee
TRIM SIZE	8 x 9 inches
PUBLISHER	The MIT Press

THE INFORMATION RESOURCES POLICY

RESEARCH FOR THE INFORMATION AGE

EDITED BY BENJAMIN M. COMPAINE AND WILL

FOREWORD BY WILLIAM O. BAKER

THE

NEW

NEW

THING

A SILICON VALLEY STORY

MICHAEL LEWIS

50 BOOKS.50 COVERS. THE NEW NEW THING: A SILICON VALLEY STORY /

DESIGN FIRM	Alfred A. Knopf, New York, NY
ART DIRECTOR	Timothy Hsu
DESIGNER	Chip Kidd
PRODUCTION COORDINATOR	Andrew Marasia
TRIM SIZE	6 1/8 x 9 1/4 inches
TYPEFACES	Weiss, Meta
PAPER	Sebago Antique Cream 55 pound
PRINTER/BINDER	Haddon
JACKET PRINTER	Coral Graphics
AUTHOR	Michael Lewis
PUBLISHER	W.W. Norton

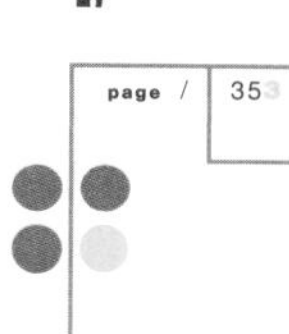

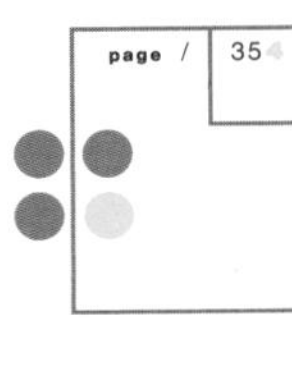

CG. CONTEXT ESSAY 03 / **left page** Exhibition view of "Communication Graphics 20" showing interactive project. Photograph © Jennifer Krogh.

communication graphics

context essay. | 03

communication graphics

context essay. | 03

communication graphics

context essay. | 03

WWW: Where Were the Websites? | **By Andrea Moed**

¶01 Recently, I got an e-mail from Jeff Bezos, CEO of Amazon.com. Bezos was contacting Amazon users to request our advice on the company's website design. It seems that Amazon is growing, transforming itself from a seller of books to a seller of, well, everything, and this requires a redesign of the site navigation. After courteously explaining to us what "navigation" is (those little tabs at the top of every page), the letter asked us to go to a specially created area of Amazon's site and review some of the design options.

¶02 So it's come to this: the original powerhouse of e-commerce, the company that practically invented it, is asking us, its customers, how best to design for e-commerce. It's curious enough to see Bezos throw up his hands and effectively ask, "So where do you want the buttons to be?" But Amazon's query was especially striking when considered alongside the results of the "Communication Graphics 21" competition. This year, a multidisciplinary jury of seasoned designers looked at a field of 271 websites, and—for the first time since the competition began accepting websites—selected not a single one to honor as exemplary.

¶03 What does all this mean? Does anyone know what he or she wants from web design anymore?

¶04 Of course, to a web designer, that's no rhetorical question. He or she knows all too well the many constituencies that make demands of her work, including business strategists, usability consultants, marketing managers, CIOs, CEOs and, of course, regular site users. All of these demands must be brought to bear on the design process. Add to that the constraints set up by engineers and project managers, which can determine the very premise of a project. Still, these are the conditions of design in all media, not just on the web. The purpose of the "Communication Graphics" competition is to recognize those designers who met the demands, transcended the constraints and created something with the aesthetic and communicative power to "make the complex clear." Did none of the websites entered achieve this?

¶05 That's certainly possible, yet it may also be true that excellence in web design is not so easily defined or apprehended right now. At a time when Amazon and other companies are exploring user polling as a design strategy, it appears that there is no agreement on what the input and role of design should be in the creation of a website—even among designers. If so, this uncertainty not only contributed to the jurors' inability to find websites worth honoring, but also affected the entries themselves.

Consensus and Its Limits

¶06 In the early history of commercial site building, it was usually clear what a designer's role was: to ensure that some attention would be paid to the visual appearance of the site. Given the rapidly evolving technologies of the web, this role involved intense negotiation. Armed with the aesthetic principles and values they had gained from training and experience, web designers negotiated with programmers over what could be made to work, at what speed, for which browsers, at what cost. (Lifelike animation, anyone? How about legible typefaces?) More indirectly, web designers engaged—as they still do—in a constant push-pull with their user base over how much effort would be required to interact with the website, and what increased insight, capabilities and conveniences the users would derive from that input.

¶07 Over the past year or so, the unthinkable has happened. All that negotiation has resulted in something like a truce. That is to say, there is now a set of web design axioms whose usefulness and applicability is acknowledged by the great majority of the mainstream, web-building business community. Among them: Hyperlinks should look different from other text, though at this point they need not be underlined or blue. The selectability of menu items should be indicated by a change of state (highlight, color change, sharpening, etc.) when the user passes the mouse over them, and again when the user clicks. Major sections or important functions of the site as a whole should be represented within a "global navigation" area that should appear in the same location on every page of the site.

¶08 These are today's Geneva Conventions of web user interface. All the most popular sites follow them, anyone who has been on the web for a week recognizes them and strong social and intellectual forces exist—behavioral studies, the ever-breaking waves of new web users, the collected works of Jakob Nielsen—to let web builders know that they violate these rules at their own peril.

¶09 The irony of the situation is poignant: Designers invented and promoted these solutions to improve the experience of the web, and they have worked so well that they've convinced some people that no further innovation is necessary.

¶10 On the mainstream web, where the stores, banks, airlines, auctions and healthcare advisors are, sameness is rampant. The looks of certain successful sites are widely imitated. A casual browsing session turns up a search engine, a community portal, a financial institution, a trade group and an electronics store all sporting the same three- or four-column layout, blue header bar and dark-blue-and-white-with-a-touch-of-yellow color scheme. Surprising sights and mind-grabbing interactions are rare. Many highly regarded experts maintain that this is all for the best.

Difference with a Mission

¶11 Designers should be countering this notion as loudly and publicly as possible. They should be arguing that innovation in web design is not over just because web users now know how to recognize links and understand what navigation bars are for. They should be demonstrating through their work how new uses of imagery, typography, color, composition and animation can make the web experience more compelling. Many great designers are in fact doing this. Unfortunately, the current market for their work is limited indeed.

¶12 Think about the websites you have seen that are not just efficient, but actually enjoyable or exciting or graceful to use; where routine tasks like searching are a pleasure; where even the experience of waiting for a download has been anticipated and designed. The companies that build such sites tend to fall into a few special categories. They include cultural institutions such as the Walker Art Center, the Brooklyn Academy of Music or the Smithsonian; marketers of trendy or upscale goods (the Viaduct furniture store, Williams-Sonoma, the late clothier boo.com); and the occasional media channel, such as Wired.

¶13 It's not surprising that organizations like these care about good website design. They need to appeal to audiences that expect vivid, multisensory experiences. They may consider a distinctive website to be vital to their image and to meeting the high standards of visual culture that they promote. On the other hand, these are far from the only reasons why a company should adopt an innovative web design strategy. Yet the case for great websites is rarely made to other kinds of clients, or it's trumped by a monolithic notion of usability that will only permit interfaces that are totally familiar.

¶14 The result is that the most innovative designers tend to go after clients in the glamour industries and market themselves accordingly in their personal sites and portfolios. Some of their sites are famously inspiring (soda.co.uk, kioken.com and yugop.com, to cite a few well-trafficked examples). But being narrowly targeted at trendy customers, they are liable to emphasize "style over design," as critic Jeffrey Zeldman recently complained. As a result, clients who don't see themselves as cultural mavericks don't see what great interface design could do for them. In some circles, in fact, cutting-edge design has developed a bad reputation, with industry commentators portraying web designers as self-indulgent artistes.

¶15 How did this play out in the context of this year's competition? Perhaps in browsing through the pool of website entries, jurors saw a great number of splashy, stylish personal and design firm sites; some corporate sites that were clean, functional and not much else; and no sites that answered jury chair Margaret Youngblood's call to "translate the client's truth into something that is clear, informative, distinctive and differentiated in the consumer's mind."

communication graphics
context essay. | 03

¶16 To recognize sites like this, arbiters of web design must come equipped with a set of values beyond the polar ethics of usability on one hand and innovation for its own sake on the other. Where would such values come from? To begin with, it's worth noting the qualities that this year's jurors admired in works in other media. Coincidentally, they are qualities that many have found lacking on the web. Yet, as a few notable websites have demonstrated, it is well within the power of designers to introduce them there.

Texture and Richness

¶17 As the jurors' choices attest, print design is praised when it engages the senses. Many of the winning entries are satisfying to touch and handle, and involved multiple and varied layers of material. It is now more feasible than ever to create similarly layered and tactile experiences on the web, yet most sites resist doing so. This may be because of the fatal wait involved. At the moment, the same consumers who will pay hidden premiums to page through gorgeously printed catalogues and brochures will not pay in minutes to download a lovely motion-graphics sequence. The current challenge, then, may be to create texture efficiently, from moment to moment and session to session, with a minimal set of elements. Sites that achieved this in the past year include Fullerene Productions' promotional site for the movie American Beauty (www.americanbeauty-thefilm.com/main.html) and Antenna Design's spare, playful site for the Cooper-Hewitt Museum's Charles and Ray Eames retrospective (www.si.edu/ndm).

communication graphics
context essay. | 03

Authenticity

¶18 There are many good reasons why the web is widely considered an untrustworthy source of information. Can design really contribute to the authenticity of a site's message the way stark, documentary photography does in the print category? It can, if designers are willing to make use of a range of content, including the contributions of users, to signify truth. This year, the Epinions site (www.epinions.com) telegraphed the unfiltered nature of its reviews and recommendations through a busy, text-driven layout that nearly bursts at the seams with voices. Documentary-style video is also having its moment on the web right now, as sites like neighborhoodfilms.com and cnn.com showcase their footage and promote a new standard of immediacy online.

Addressing Complexity

¶19 The most surprising thing to find on the web is complex information presented in a truly new way. Such designs begin with a novel concept, such as egroups.com's hub for managed e-mail lists, or artandculture.com's radically cross-referenced, start-anywhere encyclopedia of human creativity. What sets them apart, however, is that their designers understood that such a universe of information requires a truly native interface if it is to become a trusted, well-thumbed resource for users.

¶20 These are only a few of the ideas that could be brought to bear in evaluating our experiences online. Many others are needed to sharpen the soft focus of web critique. (**Send yours to 365@aiga.org**).

aiga official corporate sponsor.

aquent. | 01

AQUENT

Aquent

Aquent is the Official AIGA Talent Agency, providing an array of support services and professional training opportunities for AIGA members nationwide. Through this multiyear partnership, Aquent sponsors numerous AIGA national conferences, exhibitions and events, and offers customized packages of financial services—including insurance, retirement and cash-flow management benefits—for AIGA members. We live and work in extraordinary times. The old rules of how companies work, how work gets done and who does the work are out the window. Talented people by the millions have gone out on their own. In fact, one in four American workers today is a freelancer. Aquent is a new and very different kind of company for this new world of work. It is a worldwide talent agency for designers, assisting them in locating freelance and permanent job opportunities. Aquent's 37 domestic local offices are committed to working with AIGA's 43 local chapters to support activities that educate and inform designers about professional advancement and career-planning issues. This partnership, like all that AIGA pursues, is geared toward expanding and enhancing member benefits as well as increasing the value of the profession to the public. To that end, Aquent, as underwriter of the AIGA/Aquent Survey of Design Salaries 2000, helps AIGA expand the scope of the survey and make it more readily available not only to AIGA members, but also to companies that hire design professionals across the country.

www.aquent.com

aiga official corporate sponsor.

aquent. | 01

AQUENT

aiga official corporate sponsor.

aquent. | 01

AQUENT

Mead

Recognizing that students are the future of the industry, Mead has long offered both students and educators inspirational tools and programs like Lingo and the Mead Annual Report Student Competition. Mead's partnership with AIGA as the Official Education Sponsor is a natural extension of its position in this community, and will enhance the programs that are already in place, as well as provide new services, support, inspiration and guidance for over 4,000 AIGA student members, educators and all AIGA members who are committed to the future of graphic design. Mead's commitment as the Official Education Sponsor supports AIGA's enhanced student activities at both the national design conference in Washington, D.C., which will take place in 2001, and the business and design conference, which will take place in 2002. The company's support will also help maintain and grow AIGA online outreach to students, and increase activities with design educators and schools across the country. Mead provides high-quality products and services that help customers communicate efficiently and effectively. Mead manufactures coated printing papers in a wide variety of grades, finishes and weights suitable for virtually every printing need.

www.mead.com

aiga official corporate sponsor.

mead. | 02

Mead

aiga official corporate sponsor.

mead. | 02

Mead

aiga official corporate sponsor.

mead. | 02

Mohawk

Mohawk, a long-time supporter of AIGA, is an Official Corporate Sponsor and Presenting Sponsor of Trace: AIGA Journal of Design. Trace is printed on Mohawk Options, an uncoated line that features two distinct advantages over other premium uncoated papers: exceptional opacity and high ink hold out. And Options retains the bulk, stiffness and character you expect from premium uncoated papers. Mohawk Options is two points more opaque than other text and cover papers. As a result, customers can print lower basis weight sheets for significant savings and have full confidence in the end results. A leader in the manufacture of innovative papers for offset and digital printing, Mohawk has a long history of providing educational and entertaining content to graphic designers. Mohawk's two-year Presenting Sponsorship of Trace offers an opportunity to work with AIGA to position the journal as the critical resource for the design community. From its flagship grade Mohawk Superfine through proprietary new Inxwell products—Navajo and Options—Mohawk has engineered its papers to provide optimal performance for sheetfed, web and digital printing.

www.mohawk.com

aiga official corporate sponsor.

mohawk. | 03

aiga official corporate sponsor.

mohawk. | 03

aiga official corporate sponsor.

mohawk. | 03

Sapient

Sapient is proud to be an AIGA Official Corporate Sponsor and founding Presenting Sponsor of Gain: AIGA Journal of Design for the Network Economy. This publication is available in print and on the web twice each year and focuses on examples of the role of design in enhancing business solutions in digital contexts. Founded in 1991, Sapient is a leading creator of New Economy businesses, providing Internet strategy consulting, sophisticated end-to-end solutions and launch support to Global 1,000 and startup companies. As Architects for the New Economy, Sapient has been providing Internet solutions since 1994, and employs approximately 2,800 people in offices in Cambridge, Massachusetts, the company's headquarters, as well as Atlanta, Austin, Chicago, Dallas, Denver, Houston, London, Los Angeles, Milan, Minneapolis, Munich, New Delhi, New York, San Francisco, San Rafael, Sydney, Tokyo and Washington, D.C. Sapient is included in the Standard & Poor's (S&P) 500 Index. This partnership allows AIGA to pursue an important priority of the membership—to communicate the value of design to business, with a particular emphasis on systems integration projects and solutions requiring design as the comparative advantage in customer experiences. Gain reinforces AIGA's increasing support to professionals operating in experience design.

www.sapient.com

aiga official corporate sponsor.

sapient. | 04

Sapient™

Architects for the New Economy

aiga official corporate sponsor.

sapient. | 04

Sapient™

Architects for the New Economy

aiga official corporate sponsor.

sapient. | 04

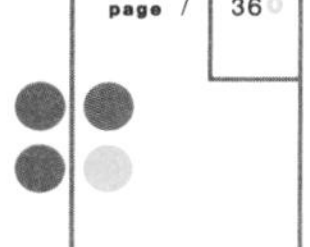

aiga 365 paper donor.

fox river paper company. | 01

aiga 365 paper donor.

fox river paper company. | 01

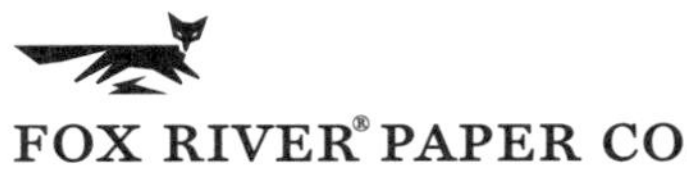

aiga 365 paper donor.

fox river paper company. | 01

Fox River Paper Company

Fox River Paper Company is pleased and excited to be an AIGA partner in the production of 365: AIGA Year in Design, highlighting the best of design and the best of designers. For the first time ever, an uncoated paper—Starwhite Sirius—is being used in this prominent and prestigious publication. Starwhite is the leading premium white writing, text and cover paper in the industry, which combines an unsurpassed printing surface with versatility for all occasions. Starwhite has long been recognized as a proven performer, offering freedom and flexibility for any job . New blue white Starwhite Sirius has a 98 brightness. Fox River is one of the nation's leading manufacturers of premium writing, text and cover papers. Its reputation for product excellence, value and innovation is driven by a commitment to meet the evolving needs of its customers. Fox River is committed to helping designers realize their vision by giving them the freedom to choose the right papers for their specific needs. The company offers an exceptional range of products in more than 150 colors and 18 finishes. Fox River = Freedom. Nothing else is necessary. Nothing else will do.

www.foxriverpaper.com

Name	Page #

A

B

Name	Page #

¶01 "The venue for Laurie Haycock and P. Scott Makela's first encounter was auspicious, a coming together of design with things unconventional, imaginative and wobbly. The occasion was the 'first and last' annual Jell-O mold competition, organized by the Los Angeles chapter of AIGA in 1985. 'Everybody brought Jell-O molds—about 25 of them—some absolutely gross and some fantastical,' recalls April Greiman, who was vice president of events for the L.A. chapter at the time. 'When you meet somebody at an important event like that, it has to be fate.' The event did not go over well with the senior members of the chapter, and never took place again. Its only lasting legacy was the 14-year relationship between Haycock and Makela, a partnership that produced—much as when you mix water with gelatin and fruit flavors—more than the sum of its parts. When friends, colleagues and peers describe the Haycock-Makela phenomenon, a picture emerges of two very different and independent sensibilities that came together in a remarkable fusion. By the time they became the resident cochairs of 2-D design at Cranbrook Academy of Art in 1997, each had a firmly established reputation. If Makela was known for his loud, vibrant, high-tech approach to design, Haycock was known for her thoughtful experimentalism and refined typography. Greiman describes the combination as upper body (Haycock)/lower body (Makela), though this, of course, depends on where you stand." (From "Truly, Madly, Deeply: Laurie Haycock and P. Scott Makela" by Peter Hall, page 20) ¶02 "Fred Seibert's career proves that it is not necessary to be a Yale/Cranbrook/RISD/SVA-educated, AIGA/Type Directors/Art Directors Club-award-winning, bona fide/pedigreed/certified graphic designer, or any other kind of designer, to create the most indelible visual identities for some of the most visible pop culture media in the world. You just have to be a fan. A fervent, ardent, passionate devotee of 'people who do fantastic work in music and visual stuff,' as Seibert puts it. Oh, yeah, you also have to have the vision thing." (From "The Instigator: Fred Seibert" by Steven Heller, page 34) ¶03 "'When it comes to design, I like to do it all,' says Michael Vanderbyl, whose lifelong goal has been to merge traditionally segregated design forms like graphic design, product design and interior architecture. As evidenced by the work that has emerged from his San Francisco-based studio over the course of his 27-year career, Vanderbyl has attained this goal—and more. A century ago, Otto Wagner, Vienna's pioneering modernist architect/designer, coined the famous term "Gesamtkunstwerk"—the total work of art—to describe what he believed was the ultimate creative attainment in the modern age. One hundred years later, Vanderbyl's talent and achievements seem to fulfill the Viennese master's criteria with startling accuracy." (From "A Man For All Seasons: Michael Vanderbyl" by Zahid Sardar, page 48) ¶04 "It is a recurring truth that when the economy does well, design awareness tends to increase in mainstream culture. Think back to the 1950s, when postwar plenitude brought forth the giddy production—and consumption—of shiny new cars and brightly decorated homes; or to the go-go '80s, when Armani suits and Memphis furniture meant prosperity writ large in the popular imagination. Well, wealth is back—at least for the moment—and material culture is flourishing. While bright colors (think orange) and flamboyant form (think Apple's iMac and Chrysler's PT Cruiser) are the hallmarks of three-dimensional hip, the graphic cultural moment is clearly dominated by minimalism. Gone are the messy, expressionistic soul-searchings so common to the early-to-mid '90s—the poststructuralist assaults on legibility, those slaps in the face to Swiss-school stricture. Instead, large, restrained type and stark photography vie for attention in a number of this year's 'Communication Graphics' entries. Indeed, there is an uncanny uniformity in much of the creative community's production—which might just make sense. If necessity is indeed the mother of invention, then innovation tends to get short shrift in flush times." (From "Up Close and Personal: Design in Detail" by Andrea Codrington, page 63) ¶05 "Faced with the threat of redundancy—or at least charges of anachronism—in a culture increasingly skewed to the digital, book designers seem to be reinventing and repositioning themselves as editors, curators and shapers of content in an effort to validate their practice. When the designers of one of the winning entries in this year's '50 Books/50 Covers' contest were asked how the advent of electronic books would affect their work, their reply hinted at some kind of genetic evolution of the designer: 'We will have to design smarter and better to make the books worth printing.' It seems that many designers are already designing 'smarter and better,' and the result is a breed of books that is intelligent, beautiful and somehow more relevant and vital than ever." (From "The Book: Rumors of its Death Are Greatly Exaggerated" by Alice Twemlow, page 193) ¶06 "Recently, I got an e-mail from Jeff Bezos, CEO of amazon.com. Bezos was contacting Amazon users to request our advice on the company's website design. It seems that Amazon is growing, transforming itself from a seller of books to a seller of, well, everything, and this requires a redesign of the site navigation. After courteously explaining to us what 'navigation' is (those little tabs at the top of every page), the letter asked us to go to a specially created area of Amazon's site and review some of the design options. So it's come to this: the original powerhouse of e-commerce, the company that practically invented it, is asking us, its customers, how best to design for e-commerce. It's curious enough to see Bezos throw up his hands and effectively ask, 'So where do you want the buttons to be?' But Amazon's query was especially striking when considered alongside the results of the most recent 'Communication Graphics' competition. This year, a multidisciplinary jury of seasoned designers looked at a field of 271 websites, and—for the first time since the competition began accepting websites—selected not a single one to honor as exemplary." (From "WWW: Where Were the Websites?" by Andrea Moed, page 355)

365: aiga year in design 21

about aiga

2000 aiga medal

communication graphics 21

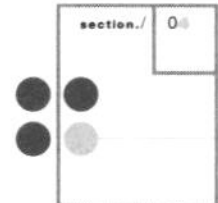